GORBACHEV

Gail Sheehy is contributing political editor to *Vanity Fair* magazine, for whom she writes extended analyses of American and world leaders. Her profile of Margaret Thatcher won the New York Newswomen's Club Award, and that of Gorbachev earned her the Best Magazine Writer award from *Washington Journalism Review* and was the starting point for this book. She is the author of eight books, including *Passages*, which sold over five million copies worldwide. In 1986 she published *Spirit of Survival*, the account of one survivor of the Cambodian genocide who became her adopted daughter, a story that is currently being made into a feature film by Warner Brothers. She is married and lives in New York.

GAIL SHEEHY

GORBACHEV

*The making of the man
who shook the world*

Mandarin

To Maura

A Mandarin Paperback
GORBACHEV

First published in Great Britain 1990
by William Heinemann Ltd
This edition published 1991
by Mandarin Paperbacks
Michelin House, 81 Fulham Road, London SW3 6RB

Mandarin is an imprint of the Octopus Publishing Group,
a division of Reed International Books Limited

Copyright © G. Merrit Corporation 1991
The author has asserted her moral rights.

A CIP catalogue record for this title
is available from the British Library
ISBN 0 7493 0708 0

Printed and bound in Great Britain
by Cox and Wyman Limited, Reading, Berks.

Contents

Acknowledgements

I express my gratitude, first, to Tina Brown and *Vanity Fair* for the unparalleled time and support given to me to do the initial reporting and magazine article which led to the writing of this book. I am deeply grateful to Elise O'Shaughnessy, my editor, for her thoroughness, stylishness and many thoughtful improvements to both the article and the book. Lynn Nesbit has, as always, been a wise adviser.

The research in the Soviet Union was made possible only through the constant efforts of Nikolai Shishlin, an esteemed friend. Sergei Ivanko at the Soviet Embassy in Washington was also cordial and helpful.

Among the many new Soviet friends I was privileged to make, none was more generous or insightful than Professor Vladimir Kvint and his wife, Natalya Daryalova, who together read the manuscript in draft with the eyes of a senior Soviet economist and a talented writer, respectively.

For meticulous research assistance I must thank Robert Monyak, a graduate student in Russian Studies at Columbia University. The fine researchers at Radio Liberty were a fund of knowledge, and I particularly thank Sasha Rahr, an author in his own right, Elizabeth Teague and Viktor Yasman. For more recent updates from their own trips to the Soviet Union I would like to thank David Aaron, former

Deputy National Security Adviser to President Carter, and William Leurs, director of the Metropolitan Museum of Art.

For assistance in translation and research while in the Soviet Union, I relied on Christopher Smart, Antonina W. Bouis and Marina Minskaya. Margot Minnini and Anne Miller of Aldridge and Miller, facilitators in Moscow, were most helpful.

I must make special mention of my editorial assistant, Allison Moir, who sustained me with loyalty and amazing resources for one so young. Lisa Garey, editorial assistant at *Vanity Fair*, gave generously of her time. And as always Ella Council nourished us all as we worked under pressure.

Finally, my thanks to Clay Felker for his unwavering personal and editorial support.

Looking for Mikhail Gorbachev

The eyes. Everyone was struck by the gleam that blazes behind his dark eyes. Presidents, Sovietologists, resident CIA psychologists, Wall Street dealmakers – all came away from face-to-face meetings with Gorbachev talking about some strange chemical reaction, as if with the intensity of his belief he had burned his image of a new world on to their own retinas and they would never be quite the same.

'His eyes are dark but the gleam is so hot, he conveys an intensity that is slightly abnormal,' I was told several years ago by a senior intelligence analyst who studied the Soviet leader up close at the first Washington summit. 'It's as though his temperature is a little higher than normal, and he's running a little faster than anybody else.'

Mark Palmer, who as the former senior Soviet analyst for the State Department had studied Gorbachev for a decade, also mentioned the intensity of his eyes. 'You feel his tremendous energy and curiosity and restlessness – he's moving all the time.' But Palmer also saw behind his ready smile a steeliness, instead of the warmth of most Russians. 'I think he's capable of a great cruelty.'

For his first five years on the world stage the eyes of Gorbachev burned with the fever of a man who saw his own world upside down, a leader who appeared to be undergoing a revolutionary transformation of vision. Where almost every world leader since the beginning of history has based his authority on military power or performance, Gorbachev tried to fashion a new style of leadership, ruling out the use of force, and lifting the cloud of nuclear dread under which billions of people walked around every day. Where every previous Soviet leader saw the necessity of closedness, he saw the advantage of openness. Singlehandedly, he transformed the image of the Soviet Union in the eyes of the West from a dangerous expansionist bear to a sympathetic if competitive partner with the courage to lead the world out of the Cold War era. That is the Gorbachev we knew, Gorbachev the statesman.

But about Gorbachev the man, we knew almost nothing.

Oh yes, we saw him so often on our TV in the West, perhaps even *were seen* by him as he plunged through the streets of our own city, that we as Americans or Europeans came to think of him as familiar, like one of ours. We gave our hearts and minds over to the belief that Mikhail Gorbachev was perhaps the last real leader, and one many Americans and Europeans would prefer to have than our own. So hungry for heroes, so swept away by the peaceful revolutionary changes in Europe, we were naturally resistant to hearing anything about this wonder man to suggest he had anything other than moral motives. As a result, Gorbachev was the first Soviet leader to be a cult figure in the West even as he became a fallen icon at home.

It is hard to believe that such a short time ago he was hailed, in December 1989, as *Time*'s Man of the Decade and the *Today* programme's Man of the Year. This book was published to coincide with his receipt of the highest accolade, the Nobel Peace Prize, on 10 December 1990. By then, the Soviet leader's position at home was so precarious he had to send an emissary to pick up the award.

But did we ever really know Mikhail Gorbachev? *Which* Gorbachev? Gorbachev himself admits, 'I feel like I've lived through three lifetimes in the last five years.' One of the men in his circle told me frankly, 'I'm quite sure there are several

Gorbachevs.'† He has changed his principles so often, and in such wild zig-zags ('I am a Communist, a convinced Communist,' he exclaimed almost pleadingly in public in December 1989, while the same month he told Prime Minister Thatcher in private, 'I'm not sure I'm a Communist any more'), it is hard to pin down the Gorbachev about which one is talking.

Andrei Sakharov, on the day he died, admitted he was having second thoughts about the 'mysterious personality' at the head of the nation. 'Gorbachev is something of a paradox for me . . .' Giving him the benefit of the doubt, he could be seen as a cautious man, Dr Sakharov said, but the human-rights crusader hinted darkly that the leader might also be unprincipled and driven primarily by his own lust for power.

It was strangely reassuring to me to hear such a statement coming from Sakharov, a contemporary of Gorbachev, but one who chose the path of uncompromising principles, suffered banishment to Gorky, and came back, if barely alive, to make his society the beneficiary of his relentless quest of truth in an ocean of lies. Gorbachev did not go to Gorky. And there is good reason that we don't know anything about him. He wants it that way. Only if he is perceived to be somehow magically free of mortal flaws and tics and failings can a leader play god. The Soviet people have always been conditioned to look upon their leader as god.

'We never knew the lives of our leaders, as you do in the US,' I was told by a Soviet law professor. 'They were a mystery for us, an icon. It was so deeply in our blood, we even didn't *want* to know about them.'

Attempts by the West to read the minds of Soviet leaders have resulted in quite monumental mistakes throughout this century. Harry Hopkins, President Roosevelt's wartime adviser, sized up the early Stalin as only the mouthpiece of a hardline clique in the Kremlin. When he later visited Stalin during the war in 1941, never having seen anything of the actual battlefront in Russia, Hopkins returned to give the President optimistic reports of the Russian powers of resistance to the German army – based entirely on the nature of Stalin's requests for American military assistance.† In truth, Stalin's secret pact with Hitler left the Soviet people open to utter devastation and prolonged the Second World War. Khrushchev was generally dismissed as a country bumpkin and no match for the deadlier Malenkov. In fact, Khrushchev turned out to be a bold reformer. Brezhnev, too, was underestimated, described as merely a 'grey-face bureaucrat'. For his first nine years as Soviet leader the betting was he'd be thrown over by the ambitious young Stalinist, Alexander Shelepin. In fact, Brezhnev ruled the Soviet Union for almost two decades.†

Gorbachev, too, turned Western predictions upside down. German officials returning from their first meeting with the new General Secretary in March 1985 indicated that he was no less dogmatic in maintaining official orthodoxy.† The *New York Times* divined that 'Foreign affairs is the field of Soviet endeavor least likely to change under a new generation.'† No one predicted that Gorbachev would move towards political liberalization. He fooled us all.

Like many Westerners, my imagination was seized by this unpredictable man. Every time I picked up the paper, which came to have a daily 'Gorbachev page', more unanswered questions swirled around in my mind.

I had first become interested in the Soviet Union in 1972. Through the Citizens Exchange Corps I arranged to spend a month there during the depths of the Brezhnev era. Furtively, our American guides put us in touch with our Soviet counterparts. Travelling from Moscow to Leningrad and through the Ukraine and Tashkent and even some rural regions, I was able to exchange life experiences with authors, journalists, artists, teachers, young construction workers and peasants. It was a sobering experience, but I was seduced by

Russian culture despite all that had been despoiled by
Communism.

So, when the editor-in-chief of *Vanity Fair*, Tina Brown,
asked me if I would like to move on from writing character
portraits about American political leaders to tackle Mikhail
Gorbachev, I was thrilled. And then stumped. Except under
controlled conditions and for his own propaganda purposes,
Gorbachev refuses interviews with writers or print journalists. Ever since Stalin's time, the Party rulers have been at
pains not to be perceived as promoting a cult of personality.

The couple of occasions when Gorbachev has given a few
scraps of biographical information about himself were set up
with planted questions, in response to which Gorbachev
gave dictation to the Soviet Communist Party Central Committee 'correspondent' or other Party organs, which were
then reprinted in the West. Occasionally, to serve his own
public-relations or policy purposes, Gorbachev will accept
written questions from an editorial group of a selected
publication, like *Time* or the *Washington Post*. After dispatch-
ing written answers, he may receive the delegation for a brief
'conversation' – which is a completely controlled situation in
which he does most of the talking. The brief film footage of
him with his family walking down the street, and the
occasional photos of him at his polling place with his granddaughter dropping his ballot into the box, are carefully
staged by the Party press agency to be sold abroad, cultivating the image of the Soviet leader as a modern, open,
Westernized statesman. The reality is quite different.

It is quite easy to play to the naivety of Europeans and
Americans, telling us what we long to hear, using the very
words we cherish in our constitutions, without being too
precise. (Democratization is not democracy; it is a slogan for
the temporal liberalization handed down from an autocrat.
Glasnost is not free speech; only free speech, constitution-
ally guaranteed, is free speech.) Gorbachev never had to
answer for his policies the way leaders do in a real political
campaign, much less face the test of an open election and a

sophisticated free press corps in search of his 'character'.

I was interested in getting behind this carefully constructed façade to probe into his personal development, life history and motivations. To begin with, how is it that a man nurtured by the Communist Party all his political life could turn out to be such a reformer? Did he have a revolutionary nature just waiting to break out of a conformist system? Or is he an inspired improviser who came to power, through connections, intending merely to make controlled changes in the existing system, but who was forced to respond radically to the reality of an economic disaster he had inherited? How much did he know and when did he know it? Is he the last true believer in Communism? Or is he perhaps the world's greatest political actor? What role is played by the beautiful, clever, calculating woman he calls 'my General'? One of Gorbachev's team told me early on, 'What Gorbachev did in the sphere of democratization and glasnost he did under the influence of Raisa.' Her background is a total mystery to Soviets, for Raisa Maximovna has never granted an interview under any conditions.

What made Gorbachev such a radical departure from all other Soviet leaders? What was it in this man's personal history and personality that compelled him to withhold the weapons of violence and fear that had been the primary tools of all his predecessors?

In May 1989 I proposed the idea of an in-depth *Vanity Fair* character portrait of Mikhail Gorbachev to Sergei Ivanko, the chief counsellor of the Information Department at the Soviet Embassy in Washington. Mr Ivanko, a charming and literate gentleman whom I had met when he was the Soviet Ambassador to the United Nations, was friendly but dubious.

'This request will have to go to the top.'

'Fine, but I was hoping to make the first exploratory trip in July. What do you think, Mr Ivanko?'

A great sucking in of breath could be heard on the other

end of the phone, either a major gasp or snicker. 'Ms Sheehy, you must understand our country. Six months will be necessary to receive an answer.'

'Six months!'

'Of course. But I can send you some of Mr Gorbachev's speeches in the meantime.'

I tried another tack. How about a trip to Stavropol, the territory over which Gorbachev had ruled as a Party boss for many years before his elevation to Moscow?

'It is possible to go to Stavropol.'

'Good, then I can get started interviewing those who worked with and for Mr Gorbachev.'

'Oh, but no one will *talk* to you about Mr Gorbachev.'

Well, what about going to his home village of Privolnoye?

'Privolnoye is closed. Impossible.'

This was not an altogether promising start. After pondering for a few days, I tried an entirely new approach on Ivanko.

'Sergei, suppose I get my feet wet by doing a story about the Soviet writers who stayed? Nothing to do with Gorbachev.'

'*Ex*cellent, Ms Sheehy, *No linkage*' said Sergei conspiratorially, as if we were in arms-control negotiations.

I quickly discovered on that trip that nothing can be done in the Soviet Union without a 'connection', meaning a fixer. One does not just arrive in town and start calling people up. There is no phone book, for starters, and Soviets from long habit don't trust talking over the phone. Every call has to be preceded by an introduction. Fortunately, I took with me as my guide and translator Antonina W. Bouis, an American-born woman of aristocratic Russian lineage who moved around Moscow like an empress. She had translated the works of most of the writers I wished to see, so introductions were easily made. It turned out that there was in fact considerable 'linkage' between these national idols and Gorbachev. Almost all were *Shestdesyatniki*, or Sixtiers – poets and novelists and journalists and historians of Gorbachev's generation whose political consciousness, like his, was formed by the brief but heady 'thaw' in the early 1960s under Khrushchev. Gorbachev frequently acknowledged the imprint of those writers on his thinking.

The next part was trickier. We managed to get to Stavropol territory and, from there, to hire a driver to take us down to the spa country of Mineralnye Vody where Gorbachev, as First Secretary for the region, used to receive the top brass from Moscow and squire them from their baths to billiards. It was a treasure trove of information and insights into how a territorial boss operates. Emboldened, I tried to persuade our driver to make an 'unofficial' trip to Privolnoye. 'What's that?' he barked. Scarcely anyone in the Soviet Union even knows the *name* of Gorbachev's home village. Our assigned Intourist guide soon informed us that the driver had reported my unorthodox request. The guide suggested I try getting permission from the present regional Party First Secretary, Ivan Boldyrev.

'Mr Boldyrev is sick,' I was told by his office.

'Then may I try him again tomorrow?'

'Oh no. He will be sick all week.'

Just as my luck was running out, I received a long-distance call from my husband in New York. 'You've got to try to get home by Thursday night – we've been invited to a dinner party for some Russian poohbah from the Central Committee.' I caught the PanAm non-stop and was back in New York with an hour to change clothes before arriving at the house of our friend, Mort Zuckerman, publisher of *US News and World Report*, and a well-informed, frequent visitor to Moscow. He did me the favour of seating me on the left of the guest of honour, Nikolai Shishlin, a consultant to the Central Committee – the ruling body of the Communist Party – and a man with sterling connections.

I made my case for the importance of the first character portrait of Mikhail Gorbachev. Shishlin was in favour of such an approach – perhaps in six months or a year he could talk

Mr Gorbachev into it. 'Oh, wonderful!' I said, probably wriggling all over. Whereupon Shishlin peered over his thick glasses with a sardonic smile and added: '*If* nothing happens.'

What happened, of course, was the collapse of the Soviet Union's outer empire, culminating that autumn in the breach of the Berlin Wall and the hurtling exodus of East Germans out of Communist confinement. Gorbachev became more mysterious and elusive than ever.

I developed the habit of rising well before six every morning to telephone Moscow before the measly thirty-eight trunk lines that service the entire country of 270 million people would overload for the day. Except for the Communist Party aristocracy, few people have secretaries. There are no answering machines, no electronic mail, just the hit or miss chance one might catch the 'connection' at his office. (If he's not there, no one else will pick up the phone on his desk, because that would only mean more work.) And so, the pre-dawn attempts to reach my 'connection' in Moscow met with only patchy success. After days of dialling, the voice of this quintessential apparatchik would suddenly come on the phone.

'Da.'

'Nikolai?'

'That's me.' The sound of a whipped dog.

Shishlin would never say no. Always my requests for an interview with Gorbachev, with Raisa, with Gorbachev's alter ego Alexander Yakovlev and others were put off with 'Maybe, maybe,' or 'Just now it is not possible,' or 'Call to me back at four.'

Once, close to exasperation, after finally reaching him in his office at the Central Committee, I asked if he could fax me an answer. His reply was astonishing.

'Unfortunately, we do not yet have fax in the Central Committee.'

I tried my luck in Washington. The resident psychologists at the Central Intelligence Agency couldn't tell me any more

than one would know about an unfriendly neighbour in a
Manhattan apartment house. Did Gorbachev have any sib-
lings? 'We *think* he does, and we're not kidding, we only
think.' Family background? 'He was born during the worst
period of collectivization but he's never acknowledged that
any relatives of his were arrested or killed.' Characteristics?
'He's arrogant, but not without reason.' More importantly,
they stressed, he is keenly intuitive; he senses the situation
and reads people on the spot, managing his inner reactions
so that he can shift from charming to tough to malleable to
menacing in the space of moments. 'He changes all the time
– his environmental attunedness is superb.' He's also an
extraordinarily goal-oriented person. Put that together with
his enormous tactical flexibility, and you understand how he
is able to pick up vibes, abandon one road because it leads to
a cul de sac, and turn on a dime.

'He's a visionary with no road map.'

In some ways, Sovietologists find it harder now to figure
out what is really going on than in the old days when they
read between the lines of monolithic Partyspeak or teased
out secrets through espionage. In the intelligence business,
as in life, there is a big difference between a secret and a
mystery, as government analyst Fritz Ermath points out. A
secret is what somebody else knows and you don't, but you
can conceivably find out. A mystery is what no one knows.
The Soviet Union used to be a nest of secrets. Now it's all
mystery – even to its own leadership.

With a promise from Shishlin that I might go to Gorbachev's
home village, I flew back to Stavropol in September. Again,
I was refused an audience by First Secretary Boldyrev.
Nobody knew anything about any 'permission' from Moscow.
I hung on a pay phone for a day and a half, trying frantically to reach Shishlin, watching my two-day local visa
run out. At the last moment, a magic telex from Moscow
arrived bearing the imprimatur of the Central Committee
of the Communist Party. It ordered local Party officials

'to devote maximum attention to the writer from USA'.

Our Intourist guide shrieked with delight. 'It's the best because it comes from the top! That's how things work in our country.'

We left before dawn for Privolnoye. It was a journey into another world, with vistas evocative of Chekhov's Russia and country people with salty tongues, the blows of history palpable in their twisted bodies and pained eyes. In the eight precious hours allotted to me in Gorbachev's village I was able to find and interview almost all of the family friends and relations on my list. Their frankness amazed me. It was a strange time; no one knew what the rules were any more. The decades of repression were gratefully thrown off when, for once, someone took keen interest in their individual lives. They took me through the terror of famine, collectivization, 'kulak mania', war and the German occupation, and of course every scrap of their recollections about Misha – the romantic, quarrelsome Ukrainian boy who stunned them all by rising to the pinnacle of Soviet power.

The Privolnoyans passed me on to the right people in Stavropol, where Gorbachev had made his career for twenty-three years. Back in Moscow I uncovered one of Gorbachev's closest friends from his Moscow University days, who, after six hours of interviews with me, satisfied himself that it was all right to open the door to Gorbachev's first girlfriend. She, in turn, gave me another entrée, and so it went. Ultimately, I was able to interview all six of Gorbachev's closest friends from his university days.

Back in New York I resumed my sunrise vigil to reach Shishlin in Moscow. But weeks went by with no answer. When I finally did track down my connection, he was staying at a hotel a few blocks from my home in Manhattan. 'Nikolai, is there something wrong?' I asked him over tea. 'All my efforts seem suddenly to be blocked.'

'You see, Gail, I want to be quite honest. Gorbachev is quite sensitive with his relatives, especially with his wife. And he said to me, Nikolai, why does this journalist from

America want to know about Raisa's barber?'

'Her what!'

'Somebody told Mr Gorbachev that Gail Sheehy was interested in lipstick, clothes, hair, everything connected with Raisa.'

'Nikolai, do you really think I would spend eight months of research to learn about Mrs Gorbachev's wardrobe and hairdresser?'

Shishlin looked chagrined.

'Where did Mr Gorbachev get this information?'

'Boldyrev.'

'Boldyrev!' I told Shishlin that Gorbachev's hardline successor as First Secretary in Stavropol had ducked me at every turn; I had never met him nor had I ever asked Gorbachev's relatives anything about Raisa's personal grooming.

'Boldyrev reprimanded me.'

'That's terrible,' I said. 'He's just trying to discredit me.'

'Maybe he's trying to discredit *me*,' said Shishlin miserably.

It was my first experience of a fact of Soviet life that still holds true – one never knows when one will be the victim of a false denunciation by a person one has never met. For all his intelligence and modernity, Gorbachev himself still cannot trust more than a small circle of his intimates to tell him the truth. Those professionals are constantly undercut by old-style Stalinist Party bosses at the regional level who correctly foresee in the publicity of glasnost and popular elections their own humiliation and defeat.

Usually Russians and Americans get on quickly and well. At first, I was constantly surprised by the many ways in which we are alike, but gradually I became impressed by the ways of thinking that make us different. Americans have a habit of breezy confidence. Soviets have a habit of fear. The personal characteristic most prized by Americans is honesty. Soviets, to survive, have had to make a virtue of deceit.

Even at the height of glasnost in 1989, the Soviet security apparatus maintained a vigilant interest in the activities of a foreign journalist.

My young tape transcriber, Arkady, a student at Moscow State University, confessed that he was afraid he would be approached to give information about what I was doing. He didn't know if he'd be able to brush it off or if he would be coerced. Others were not so open. Usually, I took my own translator, which put my interviewees at greater ease than having another Soviet in the room. But once I had to find a Soviet translator, and with that I fell into the whirlpool I came to call circles of suspicion. The translator, Sergei, arrived in my apartment wearing a black raincoat and carrying a large brief-case full of electronic gear, among which just happened to be the transformer I lacked and a printer just like mine, which had broken down. I was impressed. His language skills were superb. Sergei had started the first co-operative translating business in the country and employed seventy people in Kiev, capital of the Ukraine. The United States Information Service had used his services before he had the co-op, so he came highly recommended.

I told Sergei the nature of my questions and gave him a list of calls to try out his phone manner. He got as far as the assistant to Ivan Frolov, the editor-in-chief of *Pravda* and an intimate of Gorbachev's. I listened in as he responded to a nasty grilling: How come he was from *Kiev* and here in Moscow working for an American writer?

Within moments Sergei's confidence seemed to disintegrate. I questioned him after the conversation. He suggested that someone with connections to 'the State system' might have given a bad report on my intentions. He understood that the questions I was asking were normal for any journalist from the 'civilized world', but cautioned, 'They wouldn't like a journalist probing into Gorbachev's mafia connections, for instance.'

Then perhaps we shouldn't try to work together, I said.

Sergei assured me he was not in the state system. 'I don't report to anybody.'

'But you need to keep your operating licence,' I suggested.

Defensively Sergei said, 'I don't know what they could do

to me in Moscow, but I don't give a damn in Kiev. My co-op is very strong. Most of my employees are in the Popular Front.' Riding boldly on his v-necked sweater was an American/Ukrainian flag pin. I looked at Sergei's soft green eyes and I saw it in him too – the fear. This 'free' man – who was his own boss back in Kiev, who had the wits to corner the market on translation services the minute co-ops made it legal to go into business for oneself – was reduced with one phone conversation to a fearful child.

That evening I entertained some writer friends for dinner, including novelist Anatoly Pristavkin. Anatoly was lost until his English-speaking wife arrived, accustomed as he was to leaning on her as an intermediary in conversations with foreigners. When Marina joined us and immediately began to speak for her husband, my translator butted in aggressively.

'I will translate,' demanded Sergei, with a rap of fingers on the table.

The next time I had dinner with the Pristavkins, it was alone.

'Gail, you must know something,' they said. 'Sergei is KGB.'

'What gave you the clue?' I asked, astonished.

'Nothing. No one thing. And everything,' Marina explained in a typically Russian way. 'His fat face, his perfect English, his sudden appearance in your life with everything you need – why?'

I explained that an American woman associated with our embassy recommended him – 'He has a co-operative for translating.'

Eyebrows shot up. Marina confessed that she and Anatoly were both put off from the moment they saw Sergei. 'You must think this way – in probabilities. One out of every three Soviets is connected to the KGB. So why *not* Sergei?'

I said my sources at the Embassy were very certain of him.

'But embassy people have to live in this society of deception for two or three years,' they explained. 'They can't believe that all their Soviet friends are secretly reporting on them. It's impossible to live with that level of paranoia. So they tell themselves, "This one is OK, my real friend, and that one is probably KGB." In fact they can't be sure about anyone.'

Anatoly told me about their insurgent writers' group, April, which broke away from the official Writers' Union where the officers are appointed by the Party and have always been connected to the KGB. 'Ten of our friends – very best friends – are on the soviet [steering group] of April,' said Anatoly. 'We meet in secret and decide policy. Immediately the information goes to the top. Who whispers it? We have no idea. We know because the attacks on us are well informed and anticipate our plans.'

My face must have shown chagrin – how unsuspicious, how naive of me. 'Of course they would be watching me, I'm watching Gorbachev.'

'You can't know how to think like we must think – thank God,' exclaimed Marina, 'you live in a free society!'

After a sleepless night, I reached my Embassy contact, Margot Mininni, a flawlessly professional woman whose husband works for USIA and who has her own business as a facilitator in Moscow for Americans attempting to do business there. The moment I said the words, 'I'm worried about Sergei,' Margot's defences went up.

'My loyalty is already committed. You're just running into the suspicions and brutality of human relations here that keep this country in the dark ages.' We decided to discuss the problem over lunch at the Savoy Hotel – without Sergei. But I couldn't shake him, he followed me like a puppy. So Margot and I excused ourselves to go to the rest room.

The Savoy is noted for having the nicest toilet facilities in Moscow, but there is a unisex washroom off which the separate male and female cabins extend. As Margot and I leaned against the sinks whispering about how to test Sergei, suddenly Sergei, big as life, plunged into the common bathroom after us. That did it. Before we had to have a showdown, however, there was another twist in the circles of suspicion.

Sergei said he was apparently in trouble. He'd had a call from the Ukrainian Foreign Office saying his trip to the US might have to be cancelled. They insisted he come back to Kiev to appear in person at the Ukrainian consulate.

With Sergei out of the picture, I felt secure again. The driver who had met my plane talked his way into being my constant companion. This young man, Oleg, told me when I first met him that he had no complaints with Soviet society; he was making out very well. He was twenty-six years old, he had a wife, a child of one year, he had a car, a nice apartment and spending money. Although he had dropped out of university, he travelled abroad quite frequently. I should have been wary. This is not the biography of your average twenty-six-year-old Soviet.

After a couple of weeks I suspected at some level that my young driver was a black marketeer. He kept asking me, 'What do you need?' I'd say, 'Mineral water is impossible to buy in the restaurants or the stores.' He'd say, 'What kind do you like?' I'd say, 'You're joking. You're asking me for a brand? If I could just get a bottle of any water that doesn't turn brown when it comes out of the tap, I'd be happy.' That night he'd have six bottles of prized Narzan water in my refrigerator.

Oleg always asked to be paid in dollars. One day he opened his boot to put in my briefcase and I saw cartons of detergent and cigarettes. I also found it curious that he volunteered to clean the apartment. He did it while I was out interviewing. Nothing was ever missing, he was careful about that, but a nagging intuition told me he was up to something. By then, however, I was dependent on him.

Oleg dashed around town twelve hours a day, hardly ever going home to see his wife. He had two jobs, one with the state, which paid him for doing essentially nothing, one with a children's theatre co-op, which allowed him to travel abroad. Most of his time he spent running around doing little 'errands', as he called them, for his friends: buying and selling black-market goods. Although his parents were highly cultured members of the Moscow intelligentsia, Oleg had the sunken-cheeked, beady-eyed, wolfish look of many young Soviets. He was utterly amoral. He would fleece anyone, intimidate anyone, compromise anyone he could, if it meant getting his hands on more hard currency. I paid him very well and for a tip, when I left, I gave him my Sharp Wizard personal pocket computer.

Shortly after I returned home from that extended stay in the Soviet Union, I learned that my every move and contact had indeed been reported to the KGB. But the informer had not been Sergei, my translator. It had been Oleg, my driver.

I had not heard the last of Oleg. The day before my next trip, I was waiting on tenterhooks for the visa. Gorbachev's chief adviser had agreed to an interview date. Suddenly a fax started coming in on my machine. From Moscow! I dived for the machine, expecting it to be from the inner sanctum of the Kremlin.

> You bring me another Sharp Wizard. I know your
> arrival time. I meet you at airport. OLEG.

Amazing. The Central Committee of the Communist Party of the Soviet Union could not send a fax, but a twenty-six-year-old black marketeer could fax me his extortion order for a 260-megabyte computer worth $350.

When I managed to evade Oleg at the airport, he was outraged, and when I didn't respond to his phone calls, he turned up late at night outside the door of my apartment in the Lenin Hills. Failing to corner me, he finally had the audacity to lure a friend of mine, the wife of a top diplomat, out of the US embassy compound. Right there on Chaikovskaya Street, the young thug raged at her about my having short-changed him and threatened that the Americans wouldn't get away with this. It was a stunning display of the black marketeers' total confidence in their invulnerability from any retribution by the authorities.

After my article appeared in *Vanity Fair*, my fascination with Gorbachev remained unabated. I wanted to understand how Gorbachev fits into the course of Russian history and to look for deeper shadings in his character. Some of the leader's own aides, for instance, were quite shocked to learn from my story that their leader had lived in an area under German occupation during the war. Top functionaries in Moscow's national Press Centre, which issues the official skeleton curriculum vitae on Gorbachev, told me that 70 per cent of the biographical material in my article was absolutely new to them.

When I went back to the Soviet Union to trace the second half of his life, I was given access to Gorbachev's chief confidant, Alexander Yakovlev. Through interviews with other members of the Central Committee who worked closely with Gorbachev, and with access to the splendid Red Archives at Radio Liberty in Munich, I was able to trace his path to ultimate power. None the less, to attempt a biography of a living Communist leader in a controlled society, where public archives do not exist and the history courses are suspended until the next official version is minted, is to grapple, in Churchill's famous phrase, with 'a riddle wrapped in a mystery inside an enigma'. It soon became apparent to me that Gorbachev had succeeded in climbing up through a despotic system not because of his abilities, but in spite of them.

Gorbachev's many U-turns in policy and sacrifices of principle in the service of pleasing competing power figures – the fantastically corrupt Brezhnev, the fanatic Suslov and KGB Chief Andropov – make a revealing story. Andropov's son gave me an extensive interview which shed much light on this period in the Soviet leader's life. More exploration into the pivotal role of Raisa illuminated the psychological relationship between the two that gives her such power. Raisa Gorbachev is not just an essential support to her husband; she is close to being a full partner in leadership. I was also able to interview major US diplomatic figures who have dealt with Gorbachev at summit meetings and in private.

I persisted in asking for permission to return to Privolnoye, stressing in my sunrise chats with Shishlin, that there were still discrepancies and mysteries about grandfather Gorbachev – the member of the family banished under Stalin as an 'enemy of the people'. After months of 'maybes', I pressed for a firm answer.

'It's the responsibility of Mr Gorbachev to decide [whether I could go back to his home village],' he said. 'He understands that you are trying to make a brilliant portrait of him and his family. Maybe he'll have a chance to re-read your story.'

That hardly seemed likely, so I asked if President Gorbachev had any reaction the first time he read my piece in *Vanity Fair*.

'I think he rather enjoyed it,' said my always suavely agreeable contact.

Notwithstanding, the aides around President Gorbachev were made increasingly nervous by my inquiries. Seven months after my first trip to the village, I made one more strong appeal. My patron was uncharacteristically brusque: 'Look, Gail, they don't *want* anything more about the grandfather. If you want to spoil the whole project, then raise this question.'

So, the image-makers, if not Gorbachev himself, had become skittish about the real biographical story being told. I would have to pursue the threads on my own.

In the end I interviewed 102 Soviets with knowledge of Gorbachev, and over 50 American and European experts who have dealt with or studied Gorbachev and his country as members of the government, political or academic Establishment. More subjective analysis was possible after reading novels, poetry and histories of Russia and seeing the films of Gorbachev's era. A year and a half of research and four extensive trips to the Soviet Union to retrace his footsteps were necessary to learn about the human being behind the world leader who confounds observers again and again.

Most helpful of all was living in the Soviet Union at different intervals, which made it possible to grasp at a human level the premises and pathologies peculiar to Gorbachev's culture.

It is almost impossible for a tourist to sense the true situation in the Soviet Union without having breathed the air of industrial wastelands like Magnitogorsk or descended to a mine in Donbass or seen the expanse of the Arctic zone. Only selected cities are open to foreigners, so most stay close to Moscow and Leningrad. Foreigners are isolated from the moment they step off the plane to be ferried in a separate bus to a separate (and quiet) waiting room, then into a London-size cab for the pre-paid trip to the hotel, while Soviets stand in line for an hour or more waiting for standing room on a packed bus. The tourist may be startled to find his $200-a-night 'double room' is a dormitory-style cubbyhole with single beds, no box springs, grimy windows and malfunctioning air conditioning. Even if he has been warned to bring his own sink stopper, his smugness may be short lived when he pulls it out and feels his shoes fill up with his shaving water – Soviet workmen neglected to put in a drain pipe!

Even in Moscow's Intourist Hotel in the autumn of 1989, one day there would be no milk, the next no mineral water; there was never any coffee, just a huge samovar of hot water and a line of guests clutching their own tea bags or instant-coffee jars. Standard breakfast fare was cheese, cold peas, boiled eggs and fat boiled weiners. 'What happened?' I asked the waiter after finding that nothing on the dinner menu was available.

He fixed me with a mordant smile. 'What happened, happened seventy years ago.'

Just as baffling as the scarcity was the etiquette of entrances. The door to any hotel or restaurant is only half open. It doesn't matter if there are a dozen double doors along the front of the establishment, only half of one set of double doors will be unlocked. Never mind that people laden with baggage have to squeeze through a three-foot opening to get to their hotel room, only one half of the double door will be unlocked on every floor. The operative design factor in all Soviet architecture is the same: *control*. The flow of traffic is funnelled down until each person must file through a narrow slot where a babushka or a bouncer, some faceless petty tyrant, checks him off or gives him a chit or stamps his papers – in one way or another restricting his freedom of movement. Wishing to be polite, the foreigner attempts to learn the rules before making the next entrance. But it's no use. It's not about rules. It's about control. Babushkas derive their power from making up their own rules and scolding people for stepping out of line.

I found a deluxe dining-room secreted up on the twenty-first floor of the Rossiya, a Pentagon-sized hotel for foreigners near the Kremlin, but of course when I reached the door the bouncer barked, 'Nothing left to eat!' Even in prosperous hotels, the restaurants had nothing left to serve after 9 p.m. because the staff had taken it all home for their families, passing chickens and salad wrapped in newspapers out the back door to their colleagues. A pack of Marlboros with a five-dollar bill tucked under the lid, however, would instantly produce a platter of caviar and a bottle of champagne – never mind that a simple sandwich couldn't be obtained for love or money. The lucky foreigner could then settle back for an hour and forget 'our shameful condition', as Soviets constantly referred to their situation.

To get around in the Soviet Union it was necessary to understand that the ruble had at least three exchange rates. At the official bank rate the ruble was worth $1.66. In reality, the ruble was worth almost nothing, since it was not backed by gold or any other hard precious material and was not convertible to any hard currency. As the saying went, 'A pound of dry rubles is worth a dollar'.

Street standard was established by the *fartsovshchiki*, or

black-market moneychangers, and pegged to the ever-increasing inflation rate, anywhere between six and twenty rubles to the dollar.

Golden Ruble standard was the one required of foreigners for all hotel and Intourist-arranged services. It required you to buy rubles at the same rate dollars buy the British pound.

Lunch for four at the trendiest American-Soviet co-operative restaurant in Moscow, Tren Mos, basically a hamburger-and-coke Saturday afternoon lunch, was $100 at the Golden Ruble exchange rate.

The Marlboro standard is the most sensitive barometer of the shadow economy. One pack of Marlboros could wave down a cab driver in the summer of 1989; that autumn, it went up to two or more packs; by spring 1990 no amount of cigarettes could flag down a taxi – there were too many Western tourists in town, and more lucrative deals to be made.

All internal travel in the USSR must be pre-paid, including the cost of an Intourist driver. For a stay in Moscow I had booked a driver and paid several hundred dollars in advance. But at my hotel I was told, day after day, that no Intourist drivers were available. Meanwhile, a swarm of loutish-looking drivers stood around just outside the hotel doing nothing. I approached one, a young beefy man with shaggy hair, jeans, a big scar and a scowl, who was leaning on a well-kept grey Volga. He agreed to make the ten-minute drive to the Institute of Economics for 20 rubles and cigarettes.

'Two packs of Marlboros?' I tried. 'Nyet,' he sneered. He demanded five packs, but I'd have to go to a foreigners' gift shop and buy him Camels. Struck by his brazenness, I went back to the Intourist clerk in my hotel to ask what was going on. She confirmed that he was an Intourist driver (he had declined to say). 'So, why should I have pre-paid for an Intourist driver, and you tell me for three days you can't find me a driver, while this fellow stands around outside waiting to demand twenty rubles and five packs of cigarettes to drive me around for an hour?'

She shrugged. 'It's terrible. But it's the way things are now.'

'It's accepted then, Intourist drivers wait to demand bribes to drive?' I pressed.

She shrugged again. 'Everybody knows it. There's nothing we can do.'

I moved to Moscow for the month of March 1990 to watch first-hand the transformation of the new Gorbachev – into President of a non-Bolshevik Soviet Union. This trip had an entirely different character. I would not live as a foreigner in the isolation of hotels; this time I was prepared to approximate living within the economy like a Moscow housewife. Friends made on previous trips generously offered an apartment in the Lenin Hills, not far from Moscow University.

The Lenin Hills were leafy and pretty with the pleasant energy of a university town. Gorbachev himself had lived in the area when he attended the university, a massive Stalin-era structure whose architecture bespoke state domination over any individual identity. My apartment building was an eight-storey Stalin-era red-brick block just off the most modern boulevard in Moscow: Leninsky Prospekt. It was near where Leninsky crosses Krupskaya Street, which is named after Lenin's wife and intellectual partner. The hand of Lenin was still heavy. Factories, many inside old churches, turned out the mass-produced, Karnak-sized, Big Brother statues of the leader that loom everywhere. But on Krupskaya Street the bronze sculpture depicts a lifesize, domestic Lenin, reading a folio of revolutionary writings beside his wife. ('A wife but not a woman,' I was informed by a typically chauvinistic Russian intellectual. 'Krupskaya was a revolutionary thinker, but you can't, well, sleep with a block of wood.')

Since my apartment was in a showcase building, the construction was solid, walls thick, noise minimal, and the basic services – heat, hot water and gas – were plentiful, steady and cheap. I was pleasantly surprised to find wood parquet floors and tall casement windows in a three-room apartment splashed with light. My hosts, members of the intelligentsia, had filled the walls with bookshelves to hold the treasures they had gathered on travels abroad; intellectuals in the Soviet Union are far better read than their counterparts almost anywhere else, and are usually well versed on subjects outside their particular field. Taped to the desk lamp and the walls of the bathroom were the new buzz words – in English – 'cost-accounting', 'self-financing', 'market economics', 'currency convertibility'.

Scarcely had I turned a key in the apartment door when my neighbours popped out of their door to help. After dragging in my suitcases, they insisted my translator and I come over for tea. The Peterhovs, Irina and Alexander, introduced themselves as geologists, and laid out homemade jams and good black Russian bread as the start of a round of treats. When I tried to help clear away dishes from the first course, Irina stopped me. It is not polite, she explained. In a Russian household the guest must never see a bare table. It should look 'like in the best apartments of Philadelphia'.

This expression struck me as odd. Had the Peterhovs ever been to Philadelphia?

'Oh no, we have never *seen* a nice apartment in Philadelphia. It's just a proverb that means the very best – everybody understands it.'

The Peterhovs looked at first like any American nuclear family. Their sixteen-year-old son, Alexi, loved sports. The elder son, Sasha, twenty-one, had done his two years of military service and was in his second year of radio electronics school. Sasha had never had access to a computer, but he was hungrily reading the recently published Russian translation of *The Catcher in the Rye*. When I asked what he would do after graduating, his lips pursed tight, as I began to notice Soviets do when they are asked naive questions.

'Mmmm, they will distribute me to a research institute or

a plant, and there I shall work on communications for satellites and rockets and such things.' Military? He nodded yes. Did he want to be connected with the military?

'No! But they did not tell us until now.'

Irina had turned off on Party dogma many years before. She used to scoff at her husband, a traditionalist from the provinces, for even bothering to read the newspapers, insisting, 'They're just filled with lies and sweet hypocrisies.' She and her husband argued all the time. Her son Sasha remembered never knowing which view was right or wrong, but says, 'I was a strong patriot.' That was until he did his time in the Soviet army, which brutalizes young men. At the age of twenty he too became 'liberated' from Party dogma, and now he yearned to become a writer so he could tell the truth. After half an hour at their table, the warmth of Russian family life reached around my translator and me and drew us into its special intimate embrace.

When I first entered my own kitchen, it was with a shudder of dismay. To begin to put food away in a Soviet kitchen, one runs immediately into the total absence of products we take for granted: no paper towels, aluminium foil or plastic wrap, no napkins and no toilet paper. Then, try to do some dishes. No washing-up liquid. Nobody has it. One grew accustomed to intensely cloudy glassware, because of course there were no dishwashers, not even a dish drainer. Almost everything looked like it belonged to a standard 1950s American apartment kitchenette. Oh, the room itself was cheerful enough. A large window looked out on the twinkle of hundreds of equally brightly lit apartments in the block opposite. If the rooms had curtains, they were never closed all the way, so one lived without privacy (a word that doesn't exist in Russian), but there was something reassuring about that.

Riding the bus home at night, I would marvel at the blaze of brightly lit windows, hundreds of them, thousands, in the long boxy apartment blocks that line the broad boulevards. It is unusual in a major world capital to see each and every rectangle of every apartment filled with an identical yellow

glow. Taking this to mean that the happy face of family life
was the ubiquitous condition, I felt at first a surge of nostalgia
for a simpler time in American life. Moscow is a lively,
sophisticated city with cheap movies, first-class theatre, non-
stop exhibitions, several sports stadiums and now even rock
concerts, but it is in no way an entertainment culture
comparable to any other European city. It took me a while to
understand that the apartments are all lit up because most
people didn't have the time, money or opportunities to go
out. They were home in the evenings – usually huddled
around the vodka.

And there were lots of people sharing each of those
brightly lit rooms. In most of the apartments in my building,
for instance, the same three-room space was occupied com-
munally by three families.

As I set about housekeeping, all the conveniences we take
for granted danced through my head: electric beater; blender;
food processor; toaster; coffee maker; wall oven; large
freezer; microwave. At least three or four hours of labour
were added to every working woman's day by the lack of
household conveniences. Doing the family wash and ironing,
for instance: the small machine in every apartment's bathroom was little more than a water-swisher, with no drying
capacity. So people lived through the winter with wash
hanging from every available place in the bathroom. God
knows where three families sharing this same tiny bathroom
hung their wash! The first time I did a handwash, I made the
mistake of leaving a white cotton turtleneck to soak for
twenty minutes. It developed huge brown blotches that
wouldn't come out – the minerals and metals in Moscow
water made painfully manifest. The vacuum cleaner was a
heavy canister without wheels or flexible hoses. Without
mops or brooms, the floor had to be scrubbed with a rag on
hands and knees. Gorbachev himself pointed out the cruel
disparity between the military state and the housewife's state
in his book, *Perestroika*:

> Our rockets can find Halley's comet and fly to Venus with amazing accuracy, but side by side with these scientific and technological triumphs . . . many Soviet households appliances are of poor quality.†

March was a struggle, a dialectic between winter and not-winter, with the promise of spring an ever-elusive synthesis. Snow fell every day, turned to slush, ran into mud rivers by mid-afternoon, and clenched up into icy tracks by sundown. Each morning I jogged up the footpath in the centre of our street and became expert at running over ice.

People of the neighbourhood paid little attention to me as they went about their morning chores, all well-bundled against the unrelenting winter weather. The women wore nearly identical wool coats with fake fur collars and lapels, the same soft zip-up boots, the ubiquitous wool cap pulled down hard on the forehead; only the colours varied. The men looked less drab, their great hats often made of real fur.

At my newspaper kiosk, it was not possible to find the daily *Pravda* after 7 a.m., and to get the coveted *Moscow News* I had to pay the seller to save it for me. A Russian woman who heard me struggling with the language stepped in to help. Many Muscovites were very friendly and warm to an American, but not the staff in state stores. The babushka on guard at my neighbourhood grocery store screwed her face with a scowl every time she saw my foreign face. 'You don't belong here,' she scolded. I got the same reception as I tried to buy the chits to purchase staples like eggs and milk. 'Why do you shop here? You have beriozka!' scolded the cashier, referring to the expensive hard-currency gift shops open only to foreigners. And nobody would take rubles from a foreigner. 'Will you pay in dollars?' was always the first question.

For Soviets, there were fewer goods to buy in all of Moscow than New Yorkers can find between any five blocks along Broadway in midtown Manhattan. So while hundreds

of billions of rubles were bulging out of mattresses, everybody carried an 'opportunity' bag at all times, on the chance
they might walk or drive past an impromptu queue at a spot
where goods were suddenly being unloaded on a streetcorner. 'Beer,' my driver would pant. 'I wish I had the time
to wait.' One joke had a Moscow bus driver announcing,
'First stop is the liquor store, second stop is the end of the
queue to the liquor store.'

The one place where food could be found was in 'the
market' – open-air stalls operated by migrant sellers from the
Asian republics, who drove their goods to town in the
stripped-down cars in which they slept. So I would walk to
the nearest 'market' and marvel at the pans of pickled
vegetables and ripe fruit and a veritable Soutine paradise of
freshly butchered blue-blooded meat. The prices, however,
were staggering – 24 rubles for a kilo of chicken – out of the
question for a Soviet doctor on an income of less than 200
rubles *a month*. The same kilo of chicken at the state stores
cost less than 3 rubles. Except that there *was* no chicken in
the state stores – or much of anything else.

The apocalyptic energy in Moscow quickly envelops one
in late-night philosophizing around kitchen tables. Politics is
the national sport. Russians fill their table for a guest even if
it takes two days of manoeuvring with their fixers to do it.
As the saying goes, 'There's nothing in the stores but
everything in the refrigerators.' Toasts were always offered
to the long-suffering Russian wife 'who is assured a special
place in heaven'.

My neighbours' table was splendid whenever they invited
me over for a meal. Bright orange salmon eggs glistened on
a plate that was set atop a glass to make it look like a fancy
platter; smoked fish and devilled eggs crowded sliced pot
roast, and flavoured vodka heated everyone's tongues. Soon
we felt as warm as real family and talked easily of our lives.

Irina remarked on how Americans seem very 'excited' all
the time – always smiling, energetic, enthusiastic, open,
optimistic – they *show* their emotions. 'We are more closed,'

she said. 'It's the Russian character. It's genetic.' Another strong contrast we noticed was in the available sources of self-esteem in our two societies.

For the Peterhovs, as for many Russians I would meet, their apartment was their refuge, their books their inner life, and their children their central source of pride. But as for pride in one's job or professional position – one of the central sources of self-esteem for Americans – Soviets have been deadened by their system. Irina, for example, had prepared very seriously for her career as a geologist. She showed me the books and monographs she had written in her earlier years. That was before she realized that her institute had no use for research because it meant changing things, and the system was impervious to change.

'You are the first representative of the "other" country, and we watch you organize your work here,' she confided in me sadly after some weeks. 'We admire so much your organization – it would never be possible for us to give our work such meaning because we cannot organize those who work with us.'

Most Soviets I met believed that their weaknesses had been engineered *genetically*, and this belief was murderously self-fulfilling. Whenever I asked my Russian friends how long they thought it would be before they would feel truly free, the answer was deeply pessimistic. 'Not for my children,' even young fathers in their thirties would tell me. 'You have to be born free to feel it.' The most optimistic prediction was, 'Maybe our children's children.'

Part of the reason for this pervasive pessimism is isolation. Before Gorbachev, the Soviet people simply had no 'civilian society' of informal clubs and organizations where they could identify common ways of thinking or share new, nonconformist ideas. They couldn't trust neighbours or co-workers with their inner thoughts; even family members were part of the circles of suspicion. The *narod* – the people – did not know its own mind.

Public-opinion polls are brand-new in the Soviet Union.

Until five years ago, the very concept of investigating public opinion was outlawed. The first national polls done only in the last two years have produced some stunning psycho-grams of a population whose opinion for decades was considered irrelevant.

Unfocused rage is the overall impression given by the *narod*. 'Extremely disturbed, emotionally coloured, unstable and constantly shifting' is the usual subjective state of the Soviet people today when they respond to surveys, I learned from the premier sociologist in the Soviet Union, Tatyana Zaslavskaya. There is no issue on which they find consensus except one – hatred of the Communist Party.

But their leaders have shut their eyes and ears to all such quasi-independent polling data. 'The only polling that can be believed is from our KGB,' a moody Gorbachev told one of the nation's top news editors.†

I gave Irina a questionnaire to discuss with the women at her workplace. They seized on it, eager for the excuse to examine their lives for once. But when they looked over the questions, one woman quipped, 'She writes about the periods of crisis in adult life. Hah – in the Soviet Union our whole life is a crisis!'

Sharing the daily ups and downs of those who must manoeuvre for survival around Gorbachev's baffling policy zig-zags, watching the news with those who had had the same hopes and aspirations he did and who once saw him as their saviour, was a heartbreaking and sobering experi-ence. Irina Peterhov's mild eyes and soft voice took on a suddenly harsher cast when we spoke of Gorbachev.

'In five years he has never said the words which people are very eager to hear from him,' she told me. 'So this is the question I would ask if I ever had an interview with Mr Gorbachev. "Who is responsible for the wreckage of our society for the last seventy years? The Communist Party, or Mickey Mouse?"'

When I left Moscow, I took the Peterhovs' last request as a sacred trust. 'When you write about Gorbachev,' the family implored me, 'write objectively. Don't idealize him. Hold him to your American standards.'

I have been undertaking character studies of American and world leaders for many years. The theory in my book *Passages* is that each of us develops throughout adulthood by stages. Between each stage are points of decision between progress and regression where we are challenged to shed a protective structure, and when we do we are left exposed and vulnerable, capable of stretching in ways we hadn't known before. For exceptional individuals, like Gorbachev, such passages assume the dimensions of deep personal transformations – they become in some ways different people. And those leaps of inner psychological development ultimately become the catalyst for a transformation of the society out of which they come. It allows the pathleader, like Gorbachev, to perform those creative actions that cause leaps of growth in human societies.

Cycles of decline and comeback occur in all civilizations. The Soviet Union had several jolting 'revolutions from above' before Gorbachev gave the phenomenon a name. The model was set by Peter the Great at the beginning of the eighteenth century when that royal revolutionary began dismantling the patrimonial state. Alexander II launched another top-down revolution when he freed the serfs in 1861. And a case is made by some historians that out of the chaos of war and revolution in 1917, Lenin formulated another revolution from above, fusing a utopian vision with a brand-new kind of Party-state based on the absence of law and the institutionalization of terror. Gorbachev attempted a transformation no less stunning – a revolution that has so far destroyed the ideology of the Bolshevik revolution and is casting about frantically for a belief system to put in its place. He is in a race with history.

Usually a great leader faces a cruel repudiation or a devastating personal setback, and only after a period 'in the wilderness' of self-contemplation and despair does he or she return to make the ultimate transformation of the society. Franklin Roosevelt, Eleanor Roosevelt, Churchill, De Gaulle, Gandhi and Sadat all exemplify this dynamic. Rarely does a leader have to undergo the radical inner transformation *while managing* a revolution. This is Gorbachev's challenge.

I see Gorbachev as having already lived at least five lives. The book's structure follows the structure of his chameleon-like existence. It tracks the stunning ways in which he has changed over his life, and the fateful ways in which he has *not* changed.

By 1989 most of the world had invested great hopes in Mikhail Gorbachev – and then Something Happened. I watched it happen. Failing to deliver on the promises of his perestroika after four years in power, he began to lose his authority in the streets at home, which is why, in his fifth year, he had to formally codify the powers of a dictator. The question hanging over this book is this: can Gorbachev remake himself once more? Or has he reached his limit?

The secret of a leader lies in the tests he has faced over the whole course of his life and the *habit of action* he develops in meeting those tests. This was the plumb line I pursued in tracing the life story of Mikhail Gorbachev. The ultimate change he purported to want in Soviet society was a complete psychological and spiritual rebirth. Therefore, we must understand what experiences shaped his own psychology and spiritual beliefs. Who formed him, imprinted him, protected and promoted him? Where did it come from, this courage to take the risk of redrawing the contours of the world? And what do we see in Gorbachev's life history to explain how the zealous reformer could be transformed into the benign repressor? What are the secrets behind the feverish gleam in the eyes of Mikhail Gorbachev?

And so, this book is an x-ray of history – some of which I witnessed up close. It is the human story of the making of Mikhail Sergeyevich the man, and the political story of the making of Gorbachev the statesman. By studying the pattern of his actions from earliest boyhood to his position as the primary agent of global change in the latter half of the twentieth century, we can begin to see the world through Gorbachev's eyes.

II

First Gorbachev:

Country Cossack

1931–1949

Mikhail Sergeyevich was born into famine in a hut on a muddy river, no more than a slit in the caked earth of the Stavropol steppe. But famine here was no act of God, it was an act of state. Stalin had always been suspicious of the freedom-loving farmers in the deep south of Mother Russia, and in 1931, at the time of Mikhail's birth on 2 March into the broken ice of spring, the people of Stavropol were living through one of the most diabolical acts of political terror ever devised.

Given the odds, Gorbachev should not have survived. The artificial famine† by which Stalin sought to subdue the peasants who resisted his policy of collectivization wiped out one-third of the population of Gorbachev's village between the autumn of 1933 and spring of 1934, when food ran out completely. Watery millet soup was their sustenance, supplemented by stray kernels of corn the people could scratch out of mice holes after the state confiscated their harvest. In certain villages all the children between the ages of one and two succumbed to starvation†. One of Gorbachev's teachers remembers that 'Some people were so weak, when they went to bury their loved ones they just dropped two or three into the same grave:'

But the baby Misha came from a long line of survivors. Far

from being typical submissive Russian peasants, Gorbachev's ancestors were Ukrainian Cossacks, a band of daring and energetic people who had escaped their landowner masters and pushed down from the Ukraine and the Don area in search of virgin soil and religious freedom, settling in the southernmost wilds of the territory of Stavropol known as the Caucasus.

The vastness. That is what drew them. The shifting mirage of the Russian steppe, open prairie land, is a gentle roll of thousands of uninterrupted miles between the Black and Caspian seas. (Renowned for its natural springs, it later became the site of health spas catering to the aristocracy.) 'Just as when the energetic dynamic people came from different parts of the world to settle in America, the same kind of settlers came from different parts of Russia to settle in the Caucasian area – those who liked to work, to live the good and prosperous life,' says Professor Chuguyev, a historian at the Agricultural Institute of Stavropol. It was the equivalent of America's wild west.

The term Cossack means free people (from the Turkish), and these runaways from serfdom became the symbol of independence and free-spiritedness in Russian literature. Burned into the imagination of every rural boy was the spectacle of a band of Cossacks thundering by with drawn sabres, their horses throwing off flakes of soapy foam. They were fierce soldiers, who first learned to fight off the Tatars back in the fifteenth century, and later bargained to preserve their freedom by serving as a mercenary military force for Polish kings or Russian czars, who used them to carry out pogroms. But the Ukrainian Cossacks who pushed south were different, very much frontiersmen in the Daniel Boone mould, and this is the stock from which Gorbachev came.

Even today, ask an educated Soviet if he's heard of 'Privolnoye' and chances are he'll say, 'What's that?' Privolnoye means 'vastness' or 'free' and was the name given to the village where Gorbachev's great-grandparents settled. The family first came there from the Ukraine in the 1840s, according to records found by the local Party committee. The village is isolated in the far western corner of Stavropol, an enormous territory stretching from the Caucasian mountain ranges to the lower Volga within the Russian Republic, which is one of the fifteen constituent republics of the USSR. Privolnoye would be twenty-four hours by train from Moscow, but even today there is no train, and in winter the one road from town quickly chokes down under three or four feet of snow to barely more than a horsepath.

Privolnoye is a pretty village of 3,300 that still looks like a rural hamlet in the American midwest, circa 1930. It is the centre of the Sverdlov collective farm in Krasnogvardeiskoye (Red Guard) district. The old communal houses are wooden, with tin or thatched roofs, and every one has bright blue shutters threaded with white woodwork. Each plot, twenty feet apart, is enclosed by a neat picket fence, some with necklaces of morning glories. Only since Privolnoye's favourite son has become the power in Moscow have some of the roads been paved and new brick houses built for individual families.

The house in which Gorbachev's mother lives today, built in the 1960s, is the same folk design as the wooden cottages, but with a wooden porch and grape arbour. Her son has had the house fitted out with a special telephone line and a security system. Just around the corner, however, the paved road dissolves into dirt and a caucus of ducks slows up the car. Although the house sits on a side street only a short distance from the centre of the village, foreigners and reporters are kept scrupulously away from the dwelling. But when a reporter from the newspaper *Komsomolskaya Pravda* did get through, Maria Panteleyevna lived up to her reputation as a virago: She complained that the last time she saw her son was over three years ago – and then he only alighted for half an hour in Privolnoye for a 'photo opportunity'.† Only recently was she able to get a colour TV to replace her old black and white set.

Gorbachev's mother, though in her eighties, like many

Russian peasant women still does her own chores and bakes her own bread. In any case, her cottage is not the home in which Mikhail Sergeyevich was born and raised. After much persuasion, I was the first print journalist to be taken to the actual site of Gorbachev's childhood home.

A white hump of matted mud, dung and straw, with two or three little rooms inside, the Gorbachev hut once crouched across a dirt road from a stream called the Yegorlyk river. Here, the village falls off into big baked loaves of broken earth coughing up straw under the bleached sky – and nothing else. Misha's Gorbachev grandparents lived immediately next door. Today the huts are gone. Even in the old days only a few dwellings stood here, says a neighbour. Survival was the imperative of every waking moment and so, to borrow a line from the national poet hero of Ukrainians, Taras Shevchenko, the villagers had simply 'strewn decrepit huts along the hill just as a drunk beggar drops his satchels'.

Why would settlers have chosen so isolated a spot? When state service became compulsory and permanent under Peter the Great in 1722, the autocracy of central Russia began to erase separate national identities and cultural traditions, and there was no other choice for people of independent spirit. Gorbachev's ancestors were escaping the 'fatal avalanche rolling from the north to the Black Sea and covering everything . . . with a uniform shroud of slavery',† as Herzen described it. Here, far from the seat of power – which was first in St Petersburg, home of the czars, and later in Moscow, citadel of Soviet Communist power – the peasants were free to keep their own traditions, hunting and fishing, raising livestock, and living off the natural riches of the land. Independence is in Mikhail Gorbachev's genes. That is what makes him so different from the mass of Soviets.

Country Values

Gorbachev has confirmed that his maternal grandparents also were Ukrainian. Gopkalo was the family name, according to villagers. Growing up, Misha learned the Ukrainian language at home (though by official edict such a language no longer existed) and was firmly rooted by ballads and poetry in his Cossack past and the pride of his free peasant forebears. His personal associates today note that Gorbachev still frequently calls up the old Cossack rhymes of his youth, and in the recollections of his childhood friends is evidence that he identified strongly with the romantic Cossack ideal.

'He always wore a military Cossack-style hat,'† is one of the strongest memories of the girl who grew up next door. Another village woman recalls his gleaming patent leather boots. And his teachers prattle on about how he loved music: 'He danced, with all the girls or by himself, he always danced. A cheerful boy.'

Cossacks fancied that moustaches made them more fierce, and so young Misha grew a moustache. 'He was handsome and very smartly dressed – the mark didn't show at all then under his full hair,' adds the village girl wistfully. 'All the girls would be after him at the same time.'†

In fact, he came into this world with the blood-red mark on his forehead, his mother saw it, and it did show when he was a little boy with short-cropped hair. What did it mean? Russian peasants are superstitious about such things. Was he marked for greatness? Or stained with a curse? In a conformist society, the latter would be a more common assumption. It may have added to the reasons why his mother kept the boy so close to her, reasons which became fundamental to their survival in a society later to be crippled by an acute shortage of male labour.

Who or what ignited his romantic nature? Clearly it was not his father. Sergei Andreyevich Gorbachev was a quiet man, say neighbours, with a mechanical turn of mind. He was never active in the Communist Party, only joining it as a formality when he was sent to the Front, at the age of thirty-three, to fight the Germans in what the Russians call the Great Patriotic War. Always reliable, the father with his generous mouth and mild eyes measured out his words of advice with care and shied away from public debate. According to Grigory Gorlov, a close family friend and Party official on the district Party committee, who supervised the elder Gorbachev from after the war until his sudden death in February 1976, 'he was sometimes a little bit slow to grasp the situation and move forward'. Sergei Andreyevich was content to operate a small machine-tractor station with about twenty people under his supervision, for almost half a century. He appears to have been a relatively insignificant figure in Gorbachev's life.

The patriarch of the family was grandfather Pantelei Yefimovich Gopkalo, his mother's father. Gopkalo was the chairman of the local collective farm, which made him the first person of the village. Villagers during Stalin's time related to the chairman of the kolkhoz as the real boss. They were obliged to him for everything. Misha spent his childhood living with his grandfather.

Next in importance was his mother, Maria Panteleyevna, the sparkplug of the family and the noisiest voice in the village of two thousand people. Large and strong as a tree stump, her meaty face lumped with frown lines, 'she was not much educated and writes with difficulty,'† says a local educator, but that didn't stop her talking. Nothing stopped Maria Panteleyevna from speaking her mind.

'She was the very first to raise her voice in village meetings, a very stubborn, wilful woman,' said Gorlov, who knew the Gorbachev family well. Did she also lay down the law in the Gorbachev house? I asked. He laughed. 'Yes. Maria Panteleyevna did.'

Even at the age of four the boy Misha was painfully thin, his wrist and knees faint scribbles, his eyes gaunt and glittering. But in each of the rare boyhood pictures of Mikhail Gorbachev, his eyes penetrate straight ahead and lock on to the viewer. In one pose with his grandfather Gopkalo, the resemblance between the two is striking – the burning brown eyes, the broad face and full lips. The older man's arm sits on the boy's shoulder in a gesture of love, and the boy's hand rests trustingly on his grandfather's knee.

Misha was also very close to his grandmother Gopkalo, a tall woman with a spotless white babushka tied down over her forehead tightly as a nun's wimple. A devout Russian Orthodox Christian, she took the boy to church and made certain he was immersed in a tub of holy water and properly baptized. In open violation of the state-decreed atheism she kept icons, those shimmering images of saints rendered on wood with a veil of gold. When Stalin's Terror reached its peak, she, like other peasants of the older generation, hid their wooden saints behind ordinary pictures.

Gorbachev's mother is also a believer to this day, according to Archbishop Antony of Stavropol. Russian mothers have breathed basic Christian values into their sons for a millennium, and the Archbishop has no doubt that Mikhail would have 'absorbed the idea that connects all Christians – that God is the one who created the world and in every human we must see the image of God and treat him with love'. But there was obvious tension between parents and teachers on this point. The Communist Party had replaced religion and Josef Stalin cast himself as god the father. In school, the children had to spout back the compulsory line. 'All the parents of our students were believers,' says Misha's high-school chemistry teacher, Maria Grevtseva, 'but all the students themselves were atheists.'

It is natural for an adolescent to spurn the belief system of his elders and leap to its most infuriating opposite, hoping to demonstrate an independence of mind he does not yet truly feel. So it is believable when Gorbachev himself, in the only interview he has given on his own background, granted in 1989 to *Argumenty i Fakty* to satisfy an increasingly curious Soviet public, says that he did not feel the need to return to the Church.

The more important point is that he was raised with the natural values of country people – not those of Communist dogma. He did not grow up in a family of apparatchiks (those who serve the Party apparatus) or even one involved in politics. 'Christian values are in his genes,' says Nadezhda Mikhailova, one of those closest to Gorbachev since his university years. 'I think he inherited a love of life and love for work. He's totally indifferent to religion but he respects it. Peasants were always more respectful of religion.'

Those values – love of life and love for work – are exactly the ones Gorbachev would return to and espouse as a leader: 'Everyone should live as well as his or her work warrants,' he would later state as his starting point in the onslaught on the Bolshevik central-command system and the nation of freeloaders it has bred. As a leader, Mikhail Sergeyevich would commit himself to making possible a 'moral recovery' from his nation's deformed values. He communicates his values with the fervour of a Bible-thumping Baptist preacher. And on his historic visit to Italy in 1989, when he crossed St Peter's Square to seek an alliance with the Pope, he would make his 'confession' before the world over TV for 'our mistake in treating religion superficially'. Indeed, he casts his 'belief' in perestroika as a faith and pleads with his countrymen to take the leap of faith with him. Perhaps Gorbachev is able to take a 'leap of faith' because he learned, through his grandparents' belief in Christianity, the mystical power and comfort of an Orthodoxy that promised release from suffering only in the next life.

These were the positive themes in his early life. Darker themes threatened to overshadow them. Themes Gorbachev has gone to some lengths to keep hidden.

'Kulak Mania'

'If you want to find the key to a man's soul, look into his childhood eyes,' the poet Yevtushenko had advised me. 'Gorbachev was from a farmer's family. He saw through the eyes of his father how agriculture was destroyed, then the disaster of village life after the Second World War, when peasants thought they were working for common victory at the Front, forgiving Stalin all their poverty and hunger. But when the victory came and Stalin's emissaries went to the villages and confiscated even the seeds for the next crop, they asked themselves, "Why must we suffer again?"'

In fact, they were not farmers, but virtual slaves on state farms. Yevtushenko was certain that Gorbachev carried the wound of injustices wrought by the state on farmers. I had a hunch there was a more personal wound.

Gorbachev gave a glimpse of how his family responded to Stalin's forced collectivization in the interview with *Argumenty i Fakty*, but he mentioned only one side of the family. 'My maternal grandfather, Pantelei Yefimovich, was one of the organizers of partnerships for joint working of the land and later of collective farms, and was chairman of a collective farm for many years.' Gorbachev continued: 'My father, Sergei Andreyevich, and my mother, Maria Panteleyevna, also worked on the land – first in their own peasant economy, then in a partnership for joint working of the land, still later in a collective farm and at a machine-tractor station.'

In that opaque and condensed account is hidden the terrible contradiction that the Gorbachev of today is struggling to redress. The 'partnership for joint working of the land' was a *voluntary* association of neighbours organized by Gorbachev's maternal grandparents in the 1920s to encourage people to settle in the new territory. But collectivization, while it started out with high ideals, became a *forced* confiscation of land and livestock by the state machine that crushed more than the spirit of these people. Resistant families were arrested and deported. In the Stavropol region, six million households had disappeared by the time Misha Gorbachev was born. Though Privolnoye residents say they don't remember any killing, rivers in the Northern Caucasus were filled with bloated bodies. Terror and lawlessness racked the rural life of the Caucasus all through the 1930s.†

So the Gopkalo side of the family, according to official accounts, stepped forward to help lead the government drive to subdue the farmers of Privolnoye. Whether for reasons of idealism or self-preservation, or both, they not only surrendered their land to the state and joined the collectivization – they enforced it. That bought them safety.

But Gorbachev's *father's* father had never been mentioned, and no one in Moscow would speak about him. I only stumbled on the family secret by asking the Gorbachev's neighbours in Privolnoye. Andrei Gorbachev, Misha's paternal grandfather, never became a Party member. 'The Gorbachev family raised chickens and pigs and some cattle and sent the meat to be sold in Moscow,' the neighbours told me. 'They had their own farm, too. They lived over on the edge of the village, where all the Ukrainians settled.'

'His grandfather lived in the very last hut,' I was told by Alexandrovna Yakovenko, formerly the girl who lived next door. 'Every evening [Misha and I] went together to fetch the cows from the pasture for the families – this was our childhood.'

In 1929, Stalin announced the aim of 'the liquidation of the kulaks as a class'. Official statements instructed local Party activists to 'deal with the malicious kulak as we dealt with the bourgeoisie in 1918'. The kulak, or 'rich peasant',† was in reality the hardest worker and the most efficient and prosperous farmer, as much admired as he was envied by more passive villagers. And he was hardly rich or exploitative; only a minority owned more than two or three cows or horses, and only 1 per cent of private farms employed more than a single paid worker. The entire value of goods confiscated by the state from the kulaks was pathetic – 400 million rubles, between 170 and 400 rubles a household, or, at the inflated official rate of exchange, $90 to $210 per family.† Even more perverse was the fact that the average kulak, hunted down as sub-human for supposedly representing a wealthy class, had a more meagre income than that of the average rural official who replaced and persecuted him.

Stalin's main purpose in branding the kulaks was to antagonize relations between the classes. In villages like Privolnoye it was a struggle between the forcibly collectivized peasantry and the New Class of petty Party bureaucrats whose sole function was to maintain control. Stalin's purpose, of course, was to liquidate the natural leaders in the countryside so the Communist Party could subjugate the peasantry, rounding them up into large collective farms. And as the peasantry was brought under control, rural life as a whole began an 'almost irreversible' disintegration, according to Andrei Sakharov. No one took care of anything, because no one owned anything. Cows went unfed, farm machinery unrepaired, and the soil which had nurtured such lively national cultures was treated with barbaric indifference, for that was the essence of the new Soviet man – indifference.

The hunting down of kulaks turned into a saturnalia of arrests, the deportation of kulaks into a forced resettlement of millions. The frenzy had all the elements of the Nazi persecution of Jews. As one Party activist later explained, 'What I said to myself at the time was "They are not human beings, they are kulaks."'

'They would threaten people with guns, as if they were under a spell, calling small children, "kulak bastards", screaming "bloodsucker!"'† writes the formerly banned novelist Vasily Grossman. But the most sinister aspect of those who carried out this bloodthirsty task is that they all knew their victims, and knew them well.

Grandfather Gorbachev was a 'middle peasant', the designation for a farmer who owned his own land but couldn't afford to pay others to work for him. The elder Gorbachev never gave up his cattle and pigs, even when he had to work also on the collective farm, and went on selling his meagre produce in open defiance of the collectivization policy. The stubbornness of such resistance and the proportion of individual farms that held out in the Caucasus right up to 1933, despite increasingly harsh measures, drove Stalin to an obsession even he termed 'kulak mania'.†

Party officials recognized that middle peasants looked up to 'kulaks' as an example of efficiency and prosperity. So, to kill off their aspirations and bring them around to accepting the collective farm, or kolkhoz, as the only means of survival, Stalin himself devised a repression for middle peasants, too. The whole North Caucasus was earmarked for punishment in January 1933 by a special commission empowered 'to exact compulsory labour, and to evict, deport and punish, even with death, the resisters'.†

The Terror

When I was taken to the local Party headquarters in Privolnoye to learn more about those times, my escorts and I had to stop first before a trough meant for washing mud off our boots. Inside, inhabitants who knew Gorbachev as a boy dredged up their own painful memories of the famine, collectivization, occupation and war.

At first, there was reason to rejoice in the promise of collectivization, they report. 'At the time, we thought collectivization was the only good way to feed our large families,' says Nikolai Lubenko, a grizzled old man with a chestful of plastic-covered medals. 'For hundreds of years families wanted to live here in their villages with their own private land, but the Party propaganda did its work.'

Gorbachev's maternal grandparents, the Gopkalos, were originally 'prosperous farmers', according to Gorbachev's close friend at university, Vladimir Lieberman. Why, then, were they so eager to give up their own private land and stocks to collaborate with the repressive Stalin regime? I asked two men who had worked with the family.

'They trusted. The Soviet government made a propaganda trick – they supplied the peasants with toys,' explains Alexander Yakovenko, who worked with Gorbachev and his father in the fields.

Gorbachev's father was among the men from villages all around who came to gawk from their little horse-drawn britchkas the day the state delivered to Privolnoye thirteen shiny mechanized monsters – Ford and Caterpillar tractors – from

the planet America. Their harvests were good for the first
couple of years, but then the state deliberately set quotas
beyond any imaginable yield; and when the newly collectivized farmers failed to deliver, all the grain was removed, every
handful of food, and the Privolnians were left to starve. Even
the surrounding Soviet population was forbidden to help.

'Now we know the truth,' grimaces Mr Lubenko, that
Stalin's 'terror-famine' was designed to break the spine of
these non-submissive yeomen in the south. As the Privolnians gradually opened up to talk about the 'very difficult
times' they had during collectivization, they clutched their
hands together very tightly. Their eyes drifted into the
anonymity of distance, their sentences often broke off in the
middle, as if they were swallowing a sob.

Misha, being a keenly intuitive boy, must have felt the
crescendo of terror that heralded Stalin's great purge, even
though he was only six years old in 1937. That was the year
people began to disappear from every family. Uncles,
cousins, the loose-tongued ones first. Then brothers and
fathers. Overnight all the teachers were arrested. Children
came to school and saw all new faces. Finally students too
were expelled and condemned as enemies of the people. The
scorpions of suspicion and fear scuttled through the streets
of the village and inside their houses people sucked the air
of fear, even in the presence of their loved ones.

'Sister against sister, children against their parents – no
one had any guarantee his family members wouldn't be
arrested for any trumped-up accusation,' describes Matilda
Ignatenko, Misha's German teacher. Land confiscated from
those purged became available to the very same people who
had informed on them. Mr Yakovenko observes the grim
irony: state repression became the poor peasant's rescue from
state famine. 'Those years, '37 and '38, were pretty good –
food became more plentiful as people were weeded out.'

One of the those 'weeded out' and imprisoned for ten
years was Mr Yakovenko's father, while his brother died
during deportation – where, he doesn't even know. Yet he

seems to bear no grudge against Gorbachev's maternal grandfather, who was put in charge of collectivizing the village. The prosperous farmer who jumped to the government side to save his own skin is not hated as a collaborator but rather respected as a latter-day feudal lord. An appreciation of authoritarianism runs as the unspoken theme through everything that is said.

Mr Lubenko mashes his cigarettes with toughened gums, remembering the mass psychology that excused these brutal relations between loved ones. 'We believed we had to restore Soviet power. So we were sure all those arrested were really guilty of being enemies of the people.'

Matilda Ignatenko shakes her head in disagreement. 'My father was a gardener, a good man – one of the first to join the kolkhoz.' He, too, was 'weeded out'. She whispers the rest with the hiss of bottled-up shame. 'My whole life I had to disown my real father. People would ask me and I said he died.' Renunciation of condemned family members was the only way a student or teacher could be reinstated in school. These grim and shameful memories of families turned against themselves as part of the terrible weight of repressed memories – repressed until the era of Gorbachev's glasnost – that have kept tens of millions of Soviets bent and passive under the rubble of fear.

It is normal for youngsters to register any scandal within the family – especially an event that no one talks about – as something to be ashamed of, and this was the common reaction of Gorbachev's many contemporaries who had a family member branded a people's enemy under Stalin. 'We never remembered if family members were taken to prison when we were young,' affirms one of Gorbachev's university classmates. 'I can't imagine speaking about it.'

The Family Shame

Misha Gorbachev was not spared such tragedy within his own family. Grandfather Gorbachev, his father's father, was on the list in 1937. The lists of those to be arrested were drawn up by local Party activists, who were open to bribes and free to settle ancient family feuds. A barefoot man turned 'knocker',† or informer, might call his neighbour a kulak simply because the neighbour had a pair of boots; evidence was irrelevant. Confidential State Political Police reports cited in *Harvest of Sorrow* reveal that kulaks were stripped of their shoes and garments and left in their underclothes. Village hooligans simply looted their dwellings of boots, women's underwear, washtubs, anything. Lower-echelon Party officials also stole with impunity, drinking the still-warm soup on the stove, downing all the alcohol, even filching spectacles.

Grandfather Gorbachev was dragged out of his kitchen by secret police; they gave no reason. The women of the hut watched in dread, sobbing but afraid to scream, as he was herded off like a goat. Along with about forty other villagers, like Mr Lubenko's brother, he was locked in a wagon and taken to a transit point in the north: the city of Archangel, a major religious centre. Deportees were of every age and condition, including pregnant women, and children (15 per cent of whom reportedly died in transit). Tea or soup was the only nourishment during the several days' trip.

Their first sight on arriving in Archangel was the brilliant one of soaring golden bulbs on the many churches. It was a phantom vision of deliverance: the churches had been taken over to be used as transit prisons. Inside, the deportees were stacked in tiers on wooden sleeping platforms, unable to wash. Some roamed the town begging for help, but the locals, under strict orders to ignore them, refused even to pick up their dead. The poet Anna Akhmatova captured the horror of these years in her 'Requiem': 'It was a time when only the dead smiled, happy in their peace.'

Grandfather Gorbachev was sentenced to nine years in the gulag.† He had been done for by a neighbour, from whom a denunciation was coaxed to the effect that the old man had hidden forty pounds of grain for his family from the collective's harvest. The family believed he had been executed.

Although the morning after his grandfather was taken, young Misha probably would have awakened to the same serpent of mist crawling along the muddy river, the same comforting monotony of a life frozen in time, he would later hear his grandmother's hushed and anguished stories about that terrible night. In 1987, he reportedly confided to editors of the Italian Communist Party newspaper, *L'Unità*, that he'd choked back tears when he saw a similar scene in the mid-1980s film *Repentance*.

But that wasn't the end of grandfather Gorbachev's saga.

A few years later he returned 'by chance',† according to a consultant to the Central Committee, Nikolai Shishlin. The benign explanation is that Stalin's main henchman in the purges, Yezhov, a very small man with stiff hair whose name meant 'porcupine',† was himself executed in 1939. And to prove that Yezhov had been guilty of errors, some 38,000–40,000 people were released from labour camps that year.† The total number of prisoners then in labour camps is estimated at from eight to twelve million. So, apart from the tiny fraction released in 1939, it was almost unheard of for those sent to the gulag to be freed before Stalin's death in 1953. Moreover, the KGB recently revealed that 786,098 Soviet citizens were shot to death as 'enemies of the state' during Stalin's Terror.† Why, then, was this man picked out of the ocean of lost souls toiling in the Siberian wasteland?

The shame must have seeped through to the sensitive young Gorbachev, especially since the tragedy of the millions of innocents ground up by Stalin's cold-blooded policies wouldn't be revealed to him until Khrushchev made his famous secret speech in 1956. It would be years before Mikhail Sergeyevich dared breathe a word of the family secret. He confided to a few university friends that he had had a close relative who was repressed, describing him as a middle peasant. And decades later, as General Secretary, he showed signs that he still harboured that shame and sense of moral outrage when he spoke, at a special legislative session commemorating the seventieth anniversary of the Bolshevik revolution, about the 'injustice' and 'excesses' wreaked on middle peasants in the thirties. Shame is one of the most painful emotions, and the urge to redress its wrongful cause can be a powerful motivation in life.

Living with Contradiction

I subsequently learned what became of grandfather Gorbachev from Grigory Gorlov, the family friend on the district Party committee. He says Gorbachev's grandfather was evacuated at the beginning of the war to an area in the Kizlyarsky Steppe in the Caucasus to the south-east of Stavropol – an area controlled by Mikhail Suslov.

Suslov is a sinister figure whose name has been definitively, if mysteriously, linked with Gorbachev's rise to power. Suslov had been a member of the special commission devised by Stalin in 1932 to crush those who resisted collectivization – among them Gorbachev's grandfather.† Successful in that effort, Suslov made himself a specialist in repressions, which enabled him to rise in the hierarchy of a despotic system to become the Kremlin's chief propagandist.

When the German army pushed into Stavropol in August 1942, Suslov, then First Secretary of the territory, fled in a big Volga with a small band who went into hiding in the Kizlyarsky Steppe. Although he was not behind enemy lines, Suslov was responsible for co-ordinating partisan activity in occupied Stavropol.

It is conceivable that grandfather Gorbachev worked for Suslov in underground activity.† Russian partisans who have emigrated to the West say that former prisoners under Stalin were commonly used as agents, since everyone knew they had been repressed and would be less suspicious of them.

Those who worked with Suslov in the Kizlyarsky Steppe were also responsible for carrying out the forced deportation of the entire Muslim population of Stavropol – about a million people – who were arbitrarily accused by Stalin of 'collaboration with the occupying forces'. If grandfather Gorbachev did indeed work for Suslov, it could have forged the family connection that later paved the path to power in Moscow for Mikhail Sergeyevich.

It is almost certain that grandfather Gopkalo was known to Suslov. The significance of Gorbachev's maternal grandfather has been overlooked. But as an 'organizer of collective farms', not just the chairman of one kolkhoz, Gopkalo would almost certainly have been involved in partisan activity during the occupation of Privolnoye, and as such would have come under the supervision of both the secret police and Suslov.

What is more, Gorbachev himself worked along with his father for five years, up to the age of eighteen, at a machine-tractor station. Under Stalin, machine-tractor stations were set up to ensure control of the Party. Every MTS had a political department, directly linked to Moscow, which dictated to the collective farms their quotas and prices and made sure all their food production was surrendered to the state. So, starting at thirteen, Gorbachev combined political work for the Party with his studies. The patriarch of the family, grandfather Gopkalo, would have been in a position to give the boy such an important post so young. And Gopkalo's high status would also explain how Gorbachev managed to get the important award that paved his way into Moscow State University.

It is plain that young Misha became acquainted early with shame and betrayal on one side of the family, and compromise on the other. He lived with the secret shame of knowing that his freedom-loving grandfather Gorbachev, from whom he took his restless energy, had been branded and broken as an 'enemy of the people'. At the same time he lived with the collaboration of his maternal grandparents, the Gopkalos, whose scant privileges included the extra food that may have ensured their grandson's very survival. What's more, grandfather Gopkalo could provide Misha with literature from the farm's library and later use his connections to advance the boy's interests.

So Mikhail Gorbachev learned two opposing life lessons. One said preserve the pride of your independence at all costs. And the cost was very high. The other taught that survival entailed compromise – compromise with whoever was in power.

Living with both – conviction and compromise at the same time – became Gorbachev's moral habit of action, as the ancient Greeks defined character. It rendered his character complex and his words and actions often contradictory. As his story unfolds, Gorbachev will be seen as learning a daring high-wire act. He starts out moving in one direction, and while everyone is holding their breath to see if he can maintain his balance, in a flash, he flips in mid-air and begins moving in the opposite direction. It is a style of mental acrobatics peculiar to Soviet man – what I came to call doublethink.

A Southern Temper

It is often said in the village that Mikhail took on his mother's character, while his younger brother, Alexander, took on his father's. 'Emotionally, my mother influenced me more,' he told a German journalist. 'Intellectually, my father. Even though he was a simple man, I learned much from him.'†

Insatiably curious, his nervous system wired more tautly than most (he later sought treatment for a chemical imbalance), the boy always loved a good argument. Just like his mother. According to Alexandrovna Ivanovna Yakovenko, the girl next door, his first quarrels were about, of all things, baseball.

Alexandrovna Ivanovna emerges from a yard alive with ducks and roses, shuffling like an old woman, her legs gnarled and as thick as tree stumps. But upon hearing Gorbachev's name she is immediately transformed. The girlish delicacy of her smile and the devilry in her blue eyes push back the furrows of her face and she kicks off her galoshes and heavy burdens to take us inside to talk.

She remembers their childhood as joyful. Young Misha obviously liked his little spitfire of a neighbour. She would let the wind flutter her skirt and play with her silky hair as she climbed the slope before his hut, water pails yoked over her shoulders. The big excitement was swimming in the brown river. The boys glowed like white worms in the distance of their part of the river, while the girls, covered only with cotton underwear, slithered in, giggling, down at the other end. But just let a bunch of rowdy boys set upon Alexandrovna in her privacy and Misha would come running to shout at them or slap them on the side of the head. 'He was brave,' she sighs, 'and nimble.'

They played their own form of baseball – lapta – where the batter swats at a soft ball tossed by a teammate, and tries to gain a base before a member of the opposing team tags him with the ball. Too poor to have a real ball, Misha and Alexandrovna fashioned one out of wool. And every evening when she and Misha went together to fetch the cows for their families, they argued.

'You hit the wrong way!' he'd jeer.

'What do you know, smartie!' she would shoot back.

There was not a single game without quarrelling, she recalls, chuckling at the memory of her running argument with young Misha over who was better, the girls or the boys. 'The boys offended us girls because they always wanted to be the winners.'

It wasn't an obsession with the game – Gorbachev never showed any interest in athletics and didn't play a sport all through high school or university. No, he was just naturally argumentative. He was, after all, a hot-blooded southerner, and according to a local educator, 'People down here are as explosive as gunpowder.' But even when his emotional trigger was set off and his voice rose upwards into the sing-song pitch of the temperamental southerner, Gorbachev used his brain, rather than his considerable brawn, to impose his will.

Neighbours and teachers vow Misha never got into big fistfights with the other boys; when he shouted at them they backed off. He even challenged the military representative of the district when the man visited the secondary school to inculcate patriotism in the children. Gorbachev's classmate, Boris Gladskoi, remembers the moment vividly.

'Gorbachev had a quarrel with him, very friendly, but he told the officer he was not correct. And Gorbachev proved that he was right!' Two hundred people attended this compulsory meeting, and almost everyone applauded the outspoken boy for standing up to the military boss. 'He was decisive and strong in defending his position,' says Boris. But the critical point is that young Misha did not set himself against authority, he presented himself as a bright reformer intent on improving the authority's programme. As Boris says, still amazed, 'He convinced the military man.'

Years later his classmates at university would take notice of Gorbachev's strong opinions and testy outbursts. Later still he would learn to control his temper, to be so controlled, in fact, he used it to probe for weakness in his adversaries – 'not like Khrushchev, who used a meat axe,' reported Richard Nixon, 'but like a stiletto'.

The Germans Are Coming

Mikhail Sergeyevich was ten years old when his father went off to war, not to be seen again for five years. Gorbachev speaks with pride about his father: 'He fought in the Great Patriotic War as a combat engineer. He received a medal for valour, for the crossing of the Dnieper.' Sergei Andreyevich had seven male relatives who died in the war, only one other lived through it.†

Gorbachev was too young to experience the glory and gore of war that give the warrior his manhood. He lived the grovelling daily grind of the victims of occupation, and that makes all the difference between him and previous Soviet leaders, who paved their chests with medals and conferred lofty military titles upon themselves. It also sets him apart from men like George Bush and Deng Xiaoping and Fidel Castro and the hardline Communist leadership in Eastern Europe that crumbled in a matter of months once Gorbachev announced that the Red Army would no longer prop it up by force.

For men of Bush's generation, war was the highlight of their lives; for Gorbachev, life began after the war.

When German soldiers swept through Privolnoye in August 1942, a sultry haze lay over the steppe. The ripe floods of wheat smoked with yellow dust because the villagers had nothing left to harvest it with; all the machinery, all the horses and cows and sheep, all the able-bodied tractor drivers had been evacuated. Privolnoye had been reduced to a reservation of women, children and pigs.

Combat did not spread as far as Privolnoye. 'The Germans came like a wave,' describes Gorlov, the close family friend and an official on the district Party committee. 'They took a census of how many people lived here, then a senior Russian would be appointed administrator of the occupation, and the Germans kept going.' About sixty soldiers were left in village.

Germans were searching for food and Jews. Gorlov recalls that 'all the Jewish families were gathered together', on the collective farm he ran. It was his duty to prepare about 370 Jewish families caught fleeing from the German occupation of the western Ukraine for 'deportation'. Tonelessly, he describes how the women, children and old people were slaughtered at a nearby river; later, when the Soviets wanted to build a water reserve on the site, the remains were moved elsewhere to be burned.

Hitler's main interest in this territory was to cut off the Soviet Union from its oilfields in the Transcaucasus. He needed the help of the people in the northern Caucasus, and research by West German scholar Alexander Rahr points to considerable collaboration. 'The few Russians living there, like Gorbachev, benefited from the occupation because they went into schools, they had food enough, and the collective farm system was totally abolished, people could work for themselves.' Rahr alleges, 'They can't reveal that in reality there were schools, organized by the Germans; they brought in Russian teachers who collaborated. Gorbachev's main subject in the German school was religion.'

During the occupation the eleven-year-old Gorbachev and his mother were sent to the fields to collect what they could by hand. Their supervisors were Russians, appointed by Germans. The boy would awaken to hear his mother's withered bare feet slapping on the ground as she ran back to the hut, carrying dried dung for fuel, before the Germans could catch up with her and demand milk from her private cow.

Maria Panteleyevna headed a team of ten or fifteen women working in the fields. So Gorbachev passed through the formative years of puberty working shoulder to shoulder with women, shaking the faces of sunflowers and scratching the earth for the fallen seeds that were the only substitute for bread. His mother showed him how to be an organizer, a doer, how to proclaim, 'One doesn't have to take things as they are, there must be a better way!'

He was a male child, a robust and energetic male child, and, as such, prized beyond any possession. War was sapping the life blood of Soviet society† to a degree unimaginable in America, which saw 500,000 men perish in the Second World War. Soviet mothers and wives lost twenty-seven *million*,† and another fifteen million men were wounded or maimed. One out of every three Soviet males between the ages of eighteen and twenty-one watered the ground of Russia with their dying blood. So it is easy to understand why mothers of that generation treated their living sons like gold.

'We kept saying we'll be victorious no matter, even though things were falling apart,' recalls one of his teachers. 'We women went out into the fields and it was all done by hand. The children were given orders to pick up all the straw.' And it seems that young Misha came to respect strong women from an early age. 'That's true,' says the girl from next door. He would eventually marry the strongest-willed one of all.

Certainly his young, fatherless years left an indelible imprint on his character. Mikhail had to take on adult responsibilities prematurely, to play the part of a little husband. He read the newspapers for adults; men twice his age would seek his views on war and domestic decisions, and that must have helped develop in him the powerful self-assurance he shows today. 'He was clever enough to understand the whole thing,' says Mr Lubenko. Not famine, nor war, nor the loss of his father, nor deprivation of basic needs, could break him.

In the fatherly admonitions he gives to Soviet citizens during his walkabouts today, one can hear the legacy of his father's long absence: 'You need to say to yourself, "I will be disciplined. I will take responsibility. I will work harder."'

The occupation of Privolnoye lasted for five months, until January 1943, long enough to leave a pall of suspicion over the area throughout Stalin's reign. As Gorbachev struggled up through the Party ranks, he always had to have a protector to keep this black mark from showing up on his record. Even today members of his own ruling circle were stunned to learn that Gorbachev had lived in an area occupied by the German forces.

The stain of living in an area occupied by the Germans was not erased by having a soldier in the family who fought with valour for the Soviet Army. So paranoid was Stalin, when his prisoners of war came home from Nazi labour camps, that they were imprisoned in his own camps as suspected collaborators.

Young Misha seems to have harboured no burning enmity for the Germans. He later acknowledged that he did not see them as Nazis. His buddy, Yakovenko, tells of an encounter

on the street when a group of Russian boys came upon some
young German soldiers flirting with the local girls. The
circled around one another like angry dogs. It appeared a
brawl was about to begin. But one of the Germans knew
Russian, and soon the males found common ground in their
youth and their helplessness in the face of war. Yakovenko
recalls the exchange: 'We are not to blame because they,
Stalin and Hitler, drink wine and Russian soldier and
German soldier they kill each other.'

Moreover, immediately after the war Misha elected to
study the German language with Matilda Ignatenko, a
teacher who lived in a German settlement in the next town.
She describes one telling incident about teaching the teenagers a song in praise of Lenin. The lyrics said Lenin was 'a
friend and a führer and a leader'. Führer. That means only
one thing – Hitler. The students cursed and snarled at the
German teacher: how dare she ask them to sing 'Führer' and
'Lenin' in the same line? But Mikhail had brought his
dictionary to class, and he found in it the broader definition
of the word.

'It means, simply, leader,' he said calmly.

Remembering her surprise and relief, the German teacher
says of the young diplomat, 'He really helped me out.'

Communist Party as Parent

After the war, hard work was still the constant theme of
Gorbachev's childhood. And the deprivations continued.
'This was the wheat basket of Russia, and we had to send
everything to people in central Russia,' say the villagers
bitterly, 'so it was very very hungry and hard times here for
eight more years.'

'From the age of thirteen I had started working in a
collective farm from time to time,' Gorbachev has stated.
'The atmosphere and entire mode of life of a peasant family,
joint work with adults from a young age, naturally influenced

the moulding of my character and development of a point of view in life.'†

Gorbachev worked in the fields from the last day of school until the autumn. A state decree in 1942 legalized employment of children, and every boy and girl between the age of twelve and sixteen worked a compulsory minimum of fifty days a year. Harvesting in summer was no holiday. In the scorching heat of midday Misha and Yakovenko would dive head first into the moist, rotting straw and sleep, a couple of hours at most, invisible except for their bare soles poking out of the haystack. Snow often fell before the harvest was in, but school could not open until the wheat had been cut and baled. The combine Misha drove by himself had no cabin. To keep from freezing, the boy wrapped himself in straw. Thirteen years old, bouncing over the rutted soil as he struggled to steer, he must have looked like a little straw man.

After his father returned from the Front, Misha turned over the wheel to Sergei Andreyevich and sat beside him in the machine tractor. 'We spoke a lot about policy, also about foreign policy,' Gorbachev has said about the relationship with his father. 'However, the older I grew, the more I had my own opinion.'

School did not begin for Russian children until the age of seven. If they were lucky enough to go on to secondary school, they still had only ten years of education, and the quality of education in rural schools was sorry compared to cities such as Moscow and Leningrad. Maria Panteleyevna, who frequently visited Misha's primary school to check up on her son's progress, received orders from her husband, still away at the Front, that the boy must go on to secondary school. That meant sending him to the little town of Krasnogvardeiskoye, the education centre for surrounding villages, ten miles away. The boy would have to walk. So, Maria Panteleyevna drove the family cow to a market many towns away, had it slaughtered and with the proceeds bought her son a pair of sturdy boots.

It wasn't until Misha went off to Krasnogvardeiskoye for his last three years of school that he would have had any perspective of the wide open sweep of steppe between a gentle line of mountains that melt into a mauve blur. Icy winds whirling across the vastness made walking treacherous. 'On Sundays we had to walk three hours and bring enough food with us to last the week,' as another classmate from Privolnoye, Boris Gladskoi, recalls. Suety string and grit – they called it sausage – with a fistful of bread; that was all they had to eat. But Misha adapted well.

He very quickly took an active part in his new surroundings, according to his teachers, and was elected secretary of his class. 'He was very social, he lived life,' remembers one. 'Yes, but also very serious,' reminds another.

Juggling a thousand students in triple sessions, the school offered four or five classes a day, after which students had to wash windows and clean floors, so there was little time for sports or extracurricular activities. 'We didn't know what it was to be bored,' Gladskoi emphasizes. But the more curious students would come back in the evening. And Misha was the most curious of all, says Yekaterina Chaika, his chemistry teacher.

'Misha loved to make experiments with sparks,' she recounts, the metaphor suddenly registering in her chinablue eyes. 'Yes, he wasn't afraid.' She scrounged up phosphorus, sulphur, magnesium oxide, anything to feed his insatiable curiosity and produce simple fireworks.

Theatre also attracted this naturally gifted actor. He played the prince in Lermontov's *Masquerade*, and took part in many other sketches and plays. He was very good, say his classmates, and even talked to Boris and several other friends about trying to get into a theatrical institute in Moscow. But that dream was only a variation on his main goal: to earn a gold medal for his grades, because that was a ticket out of the steppes. So he buttered up his secondary-school teachers as he had the German teacher: 'I've done my homework, but I haven't done it carefully enough,' was one of his ploys.

And the first hand up to answer in the rote drills was sure to be Misha's.

Impatient to get on with life, Misha took the decisive step of joining the Komsomol – the nationwide Communist Party youth organization – when he was only fourteen. Just as Komsomol positions were the only leadership track in secondary school, Komsomol membership was compulsory for anyone dreaming of a political career. And for a dirt-poor fourteen-year-old longing for an education, for life outside of a haystack, for contact with a wider world and the power of ideas, there was only one gate of admission – the Communist Party.

In a practical as well as emotional sense, the Party became Misha's father, mother and god. He proselytized for it, recruited for it, and lavished upon it his loyalty – above fun, above friends, even above love.

The first classmate to describe her relationship with Gorbachev as 'young love', Julia Karagodina, was a sixteen-year-old girl possessed of a womanly beauty, not too shy to cock her head and let her wide-set dark eyes take in Misha's handsome face – even if, at first, she was only play-acting. The two played romantic co-stars in the 1949 school production of *The Snowgirl*. It may have been the only time in his life that Gorbachev wore a military uniform, looking mature and gallant in his epaulettes and gold-braided chest. Julia was costumed like Anna Karenina. As she told David Remnick of the *Washington Post*, 'We never said "I love you" to each other. He would never say such things.' The farthest Mikhail Sergeyevich would go was to put his arm around her shoulder to say, 'Let's go to the movies.'†

But a scene they played together in real life, in front of all their Komsomol comrades, was far more self-revelatory of the character of Mikhail Sergeyevich. The young twosome had just come from a Komsomol meeting to gather with others at the local moviehouse. 'He was angry with me for not finishing on time a little newspaper we put out. And despite our friendship, he reprimanded me in front of everyone, saying that I'd failed, that I was late. He was shouting a bit, disciplining me. Then afterwards it was as if nothing had happened. He said, "Let's go to the movies." I was at a loss. I couldn't understand why he did what he did, and I said so.'

Gorbachev replied, 'My dear, one thing has nothing to do with another.'

He publicly humiliated his first girlfriend in order to show Party elders his total dedication to the Communist cause. He needed their support to recommend him for higher education. It was only one of a number of such incidents reported by friends as Gorbachev grew older.

The Unnoticed Diplomat

Up until the age of sixteen, Gorbachev was an only child. It is likely that Maria Panteleyevna, Gorbachev's mother, had lost other children, since peasant families were normally large and birth control non-existent. In 1947, however, home from the front at last, Sergei gave Maria a second son. And he became the apple of her eye. Alexander ('Sasha') inherited his father's character and was more quiet. 'Mikhail is very energetic, while Alexander is a little slower,' says Gorlov. 'Sasha' grew tall as a tree and became the athlete in the family, while Misha was the talkative, pudgy intellectual. Sasha played the guitar and had a fine singing voice. Misha, though he plucked at the balalaika and sang in the school choir, wasn't musical: his classmates, making every effort to be kind, have to admit that, 'really, even a frog could sing in the chorus'.

The two boys never became close; Sasha was still a baby when it was arranged that Misha should stay in Krasnogvardeiskoye for his final year of high school. Misha and another boy from his own village, Dmitry Markov, rented a room. Their landlady, Tamara Unstentova, still lives in the tiny cottage with its cloth-covered doorway. She was a teacher and was given only enough wood to heat her own room, so the boys spent the winter in a fifteen-by-twenty-foot room with only wooden shutters to shelter them from the icy winds. It was hard to imagine, as I stared at the niche in the wall, that two strapping eighteen-year-old boys, swaddled in their bulky clothes, could have slept there, side by side, on a cot smaller than their landlady's single bed.

There were parties at school, but the two boys never brought anyone home. Tamara Unstentova says she 'never saw Misha with a girl, never'. She did notice that he read a great deal – fiction, poetry, real literature – at least when there was enough kerosene to light the oil lamps after he'd finished his homework, which, because of the post-war paper shortage, had to be written between the lines of old books. And what did the boys eat? 'The walls are so thin, and I never once smelled anything cooking so I imagine they lived on cold meat.'

'What do you want to become?' his teachers asked Misha when he was awarded a silver medal – not the gold one he'd planned on – for his high grades.

'I want to become a diplomat,' he told them.

'Of course it was a childish answer, not serious,' clucks the chemistry teacher. 'We didn't differentiate him from the mass of students.'

In fact, Gorbachev was a natural diplomat. But, for all the boy's effort back then, no one took notice of him as an individual. That was not the Communist way. So, in the summer of his nineteenth year Gorbachev distinguished himself in the Communist way – as a model kolkhozniki. Driving the harvester every day, choking in the swirls of dust from the steppe, sweat streaming from his face, a continual trilling in his ears, he worked like a demon and waited for the Party to take notice.

It was a bumper harvest. The collective exceeded its plan. And the team of Misha and his father and the Yakovenkos, along with many of the local officials, were nominated for a prestigious government award, the Order of the Red Banner of Labour. The young man had to buy his first suit and get a haircut for a formal photograph in the Stavropol Party newspaper: his first publicity picture. It was a most unusual award for such a young man – only three or four students in the entire Stavropol region had won such an honour in the previous decade – and it allowed Misha the otherwise impossible privilege of applying to enter a university.

'He himself decided to go to Moscow University,' says his history teacher. 'No one pushed him,' affirms his English teacher. 'Neither his parents not the school had influence like that.' In fact, his teachers were completely unaware that the award entitled him to any such privilege. In this provincial outpost, under a system of enforced conformity, nobody spotted Misha Gorbachev's genius for leadership. His parents, limited by scant education and a status of no importance among the local Party elite, could not help him advance any farther. He had to take the risk of finding a future all by himself. But Gorbachev possessed an unerring talent for pleasing the right people.

The person who would have placed his name on the list of candidates recommended for the Red Banner of Labour Award – his ticket out of Stavropol – was the district-wide kolkhoz chairman, Grigory Gorlov. Today, the Gorbachev family friend is a white-haired man with the lipless, trap-like mouth of a lifelong bureaucrat. He supervises a veteran's organization in Stavropol city. Back in 1949, he was the most important Party official in the district and a close associate of Misha's grandfather Gopkalo, who held the local chairmanship of the Privolnoye collective farm. Gopkalo's grandson, Misha, had demonstrated to Comrade Gorlov's satisfaction that he possessed the characteristic valued above all others: complete loyalty to the Party.

Moscow State University was the most prestigious institution of higher learning in the land. As a candidate for admission, Gorbachev was competing not only with the children of Moscow's elite, but also with highly decorated soldiers returning from the Front. Still, universities were obliged to take a small quota of 'peasants', and few of the applicants in this group would have won such an important labour award as Misha's Red Banner of Labour.

But the young man also had a great deal working against him. Every university applicant had to fill out an extensive 'anketa' or investigation of his background. Coming from an area that had been under German occupation, with a grandfather who had been sent to the gulag as an enemy of the people, Gorbachev had two of the darkest stains on his personal history. Even if he was able to lie, or avoid mentioning these disqualifying factors on his anketa, he would have needed protectors to help him cover up the black marks against him.

The District Party Committee could have checked the boy's background – and in fact Gorlov knew very well about these disqualifications – but local Party activists apparently closed their eyes to the facts, perhaps with a longer-range purpose. Hadn't Misha Gorbachev shown himself to be a model Communist youth?

By the age of eighteen, Mikhail Sergeyevich had already developed the self-confidence of the survivor, which transcends circumstance. Some of his friends referred to it as a 'blind faith' and were baffled, even intimidated by it, which is natural, because such faith in oneself cannot be taught. This steel core of self-assurance within the survivor is an inner psychological strength, centred in the knowledge that one must make – and merit – one's own happiness. As he demonstrated his charismatic power to persuade others, even formidable authority figures, to see things as he did, Gorbachev's confidence became self-reinforcing.

Mikhail Sergeyevich dared to believe he could shape his own destiny – which made him different from all the others.

To appreciate fully the guts it took to be a self-made man in the Soviet Union in the 1940s and 1950s, it is necessary to point out a fundamental difference between Russian culture and Western culture. The concept of individual choice is an integral part of our Western philosophy. Particularly in

American society, it is taken as read that the individual can determine his or her own destiny – the choices are your choices, my choices and the social choices we make together.

In Russia there were no choices. Whether under the czars or the anarchists or the Bolsheviks or the Communist Party, the individual was in no position to choose anything about his life – not where he lived, not what kind of house he had, not even how many chickens or pigs he kept. The Russian peasant moved from czarist serfdom to enforced collectivization with barely time to learn the difference. But Gorbachev is from a different strain from the average Soviet. He is in many ways an aberration. The vast majority of the Soviet population have spent their whole lives under authoritarian rule. Typically it takes more than two generations to destroy the popular memory of earlier times.

On the surface, Misha appeared to be a strident believer, a Stalinist stalwart, which made him appealing to the Party. Determined to better himself, he cunningly concealed the defining difference between himself and others: not in what he thought, but in *how* he thought. Firmly rooted in his Cossack past and the pride of a free peasant family, with parents and grandparents who were not Party activists but Orthodox Christian believers with a frontier zeal, he was able to develop as a broad-minded generalist – like most great leaders – rather than as a narrow, doctrinaire ideologue. He was open to everything, interested in everything, romantic, yes, but at his roots a realist.

Having survived hunger and persecution, Mikhail Gorbachev developed the knack for survival that has made him a master tactician. He would go on balancing in his high-wire act as a survivor of a repressive regime, a survivor of Communist Party back-stabbing, a survivor of the abyss beneath the Politburo, and ultimately as a world-class political survivor.

In this book we shall see how the character of the man – his habit of action – becomes the catalyst that is opening up and splitting apart the world's last empire.

III

Second Gorbachev:

First-generation Apparatchik

1950–1977

Mikhail Sergeyevich never forgot the train ride from Stavropol in the autumn of 1950, passing through the ghosts of cities, through Stalingrad, in ruins, through Voronezh, in ruins, through Rostov, in ruins, through Kharkov, in ruins, the winds of war seeming to have howled thousands of miles down from Europe levelling all that was civilized in Mother Russia, and suddenly *Moscow* . . . a rouged and golden city, pantheon of the gods, the shining tomb of Lenin, the spires of Stalin's empire skyscrapers, the broad boulevards with parades of trees under leafy parasols, and at the very top, swept up in the clouds of the Lenin Hills, the Mount Olympus of the intelligentsia – Moscow State University.

When he arrived, his Cossack fur hat cocked to one side, a sober blue military-style coat and strict bearing, Gorbachev plunged immediately into the role of Komsomol activist. A strident and humourless sloganeer, he gave every sign of being a young Stalin. But beneath the stony front beat the heart of a boy from the sticks desperate to be noticed – how desperate is apparent from his habit of wearing his labour medal, not just for holidays, but almost every day.

'Who does he think he is wearing a *medal*?' the savvy Muscovite students teased behind his back. 'Our war veterans, now they have *real* medals!' They giggled too at his boxy brown suit; he wore it every day for five years, until by his last year he was too porky to button the jacket.

An odd sort. He didn't like sports. He memorized poetry. He was obsessed with studying from original sources – in the true Marxist tradition. 'And he doesn't even drink!' jeered a suave Muscovite, Dmitry Golovanov, the son of a prominent newspaper editor. Golovanov chuckles, recalling his first impression of Gorbachev. 'We represented the Moscow "elite", we lived with Mother and Father in nice apartments. And he was a child from the provinces, he lived with other colleagues in the dormitory, not crude, but provincial. He wasn't very interesting to us.'

Mikhail stayed in a vast former czar's stable called the Strominka, far from the Lenin Hills campus. Ten thousand students were crammed into this hostel, up to fifteen in a room, the cots lined up regimental style and the only suggestion of individuality the suitcase under each bed. Meals were taken at a communal table, if one could call the month-old packages of mouldering sausage mailed from home meals. Showers were only to be had by trooping off twice a month to a public bathhouse. Yet the first impression Misha made on his roommates was 'tidy', 'self-contained' and 'cautious'. Always a puritan, he organized his room-mates in Room 324 so that eventually they would win the 'neatness award' for the tidiest room.†

Moscow State University educated the crème de la crème of Soviet youth. Most of its 30,000 students were coddled children of the Moscow intelligentsia and Party elite. Gorbachev's other competitors for admission were the thousands of demilitarized men staggering back from the Great Patriotic War with military honours far more impressive than Misha's civilian labour order. One might well ask, then, how a poor tractor driver's son with three strikes against him – grandson of a former 'enemy of the people', coming from a formerly occupied area, and without a single family member in the nomenklatura to pull for him – was able to levitate himself into the law school of the most prestigious university in the country.

Mikhail Sergeyevich had been sent to the university with a glowing recommendation from the Stavropol Party Committee as a favourite son – with the makings of a first-generation apparatchik. The term apparatchik refers to the army of full-time paid professional Party functionaries, including the first, second and third secretaries and department and section chiefs, and professional propagandists appointed to Party Committees inside *every organization and factory and collective farm*, as well those at the central, regional, local and primary levels.†

And indeed, the moment he was old enough – at the age of nineteen, in his first year at university – Gorbachev applied to enter the ranks of the Communist Party as a candidate member. This was as precocious an act of devotion as becoming an activist in the Komsomol at the age of fourteen. 'In Party work we have mostly people who are not intelligent or cultured,' says a member of the Moscow Party establishment. 'He stood out.' Russian émigré Viktor Yasmann, a scholar at Radio Liberty who is an expert on the KGB, points out that 'the young Gorbachev's mission was clear from the beginning. He was talented and ambitious, very courteous to people, and he didn't drink – this is very important. He tempted the Party to include him.'

The Stavropol Territory Party Committee had suggested he could be given a role in propaganda work in Moscow. He loved to make speeches – turgid, ideologically rigid, sloganeering speeches in his laughably rolling country accent. But there was nothing warm or amusing about his tone. Years later the émigré Fridrikh Neznansky would remember Gorbachev's 'steely voice' when, as Komsomol Secretary of the law faculty, he demanded students be expelled from the organization for offences as slight as telling a political joke or resisting assignment to a collective farm.

A gifted actor and natural mimic, Mikhail Sergeyevich was

simply parroting the steely voice and mimicking the tactics of Father Stalin.

Why, though, had he ended up in the law faculty in the first place? It was one of the most restricted departments of all; in the whole country there were only sixteen universities with law schools.† Nor was it a natural choice for someone with his curiosity and eagerness to learn. The law faculty was the polar opposite of a Western law school: the underlying feature of Stalinism was the *absence* of law; despotism recognized only one law, and that was whatever the despot capriciously proclaimed it to be. And there was nothing in Gorbachev's record to suggest that he had any interest in law enforcement. So this choice has remained a puzzle to Gorbachev's few foreign biographers. In fact, it wasn't his first choice. Gorbachev himself has stated that 'at first I wanted to enrol in the physics department. I like mathematics very much, but I also liked history and literature.' He took the entrance examination for admission to the science faculty, and failed. He couldn't decide from there, as he has said, 'which discipline in school attracted my special interest.'†

A likely explanation is that a deal was struck with the prosecutor's office in Stavropol and the young peasant boy from Privolnoye was sent to Moscow under their auspices. We know that the Red Banner of Labour award had opened the door for him to apply to this rarefied citadel of learning, and that the Stavropol Party Committee had enthusiastically sponsored him and suggested him for Komsomol Party work in Moscow. The local KGB directorate, which commonly collaborated closely with the provincial committee of the Party, may have also had their eye on Gorbachev as a potential future recruit.† He was exactly the sort of trustworthy type for which they would be on the lookout. The prosecutor's office might even have sponsored his application to the law faculty because from there, upon graduation, students were 'allocated' (they had no choice in the matter) to one of three law-enforcement agencies: the Procuracy (state prosecutor's office), the MVD (internal police), or the

KGB. Many students are sponsored from the start by a security agency which then receives them back.

Moscow State then, as now, allowed the KGB to have a whole floor for recruitment. The law faculty was heavily penetrated by the KGB and the Komsomol was a virtual playpen for developing and cultivating future leaders of the Party and the KGB. The two organizations worked in close co-operation, and it was normal to recruit Komsomol members as secret informers for the KGB. In fact, one of the key missions of the Komsomol organ in the law faculty was to recommend recruits for KGB work.

The Soviet secret police is far more than an intelligence agency, it is the medium through which the Politburo runs the country. A unique creation of Lenin and of the ethics of the Soviet regime, the main function of the KGB is to keep political power in the ruling Communist Party. It is designated as the *military* arm of the Party and as such has its own army: the Soviet Interior Ministry troops we read about so often today clashing with armed ethnic minorities that continue to erupt in regional civil wars. The KGB also maintains surveillance over the government army – literally sets up and monitors the army's communications systems – which is why the Soviet Army has never been considered a direct threat to a Soviet leader. There is no comparable political police system in the world.

Imagine the Postmaster General of the United States being also a general in the CIA. Imagine knowing your personally assigned KGB officer, chatting with him whenever you write something unusual, trying to outwit his psychological intimidation games. Imagine a CIA that has ten million operatives *inside* the country, 7.5 million of them paid informants† who look indistinguishable from the general population. They may be your friends, or even members of your family. The total number of operatives is a state secret, but a recent outcast from the spy network told members of the Democratic Platform in Moscow that the number exceeds the forces of all Western intelligence agencies put together. This is the reach of the KGB.

Having lived through German occupation and Stalin's purges, Gorbachev had felt not only fear of the enemy but also fear that he would be accused of *being* the enemy. He knew very well that one had to play the game to survive, and the Party was the safest game around. More than anything else, affirm his friends of that period, Gorbachev wanted to be a success in Party work.

'It is quite possible that Misha would have liked to have been a KGB officer, but was rejected for being too bright and too cultivated during that anti-intellectual Stalin period,' says Yasmann, the scholar on KGB operations. 'They may have put him in reserve, but cultivated him within the Party apparatus.' The spy organization is not officially allowed to have operatives inside the Party apparatus, so it is particularly keen to develop informers with an interest in politics who can be placed in Party jobs.

So thoroughly entrenched was the secret police in the early 1950s in every facet of Soviet life that no one advanced in Party work without a patron in the security organs. One could go about his or her life and work, as an ordinary, passive, Soviet dependant, without coming into direct contact with the secret police. But for anyone who wanted to be a mover, certainly anyone as upwardly mobile as Misha Gorbachev, it was inconceivable that advancement in Party work would be possible without explicit patronage within the secret police.

It is not possible to say for certain that Gorbachev was an informer for the KGB at university. The question must be raised, however, given his accelerated rise in Party positions during the early 1950s, how could he *not* have agreed to be an informer?

It is well to bear in mind that decades later, as General Secretary, in all his breathtaking reformist blows – to the army, Politburo, Party apparatus, territorial bosses – there is only one political institution that Gorbachev has never touched. The state security agency – KGB.

Working for the Party Thought Police

By his second term Misha had set about determinedly polishing himself both culturally and politically, and he used his newly acquired urban manners to begin climbing the ladder of Komsomol leadership. The suave Golovanov, a comrade in the Komsomol, invited him as a guest to one of the rare private apartments in Moscow, which his family had managed to hold on to ever since they had obtained it by being close to the czar. Drinking vodka was a symbol of masculinity among Muscovites, and Golovanov's father took it upon himself to teach the boy from Stavropol how: first take a sniff of bread, then throw a shot of vodka at the back of the throat with a single flick of the wrist. Gorbachev never did take to drink other than the occasional glass of wine, but he would use that lesson well.

In a telling incident, Gorbachev made the first step in his career by inviting a candidate for the class Komsomol organizer, supposedly a friend of his, to a restaurant and egging him on to drink great quantities of vodka. He left the candidate staggering down the street where the man was eventually picked up by the militia. The next day, after the police notified the university of the student's 'hooliganism', the man was denounced for his drunkenness at a Komsomol meeting by none other than Mikhail Sergeyevich. In short order Gorbachev was elevated to the very job his 'friend' had been seeking – Komsomol organizer for his class.†

'Be careful of him,' a friend warned Lev Yudovich, a third-year student who later emigrated. Yudovich and his friends regarded Gorbachev as two-faced: always buddying up to other students only to get information. Several other émigrés have characterized the student Gorbachev as a zealot and harbour suspicions that he spied on them.

'He locked on to people,' says the member of Misha's

study group who came to know him best, Nadezhda Mikhailova. It is a phrase that friends and acquaintances use
often about this magnetic man – *locked on* – and it conjures
up his eyes, his way of penetrating others' space, his knack
for captivating the right people: Moscow aristocrats, older
men like Gorlov, who had pull in the Party apparat, as well
as the brightest students in the school.

Mikhailova claims that 'he never deviated from Party line.
We didn't have dissidents in our day. We were raised not to
question Stalin, never in seminars, and Misha was a child of
his times – *nobody doubted Stalin*.'

'Inside every Soviet person there sits Stalin,' says a liberal
deputy to the Supreme Soviet, Gennady Lisichkin. 'The
question is what percent of Stalin is in each one, and in
Gorbachev, I think, there is more than people think. At the
university he was already a political worker. To be Komsomol
secretary at the university means a lot.'

Gorbachev's main task as a Komsomol organizer (according to the rules of the youth organization) was to spread
Party propaganda: 'to help the Party educate young people
in the spirit of Communism' and turn them into 'the Party's
active helper and reserve'. He took the role of hard-line
ideologue in his Party work, expelling members who weren't
letter-perfect in their paeans to Stalin, and recommending
expulsion for those whose family background (like his) held
any taint of disloyalty to the regime.

'Yes, he was strict. So was I, the first year,' says Golovanov, who was also an activist. 'We both kicked people out of
the Komsomol. That was normal.'

When another activist had a speech to make at an inter-
college conference on the laws of economics, for example, he
had to get Gorbachev's approval. The man wanted to make
mention of the theory of business and self-financing, that is
the capitalistic notion of being paid for one's own work. 'I
asked him if I thought correctly.'

Gorbachev, then, was a de-facto member of the Party
thought police.

'At the Front and in the army I was a leader of the Komsomol organizations, so I know how it was,' I was told by the man who was generally acknowledged to have been the most brilliant orator in the class, Vladimir Lieberman. The young Jew had to be brilliant; Moscow State was as anti-semitic as every other institution and the quota for Jewish students was minuscule. Lieberman, the offspring of a family of Moscow intellectuals, had survived five years at the Front and upon being rewarded with admission to the university he dedicated himself, like Gorbachev, to serving the Party. 'Gorbachev's good will towards people attracted them to him, so he got information because people were open to him,' he says.

Charactor assassination is a speciality of the KGB. I asked Lieberman if Mikhail Sergeyevich used the information he got to report on people and ingratiate himself with the KGB. He would give only an indirect answer. 'Nobody thought it was necessary to hide things from Mikhail Sergeyevich. He was trusted.' I persisted in my question: did the KGB require that Komsomol leaders report back to them? With some impatience at my apparent naivety, Lieberman replied, 'If I needed to do it, I would go to the KGB myself,' and volunteer information. But he maintains that the KGB didn't need to use them as 'stool pigeons – to provoke people, because we were spreading Bolshevik ideas'.

The towering wall of snobbism behind which Muscovites look down on anyone from *anywhere* other than Moscow is so formidable, not one peasant in a thousand would try to be accepted as an intellectual or social equal. Gorbachev was dogged, never allowing the scorn and snickers to undo his inner confidence. And, outside his Party work, he behaved with modesty, even humility.

There were four students assigned to a study group. One of Gorbachev's study partners, Natasha Rimashevskaya, never thought of him as having any aspirations to be a leader. 'He would always sit in the next to last row. Always. Yet he had such personal magnetism he would seem to push forward. Something in his internal mechanism – even though he was not overtly ambitious – there was something in the way he stood, the way he talked, the way he behaved with people, the way he *locked on*, that seemed to be pushing him forward to be a leader.'

The student Gorbachev was painfully aware of the gaping holes in his experience and especially in his knowledge of culture, reports his roommate of three years, Rudolf Kolchanov, 'and he wanted to liquidate that gap'. He was also behind a year, owing to the occupation of Stavropol. 'We all worked a great deal, but he worked more than anyone, poring over Marx and Lenin in the study room until two or three in the morning.'

'As a country boy he was unique among us,' admits another member of his study foursome. 'And the medal – he wore it the whole first year. That drew attention to him.'

'There was nothing country-boy about his intelligence,' contends Lieberman. In their second year the militia man in their seminar on political economy summoned Gorbachev, Lieberman and a Czech friend of theirs, Zdenek Mlynar. 'The girls have asked you to slow down a bit,' he reportedly said, 'because when you three and the professor talk, they can't follow your thoughts that quickly.' The impression of a country boy was based on his clothes and his manners, says Lieberman, but not on his maturity.

Kolchanov, today an important newspaper editor, wants to be accurate about such descriptions and holds that 'In fact he was *not* the most impressive student in our class by any means. It's not as if he were always a great reformer and a world leader just waiting to happen.'

The consensus of those who knew him at the time is that Gorbachev was intellectually curious with a restless mind, but a quick student rather than a reflective person. Romantic and even naive philosophically, he nevertheless challenged teachers and students who blathered on about general principles and he insistently repeated Hegel's aphorism, 'Truth is always concrete.' He drew on his own real-life experiences as a peasant to prove it, which his urban classmates found at first, well, quaint.

The Muscovites began to register Gorbachev's presence in his second term, not because he was a gifted rhetorician – he definitely was not – but because his utterances in class had 'a fundamental quality'. Rural peasant students not infrequently showed themselves to be stronger students than their citified contemporaries and gradually gained their respect. Gorbachev would eventually ingratiate himself with members of some of the oldest aristocratic families in the capital, who found him 'very well balanced, merry, optimistic'. He made himself equally at home with the older demobilized soldiers in his dorm and people who came from different provinces and the few foreigners, always taking an interest in how people's families were and how their brothers and sisters lived. 'We were several years older than the students from Moscow,' Mlynar explains their perspective. 'To us, they were nice clean young kids still living on their parents' income. We were more self-sufficient, we had student grants, and because of our life experience we were also more attractive for the girls.'

But, as in secondary school, Gorbachev was not a ladies' man. Female students were housed on the same floor, as were the men in their barracks dorm. Given the fact that eight to fifteen men slept in each room, Gorbachev's roommates had to work out an elaborate system for privacy time. A sign was hung in the hall euphemistically designating 'Cleaning Hours' when a man could have a woman alone in his room. Gorbachev wasn't in on the joke. Golovanov still marvels at his asceticism, 'While the rest of us were out chasing girls, Misha sat and worked, ten or twelve hours a day in the study room – amazing.'

An Aristocratic Romance

There was, however, one girl who caught Gorbachev's eye in that first year: Nadezhda Mikhailova. A splendidly endowed Russian woman, green-eyed, raven-haired and refined of feature, she told wonderful stories and rivalled Misha as a mimic. The attraction was mutual. Mikhailova was the first to spot the unique qualities of this unpolished yokel, regarding him rather as she would an interesting wild animal that could be taken home and tamed.

'I can't really tell you what day, how I met him but . . .' Nadezhda Mikhailova brought over a pile of pictures and she sighed as she pointed out Mikhail as one of 'our group', the foursome that studied together. 'I was a very romantic girl. Mikhail was romantic too. This romanticism enables a person to think and solve problems on a grand scale.'

Mikhailova carried herself like an aristocrat, which she was. Her mother's father had been a colonel in the Czar's army, who steadfastly refused to serve in the Soviet Army after the revolution despite pressure from his family to earn some money. It was in Mikhailova's romantic nature to carry off the style of impoverished nobility.

'Misha, you live in the dormitory, poor dear. You cannot live on bad sausages,' she consoled the peasant boy. Then, with a voice that characteristically rises like the high trill of a songbird, she'd coax, 'Come home with me to study. You will see, Mama is a splendid cook!'

Despite the fact that Mikhailova's father had a high position in the government apparat, his family of seven was allotted only two rooms in a communal apartment with several other families. But, as Chief Accountant of the Food Ministry, he came by delicacies not available in state stores. Misha spent many evenings at Mikhailova's home, often with the two others in their study group, cramming for exams. Nadezhda's mother would pour the steaming ruby warmth of homemade borscht into the boy and treat him to meat pastries and smoked salmon and cream puffs. He always loved to eat.

'He didn't have any culture,' Mikhailova says. 'He would come to me and say, "Nadezhda, if you go to a museum maybe you'll take me and tell me what this artist feels." Or

"If you're going to the conservatory, take me with you and tell me what this composer is thinking." It was not embarrassing to him at all to ask.' Another student remembers Gorbachev once asking, 'What is ballet? I've heard talk about it, but I've never seen it.'

Mikhailova lived across the street from the Bolshoi Theatre, so she would stand all night in line for tickets to take him to the Bolshoi. She herself had wanted to study dancing, acting and singing but her father said it was unthinkable for the daughter of nobility to be on the stage. So she poured her love of the arts into the ready sponge of this country boy. She taught him to appreciate the French Impressionists, but he particularly fancied a group of seventeenth-century Russian classicists known as the Peredvizhniki. 'He worked on himself a lot,' says his first culture coach, 'and still does today.'

Did he court her? I ask.

'He liked me. I knew that.' She smiles fetchingly and drops her violet-shadowed eyes over a long sip of tea. 'But he wasn't my taste. I liked tall, thin, elegant men. He was short and fat.'

But when I came to know Mikhailova better, she volunteered the real reason why she ignored Gorbachev romantically in their student days.

'Because of my noble birth my family didn't want me to have any relations with a country boy. It's in the genes.' She says it wistfully but with the prejudiced finality of her class, a striking contradiction in a society dedicated for the last seventy years to eradicating distinctions of class.

What is more, she admits, 'He didn't try to catch girls. He was totally indifferent.' Mikhailova was accustomed to impassioned Great Russian men who stayed up nights writing her reams of love poetry. Misha never wrote her so much as a note while they were classmates. 'He seemed to like me, but he never showed his attraction to girls.' It would be several years before he rekindled their relationship.

Notwithstanding, Mikhailova put the stamp of her approval on Mikhail Gorbachev. At last, twenty years old, he was beginning to be recognized for his individual identity. He _was_ different from the others, in ways his classmates found peculiar, impressive and sometimes downright dangerous.

Gorbachev's first three years at university coincided with the last three paranoid, purge-crazy years before Stalin's death. He would later characterize his student days in Moscow as the period in which he was pondering his 'moral values, the meaning of life, happiness and justice and mankind's future'.

I sat for many hours with his old friend, Lieberman, trying to understand what the 'moral values' of young Misha might have been. Lieberman sat chain-smoking rough Russian cigarettes in his tiny apartment, where two single beds beneath a double spread are shoved under the living-room window. A permanent frown is carved in a sickle over his left eyebrow and beneath his granite-blue eyes his handsome face is deeply creased. The result is a permanently quizzical expression, as if, somehow, after all these years, it just doesn't add up.

'About morality,' he began his lecture. 'Though he was poor and never had enough money, Misha was never greedy, materialistic. He didn't care about alcohol or playing cards. And though he was very handsome, with great hair, he never showed much interest in women. Gorbachev always had this amazing ability to work. Life hasn't changed that. No hobbies. No side interests. Just work.'

But did Gorbachev come to university with fixed moral bearings? I persisted, explaining that I meant a clear sense of how people should behave with one another.

Lieberman reprimanded me. 'You are breaking the order.' He is like other friends of Gorbachev, now in their fifties and sixties, on whom the Stalin years have left a strong imprint:

they insist upon order, discipline and speaking in lecture form. In the end, he found it impossible, even irrelevant, to speak of any fixed moral universe.

'He had an intellect. A person's fate depends on that. Only that.'

And so one tries to imagine the inner universe of a lively-minded twenty-year-old for whom the study of law was mainly an arid memorizing of the state penal code. Some of the professors in the law faculty were pre-revolutionary relics and truly learned, but most were Party propagandists. There was no such thing as 'dialogue' between students and professors. They studied Roman law, English common law, even touched on the American constitution. But they did not study history, not even Russian history (where Gorbachev might have learned something about the fate of earlier reformers). Andrei Vyshinsky, architect of the famous political witch trials in the 1930s, was still a professor at Moscow State University. His theories, mainstays of the Soviet legal code, were forced into the heads of the law students. Notable among them was the view that if a suspect confessed to a crime it was overriding evidence against him. 'Many of us took it as gospel,' confesses Golovanov, 'but Gorbachev didn't. He couldn't, of course, refuse it openly because he would have been thrown out. But he expressed another view among friends.'

'It's wrong, just plain wrong,' Gorbachev would insist. 'Confessions can be forced.'

'No, it should and must be done,' argued other students, parroting back the orthodox line, 'to keep order.'

Students were also exposed to Hegel, certain French philosophers and, of course, Karl Marx. 'But our fundamental teacher was Stalin,' says a classmate. 'All twenty volumes of him.' Gorbachev's curiosity made him impatient with this reductionist teaching, and led him to some tense confrontations. When Stalin issued one last book in 1952, their second year, a special course was immediately introduced, adding another two hours to the students' six-hour class day and eliminating their lunch break. The sole qualification of the professor invited to teach this course was that he had been present at the Kremlin meeting from which this utterly sterile work of Stalin's had emerged. He simply sat and read the book aloud, word for empty word.

By the third class Gorbachev and Lieberman had hatched a plot. They slipped a 'rather hooliganish' note to the professor; Lieberman claims that it was his formulation but that Gorbachev wrote it. The note was left unsigned.

In front of the entire class, all 170 students seated in an auditorium, the professor read the note aloud, in a tone of blood-curdling contempt: 'This is a university, and they admit people who graduated from ten years in school. That is, people who can read by themselves.'

Then he looked out into the eyes of the students. Such a note, he charged, could only have been written by people who did not respect Marxism–Leninism or the Party or the country, and that was why they were afraid to sign it.

Slowly, Gorbachev rose to his feet; the peasant boy with the too-tight brown suit stood frozen from head to toe. Seconds later, an utterly terrified Lieberman somehow got to his feet as well. There they were, the tough student Komsomol boss and his vice-secretary, both stalwart Communists, exposed and suddenly vulnerable.

Within minutes, Mikhail Sergeyevich was summoned to the dean's office. The Party secretary for the university was already there, waiting for him. Kolchanov kept Lieberman company as Gorbachev's deputy trembled outside in the corridor. They both knew that such behaviour was considered sufficiently 'disloyal' to get them expelled. Just one denunciation was enough to lead to their dismissal from the university; it might even get them a one-way ticket to a labour camp. Ideological purity was of utmost importance in the law faculty, where people were being trained not only to share Stalin's repressive worldview but to carry it out as the society's prosecutors.

Gorbachev emerged from the dean's office before the next lecture began, calm, unruffled, as if nothing had happened.

'Don't be afraid, Volodya,' he told Lieberman, 'everything is fine.'

Lieberman says, 'He was more trusted, in everything, than me, because of my nationality. There were no consequences for us.'

The peasant boy from Privolnoye, indeed, seemed to be able to get away with outbursts that would have held severe consequences for almost anybody else. One can only surmise that, to be so well protected, he must have made himself valuable to his Party supervisors.

Gorbachev's other close friend at university was a tall, handsome, intellectual Czech, Zdenek Mlynar, passionately political and, like Mikhail, a 'foreigner' to Muscovites. He lived across the hall in the Strominka. Mlynar knew something of the world and was already a full member of the Communist Party. Today, he lives in Vienna, where he remained after Soviet troops crushed the Prague Spring.

'The two of us were convinced Communists back then,' affirms Mlynar. 'We believed that Communism was the future of mankind and Stalin was the one great leader.'

Mlynar soon learned, however, that Gorbachev felt keenly the conflict between reality and propaganda. As they grew closer, Gorbachev occasionally felt able to drop the mask of orthodoxy that was essential to his survival.

Cossacks of the Kuban

The first and most memorable occasion was prompted by a showing to the whole class of a film made by the government in the late 1940s called *Cossacks of the Kuban*. The title refers to the Kuban river, which flows past Stravropol on its way south from the Sea of Azov. The film was a Soviet-style *Oklahoma*, a musical–comedy supposedly depicting the life happily collectivized Cossacks in the very region where Gorbachev grew up.

The film opens with great swirls of wheatfields waving in

the wind and women marching, rakes over shoulders, warbling in the sunshine, 'We should all sing a merry song so young Cossacks should be healthy and strong.'† They march up hills of grain, literal hills, and merrily shovel the stuff in unison while a line of Cossack men watch the abundant pellets gush from the harvester – it's a Rockette line harvesting! The film speeds up and we see an army of trucks flying the Red flag and racing along a ridge under a beautiful sky, while back in the fields the girls scamper between the bales to rake up every last piece of straw for the state, singing, 'There's nothing we can't do, we're always in good cheer; and carload after carload, we send off to town; we collective farmers won't let the country down.'†

As they watched the scene, Gorbachev whispered the cold reality to his Czech friend: 'If the leader of a kolkhoz does not use brute force against the farmers, they would probably not work at all.'

The film's heroine is chairwoman of a collective farm which has just won the same Red Banner of Labour award that Gorbachev's kolkhoz was given. She is trotting beside a sparkling river in her snappy racing trap, blonde hair coiffed in a chignon, wearing a satiny shawl, prettily printed skirt and conspicuously modern watch. 'Look at all the wealth around us!' she exclaims. To the sound of Lone Ranger-esque music, a moustachioed Cossack man catches up with her. 'Not a bad buggy you have,' he says. 'But isn't it time you had a car?' He's needling her, all in the spirit of socialist competition, because he, too, is chairman of a collective farm. 'I hear you have electric lights at your farm now,' he says jealously. 'Oh yes, we're going to run our whole farm by electricity,' boasts the beautiful chairwoman, leaving him in the dust.

Her workers, a bevy of beauties in heavy makeup with their labour medals bouncing on their breasts, ride beside her in a harvest truck sitting atop the watermelons they've just picked. A group of young Cossacks, very macho, come galloping up to cut off the truckload of fair maidens. They jump off their horses and swagger over in their high boots and rakishly cocked Cossack caps: 'We bachelors are seeking something we haven't lost yet.' The girls all giggle.

Gorbachev could hardly contain his grim laughter. The movie was set several years after the war, when the only men left alive in his part of the country were old, crippled or too young to lose their virginity. A car, a watch, electric lights were all fantasies; the reality was that the state had taken away even their seed grain. Farm machinery was already so antiquated, much of their harvests rotted in the fields or granaries before it could be taken to town. And nobody dared to run and pick up the leftovers in the fields: that was called 'stealing from the state.'

But the hypocrisy reached its peak in the State Fair scene: two Cossacks strut through the outdoor selling area where farmers are selling crates of fruits and vegetables at cut-rate prices. 'Why not?' they say when challenged for undercutting the state. 'We've completed our grain delivery for the state. It's our duty to multiply the wealth of our farms.' A not-so-subtle propaganda prod to farmers to sell their ungathered surplus and plough the proceeds back into their collective.

The girls from the winning collective come running out of a shop, their arms bulging with hatboxes, shoe boxes, sweets and balloons. They walk along in their summer dresses with chiffon scarves fluttering around their curly blonde hair followed by men in plaid jackets and ties who buy the girls lemonade on the way to the movies. The heroine strides through the stables, a huge pocketbook clutched to her chest, picking out horses for her collective's stud farm. Then she stops in a music store. The salesman shows her a piano, 'Made in Leningrad', and falls over himself trying to make the sale, even playing Chopin for his lovely customer. This scene could provoke only bitter hilarity in anyone who has dealt with the classic surly Soviet sales clerk, whose only sense of importance comes from successfully avoiding any work and resisting the customer's every effort to buy. When the rival collective farm chairman catches up with the chairwoman, he scolds her: 'Imagine, buying a piano.' But she counters, 'The best collectives already have stadiums, why not a piano too!' Then she flounces out, followed by her driver – yes, she has a chauffeur, with a cap, who follows her around carrying her stack of packages – the very picture of a well-rewarded winner of the Red Banner of Labour.

It was more than Misha could bear. Back in their dorm he cursed the film, telling Mlynar that the wealth and plenty people supposedly enjoyed in the countryside was 'pure propaganda, nothing to do with reality. You can't actually buy anything!'

With Mlynar, Gorbachev 'always took the side of reality'. He also confided to the Czech his doubts about the simplistic way Stalinist doctrine divided up the Soviet world between 'supporters' and 'criminals'. Gorbachev believed, according to Mlynar, that 'there can exist [among Communists] opponents, critics, reformers, who are not "criminals".'

But, while he criticized concrete facets of Stalinism, Gorbachev was careful not to deprecate Stalin himself – even when the hypocrisy of socialist propaganda hit home in a painfully personal way.

There was, for instance, the day he split his only pair of trousers. He bent over at his table in the lunch room to pick up a fork and – rrrrip. His embarrassment turned instantly to cold fury. He turned on Lieberman and began to berate his Komsomol deputy. 'Tell me as a senior comrade, where is this socialism?' he demanded. 'I have only one suit and now the trousers have split. Our other comrade here,' he glared at another student, 'he has a lot of suits, and though he can live life at the dorm, he is renting a flat instead. He is living the high-society life. He goes to the Central Telegraph and meets girls there and brings them to his flat. So *where is this socialism!*' Having delivered this scorching criticism, he turned and left his comrades speechless. The puritanical true believer had shown his first disillusionment with the reality of class privilege that lay behind the façade of socialist equality.

There was one other time when Gorbachev gave himself away publicly as an emotional southerner with basically egalitarian instincts. It was over the issue of the infamous Doctors' Plot of 1952, when Stalin ordered all the Jewish doctors in the Politburo arrested on trumped-up charges of poisoning the leadership. A wave of anti-semitism swept Moscow State University and some students saw an opportunity to earn loyalty points. They turned on the Jewish student in Gorbachev's study group, Vladimir Lieberman, who aroused jealousy as the class orator and most highly decorated war veteran. An ugly confrontation took place in a lecture room before Gorbachev's whole class.

One student tried to implicate Lieberman in the Doctors' Plot, spewing forth garbage meant to cast doubt on his loyalty. Lieberman himself rose to make an eloquent defence: 'Should I, as the only Jew among you, take on the entire responsibility for all Jews?' Everyone fell silent. Gorbachev, eyes blazing, jumped to his feet. Pointing at Lieberman's accuser, he shouted, 'You're a spineless beast!'

Mikhail Sergeyevich is in truth a highly emotional man. 'Balanced' is the adjective friends often apply to him, a compliment in a conformist society where self-preservation requires that one conceal private emotions behind a bland mask of indifference. He must have earned his reputation as a man of 'iron self-control' by repressing his feelings. But even though Gorbachev worked hard to maintain that mask, he sometimes overreacted emotionally. He hasn't changed in this regard, acknowledges Lieberman. 'He still cannot sometimes keep his temper. I know all his breakdowns and outbursts of the last five years,' sighs the former state prosecutor. 'And I am always upset by them because I know by the evening of the same day he will be thinking differently. He is often irritated. Only afterwards does he think over his words.'

And so, even though he was being groomed as a first-generation apparatchik, the country Cossack simply didn't have the ingrained bureaucratic nature – the inflexibility, narrowness and incapacity for independent thought – essential for the role. 'His is not an authoritarian personality,' Mlynar says definitively, and others who have worked with him up to the present day confirm this appraisal. 'He is open-minded, curious, he has an ability to listen, learn, and he's able to adapt,' continues Mlynar. 'All this is the root of his self-confidence.'†

Soviet society stood in total contrast to such a nature. It was isolated and inflexible; it demanded conformism; intellectual curiosity was hazardous to one's health. By the time Gorbachev reached Moscow State University, the intelligentsia had been virtually destroyed, leaving no one in the entire leadership of the country who one could say, with certainty, had had a higher education.

'Those were the days when we never spoke heart to heart,' says Mikhailova.

But Gorbachev lived a double life. 'He was a doubter,' swears one of his roommates Kolchanov and several other more liberal friends from those years. Behind the closed door of their dormitory room – a famous room it became, attracting the most dynamic thinkers from other dorms – discussions raged deep into the night and took dangerous turns.

'We could be sent to jail for such discussions!' Kolchanov would caution. The debates howled on. 'Gorbachev had a very clear understanding of Stalinist collectivization and he thought of it as an incredible injustice,' says his roommate. 'He couldn't say it openly, but he was much more knowledgeable about this than we city boys.'

Shouting and screaming and waving their fists over their heads, the impassioned students of the secret 'club' battled over the right and wrongs of the Stalinist system. When the pitch became particularly high, Gorbachev would break in and try to mediate. 'You think this, you think that, but let's talk this through,' he would say in a voice that betrayed little emotion.

On the one hand he seemed, in private, to be entirely open to seeing the evils of Communism as it was translated into everyday Russian life. On the other hand, he gave every sign of being a sincere and true believer, as evidenced in his hardline behaviour as Komsomol organizer and his probable connection to the KGB, an organization devoted to gathering information on 'political enemies'. And this is the most notable and sustaining feature of Gorbachev's stance with regard to fundamental principles: *no one was ever quite sure what he stood for*. In their seminars, Natasha Rimashevskaya remembers, he always approached debates the same way. He had one phrase he loved to say:

'As to this question, one must approach it *dialectically*.'

That meant he wanted to entertain a thesis and its contradiction at the same time; always he sought to take into consideration all sides of an issue. But in the process he was never specific, never committed himself. Pressed to draw a conclusion about Gorbachev's character from this habit of action, Rimashevskaya says carefully, 'Maybe that eventually transforms into a person who would work for compromise.'

Lenin is in his blood, say Gorbachev's friends. And Lenin's doctrine of 'one step backward, two steps forward' – or complete tactical flexibility – appealed particularly strong to him, according to Neznansky.

And so, while the suit of apparatchik did not quite fit him, a decisive change of character was in the works. The price of maintaining his cossack independence of thought would have been expulsion from the Establishment and the lonely road of the outsider – and Gorbachev was not by nature an outsider. It was becoming ever clearer to him that to advance in Soviet life one had to cut one's convictions to fit the prevailing Party line and find a way to compromise with whomever was in power.

He began to make this knowledge work for him. The Communist Party machine – not more than 300,000 people†

– was the Establishment, the equivalent of the Ivy League class in America or the titled gentry of Europe. The ruling elite itself was drawn from a fraction of the population admitted to the Communist Party. In 1952, in a country of 184.8 million people,† only 6,882,145 were Party members.† And the Party hierarchy is a very closed world, difficult, almost impossible to enter except through one's parents or grandparents or powerful connections. Although Gorbachev had this entrée through his maternal grandfather, he also carried the stain of his paternal grandfather and the occupation. Gorbachev would always have to work hard to convince Party big shots that he could be trusted. He had to be more ambitious and clever and determined than anyone with pull in Moscow. And he certainly had to put aside those foolish thoughts about how the system had victimized the peasantry and was lying about it through propaganda.

He was rewarded for his efforts. At the exceptionally young age of twenty-one, in only his second year at university, Mikhail Sergeyevich was accepted as a full member of the Communist Party. And in his fourth year he was appointed Komsomol boss for the whole law faculty, making him an official Communist Party functionary. This was not a position to which one was elected by fellow students. When the Party decided to promote anyone, even to such a relatively small position, a message would be sent to the KGB to consult the files and decide if the person is to be trusted. At that point if Gorbachev had withheld damaging information on his anketa, the KGB would have caught up with him. But he was given full clearance and placed in the highly esteemed position of the Party's chief functionary in the law faculty of the country's most prestigious university.

Golovanov insists that once Mikhail attained the top Party job in the law faculty, 'He was prepared for compromises. And that showed up later, a talent for compromise.'

The hot-blooded cossack glimpsed by more liberal classmates like Mlynar and Lieberman had to be pushed even deeper below the surface. One of his roommates could never remember Gorbachev being angry in any sense. 'He always held in his feelings,' says Kolchanov. 'He never lost control. Never.'

Well, once. Fatefully. Over a girl named Raisa Maximovna Titorenko.

Falling in Love with a Prestige Object

Graceful and slim as a willow branch, haughty and ethereal, wherever she walked Raisa left a gaggle of gaping men behind her. 'She had an exceptionally beautiful figure, Russian style,' says Kolchanov. These awkward boys tried every ploy to win her, but Raisa cut them down with a cold stare. She was a gold-medal student in the philosophy department, which was housed in the same building as the law faculty. Gorbachev's friends considered women philosophy students a little strange, 'somewhere up in the clouds, far from life,' says Kolchanov, 'and Raisa had some of that in her'.

'She was a prestige object,' Mlynar explains. 'Just as she is today.' And certainly Raisa, despite the fact that she roomed in the same rough Strominka dorm with Gorbachev, was a woman who expected to be deferred to. When she spoke, *if* she deigned to speak to someone at all, 'Each word was a labour to which she had to give perfect birth.' She appeared unattainable.

Gorbachev first laid eyes on her at a ballroom dancing class. He was teasing his awkward male friends from the safe remove of the doorway, when Raisa started to dance with one of them, a gawky giant named Tapilin who pitched forward like a giraffe. Big tall Tapilin and little tiny Raisa – Gorbachev laughed aloud at the ludicrous sight.

'Let me dance with your partner,' he insisted as he cut in.

Raisa, only five foot two, with great dark eyes and silken skin, so elegant in her speech and so polished in her dancing, was a vision to this country boy. Gorbachev returned to his dormmates a lovesick man.

'He fell for Raisa right away,' said Kolchanov, head over

heels, and walked about numb for weeks until she showed a response. 'I think it was more him falling in love with her. He always loved her very much from the very start. I would go and visit them in Stavropol in the 1960s and I would see that their love had only grown stronger.'

By now Gorbachev had become matinee-idol handsome, with a sensuous Rudy Valentino mouth, dimpled chin and those smoking-coal eyes. But Raisa came around, according to Mlynar, because she felt this Mikhail was a reliable person, 'reliable' being an important mark of character for Soviets. She also liked him for his 'lack of vulgarity'.†

Raisa's background is a black hole to Soviets. She is even more secretive than Gorbachev. She was born on 5 January, 1932 in the Altai section of Siberia, in the city of Rubtosovsk. Her maiden name, Titorenko, is Ukrainian but she was raised mostly in the mountainous, industrialized territory in southern Siberia that is known as a spiritual place for the yogis who practise meditation there. Raisa later moved with her family to the Rostov territory, not far from Stavropol, where her mother still lives today. Because of her wide cheekspan, she is believed to have Mongol ancestors, an unappealing feature in a society that bears undisguised hatred for the Tatar–Mongols stemming from Russia's long subjugation by both.

Rumours persist that Raisa is related to an important member of the Party apparat and that this is how Gorbachev got his pull. In a closed society rumour is the substitute for fact and takes on the weight of absolute certainty, but no evidence has been produced to support the long-standing rumour that she is related by marriage to Andrei Gromyko.† One of their university classmates was told that Raisa is related to a Khrushchev-era member of the Politburo.† Another insists that her connection is to Suslov.†

But a classmate who has been at the Gorbachevs' home and knows the whole family well says that Raisa is not from a well-educated family. 'Her father was a simple railway worker, she never had any very important family.' Raisa herself much later admitted to a group of high-powered American business and academic women that she 'came from a very poor family'.† Members of the Moscow intelligentsia like to point out that hers is an uncultured voice. Sounding every bit as class conscious as the British, they say, 'Yes, the grammar is correct, the accent is correct, but the *intonation* gives her away.' They insist that Raisa is 'strongly provincial', just like Gorbachev, but has always put on airs and graces.

And so, although Raisa was beautiful and ambitious, the chip on Raisa's shoulder was probably more a manifestation of insecurity than arrogance. She was culturally aware and had come to the capital hungry for the kind of intellectual polish that someone like Mikhailova had absorbed naturally. Her brother is a writer, according to a Stavropol professor, and Raisa came to Moscow University with some reading knowledge of English (although she still speaks only a handful of English phrases today).

'Raisa was a very mediocre student,' says one of her professors, the renowned émigré writer Dr Alexander Zinoviev. 'She studied so-called scientific Communism. Only the stupidest students studied this subject. Then she was a Komsomol and Party activist.'

Gorbachev, however, was inordinately proud of Raisa from the first. To him, she could have appeared lofty. And indeed, she was superior to him in the early years. She had come to university with a gold medal, while he had only silver; she made '5s', or top grades. She picked up where Mikhailova had left off. She marched Misha off to book stores and museums and to the theatre to see Chekhov, Gorky, all the classics. Together the couple turned up at every foreign exhibition – 1953 and 1954 saw the first opening to the West – and hotly debated Abstract Expressionism. 'By the third year, he knew as much about art, literature, culture and sports as any other person in the class,' says Kolchanov.

'Like Mr Gorbachev, I come from a rural area near Stavropol,' a local official confided anonymously. 'He was a . . . a . . .' he gropes for a polite word.

'A hick?'†

'Yes, exactly. And I think it was Raisa who brought him up. Raisa saw in Mikhail Sergeyevich good clay. He was intelligent, open, courageous, a hard worker – but a hick. She refined him.'

Even Mikhailova offers this assessment: 'Raisa Maximovna of course played an early role in his cultural development.'

All his life, Gorbachev has been nurtured and made much of by exceptionally strong-minded, outspoken women. One of his strengths is that he is not competitive with women who have some superiority; instead he says, Share it with me, teach me. He was always a willing and eager student, looking for imprints that could help him advance. Raisa was perhaps the strongest imprint on his adult life.

'Raisa Maximovna is the alter ego of Gorbachev,' confirmed Lieberman. 'She read more political theory books than he did. When he was made Komsomol secretary for the whole faculty, he had a lot of administrative work. He couldn't study so much, and he began to get "4s"; he sometimes missed classes. So she helped him even then with his studying. She is always helping Gorbachev.'

Their wedding was a sterile formality, the signing of books in a registrar's office. What followed, though, was a surprisingly affluent bash at the students' residence, a Komsomol wedding party, with dancing and food and unlimited drinks that no peasant on a grant could possibly afford. Assistance may have come from the KGB, which has an entire directorate devoted to dispensing luxuries to the Moscow party faithful and helps students who have been helpful to it. There were toasts, and toasts, and more toasts – to the point where Mlynar accidentally smeared his new suit with butter and then suddenly everyone stopped to wonder, 'Where will the wedding couple spend the night?' After some manoeuvring, the two managed to stay the night alone in one of the dormitories, but in the cold light of morning they had to go back to separate rooms until the following year, when they obtained a room in the new students' residence in the Lenin Hills.

'Raisa was always very hospitable,' remembers Kolchanov. She cooked a little in those days, fried meat or soup or piroshki. Friends could scarcely pass their room without Raisa catching their attention and coaxing them in, insisting, 'How can you possibly not come in for tea, just for a second, a "minootichkoo"?'

And so this gregarious young man, with the help of his attractive wife, went out of his way to make contact with all sorts of people. Among his friends were Jews and Persians and Tatars, Czechs, Poles and Bulgarians. He learned about the war from the veterans he roomed with – Tapilin, Shapko and Safronov – older men, with wives back home. And through his relationships with cultured women, he bootlegged what he couldn't get from his own background or from the stultifying academic programme.

'He wanted to know everything,' as Mikhailova says. 'He took a little from me, a little from Raisa, from Mlynar, from Kolchanov – but mostly he did it himself. He grew before our very eyes.'

Death of God

At 6.00 a.m. on 9 March 1953, night workers at Moscow's Dynamo auto factory huddled in disbelief around a radio from which the disembodied voice of their trusted commentator, Levitan, a Soviet Walter Cronkite, delivered the news. Stalin was dead.

A shudder moved across the land, people trembled at the impossible thought of going on without the omnipotent leader. Stalin made the day begin, Stalin made everyone work at night, because he worked at night, Stalin made every decision there was to make, Stalin gaveth life and Stalin took it away. Even those who had suffered under Stalinism felt helpless and were afraid to think of the future. Out in the provinces people wept in the streets. Millions swarmed into

central Moscow, where he lay in state, pushing blindly
through the crowd to gaze one last time on the face that had
overshadowed their tiny lives in every way – in the extravagant mass-produced statues in every square, in the gigantic
red banners that bore his hallucinatory likeness in mandatory
parades, in the trillions of posters churned out by his
propaganda machine and posted in every school and workplace – and they shrieked upon seeing the waxen black-
lipped deathmask of a leader whose brain had haemorrhaged
and whose features had been contorted beyond recognition
by a horrible, very mortal death.

The crowd spun out of control.† Hundreds, possibly
thousands, were trampled to death by the mass hysteria that
exploded over the evidence that, yes, it was true, god was
dead. The people were crying, not because they were monsters like Stalin, but because they had been utterly deceived
by Stalin's lies and psychological manipulation.

In the Strominka, as well, life seemed to come to a
standstill. When they first awoke to the news, the shocked
students listened as Moscow Radio appealed to the Soviet
people to unite behind the Communist Party. The men
drifted out to attend their classes but were called instead to a
mass meeting in an amphitheatre, after which they broke up
into separate faculties. Gorbachev crossed Herzen Street and
headed for the House of Culture where all students from the
humanitarian faculties were to meet.

'Wait, Misha!' It was Lieberman, in a fever, running to
catch his friend. 'Misha, wait!' But Misha didn't hear or
didn't stop.

'I met Stalin's death with joy,' says Lieberman, almost
whispering as he relives that momentous day. 'I wanted to
smile and share my joy.' But inside the House of Culture,
when Lieberman finally caught up with his friend, pushing
his way next to Gorbachev, he looked in his face and –
recoiled.

The eyes of Gorbachev – sad, serious, imperious eyes –
made it stonily clear: Don't approach.

'He didn't cry but he was taking it all so seriously. I wanted so desperately to talk to him. But I didn't dare. I was really tormented,' and Lieberman's eyes redden in the retelling.

Mikhailova sat next to Misha at the memorial ceremony that was held the same day. The student representing their group stood up and emoted: 'If Stalin's life could have been extended by one day, I would have given away all of my blood, drop by drop.' Mikhailova recalls the mood of the times. 'Each of us would have done the same. We worshipped Stalin as a god, an icon. I felt I would have given my own blood that same day.'

On the day of Stalin's funeral Gorbachev stood at the window of their student hostel, Zdenek Mlynar beside him. Sirens raked the skies, then there were two moments of silence, and Gorbachev's face registered the fearsome rapture. Gorbachev's own recollection of that day was: 'Lots of us were in tears.' Zdenek said, 'Misha, what will become of us?'†

'Stalin's death wasn't a liberation for us,' Mlynar confided to me, his voice even now thick with emotion, 'for we were Communists.'

After the first shock was over, however, tens of thousands of Muscovites and their families sighed with relief. With Stalin gone, it was almost easier to breathe. People were no longer forced to work at night. The renewal of the country began, and the first steps of Stalin's successor, Nikita Khrushchev, brought a glimmer of hope for the future. Under Stalin, no one had dared even to talk about the future.

For the students at Moscow State University, it began to sink in: the new era would depend on them. Soon after Stalin's death people began to return from the labour camps, and such bright idealistic young men must have realized that the system of law was a sham. Public prosecutors who had tried to be honest were incarcerated. New graduates of the law faculty would either have to carry out the existing system and be corrupted by it, or change careers.

'I answered that question for myself in our fourth year, 1954, a year after Stalin's death,' says Golovanov. 'I stopped studying law, I just couldn't do it.' He became a journalist. 'But I think even Gorbachev was full of doubts. And today we see how he tries to build a state based on laws. Not a single leader before him, not Khrushchev, not Brezhnev, was concerned with these questions. For them law was them themselves.'

Many of Gorbachev's classmates went on to become pillars of the Moscow Party Establishment – members of the Ministry of Justice, the Central Committee, the militia and two generals in the KGB. Kolchanov today is the editor of *Trud*, a mass-circulation trade union newspaper. Golovanov rose to become director of the nightly evening news show, *Vremya*, and used to be among the several hundred top opinion-makers whom Gorbachev would call together regularly to enlist in his reform programme; he has since been banished for some offence to the Tass office in Sofia, Bulgaria. Natasha Rimashevskaya remained in Moscow and rose through the academic ladder to become a director of an institute of research studying socio-economic problems. Anatoly Luky-anov, two years ahead of Gorbachev, would eventually become chief of staff of the Praesidium of the Soviet parliament, and advance under Gorbachev to become its President. And Lieberman, the brilliant orator, joined the Moscow state prosecutor's office, but his career never went anywhere and today, semi-retired and sick, he teaches one course at a management institute and lives with his wife in two rooms.

Not one – not a single one of them – would have predicted that in the future their friend Misha would become leader of the land. Gorbachev wanted desperately to stay in Moscow, confirms Golovanov; he told Mikhailova that he badly wanted to get a job as an assistant in the Moscow prosecutor's office. That was all they knew of his hopes for the future.

The fact that he escaped conscription into the armed forces, which is still compulsory in the Soviet Union, has stumped his biographers.

Gorbachev had never shown any interest in the military. He and Mlynar stood out from the former soldiers in their dorm as younger men with a very different generational perspective. 'For them, the war was the highlight of their lives,' explains Mlynar. 'They would carry on about "Why did Stalin stop us on the Elbe, we could have fought on to Paris!" and they were all caught up in the cause of world revolution. But for Gorbachev and myself, we wanted never to have another war. We had experienced the war from the point of view of the civilian population, as the victims. In the fifties we all believed that the Cold War could turn into a hot war. We saw the cause of this danger in the West, because of the monopoly by the United States of the atom bomb until 1949.'

Satisfying military service with a one-month military course during the summer vacation,† Gorbachev seemed assured that the Party had another kind of service in mind for him. Entering his fifth and final year at the university, he must have been fairly sanguine about his chances of being granted a post in the Centre. But, in his last year, everything went awry.

That year, the faculty and students who were housed at the Strominka downtown were moved up to join the loftier Lenin Hills law school. One Komsomol leader had to be chosen for the merged law faculties. Gorbachev lost out to a well-connected Muscovite. It was a serious setback to his hopes of launching a political career in the capital. But worse was in store for the boy from Privolnoye.

After graduating, when Mikhail Sergeyevich went to the Moscow state prosecutor's office to apply for work, there was a bad odour about his interrogation. Something was wrong.

'I don't have any apartments,' the prosecutor told Gorbachev brusquely. 'You come from Stavropol, you should think about going back where you came from.'†

Had they found out more about the stains on his background?

'He was unable to stay in Moscow, because there was a serious check-up and everything came out into the open,' claims Dmitry Barchevsky, a well-known Soviet filmmaker who is researching a film based on Gorbachev's life. True, upon graduation each student was thoroughly investigated before being 'distributed' to a prescribed place for three years of work. The investigation of graduates of the law faculty, who would be placed in law enforcement or intelligence agencies, was particularly rigorous: the KGB would produce a complete psychogram. According to scholars at Radio Liberty, 'From generation to generation they know what your mother and father, your grandparents and great-grandparents, have done.'

Viktor Yasmann, a senior researcher at Radio Liberty who is an expert on the KGB and a former Soviet citizen of this period, has another speculation. Before Stalin's death, the precursor to the KGB – the NKVD – was under the rule of the ruthless Lavrenti Beria, and the secret police had reached its apogee vis-à-vis other state institutions, including the Party. Gorbachev's career surge took place in the last three Stalin years (1950–3), when those who advanced needed protection by Beria's compatriots in the organs of the secret police. Beria was then seen as a potential successor to Stalin. But he was arrested and subsequently executed shortly after Stalin's death, and the NKVD was split into two institutions, the Ministry of Internal Affairs (MVD) and the KGB, in an effort to bring it under firm Party control.

'The Party didn't want Beria-linked functionaries. That's why Gorbachev lost his position as Komsomol leader and why he was sent back to Stavropol,' believes Yasmann. 'Suddenly, he wasn't so attractive to the Party any more.'

Back to nowhere. It was a bitter blow – Gorbachev's first failure. There was no arguing. One was never told why. After all his efforts to learn how to play by the Party rules, despite his charming of Moscow's elite, his exemplary personal behaviour, and his flawless performance for the Party overseers as a propagandist and as a recruiter for the KGB, in the face of such an immaculate record built up over five years at the university, this was his reward: back to Stavropol. The only answer was to swallow the humiliation and go back and start all over again, trying to recultivate the trust of the Party apparat.

It was a blow to his wife as well. Raisa was already pregnant, but she had every hope of pursuing a doctoral degree in the Centre. For a couple with ambitions to rise in the Party and in academic life, Moscow was the only place to be. 'You can never imagine what it meant to have a chance to stay in Moscow and continue your studies, to enter the circle of the scientific intelligentsia of Moscow – and then, to be told you have to leave for *Stavropol*,' says Barchevsky.

'Gorbachev himself had doubts about which was better for Raisa, to stay in Moscow or go with him to Stavropol,' says Lieberman. 'It was her decision to accompany him – and a sacrifice. She lost ten years before she could go to graduate school,' he adds. Perhaps the blow was cushioned by her faith in her husband's natural abilities. Since it was very difficult for a woman in the Soviet Union in the 1950s to realize any political ambitions on her own, she must have seen Gorbachev as a promising instrument – with a little fine-tuning, there was still hope that they could go far.

Back to Stavropol

'Warm Siberia' they called it. Stavropol was a sleepy, rude and dirty place of secondary exile to which lesser members of the nomenklatura and literary free spirits such as Pushkin and Lermontov were banished. It was hard to go back. Mikhail and the pregnant Raisa boarded the slow train for the trip south. There were two classes of travel, soft class and hard class. They would sleep hard for the next twenty-four hours.

They awoke to the sight of a one-street town, veiled in dust, with no indoor plumbing, no tap water and no gas, despite the fact that the first gas pipeline in the Soviet Union originated in Stavropol. It was just another of hundreds of little cities (110th in size of population) that pumped its precious resources into the Centre. Stavropol, which means 'city of the cross', was originally designed by Catherine the Great's favourite architect, Potemkin, as a fortress of Russian Christianity against the infidel Muslim armies father south in Turkey. Later, when the great mail railway was being built to run from Moscow all the way south to Tblisi and the Black Sea, Stavropol was planned as a stop on its route. But the surrounding soil was too sandy, and so the main rail route bypassed it, leaving the southern city to develop slowly, under graceful poplars and scissor-leaved acacia trees, as a forgotten backwater. A one-track railway town.

The couple rented a single tiny, heatless room.† With only a kerosene lamp to cook by, it took Raisa twenty minutes just to boil the water for a cup of tea. When their baby, Irina, was born, the landlady took pity on them and suggested they live in her room because it was warmer than theirs.

The prosecutor's office in Stavropol took Misha as an investigator. It had to be distasteful work: to be a prosecutor at that time meant carrying out a grotesque parody of justice, or being recruited as an informer by the KGB. 'Lawyers used to be the most despised profession and the most lowly paid in Soviet life,' recalls Mikhailova. No mention of this step in his career is included in the official record.

By now Gorbachev must have grasped the dimensions of Stalin's arbitrary purges. Millions, literally, of the wretched victims of Stalin's political Terror began straggling back from the gulag into the light of cities and villages. Five per cent of the population were still in the gulag, most of them appealing the false allegations used against them. Historian Zhores Medvedev, who chronicled Stalinism, writes, 'Particularly for someone who wanted to be a lawyer, it was a shattering blow to previously held notions of justice.'†

Gorbachev saw, but with what Wordsworth described as 'that inner eye' – memory. It would be a locked and silent safe for the next twenty-three years while he picked his way through the treacheries of a parasitic provincial aristocracy dependent for its privileges on one man: the non-elected regional Party boss.

In his only interview about his life, given to a correspondent of the Communist Party Central Committee, Gorbachev said vaguely, 'It so happened that I did not work in my profession for long. I was soon recommended for work in the Young Communist League, and I have been in Komsomol and Party work since then. Over the many years I worked with the territorial committee of the Party, including almost nine years as First Secretary of the Soviet Communist Party territorial committee. Those were also significant and important years in our life.'†

But, until he got on his feet, Raisa had to carry the day.

According to Mlynar and others, Raisa was one of the key factors in his early success in Stavropol. The fact is, Raisa was offered a more prestigious job than her husband. She was young and she had a university education, a rarity in Stavropol. Soon after they arrived, the local community college lured her away from her first job in a medical institute by offering her a more generous salary – 1,250 rubles a month, big money at the time, considerably more than her husband was paid – to teach in their philosophy department.

'To tell you directly, we weren't all at her level,' says the chairman of her department, Professor Chuguyev, a sensitive man who speaks of Raisa with some awe. 'She had great respect from all of us at the institute, both as a teacher and as a person.' Not everyone shared the professor's high opinion. When Mikhail first brought his bride home to Privolnoye, the jealousy of the local peasant women was blatant. 'Who is she? What is she? Where did he take *her* from?' they demanded. Mrs Yakovenko, the girl who grew up next door, recalls how 'all our girls didn't like her'. They wanted to know 'Why does she always have to go with him?'

Nor did Raisa have much in common with the ladies of Stavropol, who slapped down the street in their cork-heeled mules and shapeless sweaters. Workhorses for their husbands, lugging home bulging sacks and keeping house under the most primitive conditions even as they worked at sterile jobs and waited in interminable food lines, most were old before forty, with withered breasts and stumpy legs. Even the pretty ones, ravaged by indifferent medical care and dentistry, had smiles that resembled a pile of broken china. Their husbands, meanwhile, gradually turned livid with drink.

Raisa always took care to look and dress more like a European woman. She too worked long hours, but a teen-aged cousin of Gorbachev's came to Stavropol to care for the newborn baby, Irina, and the Gorbachevs later had a full-time housekeeper who cooked the meals and eventually accompanied the family to Moscow.

From the start, Raisa's relationship with Mikhail was strikingly different from the Soviet norm – a partnership between equals. 'They were so close to each other, sometimes people were irritated that she always accompanied him,' notes Professor Chuguyev, echoing the women of Privolnoye.

Professional Son

The full politicization of Gorbachev took place in 1956. That was the year Nikita Khrushchev made the famous secret speech at the 20th Party Congress that split open the Stalin cult of personality. After the Congress in Moscow, the speech was read to Gorbachev and other Party members by the Stavropol territorial Party committee, allowing for no discussion. The message of this speech, which was given without the consent of the Politburo, was that Stalin had brutalized his own people. But the Politburo never permitted the contents of the speech to be published, and so Khrushchev's revelations never reached beyond a small group of Party intimates. 'I made the first step, the word has been said,' Khrushchev told his granddaughter, Julia; but after he died, his widow, Nina Petrovna, lamented that 'Nikita will be forgotten.'†

He would not be forgotten by Mikhail Gorbachev. That speech had an extraordinary impact on Gorbachev, according to Mikhailova, who saw him shortly thereafter. 'It was totally unexpected, he was really shaken by it. He talked about Khrushchev's great political courage.' It was a turning point for the twenty-five-year-old believer, shattering for good the protective capsule around his boyhood faith in the system under Stalin. But the speech also offered a dangerous bromide that Gorbachev would take as his new belief and stick with, blindly, up to the present day. Khrushchev rationalized all the brutal realities of socialist history by blaming them on human perversion. The glorious goals of socialism were as noble as ever and the system superior to all others.

'Gorbachev was young at that time, I was young, we belonged to the same generation and we were enthusiasts,' Gennady Gerasimov reminisced recently, 'we wanted to change Soviet society for the better.' Gerasimov, who has served as Gorbachev's spokesman in the West and is now press secretary for Foreign Minister Shevardnadze, points out that the Khrushchev speech 'is not very good if you read it today'. Yet Gorbachev is still using the same rationale: first, blame the leaders of history for perverting the noble goals of socialism, and when that doesn't work, blame the people: but never, under any circumstances, admit that the *system itself* might be to blame.

'If you listen to him today,' says Gerasimov of Gorbachev, 'he says that he thinks the socialist idea is valid, and that his job is to give socialist ideas second breath.' The suave spokesman comes very close to a sneer, and out blurts an extraordinary confession of lifelong frustration. 'My generation waited in the wings for too long. We wanted to start in the 1950s. Now it's the 1990s. We spent all of our lives beating around the bush, and now this is our last chance, and that's it.' But at the time – despite the Politburo's attempt to squash it – Khrushchev's speech opened the floodgates for new magazines and books publicizing Stalin's misdeeds, initiating the 'thaw' of the early 1960s that gave Gorbachev's generation its nickname: the Shestdesyatniki, or Sixtiers. For Gorbachev, there was also a personal catharsis of the family shame he had carried secretly since 1937, although it still was not possible for him to speak openly about the injustice done to his paternal grandfather, whom he refers to even today only as a 'relative who was a middle peasant'.†

And so Gorbachev gave up Stalin as the god-the-father figure and began a thirty-year saga of looking for new protectors.

In the Soviet Union protection is everything. Particularly in the blood sport of politics, it is impossible to advance without a patron. And the way one makes oneself attractive to strong patrons is not by demonstrating ability or talent, but by blind loyalty. After landing back at square one, in the Stravropol prosecutor's office, Gorbachev was in dire need of a powerful sponsor. So he set about cultivating and manipulating older men with the power to protect and advance him. The fact that his own father was absent for the five years of adolescence when a boy needs a male figure to identify with, and to endorse him as worthwhile, could easily have turned Gorbachev against the 'fathers' he met in adult life. Instead, he listened attentively and followed with filial loyalty each of the patrons he attracted. He didn't compete with them, and he *never* turned against them.

He did have to hide his doubts. But he became expert at knowing intuitively what each of his protectors needed to hear, and adapting himself in every way – his tone of voice, his body language, his dress and even facial expressions – to imitate the idiosyncrasies of his patrons. 'Gorbachev has yet to show in his career the "killer instinct" needed to get to and stay at the very top,'† the Western press was writing as late as four months before Gorbachev ascended to the highest post in the Kremlin in 1985. True, violence and force were not his weapons, but he had a different sort of instinct, that of a covert 'killer', of a natural propagandist. If the suit of the narrow-minded, lock-step apparatchik still didn't fit him, he would get ahead by tapping other aspects of his character: his intuitiveness, his natural ability as an improvisational actor, his ease in changing colours.

He would become a brilliant chameleon.

Pragmatic politicians the world over would see this as a defensible path to power. American congressmen, for example, marvelled at Lyndon Johnson's ability to make liberals think he was liberal and conservatives think he was conservative, and to make even those who knew he believed differently excuse him anyway. As Robert Caro's revealing examination of the American President makes clear, Johnson would make almost any compromise, and shift in almost any direction on a given issue, if he thought it necessary to keep him in Congress. 'He could talk so much – and no one ever knew exactly where he stood,' which may be the ultimate political gift.†

And so the peasant from Privolnoye pleased, charmed and mirrored his patrons, finding his way into their hearts, ensuring in *every case* that they would recommend Mikhail Gorbachev to replace them as they moved up the ladder of power or shuffled off their mortal coil.

Within a few months of his return to Stavropol, he was bailed out of a bad situation by his first patron. Grigory Gorlov, the same man who had smoothed his way into Moscow University, now a territorial Party committee official, enabled Gorbachev to leave the prosecutor's office. 'I recommended him as deputy head of the ideological section of the Komsomol in Stavropol city,' Gorlov told me. 'My wife was ill and I couldn't take the position myself, so I recommended the boy in my place.'

Komsomol work at the city level was a lowly position for a graduate of the law faculty of MSU. Yet all those who worked with Gorbachev in Stavropol say he had a certain aura –

'untouchable, not like a common guy't and his work habits
became legendary. Rising swiftly as a professional propagandist, he was only twenty-nine when he was recommended for the job of Komsomol leader for the whole
territory.

A photograph taken around that time shows Gorbachev
standing on the street just outside the regional Party boss's
residence between his four-year-old daughter and his
mother. Little Irina is well dressed in a coat of velveteen
plush, Maria Panteleyevna is wearing high boots and a
babushka, and Mikhail Sergeyevich looks every inch the up-
and-coming Soviet politician. What's more, in his wide-
legged trousers and old man's hat and heavily padded
overcoat, his chin tucked in to exaggerate an incipient double
chin, Gorbachev is almost a mirror image of the man who
was then the ultimate power in the country – Nikita
Khrushchev.

Then, on 14 April 1962, Gorbachev was 'unexpectedly't
moved from his comparatively important Komsomol position
into what appeared to be a rather obscure Party job as the
political supervisor for four united regions of agriculture. It
looked like a demotion,† or else a bad move for an obviously
ambitious workaholic to be making at thirty-one, an age
when most people feel restless and impatient, pinched by
the restrictions that stem from the choices of their twenties.

But the new job was neither a demotion nor a mistake. It
was part of a calculated strategy. Once again, Grigory Gorlov
was watching out for his old friend's son. Gorlov told me
that he, along with two other local Party leaders, had
recommended Misha for the position because it would put
him under the tutelage and protection of the fastest-rising
power in the whole territory – Fyodor Davidovich Kulakov.
(The KGB might also have had a hand in this latest career
decision. At the time, it was co-ordinating its activities with
those of the Komsomol at every level.† And, since it is
officially barred from placing operatives inside the Party, the

KGB has always been particularly keen to help promote their informers within the apparat.)

Gorlov had done as much as he could for Gorbachev. At this point, the young man would need a patron with more power, particularly since the winds of command were shifting once again.

For all the fervour it had awakened in the progressives of Gorbachev's generation, the Khrushchev thaw was turning out to be a false spring. In 1961, as a delegate from Stavropol, Gorbachev attended the second Party congress presided over by Khrushchev, and this time Khrushchev took his ardent anti-Stalinist campaign too far. He declared some serious reforms, reforms which threatened the monster known as the Party apparat, that headless jellylike bureaucracy whose tentacles reach into every aspect of Soviet life and whose sting is both formidable and untraceable. By insisting that at least one-third of the regional Party committee members be replaced at each election, he threatened the apparatchiks in their most jealously guarded preserve of power. The delegates at the Congress rubberstamped Khrushchev's plan – and then went home to lie in wait for their chance to trap him.†

Gorbachev's new patron was one of those delegates who had decided that Khrushchev was going too far, and had to be stopped. 'The peasant from Penza', as Kulakov was dubbed, had much the same country-bumpkin background as our Cossack from the Kuban. A Great Russian, he had begun his career tending sugar beets on a state farm and was awarded a medal 'For Valiant Labour'. He too had joined up with the Party at an exceptionally young age, twenty-two, and he too saw it as the smartest move he had ever made. Party influence had propelled him into the post of Deputy Minister of Agriculture for the Russian Republic and then to the appointment as First Secretary of the Stavropol region.

But there was nothing of the country bumpkin about Kulakov's manner of doing business.† Whipsmart, sleekly dressed and highly ambitious, this progressive territorial

Party boss believed in doing things on a grand scale. He worked hard and demanded hard work, moving about his enormous territory to give hands-on direction for his agricultural experiments. His thick lips, large nose and kinky hair, together with his patronymic, Fyodor *Davidovich* (indicating that his father's name was David), gave rise to whispers that he was Jewish.

Kulakov had supplemented his college degree with a correspondence course at a Moscow agricultural institute, earning a diploma in agronomy. And so, as soon as he went to work for Fyodor Davidovich, Gorbachev signed up for an identical course of study at the Stavropol Agricultural Institute. The thirty-one-year-old disciple attended night school for the next five years.

By 1967, when Gorbachev was thirty-six, he too got his diploma in agronomy. Just as his law degree was less like graduation from, say, Yale Law School than from a police academy, his 'degree' in agronomy was basically a paper certificate verifying his completion of a correspondence course. Raisa, then thirty-five, finished her dissertation and prepared to defend it, a daunting interrogation process in the Soviet Union, but one for which her steeliness stood her in good stead. She passed.

Gorbachev hit the fast track at thirty-two when Kulakov gave him the added responsibility of attracting talented people to join the Party cadres. It was plain that Gorbachev had become a member of his boss's clan. 'Kulakov was his teacher,' says Gorlov, 'and Gorbachev took all the lessons of Mr Kulakov.' But Gorlov is quick to add that Gorbachev never sank to the level of mindless sycophancy. 'He was always very objective. He listened all the way through and if the person was not correct, he would tell them directly.'

Gorbachev stuck close to this new patron for the next eighteen years, paralleling Kulakov's ambitious ascent up through the hierarchy and into the Kremlin inner circle. He showed respect and submission when Kulakov threw his authoritarian weight around and ignored the fact that the man was a wild and heavy drinker, even though, says one co-worker, 'Mikhail Sergeyevich didn't have any patience with drunkards.'† Kulakov was a career Party functionary. 'Maybe Misha was also a functionary in those years,' acknowledges Mikhailova.

The cunning peasant from Penza had a talent for functional survival. Although he was determined to turn his region into an agricultural success story, Kulakov dutifully accepted Khrushchev's orders, even speaking in favour of the Kremlin chief's absurd anti-grasslands programme and proclaiming that Khrushchev 'is quite right in aiming for a complete reorganization and strengthening of agricultural administration from top to bottom'. Khrushchev's chair was barely cold, following his ouster in 1964, when Kulakov eagerly stepped forward to reverse himself, agreeing with Leonid Brezhnev's new Kremlin clique that Khrushchev's agricultural policies had been 'harebrained'.

Gorbachev watched as his patron navigated the treacherous shoals of Party politics.† And he had a ringside seat at Nikita Khrushchev's downfall, since it was Kulakov who held the plotting party that deposed the Soviet leader. On a 'hunting and fishing' holiday in the Manych lakes down south, according to Roy Medvedev's account, 'a detailed discussion of the Khrushchev question took place among a group of members of the Praesidium and the Central Committee in September' while they were 'guests of the First Secretary of Stavropol, F. Kulakov'. The main instigator of the back-stabbing was Mikhail Suslov, the sinister propagandist who had been Stalin's bloodthirsty henchman in Stavropol during the Second World War. Suslov engineered the coup with the support of the KGB.

So Gorbachev saw up close what happens to a reformer who tries to act independently of his power source, which in the Soviet context has always meant the Communist Party elite. Sympathetic with Khrushchev, he none the less learned a lesson he would later repeat at a Writers' Union meeting in 1986: the bureaucracy had managed to 'break Khrushchev's neck',† he told his audience, and it would like to do the same to his.

But Gorbachev had a secret weapon, a full partner in the power game, a most unusual circumstance in the Soviet Union. His wife, Raisa Maximovna, discussed with him every move he made and furthered his career in many different ways. Raisa even became her husband's teacher – literally as well as figuratively.

Raisa, Prophet of Perestroika

In 1962, Gorbachev enrolled in his wife's philosophy seminar at the same Institute of Agriculture where he had begun his agronomy course.† In her high-ceilinged, fin-de-siècle class-room hung with the huge, child-like, methodological posters she'd invented for the strict teaching of Marxist–Leninist philosophy, he squeezed into a tiny desk chair and listened to Raisa's brittle, high-pitched voice at weekly lectures.

Raisa's degree in philosophy was not equivalent to a philosophy degree in the West; it was a degree in orthodoxy, the equivalent of a diploma from a Bible college. Rather than grappling with Descartes and Schopenhauer, she had been thoroughly indoctrinated in the methods of teaching Marx-ism–Leninism, the sole purpose of which was 'to put the ideology of the country in the people's heads'. The curricu-lum was ordained by the Communist Party Central Com-mittee as a form of political control and a mechanism for training the future Party elite. (Such courses have since been eliminated in Eastern Europe.) But every Soviet student, regardless of their prospective profession, paid close atten-tion in these classes, since their grades would be the basis for future scholarships and jobs.† Raisa Maximovna's word was gospel and her students cowered before her.

Grigory Gorlov, who took Raisa's course at the same time, describes the heated arguments she would have with her student–husband. Gorbachev would make a speech about

Kant. 'You're wrong,' Raisa would snap. 'It is better understood this way.' And when his curiosity would prompt him
to ask searching questions, she would cut him off: 'We don't
go into verifying questions.' Or 'Such questions are obstruc-
tionist.' She granted him no privileges.

'They have the same character,' says Gorlov, an assessment echoed by many who have known the couple over the
years. But Raisa always had a sharp edge. If she comes across
as bossy or supercilious, it is a common female response to a
system that purports to be gender-equal but is in fact male
supremacist at every level. Women have so little real power
in the Soviet Union, whatever small domain they do control
they dominate by the cheerless intimidation of all who dare
pass through; hence female bureaucrats are the most feared,
female teachers and doctors are often little dictators, right
down to the babushkas in the park who insist upon helping
you so they can scold you.

At home, too, 'they had the same position within the
family', recalls Gorlov. 'Sometimes she would quarrel with
him at home about politics or international relations. She
would disapprove of his ideas. But he'd come right back and
prove his personal view of events.'

The fearsome Raisa even faced down the Party mind-
control police. During her time as a teacher, there were
always inspectors going around to check up on how courses
were being taught. One day they tape-recorded Raisa's
lecture secretly. When she learned of it, she marched straight
to the director of the institute and demanded that he
summon the offending inspectors.

'She invited the director and vice-director and me here,
too,' remembers Professor Chuguyev. Then Raisa shook her
finger in the faces of the so-called authorities and spat out
her scorn. 'This is the *last time* you'll do this!' she admon-
ished. 'If you need to check up on me, come and ask me. But
don't you do it this way. It's not morally acceptable. It's not
honest. Do it *openly*.'

Thoroughly chastened, the half-dozen men meekly apologized: 'Raisa Maximovna, we won't do that any more.' Tails between their legs, they left her monarchical domain and did not return. Until she refused to teach atheism.

'I don't like it, I just don't *like* to teach atheism' – again Raisa delivered her edict to the investigators – 'and I'm *not* going to do it any more.' Period. End of discussion.

Raisa's aggressive wrath was all the more extraordinary given the fact that her husband was still a mere city-level clerk at the time. 'She wouldn't permit vulgarisms against capitalism, or any other system,' notes Professor Chuguyev. 'She held firmly to the view that only scholarly criticism was acceptable. And she was very firm on this point that people should talk and criticize only *openly*.' Thus was Raisa an early practioner of glasnost.

(Gorbachev's first recorded use of the term occurred in 1971,† when he proposed that discussions of the local Party committee should be controlled by glasnost and democratic methods. He probably picked up the idea from Kulakov, who had spoken freely of the need to 'democratize' interregional management of collective farms.)

Ironically, given her record as a propounder of Marxist–Leninist orthodoxy, Raisa would also prove to be a prophet of perestroika. The field of sociology had been crippled by the same anti-intellectual fanaticism that was helping to destroy Soviet agriculture, but Raisa Gorbachev was one of the rare people who dared to do independent research among the farmers – the kolkhozniki – during the sixties.

In the neighbouring Krasnodar territory Raisa studied the first collective that refused the system of being paid by points and demanded money, daily pay. The 'self-accounting' system they called it – khoraschet – which meant that their payment and bonuses depended directly upon the size of the harvest, rather than being a fixed amount guaranteed by the state to shiftless drunkards and hard workers alike. While she continued to teach up to eight hours a day, the young

mother wrote a dissertation demonstrating that this unorthodox initiative had earned the farmers a higher standard of
living and awakened dreams of foreign travel and consumer
goods. She then turned her research into a chapter in a book.

Raisa's doctoral dissertation would also serve to advance
her husband's political career: 'self-accounting' became a
cornerstone of Gorbachev's programme for restructuring the
Soviet economy. Was it in truth an idea that he gleaned from
Raisa's research? I checked with Professor Chuguyev. 'Without a doubt,' he says. 'She would discuss these things she
learned with Mikhail Sergeyevich. This has been in his mind
for a long, long time.'

Raisa's proud husband boasted to Mlynar that the farmers
were thrilled to be asked questions for the first time. Even
more unorthodox was Raisa's interest in the low status of
women in kolkhoz villages; she pointed out in her dissertation that the men got all the technical education while the
women did the meanest manual labour. 'Raisa got a lot of
enjoyment out of talking about her work and loved to tell
what she was doing,' recalls one social acquaintance. 'One
felt a great mutual respect between the two. Gorbachev knew
all of her stories and details of her life. I was even surprised
at how close and good their relationship was, and the
equality of their relationship.'†

Filling the Party Father's Shoes

Gorbachev had not yet turned forty when he was named a
full territorial Party boss, in April 1970. It was a heady time
for the young couple; they seemed to be living a charmed
life. Kulakov, who had been sent to Moscow to become
Agriculture Secretary, recommended that Gorbachev replace
him as First Secretary of Stavropol. The peasant from Privolnoye had become one of only a hundred or so territorial
Party bosses who played a crucial role in deciding who runs
the country. Furthermore, Gorbachev was now under the
wing of another powerful 'angel' in Moscow: Mikhail Suslov,

the ruthless conniver who would outlast no less than three General Secretaries. After serving both Stalin and Khrushchev, Suslov was now a kingmaker in the Kremlin of Leonid Brezhnev, and he had supported Kulakov's recommendation that Gorbachev be promoted.

But when Misha's father travelled to town for the occasion, the older man's words reflected the fear of one who remembered what had happened in the recent past to ambitious young men like his son.

'Misha, don't you think it's a little early for you to have such a high position?' the father asked.

'They trust me,' Gorbachev replied. 'I will try my best to do my job so I should not deceive them.'†

A year later Gorbachev was admitted as a full member to the Central Committee, the ruling body of the Communist Party. There he would meet another man destined to play a part in his future, who would become perhaps his most important ally besides Raisa, Alexander N. Yakovlev. Even then, Gorbachev and Yakovlev were potential intellectual allies. Yakovlev had been chosen by the KGB as the first Soviet exchange student to go to America and attended Columbia University in 1959–60.† But in the late sixties, when Yakovlev was working for the Central Committee in the republic of Uzbekistan, he fell foul of the Brezhnev clique by refusing to compromise himself in accepting 'presents' from Rashidov, the territorial boss and a member of the Politburo, according to the respected economist Tatyana Koryagina.

'Rashidov was a real mafioso and a great friend of Brezhnev. So they made a false accusation against Yakovlev and he was sent to Canada,' says Koryagina, who claims the story came to her from Yakovlev himself. Indeed, Yakovlev was sent into 'soft exile' for ten years as the Soviet Ambassador to Canada.

Over most of his tenure, from 1970 to 1978, Gorbachev was by all accounts an unusually popular Party chief. He was known as reasonable, good-tempered and entirely approachable, with an ability to inspire those who worked for him. He also began to look older, fuller, with bare wedges of skin pushing back from his forehead on either side of a thinning patch of hair. He and Raisa moved into the pretty, pre-revolutionary stone house with six bedrooms that was assigned to the First Secretary. On the short walk from the residence on Dzerzhinsky Street to the monolith of Party headquarters Gorbachev was often buttonholed by citizens, and he always stopped to listen. 'For those ten years all the churches were allowed to function in Stavropol,' says Archbishop Antony, who came to the region in 1975.†

The new First Secretary and his wife were eager to receive members of the intelligentsia from all over the area. 'They liked the company,' says his lionfaced deputy, Georgy Starshikov. 'He was a popular man, he loved to dance and sing and recite poetry – he knows Lermontov and Pushkin poems well. He especially liked to welcome the cultural people coming from Moscow.' Word leaked back to a small circle that the First Secretary in Stavropol was very much opposed to Brezhnev's repression of all that was new and progressive in the arts. When writers, actors and directors ended up in Stavropol, Gorbachev would question them with close interest, Moscow journalist Arkady Vaxberg remembers.

'Why are they persecuting Solzhenitsyn?† He is my favourite writer,' Gorbachev would demand.

'Why are you asking *us*, we're the ones who should be asking *you*,' the incredulous artists would respond.

'If you ask a question like that, obviously you don't understand how things work,' Gorbachev told them. 'I'm a member of the Central Committee but I don't know anything except the official version. I have no idea what is happening. But I'd like to find out.'

Other than these infrequent visitors, entertainment was non-existent in Stavropol. To relieve the boredom the Gorbachevs liked to read to each other; Raisa particularly liked Dostoevsky, and having learned to read English she also summarized foreign books for her husband. When he received gift books from Western authors, Gorbachev would say, 'Raisa will help me read it.'† But if their life was dull at times, it was far from difficult.

Perhaps the most coveted of their new perks was the permission to travel abroad, to see the West. No Soviet outside the ruling elite, unless he or she was useful as a showpiece, like ballet stars or Olympic atheletes, could even dream of such a privilege. (The anketa, or written interrogation, for admission to any university or institute asked if any relative had travelled to the West; a 'yes' meant disqualification.) Permission for foreign travel had to come from the top – from Mikhail Suslov in fact, according to the respected émigré historian, Zhores Medvedev.† In exchange for organizing the leisure activities of Suslov's family and friends when they came south to the Soviet 'Florida', the Stavropol Party Secretary and his culture-hungry wife were treated to more than a taste of the good life. They got themselves invited on junkets to France, Belgium, Italy and West Germany. Thus began the Gorbachevs' serious flirtation with the modes and manners of the West.

They had taken their first trip even before Gorbachev became a top provincial boss. At the invitation of a leftist French businessman, Jean-Baptiste Doumeng, who footed the bill, Misha and Raisa went to France with a group in 1966.† Once the ritual visits to factories were over, the couple rented a Renault and indulged themselves in a leisurely drive, taking several weeks to travel up and down the country. Back home, Moscow's heavy hand in local affairs became more and more oppressive to Mikhail Sergeyevich. Conditions of political life in the Soviet Union were nothing like what he had seen in the Communist Party in France.

Zdenek Mlynar, Gorbachev's closest friend at university, visited the couple in Stavropol in 1967. Misha took the man out and they had a few drinks. Mlynar bubbled over about the exploding liberalization movement taking place back in his native Czechoslovakia under the leadership of Alexander

Dubček, for whom Mlynar was the chief deputy. Dubček was espousing the same goal Gorbachev would embrace twenty years later – 'to get the Communist Party at the head of the process of solving society's problems'. Mlynar found Gorbachev most sympathetic and, what's more, convinced that Eastern Europe would one day be independent of the Soviet Union. His openness to the idea was startling at the time, foreshadowing a historical process that would come to a head under his own leadership.† But he was sadly pessimistic about the prospects for reform within the Soviet Union.†

'Perhaps there are possibilities in Czechoslovakia because conditions are different,' he told Mlynar with a sigh.

When the two old schoolmates came back to the house all fired up with these heretical dreams, they fell foul of the thought police – in the person of Raisa. This was not the kind of loose talk the teacher of Marxist dogma would tolerate, in her classroom or her home. She threw Mlynar out.†

Gorbachev's private sympathies must have gone undetected outside his home, because he was sent to Prague with a fact-finding group in 1969 – after the crushing of the Prague Spring – to appraise the success of the reimposition of Soviet rule. Only a complete Party stalwart would have been approved by the KGB for such a sensitive mission, and it is hardly surprising that Gorbachev made no contact with Mlynar while he was there.

In 1972, he asked to be included on an 'exchange' with the Communist Party of Italy.† Suslov must have waved his magic wand, for suddenly the young Secretary Gorbachev turned up as number three in a choice delegation sent on a delectable junket. Of course, Raisa went along. Taken to a jewel of a resort town, Città del Mare, south of Palermo on the island of Sicily, the young couple spent a week in a villa flung out on a steep promontory over the Mediterranean. They swam in a cascade of natural pools awash with seawater and slid down slides to the sea. Raisa indulged her passion for ruins and Mikhail fell with gusto upon spaghetti *con vongole* and ripe Italian fruits. The place was run just like Club Med. Gorbachev was tickled by the play money the guests wore on necklaces – 'just like primitive times' – but he told a comrade he had to be very careful because 'you lose your sense of value' and Raisa could buy everything.

But, for this provincial Soviet couple, the truly amazing aspect of their trip was that the whole resort village had been built by the socialist and Communist co-operatives of Bologna. 'Raisa and Mikhail were very impressed with Italian culture and particularly with this strange Italian Communist Party,' remembers Adalberto Mennucci, then Communist leader of Turin, who hosted the couple for another week at a Party festival. 'They were shocked at the pluralism in our Communist Party, the informal relations between the highest leaders and the rest.'

'They gave the impression of being a young couple very much in love,' is the way Mennucci's wife, Luccetta, remembers the forty-year-old Gorbachev, who was always making jokes, and his more sober wife. Raisa wore big flowered beach shirts and trousers; she was plumper then, and much less stylish than she is today. But she participated fully in conversations with the men and asked a million questions about the role of women in Italian society.

'Immediately I realized Gorbachev and his wife were completely out of the cliché of Soviet leadership and bureaucracy,' says Mennucci, who is now a leader of Italy's opposition. But although Gorbachev was 'very lively' he was also 'very careful', and he did not voice his criticism of the Soviet Communist Party.

It was the third of a half-dozen trips the Gorbachevs made to Europe and the more liberal Eastern-bloc nations to see how people in freer societies lived. The one that may have made the greatest impression was Gorbachev's trip to West Germany in 1975. On his return, he exulted privately to his university classmate Rudolf Golovanov 'about the German land, how rich and nice and civilized a land it was'.† This sponging up of ideas from the West became a pattern for the Gorbachevs.

The Making of Homo Sovieticus

One of Gorbachev's first Western-style reforms – and one of his few successful experiments in agriculture – was designed to get more yield for the state out of collective farms. His inherent instincts were progressive and sound: he wanted to experiment with something resembling self-employment.† The idea was to release large numbers of rural workers from obligatory work in collective forms of labour and let them try independent farming.

With the blessing of the territorial Party committee, Gorbachev tested the method at farms in different parts of the region. Several individuals or families would work a given piece of land for several years, on their own initiative and discretion, without yields dictated by the state, and being paid on the khoraschet system – according to their harvest results. It was dubbed the zveno-group system – exactly the system Raisa had documented where it was first used in the Krasnodar region in the late 1950s with complete success.

Under Gorbachev's leadership the zveno groups, or small production teams, were introduced gradually in many parts of the Stavropol area. There were almost 1,500 such small teams by 1976. Gorbachev travelled around the great agricultural region cheerleading for his brainchild and building a reputation as something of an innovator. He struck a responsive chord with the farm managers, who had been yearning for years to free themselves from the stranglehold of the local Party committees, when he said things like 'The main duty of raion district committees should be not to tell workers on the land what to do and when, but to work systematically to enhance the level of responsibility of cadres for matters entrusted to them.' The result was something never seen before – or since – in Soviet agriculture: a sixfold increase in labour productivity.

The implications of untapped potential in Soviet agriculture were staggering. At the turn of the century, prerevolutionary Russia led the world as a grain exporter.† Today it is 117th, after South Africa and just ahead of Romania. What's more, the farms were well kept, with weeds controlled and the soil given a rest between crops.

The Party Committee of Stavropol region passed a resolution turning over all arable land to small zveno groups. Suddenly, the very next year, 1977, Boss Gorbachev turned on a dime. Instead of small teams of individuals taking responsibility for ploughing, sowing, tending and harvesting, according to local conditions on land in which they were personally invested, now huge *brigades* of combines, tractors, trucks and outside labourers were to be moved around the region – all according to a centralized, depersonalized plan. Huge armadas of machines would be sent off to one corner of the territory, where two combines would have been enough, leaving other ripened fields to sit and rot. Outside labourers assigned to the brigades didn't give a damn, leaving flax seeds to drop out of their pods or wheat to turn to yellow dust. Called the Ipatov method, it restored control to the district Party committees. It also assured that no one would take responsibility for the land.

All over Stavropol territory, Gorbachev's abrupt volte-face was the burning issue of the day. Asked about the rapid disbanding and disillusionment among the formerly enthusiastic zveno groups, residents explained that small teams of individuals or families 'have laboured for a whole year, taking care about the harvest and pinning certain material hopes on it too. But then machine operators "from outside" arrive at the field. The principles of zveno are destroyed.'†

The first harvest under the Ipatov method was none the less excellent, a result of the soil preparation and sowing methods that had been followed by the small zveno groups. But this factor was ignored; all the credit was given to the 'Ipatovites'. Leonid Brezhnev himself praised the workers of the region for their triumphant labour victory and announced that this

'revolution' would be extended to the rest of the country.†
The greatest commendation went to the 'originator' of the
Ipatov scheme – Mikhail Sergeyevich.

Gorbachev had abandoned his concept of restoring personal responsibility for use of the land in favour of a scheme
that had been proposed by the territorial Party committee
and was close to the hearts of the conservative Old Guard.
The second harvest under the new system proved the
'revolution' to be a fiasco. The Ipatov method, a grotesquely
inefficient, dehumanized system that had actually been
devised long before, was obviously meant to crush the zveno
system. And it did, along with the incentive and trust of the
people. They watched, helpless, pessimistic and ultimately
indifferent, as their beautiful vastness was suffocated by a
grand-scale infestation of weeds.

Eighty aircraft summoned from Central Asia to rain herbi-
cides all over the region could not control 'the green blaze',
as it was called.† Betrayed once again, farmers were reas-
signed to the very collective farms that their apparently
innovative new Party boss had pronounced obsolete. By
1982, the apathy of the peasantry was so widespread that
about 19,000 workers had to be drafted from urban centres
to rescue the harvest in Stavropol territory.†

It was a striking example of the policy zig-zags that would
characterize Gorbachev's leadership from then on. It is true
that as First Secretary he had many quarrels with the chairman of agriculture for the Russian Federation, the top boss
back at the Centre. 'He took on the struggle himself and
personally fought over the issues,' remembers Gorlov. And
he always backed up his position with a barrage of facts that
would bolster his arguments. It wasn't easy to get reliable
data; he had to coax it out of his deputies by promising to
protect them under fire, persuading them to work, and work
hard, staying with him until nine or ten in the evening. If
that didn't work, there was always intimidation, the natural
management technique of any territorial Party boss. Gorbachev would pick out the most clever and energetic for

speedy advancement; the usual dead-wood Party workers got a year or two to prove themselves and then – out.

'To show the light, you have to burn yourself,' was his motto.

But in the end, and despite his exemplary hard work, the requirements of pleasing his prospective patrons in Moscow took precedence over the needs of his territory, and left the region with a declining agricultural base. Gorbachev knew only too well from his own experience that free peasants, like his forebears, were the only ones with incentive to produce and that heavy agro-industrial complexes didn't work. Yet he launched the disastrous Ipatov plan with optimistic, high-blown speeches, as if his own propaganda were enough to make up for a rotten system.

Gorbachev had made himself into a specimen of Homo Sovieticus par excellence. The term, coined by émigré writer Dr Alexander Zinoviev, refers to the acquired characteristic for total flexibility: the Soviet-bred man who can change his views or his opinion in a matter of minutes, suspending principles for expediency. Gorbachev had thwarted a positive development in agriculture in order to curry personal favour with a leader for whom he had contempt. He also lent his voice to the frog chorus publicly singing the praises of Brezhnev, and when the first volume of Brezhnev's memoirs was published, Gorbachev swallowed the disgust he had dared to express over an empty work by Stalin back in his university days, and extolled the book's publication as 'a great event in public life'. In his own long, monotonous speeches, delivered in wooden Partyspeak like a good apparatchik, there was little evidence of his extraordinary political skills, nor any trace of the Gorbachev who would emerge in the mid-1980s as a great reformer.

'When he worked in Stavropol he didn't have these ideas he now has in his head,' stresses the delegate to today's Supreme Soviet legislature, Gennady Lisichkin, who is the expert on Soviet agriculture. 'Like Khrushchev, he's a child of his background. Our leaders thought until very recently that these were the inevitable sacrifices for the sake of socialism. If he believed differently, he would never have become Komsomol secretary at the university, or First Secretary in Stavropol, or found his way to Moscow.'

Indeed, after introducing the Ipatov disaster, Mikhail Sergeyevich would have to wait only one more year to receive his reward for playing to the powers in the Kremlin.

Gorbachev's World

In retrospect, being sent to 'Warm Siberia' turned out to be a fortunate fate for Mikhail Gorbachev. Years later he was asked, 'You were hidden for so many years in Stavropol. How did you finally turn up in Moscow?' Gorbachev's reply reflected the realities of the Soviet power structure: 'Well, there are many ways to hide in the Soviet Union,' he said.†

Only if Gorbachev had gone back to the countryside could he have come to power as General Secretary, argues Vladimir Kvint, a Soviet economist and recent émigré to America who has studied political power structures in socialist countries. 'The hierarchy of despotic power is in the shape of a triangle. Only one person can make things happen – the man at the top,' he explains. 'That is the way it was here up through the Brezhnev period. Those who stay in Moscow are eaten alive by competition from hundreds of others waiting in the same line. They have to become lackeys, their backbone is broken, and almost inevitably they become corrupted.' Kvint believes that if Gorbachev had stayed in Moscow for those twenty years, 'today he'd be a clerk – just like his brother is'.

It is true that Gorbachev's only sibling, Alexander, is today a mere lieutenant-colonel, a mid-level bureaucrat in the Ministry of Defence in Moscow. The two men never became close, and on the infrequent occasions when Alexander has asked to see his brother, Mikhail Sergeyevich has treated him with the brief, cool, correct manner he would use with any petitioner he suspects of asking favours. 'He's afraid of charges of nepotism,' explains Gorlov.

Gorbachev must have known and understood the perils of Moscow. In the early 1970s he was offered the job of Minister of Agriculture, a cushy post in the government apparat in Moscow. He refused. On his next visit to Mikhailova, she told me, he confided that he didn't want to move to Moscow. He preferred Party work to ministerial work, and he believed the best place for him to experiment with improving agriculture was Stavropol. He may also have feared that he did not yet have enough power or protection to survive the endless power struggles in the Centre.

The distance between Moscow and a provincial capital is not measured in kilometres but in degrees of safety; throughout Russian history the farther one was from the czar, the more creative and individual one dared to be.

Moreover, although the world over which Mikhail Gorbachev presided was small and isolated, it embraced the mountainous area of Mineralnye Vody, one of the most desirable resort spa regions in the country. In the 1970s, Gorbachev's position as boss of this uniquely endowed territory made him, in effect, the maitre d' of one of Russia's most exclusive pleasure grounds. For two hundred years the Mineralnye Vody area had been a watering hole for the aristocracy and military. Elegantly decorated carriages had clopped along its broad esplanades and past its terraced gardens. Many charming wooden pre-revolutionary private houses survive to this day, interspersed with ugly cheap concrete worker housing and state tourist hotels.

Wearing a panama hat, with the wedding cake steeple of the 'Stalin Empire' style station behind him, Gorbachev would welcome the best touring companies, Soviet and foreign, who came to perform in the resort area's chandeliered concert halls and the grand proscenium arches of Tolstoy-era theatres. Trains came from as far as Moscow, Leningrad and Minsk to deposit the privileged members of the Party apparat on the railway platform of Mineralnye Vody, and the First Secretary was expected to meet and entertain them. Operating in such a relaxed atmosphere, where he was in a position to cater to the big shots' every whim, gave Gorbachev the chance to forge intimate ties with the top brass in Moscow. His deputy, Georgy Starshikov, tells a story that shows what a master strategist Gorbachev had become.

The Minister in charge of capital construction for the whole country, Mr Isayev, was staying at one of the dachas (country houses) of the Supreme Soviet, and taking treatments in a sanitorium in town. Gorbachev escorted him back and forth. One night the Minister invited the two men to the dacha for a game of billiards. Starshikov played with Isayev, he recalls, since 'Mikhail didn't play pool well or often.'

Suddenly Gorbachev yanked him out of the billiard room and hissed, 'What are you doing? We have to settle some business questions with Isayev, and you're beating him!'

Starshikov got the message. He went back to the table and started to lose. 'The man was pleased. When we sat down with him later and started to ask him to raise the capital budget for construction in our area, he was very friendly and said the magic words: "Come to Moscow and we'll discuss it further."'

Gorbachev told him in the car on the way home, 'You have lost a game, Grigory, but definitely, we have won.'

A territorial Party boss is a local god.† Everybody in the region has to come to him for a blessing before undertaking any scheme, no matter how small. Everybody fears him, flatters him, and bows before him, because the First Secretary is the person who can do anything. He becomes the centre of a 'clan' of densely interconnected relationships and is able to establish ties with the Party bosses of other territories, rather like relations between feudal lords.

It was in this capacity that Gorbachev and Boris Yeltsin first met. Yeltsin being First Secretary of the northern industrial region of Sverdlovsk and Gorbachev First Secretary of an agricultural region, they struck up a useful barter arrangement:† Yeltsin helped his peer to the south with supplies of

machinery and Gorbachev saw to it that Sverdlovsk received
more than its share of food.

'To preside over such a resort area as local Party Secretary,'
describes Mark Palmer, the former American Ambassador to
Hungary and veteran Gorbachev-watcher for the State
Department, 'means you can do all sorts of favours for the
big shots, you can provide women, booze, better housing,
and not only for the man himself but for his whole "mafia" –
his cousins, his mistresses, etc. Because everything in the
Soviet Union is done through connections, "mafias", large
clans.'

Brezhnev's World

Leonid Brezhnev ruled the Soviet empire for the eighteen
years, 1964–82, during which Gorbachev was trying to climb
towards power. He was not chosen to succeed Khrushchev†
for the brilliance of his mind or his scintillating personality –
he couldn't speak a simple sentence without notes and had a
generally dour disposition – but because the very void he
represented made him an acceptable compromise figure to
opposing forces in the Politburo. Brezhnev did not return
the country to the pure form of Stalinization but furthered
the central administrative–command-style government,
which grew into a quiet disaster known as 'the stagnation'.
His motto was 'The less you know, the better you sleep.'

'Brezhnev became a living god,' recalls Golovanov. Mikhail
Suslov, his chief of ideology, would sit at his feet and say, in
front of him, 'He seems like an ordinary person, but he's not
– he's a genius of a leader.' Brezhnev could also be brutal.
Andrei Brezhnev, his twenty-nine-year-old grandson,
describes the pleasure his grandfather took in keeping
pigeons and doves – symbol of peace – and hitting their cage
to see them all fly around, terrified. Young Andrei laughs at
the overwhelming symbolism.

When Czech leader Alexander Dubček made the reforms
which culminated in the Prague Spring that Gorbachev had

heard about from Mlynar, Brezhnev sent Suslov to Czecho-slovakia to size up the situation; on Suslov's recommenda-tion, Brezhnev sent tanks into the streets and had Dubček flown to Moscow in chains for a showdown.

It was dangerous to cross the Brezhnev crowd.

Brezhnev spawned a system of colossally casual corrup-tion. His coterie lived like feudal lords. At his dacha on the Black Sea, Brezhnev liked to impress visiting American officials† like then Secretary of Commerce under Nixon, Peter Peterson, by pressing a button and watching their faces as a wall rolled back to reveal an Olympic-sized swimming pool. For the personal delectation of his clique he would order private performances by the outlawed folk singer Vysotsky, and the very same avant-garde artists and poets he had officially banned.† According to the celebrated poet Andrei Voznesensky, Brezhnev also loved vodka and cham-pagne and girls and gambling. His taste ran to gypsy singers whose fast violins would create the frenzied romanticism that set the girls' souls tingling until tears and passion poured forth, ensuring ultimate satisfaction from his drunken orgies.

'The story of the mafia's power begins with the personality of Brezhnev and his circle, many of whom were thieves and scoundrels,' says Igor Andropov, son of the former KGB chief and Soviet leader. He refers to the 'very shady' dealings of Brezhnev's daughter Galina, and the highly publicized relatively recent trial of her lover, Cherbonov, and to figures such as Rashidov, the tall, silver-haired Asian crime boss who was First Secretary of Uzbekistan. Brezhnev made a public show of kissing Rashidov on the lips to show his appreciation for the loyalty of this fantastically corrupt chieftain, who compromised almost everyone in the power structure of his republic.

While figures like Rashidov might come to power outside the strict confines of the Party hierarchy, 'the corruption also took place inside the state apparat', Igor Andropov acknowl-edges. Mikhail Suslov, for instance, accepted a sort of feudal rent from some of the Party bosses in the provinces, such as

Sergei Medunov, the First Secretary of Krasnodar territory. 'Most of them paid respect just with expensive gifts,' says Leonid Sedov, one of the few surviving Soviet sociologists from those days. While the Kremlin leader himself preferred to take his bribes in the form of Mercedes cars from Western politicians (he collected an entire fleet from the Germans), Brezhnev's personal secretary, known as Big Brows,† demanded bribes for simply putting through telephone calls from regional secretaries. It was simply the way one did business with those in Brezhnev's retinue.

> I'm warning you! Take your bribes according to
> your rank!

These lines are from Gogol's satire, *The Government Inspector*,† which depicts a quintessentially imperious corrupt official, a traditional comic figure of the Russian stage. It gives the full flavour of the paradox in being a territorial Party boss: a god at the local level but a mere groveller before the masters who descended from the Centre. The arrival of any official from Moscow aroused fear and submission among the corrupt petty office-holders in the provinces. They would bow and scrape and lavish gifts on the man without so much as questioning his rank or real position. In Gogol's play, Khlestakov, a fashionably dressed but dissolute gambler unable to pay his hotel bill, passes himself off as a government inspector from the Centre, travelling incognito with secret instructions.

> Accustomed as I am, *comprenez-vous*, to moving in
> the best society, and suddenly to find myself on the
> road – filthy inns, the dark gloom of ignorance . . .

The Mayor and other town officials groan in sympathy; any top gun from the Centre is automatically expected to have the best of everything.

> When I made my rounds of the ministry, you'd
> have thought an earthquake had struck – everyone

quivering, shaking like a leaf. (Mayor and others tremble in terror. Khlestakov is carried away.) Oh! I'm not one to play games! I put the fear of God into every last one of them! Even the cabinet is scared stiff of me. And why now, I ask you? That's how I'm made! No one gets in my way . . . I'm everywhere! Everywhere!

Like Gogol's false official, Brezhnev's retinue made it their business to inflate their importance and to exact gifts and bribes for the most routine of services. Just to get an appointment with Brezhnev, First Secretary Gorbachev would have had to reward Big Brows. But he apparently kept his distance from the Brezhnev crowd when he could.

'Gorbachev never came to the dacha,' says Andrei Brezhnev, whose soft childish features are eerily stamped with the bushy Brezhnev brows. 'My grandfather never thought of Gorbachev.'

Mafia Virus

What Soviets mean when they speak of their 'mafia' is a completely different animal from the literal American understanding of criminal organizations, bound by blood ties, that have their origins in large Italian families from Sicily or Naples. That is to say, there are no discernible ties of family or ethnicity within the organizations that have flourished in the Gorbachev era.†

A top Party official confirmed the view that large clans often dominate political and economic relations in the republics,† in particular Uzbekistan, Georgia, Crimea and Krasnodar, which borders the Stavropol region. Certain clans have existed for hundreds of years. Although Soviets refer to them as 'mafia', these clans are not necessarily connected by blood ties but by the more feudal ties of territory. There have been instances where a criminal boss comes to power as territorial leader and the criminal mafia he brings with him are all people born not just in the same city, but within the same few blocks, even on the same street.

The best quick insight into the difference between 'mafia' in the American and Soviet contexts came out of a long interview I had with Igor Andropov. The son of former KGB chief Yuri Andropov is today vaguely designated an 'ambassador at large'. A tall thin man who wears well-tailored European suits over cashmere v-necked sweaters, a gold Cartier watch and Italian leather slip-ons, he received me in the book-lined study of his spacious apartment, where he sat on a leather cordovan sofa beneath a blowup of his famous father. The faces are almost identical, although Igor is only in his mid-forties, featuring a long, razor-thin nose, narrow eyes, pewter-grey hair with the obvious comb marks of a meticulous man, and the surprise of a wide, dimpled, almost pretty mouth. I asked Igor Andropov if the mafia in his country was like the 1930s mafia in America under Al Capone. The son of the former KGB chief drew back indignantly, as if by association I had sullied one of the legends of his professional tribe.

'Al Capone was a brilliant man!' he shot back. 'He was a singular figure. Not like here, not closely connected with political institutions as our mafia is.'

The implication was that in the Soviet Union one cannot distinguish between the criminal element inside the Party apparat and the government bureaucracy, and the criminal element outside in the clans of the republics. Andropov's contempt for *his* country's mafia was that of a professional for a sloppy and undisciplined amateur operation that lacks even the dignity of a proper nomenclature – that is capo, tutti di capo, godfather and so on.

'Organized crime' is indeed an oxymoron in the Soviet context. Crime is no more organized than agriculture. But corruption is as common as food lines; it is the only means of obtaining what one needs and its leading figures are as faceless as those of the reactionary right – enemies without names, power without accountability.

Gorbachev cannot order a manhunt for his equivalent of Al Capone, for example, because his country's vast black market is operated by thousands, maybe tens of thousands, of low-lifes who would be lucky to have more than a double-digit IQ. 'It is said the bureaucracy, the apparat, is against Gorbachev,' laments Andropov. 'But our political life is so complicated today, it's difficult to say who exactly is against Gorbachev.'

Andrei Brezhnev, the former leader's grandson, confirms this view. 'There are two mafias here, the criminal mafia and the government mafia. They have their own rules, their own system.' He adds, 'Nothing has changed.'

But the Party mafia and the criminal mafia were nourished in the same petri dish. They are inseparable. This linkage between large parts of the Party bureaucracy – from the local level up to the Central Committee and Politburo, as well as to government ministers in Moscow who control the supply of raw materials – and the criminal clans out in the republics who control trade and transportation is something like a spliced gene for corruption that has spread throughout the population over the past twenty-five years. This is the virus that, along with others, has 'genetically' altered the personality of Homo Sovieticus, among others.

(Over and over again I heard Soviets refer to their belief that seven decades of fear and hypocrisy under their system had 'genetically' deformed them. This conception may be in part the intellectual legacy of Trofim Lysenko, dictator of the Soviet sciences from 1948 until the fall of Khrushchev, who completely denied the existence of genes, chromosomes and Mendel's theory of inheritance. According to this charlatan, environment alone determined heredity.)

This mafia virus would one day be the invisible enemy threatening to strangle Gorbachev from within. It throttled Khrushchev in a matter of weeks by sabotaging the food supply to Moscow. The question still unanswered is, Was Gorbachev compromised by these mafias as a territorial Party boss? He was certainly tied to them; that was the system.

Ties go both ways. To what degree do those ties now keep his hands behind his back when it comes to true economic reforms?

In my interview with Igor Andropov, I asked to what degree Gorbachev was part of the system of corruption.

'I am sure it was not Gorbachev's style, what you say about the presents,' answered Andropov.

But how did he compete? I wondered aloud. He was maitre d' of the premier spa in the country. He had to greet all who came and make sure they were comfortable. They must have expected gifts and favours.

'Madame, I want to put a limit on what you are saying.' Igor Andropov stiffened. 'Sure, in many of our magazines today there are stories about such things. But to say that one leader brings to another leader always bribes, is to put a very cheerless perspective on things.'

Mark Palmer, the former American Ambassador to Hungary, was less limited in what he could say. 'What you're measured by is whether you're good at this connection business,' he told me. 'Gorbachev's genius as a young Party secretary in that region was to be good at making people feel comfortable, flattering them, and being the fixer for Andropov and Suslov.'

Ambassador Palmer describes seeing crates of presents whenever he visited Brezhnev or his staff: imported china, crystal, furniture, electronic goodies, piles of watches and fleets of cars. 'I'm not sure that Gorbachev himself was engaged in that, but he's part of that world. The way Raisa dresses – she didn't sew all those dresses herself – suggests she loves all those connections. So, I don't think these people are puritans. And the society is extremely corrupt.'

Corrupt or not, the First Secretary of a territory never had to worry about money. A young editor at the maverick magazine *Ogonyok*, Valentin Yumashev, researched the habits of territorial Party bosses for the recent autobiography by Boris Yeltsin. 'Such a person doesn't need a million [rubles], because he already has it. All he needed to do was to go and collect it, and let those below him worry how to account for it – the uncontrolled Party budget provided for everything.' Yumashev estimates that the budgets provided to the district Party committee and the territory-wide Party committee, taken together, probably ranged between 50 and 100 million rubles a year in those days. As for entertaining, special departments were set up to take care of every aspect. The First Secretary never had to wonder why there were so many cognac bottles in the plane of the official he was seeing off. The system of gifts or Party privilege worked independently of him. Today there is an outspoken campaign in the new Soviet congress against these uncontrolled provincial Party budgets. None the less, regional and district Party officials raised their own salaries by 60 per cent in 1990.

The secret Party sanatoria scattered between the Black and Caspian seas, and their use by members of the Politburo, Defence Department, KGB and all the government ministries, later became another subject of loud censure in the new Soviet legislature. Reeking of class privilege, the spas are still hidden behind *allées* of poplars and long gated driveways, huge parks surrounded by bed after bed of roses and balconies soaked in the sweet smell of honeysuckle. The clientele is served in marble interiors by a large staff, in order of Party rank; their body language is imperious, and their wives are noticeably better dressed than most Soviet women, with real jewels in their ears. This was the glamorous world over which Gorbachev presided as Party boss of the Mineralnye Vody spa region.

The KGB Clan

By the standards of his world, however, Gorbachev seems to have been an honest apparatchik. Particularly in the Stavropol years, he went to some lengths to demonstrate that he was clean.

There are several incidents reported by friends who went to Gorbachev over the years with offers of black-market goods or requests for the sort of favours Party bosses often blink and grant, and got nowhere. While he was Komsomol secretary of Stavropol city and waiting, as does everyone, on interminable lists to be eligible for a car, a good friend offered him an automobile under the table, for a price. Gorbachev threw the man out of his office.† Still later, when Gorbachev was an initiate in the Central Committee, Julia Karogodina wrote him a letter asking for help. She reminded him of their warm relations back in secondary school, in case he'd forgotten, and then pleaded for the *propiska* (certificate of permission) to move into Moscow and get an apartment.

'I got the letter back soon thereafter . . . not one warm word,' Julia recently told David Remnick of the *Washington Post*. 'On it he had written simply that it wasn't his area, wasn't his competence, and that I should apply to the city authorities, not him. Just like that, so businesslike.' Just as with his brother, Gorbachev was apparently going to great lengths to avoid even the appearance of favouritism or nepotism, behaviour that was rampant among the Brezhnev crowd.

He was in Moscow at a session of the Central Committee on 24 February, 1976 when a call came saying his father had collapsed of a heart attack in his garden in Privolnoye. A plane was provided to fly him home that night, but Gorbachev was back at the session the next day: this dutiful son of the Party didn't miss a beat, recalls Gorlov approvingly. Later that year he was rewarded with a trip to Paris.

Gorbachev's motto – 'Show the light, you have to burn yourself' – is straight out of the KGB code of ethics, according to Radio Liberty researcher Yasmann. KGB officers are by and large scrupulously clean;† the institution may be the only clan in the Soviet Union where corruption is not a way of life. The officers are the most technically modern, professionally trained, linguistically versatile and hard-working corps in the population. 'In the late seventies the KGB was the only organization not corrupted,' insists Igor Andropov, citing supporting statements from none other than Andrei

Sakharov, 'who had no sympathy for the KGB'.† He points out that his father, who worked for fifteen years in the KGB, was in a unique position to understand the 'inner life' of the country. (Quite true, given the network of millions of paid secret informers and constant mail and phone surveillance.)

Gorbachev may have resisted taking bribes because he was playing an infinitely more sophisticated game, where the stake was not money but power. The KGB, though it was the official source of all the luxuries funnelled to the Party faithful, was headed by a man who saw two glaring realities that threatened to plunge Soviet society into the very abyss over which it still hovers: 'The first crisis was before everyone's eyes – economic stagnation. The second was the corruption and mafia, which is now manifest on such a terrible scale, but was at that time hidden,' as Igor Andropov describes his father's views. Engaging in petty corruption or bigtime graft with local clan leaders would have jeopardized Gorbachev's budding relationship with the increasingly powerful Yuri Andropov.

The two men first met in the sanatorium colony of Kislovodsk. First among equals in the string of health spa towns, Kislovodsk is surrounded by mountains ribboned with curly streams that pour into gorges, from which the spas pipe in the healthful natural springwater sought by privileged Soviets for its curative powers. The KGB chief came to Kislovodsk many times, and the young Party secretary had to meet his train each time, accompany him to his state dacha, Red Rocks, settle him in, then see him to the public spas for his baths in Narzan water and treatments for his chronic kidney problems. It was during these visits that the alliance between Gorbachev and his ultimate patron was forged.

Andropov took an immediate liking to the young believer. Compared to the usual bribe-rich Party boss, Mikhail Sergeyevich's existence was almost spartan, and his family too was unmarred by any suggestion of corruption. His mother, Maria Panteleyevna, still tended her chickens and pigs in the back yard and lived on a miserly pension of 29 rubles a month.† And his relatives lived as they always had in Privolnoye, farming, although now acclimatized to working on the local collective farm. Only a cousin, Ivan Vasilyevich Gorbachev, was active in local politics, at the district level.†

'When Andropov met Gorbachev, I think he was just delighted with him,' says the journalist–classmate Golovanov. 'Gorbachev's intellect was of course much higher than average. He was much younger. Andropov saw in him simply a fine, honest young man. They had a father–son relationship.'

Igor, Andropov's only real son, confirms their closeness. 'They were two intelligent, honest, uncorrupted persons with a lot in common, but they were completely different in their personalities.' The two men were never 'buddies', according to Igor. The stern, rigidly conservative and reserved Andropov did not have the openness and easy familiarity with which Gorbachev won people over. The KGB chief always addressed Gorbachev formally, by his name and patronymic, as Mikhail Sergeyevich.

After all, Mikhail Sergeyevich was only in his early forties, a mere pup in the political chronology of a country where every member of the ruling Politburo was over seventy. But the young Gorbachev knew how to draw out the hidden personal side of the enigmatic spymaster. No one else knew until years later that Andropov was a closet poet. Given his overzealous superego, he was not the sort of man who would have wanted his amateur efforts publicized (and would have turned in his grave if he had seen the TV show devoted posthumously to his poetry, says his son), but to rhapsodize in private about Pushkin and Lermontov on the walks with his young companion must have been immensely rewarding for him. The Gorbachevs were also often invited as a couple to Andropov's dacha in the Kislovodsk resort. The company of the up-and-coming Party boss and his literate wife was a great pleasure to the sickly older man and his wife, who also suffered from diabetes. Raisa could switch from a discussion of Plato to a discourse on her sociological research among the peasantry.

Vivid in personality, powerful, healthy and robust in his physical impact – these are the strong impressions that Gorbachev registered with his mentor's son. 'I am younger by ten or twelve years,' says Igor, 'but Mikhail Sergeyevich could always walk farther than me by three kilometres, and to a higher altitude.' From his son's description, slightly tinged with jealousy, the elder Andropov seems almost to have put Mikhail Sergeyevich on a pedestal. 'My father did remark about the envy he felt for Mikhail Sergeyevich and his bi-polar education – both law and agriculture – and this fact helped my father.' Andropov felt confident handling the problems of factories, but agriculture was foreign to him. Most of all, Igor emphasizes, 'My father saw in Mikhail Sergeyevich great political potential.' Deputy Starshikov remembers that 'Mr Andropov was always very close to Mr Gorbachev at official ceremonies.'

Andropov was in no physical condition to play sports, and Gorbachev had always disdained outdoor activities as well, but both men liked to walk in the woods. They would routinely set off on long, rigorous strolls through the mountains of Kislovodsk. In a society crawling with spies, the woods were about the only place to talk. And the two men talked incessantly, of politics and international affairs. Andropov's own son had little interest in such topics.

Andropov had been responsible for the military crackdown on Hungary in the mid-1950s and the hanging and shooting of many prisoners. He was the quintessence of the KGB man: specialist in persecuting and torturing the intelligentsia and sending into exile the most brilliant writers and scientists of the seventies: Solzhenitsyn, Sakharov and others. 'But here you should understand the personal drama of my father,' pleads the son. 'By 1982 [when Andropov became General Secretary] he was already sixty-seven, not in very good health, and he foresaw very well that all the deeds he had just begun, he would not live to complete and would be done by the hands of another. Back in 1976, I could not imagine that person would be Mikhail Sergeyevich Gorbachev. My father then did not know either. He knew only that in the young Gorbachev was growing an absolutely nonstandard way of thinking. He was a man of thoroughly another perspective.'

Gorbachev always spoke of the secret police chief with great respect, despite the fact that this was the man responsible for persecuting the artists and writers with whom Gorbachev sympathized. 'I can imagine that there were activities of the KGB that did not please Mikhail Sergeyevich,' admits Igor, though he stresses that to have demonstrated such feelings for the nonconformist element would have been to risk 'a lot of unpleasantness'. Again, Gorbachev compromised his own moral values to go along with a powerful patron.

But on most matters Andropov and Gorbachev shared a very similar philosophy. The KGB chief had the facts at his disposal to underscore the true situation in Russia, and like the younger Gorbachev he was not reticent about pointing out the gap between the fantasies of Soviet propaganda and the dismal reality of Soviet life. Ultimately, however, the two men could not have grown close on so many levels if Andropov had not had utter confidence in Gorbachev's loyalty. The secret police chief, not surprisingly, was known to be highly paranoid. The ultimate sign of character sought out by a professional paranoid is a person absolutely certain not to betray. And so, seven years later, when Andropov began thinking about his successor and the KGB brought out the file on Gorbachev, the Kremlin chief could satisfy himself that his professional son, Mikhail Sergeyevich, was the Right Stuff. As Igor puts it, his father had to find 'those with clean hands – those genetically capable of giving birth to perestroika'.

The Diabetes Connection

But Yuri Andropov was not yet in the seat of ultimate power. He only headed the second of two groups rising in the Party leadership, a KGB 'mafia' that included Fyodor Kulakov, Gorbachev's primary patron. The other clan – the clique around General Secretary Brezhnev – was naturally stronger, and Mikhail Suslov belonged to the Brezhnev clan. Tensions ran high between the corruption-fighting Andropov clan and the greedy Brezhnev boys, putting Andropov and Suslov on opposing sides of what would ultimately be a fatal power struggle. Caught in the middle, young Gorbachev would need every ounce of political cunning to remain on good terms with both men.

Suslov had risen through the Party hierarchy under Stalin by wiping out his rivals with mass arrests and murders among the Party leaderships of entire regions. Most men feared to tread within sight of this ruggedly handsome, fearsome man, but Gorbachev courted him in the same way he seduced one powerful Party boss after another. 'Without question,' intones Golovanov, *'without question*. Otherwise, he would have been destroyed.'

Suslov had maintained a special interest in the Stavropol territory ever since his reign as First Secretary when Gorbachev was a boy, and one or both of his grandfathers became well known to Suslov. He sent his family to 'Warm Siberia' for the summers and his minor enemies there for exile. Gorbachev, as maitre d', looked after both. Just how warm and familiar Gorbachev was with Suslov's family only became publicly apparent on the occasion of Suslov's funeral in 1982.†

Cosying up to Suslov must have required, shall we say, considerable detachment on Gorbachev's part. Born in 1902 to peasants living in the region halfway between Moscow and the Urals, at age sixteen Suslov joined a paramilitary police unit activated by Lenin to seize food and confiscate private property from kulaks and middle peasants. In the 1930s, under Stalin, he collaborated with the secret police (NKVD) in Party purges that destroyed hundreds of lives.† Convinced of Suslov's 'aggressive orthodoxy, cool nerves and minimal sentimentality',† Stalin gave Suslov 6,000 Russian officials and sent him off to Lithuania right after the war to smash the partisan movement and reinstate Soviet rule. There Suslov earned his reputation as 'a cold and ruthless automaton'. He imposed the first major wave of deportations in late 1944, sending over 40,000 Lithuanians to Siberia, relying on starvation, disease and freezing temperatures to eliminate many deportees along the way. Impatient with the inability of the 'Western-oriented population to adjust in a matter of a few years to the Stalinist Soviet system',† Suslov inflicted on them one of the most pitiless occupations in a long history of Soviet colonization. Those who tried to run were shot on the spot and those farms and villages where the hunted took refuge were burned to the ground. Another 60,000 men, women and children were deported from the little Baltic state in 1945, followed by an estimated 40,000 more in 1946.

For his 'unsentimental' service, Suslov was made editor of *Pravda* and on his fiftieth birthday, in 1952, awarded the highest Order of Lenin. Even as he was photographed jollying up Khrushchev in a private moment – flashing an immense smile, his long white pointy teeth magnanimous as a shark's – Suslov was hatching the plot to bring down the Kremlin boss, and openly criticizing Khrushchev's attempts at a rapprochement with the US.

There were moments when it seemed he might fade from power. In 1963, he dropped out of sight for a month, and was hospitalized after a diagnosis of adult diabetes. In 1976, he was struck down with a heart attack. But by 1977 Mikhail Suslov was once again sitting at the right hand of power: supervising ideology, inter-Party relations, the Komsomol, the KGB and even Soviet foreign policy for Leonid Brezhnev. No wonder that he was held in awe as 'the grey eminence'.†

Brezhnev's health went into decline in the mid-1970s, a decline paralleled for Soviet society in the period of 'stagnation'. In fact, the official life expectancy was *declining* among Soviet males,† mainly from chronic degenerative diseases associated with drinking and smoking. In the late 1970s, a man could only expect to live to the age of sixty-two. It was literally a sick society. Suslov, no healthy specimen himself, increasingly sat in for Brezhnev at Politburo meetings, becoming known as the 'Second Secretary'.

And so, as Gorbachev worked to cement his ties with Andropov, he could not afford to neglect his relationship with Suslov, and continued to cultivate the trust of Brezhnev's henchman during Suslov's stays at a spa in Pyatigorsk. One thing that made it easier was the diabetes connection.

Andropov, Suslov and Gorbachev all shared this hereditary disease. It was no great coincidence: diabetes is definitely a familial disease, and would therefore be widespread in a closed ethnic society such as Russia, where people marry and reproduce, for the most part, with other Russians. Diabetes usually manifests itself in adulthood, as it did in all three men, and often appears for the first time during a period of severe stress. Given the demands of political survival in an illegitimate government, Gorbachev and his two patrons must have experienced more than their share of stress.

Both Suslov and Andropov came regularly to Kislovodsk for treatment of chronic kidney disease, which is one of the symptoms of diabetes. Gorbachev made himself knowledgeable about the best waters and folk remedies for this medical problem and thereby took on the comforting role of male nurse.

He could also empathize. According to Mikhailova, Gorbachev's diabetes was not severe, at least not up to the early 1980s, but he has had to limit his sweet intake. 'Raisa watches his diet very carefully, he couldn't have that discipline himself.' This is another reason for Gorbachev's abstemiousness with regard to alcohol. He drinks milk at supper and regularly takes tea with milk.

When Gorbachev wasn't cosseting his superiors he was able to take advantage of his own privileges. As a territory leader he had a free voucher to take his holidays at the

Imenikirovna Sanatorium in Pyatigorsk. Gorbachev's sanatorium, built in the mid-1960s, is a white concrete, hotel-like
structure not far from the drinking galleries where spa-goers
dutifully file in before breakfast carrying their porcelain cups
to line up for sulphur or carbon spring water. After drinking
a glass, one feels very languid. Gorbachev would chat up
members of trade ministries and union bosses before going
off to the baths and treatments that fill up the day until the
mandatory 11 p.m. bedtime.

Raisa, too, was becoming accustomed to living an existence
the vast majority of Soviets thought possible only in the
depraved capitalistic West. She would have her chauffeur
drop her at Piragovsky Bath Establishment. 'People didn't
make a big thing about her visits, we saw her rather often,'
the director of the bath establishment told me. One day
Raisa's treatment would be submersion in hydrocarbon and
sulphur water to normalize her blood pressure and give a
sedative effect. The next it would be a 'rain massage' for
stimulation. Then she would join the others relaxing in
Oblomov-like stupors in deep lounge chairs under a skylit
dome.

All in all, those years were golden ones for the Gorbachevs,
and by the late 1970s it looked like everything was coming
up roses for the Stravropol clan. With Kulakov pulling the
strings from Moscow and Gorbachev the popular boss back
in the region, they produced a successful computer model
for harvesting which received praise and publicity in *Pravda*.
Kulakov was decorated with the highest award by Brezhnev
himself, sealed with a kiss on the lips from the head
Godfather. For the first six months of 1978 he stood in the
honorific position at the right hand of the General Secretary
whenever the Politburo appeared in public. In February 1978,
on his sixtieth birthday, the message of congratulations from
the Kremlin was longer and more effusive than the norm,
and he was given a vanity publication of his collected
speeches. In Moscow corridors, as well as in Western intelligence agencies, such signs were taken as predictions that

Brezhnev's successor might well be Fyodor Davidovich Kulakov.

Gorbachev was counting on it. With his surrogate father Andropov at the helm of the KGB and his longtime mentor in line to inherit the mantle of General Secretary from Brezhnev, all was well for the maitre d' of Mineralnye Vody – his connections and protections secure. Then, suddenly, Mikhail Sergeyevich went from the peak on to the precipice.

On 17 July 1978, he found himself high on a reviewing stand over Red Square, surrounded by the elite of the Party, and given the plum of a speaking part at a state funeral. But he was behaving as though it were his own burial. The urn being drawn through the streets to Red Square on a gun carriage contained the ashes of his patron and protector. While hundreds of soldiers and civilians walked behind, holding huge wreaths over their chests, the stony-faced Politburo leaders carried the urn to the Kremlin wall.

'THE SUDDEN DEATH OF KULAKOV LEAVES A VACUUM IN THE SOVIET LEADERSHIP't read the headlines in the Western press on 18 July 1978. The brief report in *Pravda*, the official Party newspaper, aroused much suspicion. Kulakov was said to have died very 'suddenly' earlier that day, having developed 'an acute heart insufficiency' in the night that brought this vital organ to a 'sudden standstill'. A curious fate for the youngest and ablest member of the Politburo,† a man with no history of previous illness who, according to journalists, had shown no signs of any ailment. If Kulakov had indeed suffered a first heart attack, it is mysterious that he couldn't be saved, since the best possible medical assistance was on twenty-four-hour call to members of the Politburo. There was another curious anomaly: diagnoses and treatments of top officials are invariably agreed upon by a group of five to ten doctors,† so that no one of them is forced to take responsibility. But, in Kulakov's case, Brezhnev's personal physician, Yevgeny Chazov, wrote the medical report,† and was then immediately relieved of his post as Minister of Health to the Fourth Department.

Mikhail Sergeyevich's shock filtered through the boiler-plate statement he had to read at the funeral: 'The name Fyodor Davidovich is connected with the solutions of large problems in the development of the economy and culture of this region. It is painful and difficult for all of us today, as human beings, to believe the Fyodor Davidovich has left us in the very blooming of his creative strength.'

Gorbachev's face was waxen, remembers a minor official. Between the forty-seven-year-old regional Party boss and the once-towering father–protector he had cultivated for so long there now gaped a sinister chasm. Kulakov's death might have been suicide. Or he could have been 'liquidated' by the KGB on orders from the Party mafia. But now the ashes of his heart would be stuffed into a cold niche in the Kremlin Wall, where not even the crows could peck out the mystery of why it had stopped.

Only nine of Kulakov's thirteen Politburo colleagues attended the funeral. Brezhnev was conspicuously absent.

Third Gorbachev:

Disciple of Doublethink

1978–1984

'Misha, we have a place for you in Moscow,' Nadezhda Mikhailova prophesied.

Gorbachev was in the habit of telephoning his first girlfriend from university days whenever he came up to Moscow. This time, he sounded jumpy and depressed.

'What is that supposed to mean?' he demanded.

'You have just attended an important funeral,' she replied, 'and now, Misha, this position is available for you.' Her words did not sink in. Rumours were flying around Moscow that Kulakov had committed suicide under pressure from furious behind-the-scenes attacks for the failure of the country's agriculture system. Shorn of his protector, Gorbachev did not know what his own fate would be. But the shadow of a patron who had died in disfavour was a long, dark shadow indeed.

Gorbachev had stayed in touch with Mikhailova since 1955 – twenty-three years. 'I was the only person from our university group who had contacts with him this often,' she told me. 'It was a thread from his younger years.' Mikhailova could talk to him intimately, coach him, she could make him laugh and forget his troubles. She told him jokes about the aged troglodytes who hobbled out of the Kremlin to stand on Lenin's mausoleum in their big black coats and ferocious fur hats, looking like stuffed bears. She could do a hilarious imitation of Brezhnev, and would regale him with true stories, including this one:

Brezhnev is at Moscow Airport welcoming Margaret Thatcher. He's reading from a paper as he addresses the British Prime Minister.

'Dear Indira Gandhi,' he begins. His aide whispers, 'Mrs Thatcher,' but he says, 'I can see Mrs Thatcher, but right here it says Indira Gandhi!'

'Such is the level of our leaders,' she would lament. 'Brezhnev's stupidity is written on his face.' But not once did Gorbachev ever say a rude word about Brezhnev, even in their long private chats. 'He was always very correct and polite about the leaders.'

Indeed, Mikhailova remembers him telling her 'Brezhnev likes me. Better than the others.' Brezhnev was sympathetic to her Misha, she believed, because Gorbachev was handsome and nice, and young.

On this brief visit to Moscow for the Kulakov funeral, Misha was too hurried and upset to visit Mikhailova in person. But she took it upon herself to begin preparing him, over the telephone, for the imminent leap into the big leagues that she foresaw for him. She told him his funeral speech, which she had seen on television, had been stilted and amateurish. She teasingly chided him for speaking too quickly and mimicked his mispronunciation of words. 'And really, Misha dear, you must work on your provincial accent.'

He took it in his stride. 'You should forgive me such mistakes,' he said, 'I'm just starting.'

It was a lifelong habit for Gorbachev to welcome strong words from strong women, beginning with his mother and culminating in the affectionate world-class competition for the last word between him and Margaret Thatcher. Raisa would later take charge as his speech coach, calling their university classmate, Golovanov, who was director of the prime-time Soviet news programme, for videotapes of all Gorbachev's speeches, including this undistinguished funeral oration. 'And she was as tough a coach as they come,' chuckles Golovanov.

Mikhailova's style differed from the industrial-strength drill-bit didacticism of Raisa's lectures. More delicate, more amusing, Mikhailova was constantly building Gorbachev up by comparing him to the geriatric cases in the Kremlin. 'You're well educated, Misha, and you're so young for a politician. You will go far!' Their relationship had begun to flourish in the mid-1970s, at a time when the Gorbachevs' marriage was rumoured to have turned rocky. Whenever Misha came up to Moscow for Party congresses or Central Committee meetings, he would call Mikhailova and ask her to have dinner. Because it was always last-minute, and therefore almost impossible to get a reservation at one of Moscow's few decent restaurants, sometimes they just walked around the streets and talked.

He would come by her apartment on Pushkin Street, and 'he shared his impressions about the 25th and 26th Party Congresses' (in 1976 and 1981, respectively) with his avid listener. But he never spoke about his frustrations in trying to promote his innovative agricultural schemes, 'and I never asked him about productivity or breeding', says Mikhailova, 'just private things'. He inquired about her family, her private life. Family, friends, memories, that was the stuff of their conversation. She kept him up to date on the doings of their classmates. He sometimes grumbled about Raisa but he never complained about his daughter, Irina, of whom he was very proud. 'Except that she was a nervous girl.' An intelligent student, Irina studied medicine, became a doctor and eventually married a colleague. In the long absences between his short Moscow sojourns Misha kept in touch by writing Mikhailova letters and simple messages on holidays. Mikhailova's eyes sparkle and dimples dance in her cheeks as she talks non-stop about him, although she is demure in describing their long relationship.

'His warm feeling for me remained from our university

days. He was even a little bit in love with me. We weren't lovers, it was just friendship.'

Today, plump and rather lonely, Mikhailova has never married; she gets by on 550 rubles a month teaching law at a correspondence school and lives in a tiny co-op apartment piled with newspaper clippings and bulging briefcases holding notes for various professional articles she has in progress. One of their classmates says openly, 'I think she's still in love with him.'

Another classmate, Vladimir Lieberman, doesn't believe Gorbachev was in love with Mikhailova in their university days. 'He had no interest in women,' he says. 'He was just using her to absorb culture.' As for Mikhailova, he says, maybe she was too pretentious. 'She came from Moscow. She didn't think he was good enough – she wanted something more. After he became a leader in Stavropol, then she started to think about him, but it was too late. She likes that he still calls her sometimes. She still had connection with him while he was a Secretary of the Central Committee, and she stayed his friend long after he stopped communicating with the rest of our group.'†

Catapulted to Power

After Kulakov's funeral, Gorbachev went back to Stavropol, and remained depressed and taciturn for several weeks, according to his burly deputy, Georgy Starshikov. It was not clear who would be entrusted with Kulakov's job as Secretary of the Central Committee for Agriculture. His patron's death had left a vacuum in the Kremlin power structure, but politics, like nature, abhors a vacuum, and the forces shaping Gorbachev's future were already in play.

Gorbachev's family, from the start, was highly trusted by the Party cadres because of his grandfather Gopkalo. The two most prominent patrons behind Gorbachev's charmed career were Mikhail Suslov and Yuri Andropov, both of whom would have had files on Gorbachev's family, so he was patronized by the Party as 'one of ours'. He didn't need special checking and was able to make stunning leaps in his career. He was advanced most rapidly between 1950 and 1953 in the last years of Stalin, when the KGB (then called NKVD or secret police) was at its peak. Again he enjoyed rapid advancement between 1967 and 1969, when the KGB was under the supervision of his patron Andropov and regained great power.

Yuri Andropov had a strong motive to try to bring Gorbachev to Moscow. 'Kulakov's unexpected death narrows the choices for a possible successor to Brezhnev,' noted Radio Liberty researchers at the time. 'The primary beneficiary would seem to be Andropov.'† The KGB chief hungered deeply for the General Secretaryship, and he would need every good man in his clan marshalled at his side for the battle ahead. Kulakov's demise had brought the number of members on the ruling Politburo down to thirteen, the very men who would choose the next leader of the land. There was no technical vacancy – the ruling body consisted of anywhere between nine and fifteen members at a given time – but if Andropov could manoeuvre Mikhail Sergeyevich into the Politburo, he could count on the vote of his surrogate son when the time came.

And so, over the summer, before leaving for his annual vacation, Andropov almost certainly discussed with Suslov bringing Gorbachev to Moscow. Gorbachev had played his hand so well that Suslov also thought of Mikhail Sergeyevich as a loyal follower. And Suslov himself knew Gorbachev well since he continued to send his enemies as well as his family to Stavropol. But Machiavellian and powerful as Suslov was, only one man ultimately had the power to admit young apparatchiks into the land of kings. He and Andropov would have to engineer Brezhnev's blessing for any Moscow appointment.

While Gorbachev was First Secretary, he tried to get an audience with Leonid Brezhnev himself. He had a scheme for shifting the Stavropol territory's economic base from grain production to sheep-breeding and he needed seed money. He was determined to see Brezhnev face to face, and called the chairman's assistants again and again, asking for an appointment. Brezhnev's retinue kept brushing him off. 'He pushed and pushed,' says Starshikov, 'he'd asked Kulakov's advice [before he died] and Kulakov told him to push it.' After contending with Big Brows, the chairman's venal private secretary, Gorbachev was finally granted an audience. He brought with him a fat picture album he had prepared with a quotation from comrade Brezhnev on the frontispiece.

'Where did you get this!' Brezhnev's ferocious eyebrows flew up. 'I never said this.' But Gorbachev's flattery soon won him over. Brezhnev asked how much money the First Secretary needed.

'Two million rubles,' said Gorbachev, fervent in his sales pitch. If he was so smart, he should become a member of the Politburo, said Brezhnev. At the next meeting the chairman himself introduced Gorbachev's plan, which was of course approved. Thereafter, whenever Brezhnev saw Gorbachev, he'd tease, 'How's your sheep-breeding empire coming?'† So, Brezhnev knew quite well who the young man was.

That August Andropov settled in at Red Rocks, his state dacha high above the Kislovodsk spa, and summoned his protégé. The two took long walks in the woods and talked over bottles of the sulphurous local water, Narzan, an acquired taste but recommended for the older man's stomach because of its high iron and oxygen content. Gorbachev drank with him; they were the equivalent of Perrier-quaffing Western technocrats. The stage was being set.

The following month, Chairman Brezhnev would be travelling by private train up from his holiday in the Black Sea resort of Baku, accompanied by Chernenko. Andropov had persuaded the big boss to make a quick stop at the spa station.

The lush red tropical krans flowers in the garden beds of Mineralnye Vody railway station fairly sizzled under the southern sun on 19 September 1978, the appointed meeting day for this incongruous quartet. Gorbachev stuck close to Andropov in the second-floor waiting-room set aside for Party big shots – the men in panama hats – hidden from the common folk behind curtained windows. It would be a make-or-break performance for the First Secretary of Stavropol. Brezhnev would also be making other stops, to look over Gorbachev's rival territorial chiefs: Medunov, the First Secretary of neighbouring Krasnodar, who was much closer to Brezhnev and on the take; and Romanov, the Party boss of Leningrad, who had got publicly drunk on an official trip to Finland. Gorbachev, using his old tricks, had tried to discredit Romanov, but drunkenness and dishonesty were de rigueur in the Brezhnev clan. It was Gorbachev's unsporting way of life that was suspicious.

When the two massive, slow-moving men disembarked from their private carriage to face the 'father–son' team on the cleared platform, Gorbachev gave an account of his territory's record harvest. Brezhnev's face remained impassive.

Two months later, to the astonishment of most Sovietologists and Party insiders alike, the young unknown from sleepy Stavropol was catapulted into the ranks of power. He was 'elected' to fill Kulakov's cold shoes as Secretary of the Central Committee for Agriculture. His name was last on a list of promotions,† but it was none the less a plum appointment: there were only nine such Secretariats. Overnight Gorbachev had become part of the uppermost circle of the Party elite – one of the top thirty leaders in the country.

Through Lenin's system, the Party had controlled the appointments of everybody who matters, from prime minister to factory managers, newspaper editors to academics, and ensured their loyalty by lavishing on them secret food stores, imported clothes, country houses and limousines – all on loan. This Communist Party machine by 1978 probably accounted for 300,000 apparatchiks out of the then seventeen million Party members, and it had become a self-contained world of privilege.

The first factor that made the forty-seven-year-old Gorbachev's appointment so surprising was his 'breathtaking youth't in a power structure devoted to gerontocratic prerogative. Second, his entire experience consisted of being a regional farm boss; what did he know about the rest of a nation that covered one-sixth of the earth's surface? And how would such a plain-speaking yokel survive in the murderous corridors of the Central Committee Secretariat, where men spoke one sweet sycophantic language to their superiors and another, insulting and intimidating, to their inferiors?

Several insiders told me that the element of chance played a large part in Gorbachev's move to Moscow and meteoric ascension to the Politburo.† While acknowledging that Suslov, Andropov and even Chernenko had a hand in it, they were consistently vague on how and why it happened.

It turned out that the decision to appoint Gorbachev to the Secretariat was a trade-off between Suslov and Brezhnev, the promotion of the Stavropolian being the quid pro quo for Suslov's acceptance of Chernenko's elevation to the Politburo.† Chernenko was Brezhnev's yes-man. Gorbachev was reaping his reward for having managed to ingratiate himself with two giants – Suslov and Andropov – who could have crushed him between them as they wrestled for control of the Kremlin. But he was also little more than a pawn in their political chess match.

'I think Gorbachev himself was probably somewhat surprised by what happened to him,' says Ambassador Palmer. Mikhailova is certain of it. Her old friend called her the very same day with his news.

'How could you predict this!' Gorbachev exploded. 'You are a real Cassandra!'

He laughed heartily at his own tease, but this time he listened carefully as Mikhailova continued to spin her fantastic predictions.

'Don't be surprised,' she said in her lilting sing-song. 'You will have more successes.'

Like Macbeth with his witches, Gorbachev took the omen from Mikhailova with some foreboding and much resistance. If he did dream of rising to the top Kremlin post, his ambition was hidden even from himself. Mikhailova is very definite on this point.

'It would come as a surprise to him later that he became General Secretary. He wasn't a man of high ambition. He knew what he was worth.' Using the word ambition in its more pejorative Russian sense, to mean raw self-interest, she adds, 'Raisa has more ambition than he does.'

Other Party insiders insist that Mikhail Sergeyevich must have been dreaming of coming to Moscow; there was no other way to move from the position of a territorial boss, except sharply down to a very shabby life.† It is certainly believable that he was surprised and a bit overwhelmed. The day he was elected, 27 November 1978, Starshikov was with him in Moscow. 'He smiled happily. And then suddenly, he got serious. "You know, Georgy, this time, it's not just our little region we're looking after. This time, it's another job altogether."'†

Blind Alley

'My God, what did they think they were doing!'† Gorbachev exclaimed when he got his first inside look at the country's economic condition. 'Maybe I should go back to the provinces now.'

The disastrous state of affairs was another reason Yuri Andropov had wanted the unorthodox thinker in Moscow. Marshalling the resources of a vast secret police organization, Andropov was, as his son told me, in a unique position to 'analyse the inner life' of the country on two levels: the obvious economic stagnation and the hidden operations of the mafia. The KGB could draw detailed psychograms of every segment of the population. Andropov knew the worst, but, without political power, he could do little about the ruble millionaires created by Brezhnev Inc. For example, a single man represented all five Central Asian republics on the Central Committee – Sharaf Rashidovich Rashidov, the flashily corrupt First Party Secretary of Uzbekistan on whom Brezhnev had bestowed his public embraces.

'My father had an absolutely clear understanding that it was impossible to go on with the old style of life,' explains Igor Andropov. 'He saw that the old methods and forms that we held correct for the development of a society had completely outlived their usefulness.

'It became clear in the middle of the seventies, and with every year it became clearer and clearer, that the economic system was approaching its limits,' is the gentle locution by which Igor Andropov means to say that growth in the Soviet socialist economy virtually stopped *as early as the middle of the 1970s* ten years before Gorbachev came to power – and Gorbachev knew it all along. By 1978, Abel Aganbegyan, a radical economist, was using the first Soviet-devised computer models to make a prognosis for the next five-year plan. He and other scientists at the Novosibirsk Institute had come to the conclusion that 'our society is on the verge of economic catastrophe'. Aganbegyan wrote a report sharply critical of the policy of the Communist Party. It was shown only to Prime Minister Kosygin, although many others, including Gorbachev, heard about it.†

By the dawn of the 1980s, the Soviet economy had shrunk to one-third the size of the American economy, while the share of the Soviet GNP earmarked for the arms race had mushroomed to an insupportable 22 to 25 per cent.† Renewal of Soviet equipment was creaking along at an annual rate of 2 per cent a year, according to Professor Vladimir Kvint, an economist then at Novosibirsk. 'That means it took *fifty years* to change old machines to new ones,' says Kvint. After developing a computer model to plot Reagonomics, he proposed using the new American timetable for amortization, which was helping the American economy to leap ahead. But the political leadership in Moscow didn't believe in computer models and probably didn't want facts about the American economy that might shake up its military–industrial complex and all the personal fortunes that flowed from it. Kvint's report was 'lost' in the deep drawers of the Central Committee.*

The blindfold over the Soviet leaders' eyes was self-imposed: their economic catastrophe was in reality a massive political problem. So Andropov, who was more of a politician than a professional intelligence chief, set his sights on tearing down the corrupt Brezhnev clan.† He had the power of the KGB files and secret police network to attempt it. Andropov used his information selectively, politically. He knew, for example, that Kulakov's family had been imprisoned during collectivization but had offered no information against Gorbachev's patron when the man was elevated to a high position in Moscow. He knew about the stains on Gorbachev's past as well.

'Andropov was able to protect Gorbachev from many different blows,' sayd Golovanov.

He was a shrewd judge of character as well, and he looked for men with curiosity and a love of learning like himself. Before becoming KGB chairman in 1967, Andropov had attracted a circle of 'consultants' which brought together some of the best and brightest in the Party: Georgy Arbatov, director of the USA and Canada Institute; Fyodor Burlatsky, political scientist and today prominent editor; Georgy Shakhnazarov, futurologist and eventually a personal assistant to Gorbachev; *Izvestia* columnist Alexander Bovin; and Nikolai Shishlin, today an international media liaison official.

---

* The CIA, one of whose main missions is to gather and analyse data on the economic and military might of the Soviet Union, kept telling American government leaders all through the 1970s and 1980s that the Soviet economy was more than half as large as the American economy and that 15 per cent of its budget was devoted to arms. It was this wrongheaded analysis on which US defence spending was based. It took the CIA almost *fifteen years* to catch up with the reality that the Soviet Union was in 'near crisis' and might soon be pushed 'over the edge into sharp deterioration' – a view not expressed until the agency's anachronistic report: 'The Soviet Economy Stumbles Badly in 1989'.

During his brief tenure as Soviet leader, Andropov would also promote from obscurity virtually the entire retinue that later surrounded General Secretary Gorbachev, including his Prime Minister, Nikolai Ryzhkov, and his loyal right-wing ideologue, Yegor Ligachev.†

This is not to leave the impression that Andropov was just a nice cultured man who liked to chat about ideas and literature. As KGB chief he also persecuted thousands of political prisoners, and it was Andropov who gave the command to shoot down the Korean passenger airliner in September 1983, killing 269 civilians.

The task which faced Gorbachev on his arrival in Moscow was daunting: to improve the efficiency of Soviet agriculture. But he was youthful and energetic, and, above all, carried himself with an inner assurance that seemed strangely *detached* from the sordid and sorry state of the Soviet socialist experiment. He started out as a jolly person to work with, very communicative, according to Alexander Bovin. He sang, though not well, and danced and displayed a lively sense of humour. Even Boris Yeltsin begrudgingly acknowledges, 'When he first came to work at the Central Committee he was different than he is today – more open and frank. We thought that at last Soviet agriculture might really get moving . . .'† (However, their relationship soon cooled when Gorbachev reprimanded Yeltsin for 'violating Party discipline' after Yeltsin took exception to inaccurate statements in a Central Committee memo.)

Ambassador Mark Palmer first became aware of the new man in Moscow over a drink with Anatoly Dobrynin, the long-time Soviet Ambassador to Washington, who was passing through Budapest.

'There's this incredible man, Gorbachev, who asked me to come over on a Saturday morning to talk,' Dobrynin related, still somewhat dazed. 'We talked for four or five hours straight – he asked me over a hundred questions about the United States and the rest of the world. This Gorbachev, he's an insatiable hurricane of a person.'

That conversation first tipped off Palmer that there was 'something unusual' about the man. A few years later Dobrynin added to the assessment that Gorbachev was very open-minded and not only curious but also *flexible* in his thinking.

Despite the fact that in 1979 the USSR gathered in the worst harvest in four years, Gorbachev was pushed even higher in the political firmament: named candidate-member of the Politburo. Encouraged, the Agriculture Secretary tried to resurrect 'an open debate't on the usefulness of small group farming in the Soviet Union. He spoke in favour of easing restrictions on farms that wanted to transfer to full economic accountability. (Only 8 per cent of Soviet farms were operating at anything like a profit; the indebtedness of the large collective farms had in fact increased from 2.5 billion to 25.7 billion rubles in short-term credits between 1970 and 1980.)† He took a big risk in raising the dreaded zveno small-team concept again; it had become such a highly charged ideological issue that one proponent of the zveno had been sent to jail for his heresy and died there.

But President Carter's US grain embargo, imposed in protest against the Soviet invasion of Afghanistan, helped Gorbachev argue his case. The Party apparat was panicky over the threat of grain shortages. In January 1981, the Agriculture Secretary was able to pass a remarkable resolution that removed some of the limits on collective farmers' small independent farming operations. Most radical of all, the resolution provided for the selling of vegetables and meat to the socialized sector at free-market prices! But the guardians of the status quo struck back before the decree ever saw printer's ink. Publication of the document was blocked. Gorbachev had fallen foul of the real game.

'Decentralizing agriculture, even a little bit, would present a threat to Party control over the peasantry,' observed a Western diplomat.† And when the US administration lifted its grain embargo, the liberal decree was buried forever. In practice, after this nothing in agriculture was changed for the better, according to Professor Kvint.

Gorbachev met his first American in 1980. John Crystal, a Sioux City, Iowa, agribusinessman and banker, was invited to the Soviet Union because he was the nephew of Roswell Garst (Khrushchev's idea of Mr America, the one businessman the Soviets could turn to for sound advice). One of the first things Crystal registered when he entered Gorbachev's office was that the ubiquitous portraits of Lenin and Marx were nowhere in sight. He found Gorbachev extraordinary in other ways as well: the Russian seemed to appreciate the enormous productive capacity of American agriculture, and he accepted criticism with complete equanimity.

'He didn't seem to have an inferiority complex at all, and I think most Soviets do. Gorbachev really believed he was in the ruling body of a superpower,' says Crystal.† He was not in the least intimidated by the affluence of the US. Why? Because he believed down to the letter the editorials he read in the Party newspaper, *Pravda*, painting American society as made up of huge armies of the near-starving. When Crystal mentioned the size of the American middle class, Gorbachev complacently insisted that there were many more Americans living in poverty.

Two years later, the Sioux City farmer stopped in to see the Soviet Agriculture Secretary again. This time Gorbachev talked a bold game of geopolitics: 'The technology war has changed between the superpowers,' he told Crystal flatly. 'What good are all these tanks, armoured personnel carriers, all this stuff, when we both have so many nuclear missiles?' He spoke with the voice of a new generation: a post-Second World War perspective. Crystal went home excited. It was clear to him that the Soviet Union, crippled by its defence expenditures, was 'ripe for the plucking by a guy like Gorbachev'. It was going to happen anyway, Gorbachev just happened to be coming along at the right time. Crystal called the State Department to say, 'I've just met the next leader of the Soviet Union.' He offered to come to Washington and fill them in. 'Don't bother,' was the response.

But, despite the geopolitical razzle-dazzle, Gorbachev was still failing to make a dent in the area for which he was responsible. That same year, the Soviet leadership was presented with a grim report on the food crisis: a tenfold increase in Soviet food imports over the preceding decade, staggering mishandling of agricultural equipment, catastrophic losses in crop harvesting (20–33 per cent), and a national diet that was well below the minimum standard in protein.†

'But Gorbachev is like Reagan – Teflon – everybody else gets blamed but him,' observes Crystal.

The Agriculture Secretary did make one last attempt to persuade the Politburo elders to embrace the dreaded zveno system, but as soon as he ran into political resistance, he pulled back and reversed himself. It had become a pattern, touting the need for reform, then changing tack the next week, then shifting again, always starting and ending with half-measures.

Gorbachev would spend four years banging his head against the Kremlin Wall. What did he actually accomplish as Agriculture Secretary? Nothing, absolutely nothing, acknowledges Bovin. But wasn't there some contribution, even one concrete experiment that he launched? I asked the expert agriculturist in the Supreme Soviet, Gennady Lisichkin. 'There is no such example,' he replied with finality.

But the fact that Gorbachev could not point to one positive result during his four-year tenure as Agriculture Secretary made absolutely no difference. Mikhail Sergeyevich had already been inducted into the circle of kings in 1980 – named a full member of the Politburo, the crowning achievement in his meteoric career. He was all of forty-nine years old, a mere babe by the reckoning of the Soviet gerontocracy. Gorbachev had become initiated into the real, unwritten rules of Party life.

'Advancement is never based on success,' is the way

Lisichkin put it. 'It depends only on personal loyalty.' The path to power was paved by patronage, and that required being 'flexible' about one's principles.

The salient question here is this: what did Gorbachev know about the failure of the socialist system, and when did he know it?

He understood large numbers of irrefutable facts which pointed in the direction of disaster as early as 1980, confirms Crystal: 'I think even when he came to power [in 1985] he had a vision, but no plan.'

Alexander Bovin, another pet of Andropov's, worked briefly with Gorbachev when Bovin was a deputy of the Supreme Council of the Russian Republic; he depicts a more duplicitous stance. In the Brezhnev days Bovin became famous for his provocative writing and wit as well as the eccentricity of a Kaiser-style moustache. Today he is a huge barrel of flesh barely restrained by red plaid braces, and occupies a large, inactive office at the newspaper *Izvestia*.

'We did understand under Brezhnev that we were headed for a blind alley. But we lacked the courage to state that openly. I couldn't do what Sakharov did.' Bovin broods a bit, the flesh of his face collapsing into a pudding beneath his chin. 'I kept silent. Like a majority of people – like Gorbachev.'

Early in 1980 Andrei Sakharov, the pioneering physicist and creator of the Soviet H-bomb, was seized on the streets of Moscow by Andropov's KGB and forced into exile in the closed city of Gorky, where he would keep the flame of conscience alive despite being cut off from his family, and most painfully, from his own writings, which the KGB repeatedly stole and destroyed. Sakharov was an exact contemporary of Gorbachev's, though a far more influential member of the elite, when he underwent an inner transformation. He broke with the leadership and gave voice to his true beliefs, becoming the standard bearer for the dissident movement. The pretext for his exile was his open letter to Chairman Brezhnev calling the Soviet actions in Afghanistan 'a clear example of expansionism', but when asked what was the last straw that caused his banishment, he replied, 'My life, my whole life.'†*

It is rather striking that the same year Sakharov was banished to Gorky, Gorbachev was elevated with Andropov's help to the ruling Politburo. Since Bovin admitted lacking the courage to speak what he knew to be the truth, I asked him to describe how he lived with himself day by day, knowing that the country was headed down a blind alley but not doing anything about it.

'Somehow you get used to it. You do your everyday things. Concrete things.' He worked as a journalist. He tried to make his articles witty. He had his family, his friends. 'But I felt a kind of' – he sighs – *split personality*. That was very painful, of course. But it's not a steady, non-stop feeling. The course of everyday life does not allow you to think about it all the time.' Does one have nightmares? 'My wife did. It depends on how strong your nerves are.'

Fight or Flight?

Gorbachev's dizzying rise through the ranks did not change his work habits. Just as he'd burned the midnight oil in his Stavropol headquarters, he stayed late in his office in the most elevated of twenty identical Central Committee buildings on and around Staraya Square, a block from the KGB headquarters. Everything about the Central Committee apparat building, the traffic going in and the work product that comes out, reflects the rigid hierarchy of Communism and the fact that the Central Committee is the real bastion of power in the USSR. It takes up several blocks and its inhabitants are assigned one of twelve entrances according

---

* Gorbachev did not have to vote on the invasion of Afghanistan, since he was only a non-voting candidate member of the Politburo in December 1979, but in 1981 he justified the Soviet invasion as a 'legitimate defensive action provoked by attempts to foment counter-revolution' by the US and Pakistan. By 1989, he made a full about-face, publicly condemning the invasion as 'a crime against humanity'.

to their rank in the hierarchy.† The army of chauffered cars provided to the Party elite are also ranked: Volgas are surpassed by Chaikas which are superseded by the mighty Zil limousines handmade for the top brass. Gorbachev had immediately started with a Zil.

But the truth behind the Central Committee Secretariat's grandiosity is that most of the work is make-work: stacks of useless reports based on incomplete or deliberately falsified statistics, streams of unrealizable programmes, and always the slogans, bombastically upbeat slogans. More than anything, the Secretariat is a vast house of propaganda meant to keep the Party in power by massaging its own delusions.†

The jolliness and equanimity that Gorbachev displayed during his first year in Moscow had worn thin under the frustrations of life on the fast track. The only two physical activities he had enjoyed in Stavropol were swimming and walking aimlessly in the woods; now even those had fallen away. He told Mikhailova he couldn't enjoy walking with a pack of bodyguards nipping at his heels. Apart from avid theatre-going with Raisa and reading the odd mystery novel, his life was entirely devoted to work – or rather, make-work. 'I don't think he completely relaxes,' worries Mikhailova, who says she saw Misha more often after he moved to Moscow.

Gorbachev developed a 'nervous condition', serious enough for Kremlin doctors to order him to take a course of spa treatment.† They recommended radon baths. Gorbachev took a week off to ensconce himself in the Imenikirovna Sanatorium in Pyatigorsk, a short drive away from the new pride of the spa town, the Upper Radon Baths.

'Gorbachev came here when he was First Secretary of Stavropol krai – and later, he came down from Moscow for a cure for a nervous disease,' confirmed the establishment's director, Vitaly Pavlovich, doctor of 'bulneology'. Radon! Isn't that the radioactive stuff Americans sell their homes to flee if it's found underground? I inquired. 'Many of our leaders have gone to radon baths and see, they're all fine,' was the unconvincing answer. Radon is believed by Russians to be useful for almost all diseases, and 3,500 procedures are done in Pyatigorsk every day. One sees women enclosed in what look like plastic-hooded skimobiles, taking a radon air bath with the radioactive gas piped directly to their lungs. In the basement, they line up to lie on their backs and receive a vaginal douche of radon water through six-inch glass syringes. To a foreigner's eyes it looks like a chamber of Mengele's horrors, but the director insists, 'Almost all gynae-cological diseases are treated in this way.'

The 'nervous disease' that brought Gorbachev to these baths may have been his diabetes. A person with the gene for diabetes often manifests the illness first during a period of severe stress. Too much stress for too long – stimulating a fight-or-flight reaction – is dangerous for a person susceptible to diabetes. It is the body's emergency reaction to the unexpected: the blood flows faster, the heart beats faster, blood vessels constrict, and the body is readied to act with all available energy either to fight or run away. Whether or not Gorbachev's 'nervous disorder' was related to his dia-betes, he certainly must have suffered at that time from chronic fight-or-flight frustrations.

'The baths strengthened and stabilized his nervous system,' claimed the burly director of the Upper Baths, whose own purplish skin looked glaringly cancerous. He told me Gorbachev was 'cured' there in 1980 or 1981. Today, the General Secretary goes to a sanatorium on the outskirts of Moscow where the radon is synthetic.

Gorbachev was not prepared to take the fighting path, like Andrei Sakharov, but his constitution was showing the strain. So he found a third way out – beyond fight or flight. He began creating a policy to fit the personality of the man he most needed to please, even though it represented a contradiction in every respect of the zveno reforms for which he was campaigning at the very same time. Knowing that Brezhnev opposed the wider adoption of the zveno groups

as undermining the socialist character of agriculture, Gorbachev offered the Chairman a heavy investment scheme for
rescuing agriculture through even greater central control. But
no sooner had he offered the plan, than he began backing
away from it. Writing in *Kommunist* he built up the programme:†

> Despite indisputable achievements in the develop-
> ment of the agrarian sector of the economy, the
> food situation has still deteriorated . . . the Food
> Programme plans to link in a single organism all
> the components of agriculture and the sectors
> which service it. The end result must be not only
> the creation of a reliable food stock, but a significant
> improvement in the functioning of the country's
> entire economy.

Then, in the same essay, he expressed the contradictory
thought – the reality – that the food supply could not be
improved so long as farmers were fleeing the dismal conditions in the countryside: 'The mass migration of country
dwellers . . . to the city upsets the development of agriculture.' Here, for the first time, Gorbachev mentioned
perestroika: 'the need for an appropriate psychological
restructuring. All agricultural workers are now required . . .
to display initiative and enterprise.'

No decree from the Centre *requiring* workers to display
initiative and enterprise had the chance of a snowball in hell.
So Gorbachev called together a group of six radical academics
from Novosibirsk and invited comment on his Food Programme from these theoreticians. Leading them was Abel
Aganbegyan, the radical economist who had been branded
'an unreliable man' back in Khrushchev's time, and Tatyana
Zaslavskaya, a pioneering sociologist. The six had all made
their way to this most distant of institutes, in the city of
Novosibirsk (New Siberia), where there was a free spirit and
favourable conditions for serious work. They were able to

work together as a community of young, progressive empirical thinkers with similar opinions on economics and social research.

'Gorbachev produced an impression of a person who doesn't know anything about economics,' recalls Aganbegyan. But they were all impressed with his openness: 'He conducted the meeting in a very democratic way and he didn't tell off anybody who criticized him.' The bombastic Aganbegyan, an Armenian Jew accustomed to being on the wrong side of Soviet leaders, blasted the central-control scheme and for good measure vented his spleen on the 'economy of shortages', where all the power was in the hands of the producers and none in the hands of consumers. Gorbachev calmly took notes on a yellow pad.†

Zaslavskaya, an intellectual of considerable elegance and dignity, speaks with a soft voice that mutes the sharpness of her message. In the same meeting, she pronounced the Food Programme one of 'compromising character' and 'semi-measures' – two charges that dog Gorbachev to this day. Gorbachev was creating yet another organization, Gosagroprom, on top of all the other ministries that already had their hands in the agricultural till. The group of academics urged him to keep the ministries out of the new structure.

Gorbachev turned to an aide. 'What do you think if I wrote this recommendation into the proposal?' Then he answered his own question: he couldn't support their proposal to dilute the authority of the ministries – the inside levers of the Party apparat – because 'I will be gone from my chair.'†

Nevertheless, the meeting did eventually bear fruit. Gorbachev had been stimulated by these unorthodox thinkers. Eventually, they would become the core group of his perestroichiki, and Aganbegyan briefly became one of his top economic advisers.

Eighteen months in the making, the Food Programme was launched by Brezhnev at the plenum of the Central Committee on 24 May 1982, with appropriately inflated rhetoric. Gorbachev kept a low profile in the media campaign. 'If Gorbachev is not particularly pleased with Brezhnev's Food

Programme, then where do his sentiments lie?' asked
puzzled Sovietologists at the time. 'As with most Soviet
leaders, it is difficult to tie him firmly to any specific policy
position.'†

Not surprisingly, the plan turned into a massive swindle
by corrupt ministers and a further disaster for Soviet agriculture. 'Gorbachev was the inventor of Brezhnev's Food Programme,' admits Central Committee denizen Nikolai
Shishlin today. I ask if he thinks his then-colleague really
believed in the ill-fated scheme. 'It's certainly difficult to
answer this question,' Shishlin replies. 'He did understand
that this programme wouldn't work when he designed it. He
hoped' – Shishlin flutters his lids in mock-naivety – 'he hoped,
just as he hoped in 1985, that a few improvements and
everything will be all right.'

Was Gorbachev still a romantic in 1985, when he first took
power?

'I think we are romantics even now,' says Shishlin with an
edge of self-contempt. 'We think that democracy will work
by itself.'

Thinking on Two Levels

A Westerner would naturally ask, How does one live with
the conflict of holding two mutually antagonistic ideas in
mind at the same time, of *consistently* believing one thing and
doing the opposite? We call this thought process *cognitive
dissonance* – the private perception that one is not acting
according to the values or principles one claims to espouse.
Of course, all societies and most human beings continuously
make compromises. But Western-educated thought processes are such that we continually struggle to *resolve the
contradiction* or reduce dissonance, because if we don't, we
will live in a constant state of confusion and psychological
discomfort. As a result, cognitive dissonance acts as a motivating force.

From my observation, Soviets do not think in the same

way. They do not struggle with cognitive dissonance. They are trained by their ideology to struggle with the concept of *dialectic*: namely, that there are always two possibilities, and even though they may stand in opposition to one another, both can be accepted, both can even be followed. Soviets trained to this dualistic thinking are accustomed to *living with both*. This explains why, for example, Gorbachev the country Cossack could be aware of the evils of Communism and confide to his roommate the reality that he knew from his everyday life as a peasant, but at the same time be a 'pure Communist' in his heart. The incongruity does not create inner conflict for a Soviet – so long as a larger structure or framework encompasses all such contradictions. And that structure was the monolith of the Communist Party.

In Marxian theory Communism is so utopian in its ideals that its apostles are granted the right to rewrite history and reality. This is justified as the necessary means of creating a New Soviet Man to fit the ideological end. Indeed, in the 1988 edition of the Moscow-published *Short Political Vocabulary*, the word 'personality' is still defined solely as an instrument of the state: 'every socio-economic formation gives rise to a new type of personality'. The Marxist design for a Communist society pays no attention to the inherent qualities of the human being or the universal values according to which large numbers of people, if allowed majority rule, organize themselves into a civilized whole. For Marxists man is an 'aggregate of social relations', and the hierarchy has only to establish the correct conditions of life for people to be transformed into the embodiment of virtue.†

In other words, the individual is to be rewired – by fear and repression as under Stalin, or by propaganda and persuasion as under Gorbachev – to be the mass expression of a philosophy dreamed up by men who assume the powers of gods. Lenin, too, was a romantic and a utopian, on the philosophical level. His ideals were noble, but on the tactical level his actions went almost beyond cynicism.

Like their leaders, Soviet citizens must also adapt to

thinking on two levels at the same time. As explained to me by one of the editors at the maverick Soviet magazine *Ogonyok*, Valentin Yumashev, 'The first level is protective. You believe that you mean well and cast your actions in the name of romantic ideals. At a deeper level, the level of heart, you understand that it's a compromise or a betrayal and you shouldn't do it. Truth is mixed with lies, compromises with attempts to justify them. But you can't let yourself think at that level, except in rare moments, or people would have gone crazy years ago living in the ocean of lies.'

Hence the development of doublethink. George Orwell coined the term in his novel, *1984*, as a way of encapsulating the absurdity of totalitarianism. I will use it as a way to analyse the way Soviets live with the hypocrisy of the Communist Party. At the first level you believe you are sincere, but at the level of heart you realize you are lying. Ambitious Soviets, the leaders like Gorbachev, become chameleons accustomed to acting many parts, and drift into the condition described by the writer Zinoviev as Homo Sovieticus. 'Homo Sovieticus or Communist man is very flexible, he's like a chameleon. He can change his views, his opinion, in a matter of minutes. One minute he will be speaking with an American spy and blaming the Soviet regime for every evil. Five minutes later he can go to the KGB and denounce this American spy. In this state of mind one can easily betray.'

For those being led, the condition of Homo Sovieticus is that of the walking dead. 'Indifference is their chief characteristic,'† says novelist Anatoly Pristavkin. Because they were never able to speak the truth, they couldn't even *think* the truth. As a result, the masses have accumulated a perverse talent for not seeing what they see, for not believing their eyes, as though they had been rewired into a single, nerve-connected social organism.

What Gorbachev's life story makes clear is that although he was a risk-taker he was never an outsider. He worked *within* the structure he found. And, as a reformer from within, he always kept his eye first on the political currents, on pleasing whomever he needed to in order to secure his own position. As his university classmates testified, no one was ever quite sure what he stood for. In debate, he would use the same revealing aphorism: 'As to this question, one must approach it *dialectically.*' That meant he wanted to entertain a thesis and its contradiction at the same time. Always he sought to take into consideration all sides of an issue, but in the process he was able to avoid being specific, to keep from committing himself.

The first-generation apparatchik adapted to the treacherous culture of Moscow by changing character again. He became a disciple of doublethink.

The Reformers' Rise

The long war of nerves between Suslov and Andropov came to climax in January 1982. The man with the most feared information bank in the world had been beating the drums of war with an increasingly noisy anti-corruption campaign. Now he confronted Suslov face to face with evidence that was too close to home to be dismissed: Brezhnev's daughter, Galina Cherbanova, was up to her ears in selling state diamonds for private gain. Suslov insisted the scandal had to be hushed up. Andropov refused to back down – this was his chance to expose the fact that the iniquities of Brezhnev's leadership went all the way to the top.† But just before his death, Suslov came into conflict with Brezhnev. He was the only Politburo member of whom Brezhnev was afraid.

The fatal stroke suffered by Suslov on 20 January was widely rumoured to have been provoked by that head-on confrontation with Andropov. In the long funeral procession through Red Square, everything looked as it always did at the frequent funerals of the ossified leadership: snow lying heavily in the dark arms of evergreen trees, the body of the deceased borne in a coffin on the shoulders of Politburo members, and the rows of bulky black-coated men in big fur hats marching behind in a manner befitting their killer instincts. But now, for the first time, Gorbachev was marching in the row right behind Brezhnev. He walked beside his surviving patron: just he and Andropov. But he made certain also to hug and stroke Suslov's family members.

Andropov left the KGB (one cannot ascend to Party chairmanship from there) and returned to the Central Committee to take over Suslov's job as chief propagandist and the second person in the Party. With a new power vacuum in the Kremlin, the relationship between Andropov and Gorbachev flowered into a full-blown conspiracy to tar and feather their respective rivals. Andropov was attacking corrupted Party leaders (though never exposing any corruption in the KGB, where the mechanism of flattery was widely used). But when it came to showing his leanings in the tug of war for the mantle of succession between Andropov and Chernenko, Gorbachev again played to both sides. Andropov's natural son, Igor, says only, 'I *think* he supported my father.' Gorbachev himself boasted to Mikhailova, 'Chernenko has high regard for me.' He intended to talk Chernenko into giving him the plum responsibility for cadres: to groom the next leadership team.

Before the year was out Red Square was the site of another funeral procession. Again, snow lay in the arms of dark trees and again the rows of bulky black-coated men in big fur hats marched behind an open coffin. But this time the face on which they would bestow their last, carefully composed grief-stricken looks was that of Leonid Brezhnev himself.

Andropov swept into power in November 1982, and Gorbachev became the second man in the Party with responsibility for the entire economy. Together they set about purging one-fifth of the regional first secretaries and nine of the twenty-three Central Committee department heads. Gorbachev kept in touch with the team of economists and sociologists at Novosibirsk and asked them to advise him about what he described as 'the high degree of social protection in our society' – a delicate way of asking: what do we do with a nation of freeloaders? Their conclusion was that no meaningful economic reform could be introduced until or unless Soviet leaders were ready to bite the bullet of Bolshevik egalitarianism: uravnilovka, or *levelling off* of incomes, which ensured that none could become rich, but all had the duty to remain equally poor.

But if Gorbachev was formulating any actual plans for economic reform, he kept them to himself. He had nothing to say in speeches or Party meetings about the defence or industrial sectors. He made the ritual calls for improvement in consumer goods but nowhere suggested how such goals might be achieved.

The high point of 1983 for Gorbachev was his eye-opening ten-day trip to Canada in May. It was most unusual for a Politburo member to take such a long official sojourn in a Western country. By now, Gorbachev had probably had more foreign exposure than almost anyone in the Soviet leadership, past or present, with the exception of Foreign Minister Gromyko, but his contacts had been with fraternal Communist parties rather than Western government leaders. In candid discussions with members of the Canadian Parliament, he was well prepared for hostile questions, and showed annoyance only once, when asked why the Soviet Union preached greater trust but packed its embassies with KGB agents.

'Do you really think we are such simpletons?' he demanded.† He told them they were prisoners of the 'spy mania' that America was whipping up. 'It is calculated ideological sabotage to discredit the Soviet Union, to strike a blow at her authority.'

But he more than balanced this outburst with humorous banter and uninhibited policy innuendoes that made Canadian conservative and liberal MPs alike sit up and take notice.†

Canadian diplomats were hit with a mild form of the Gorbymania that would sweep through Europe and America later in the decade. Gorbachev more than passed his first test as a potential statesman, but there was almost no US news-paper coverage of his visit. The Soviet Ambassador to Canada, Alexander Yakovlev, later remarked frostily that it was interesting that Americans didn't want to know anything about a future Soviet leader, since by 1983 Gorbachev was already an obvious potential successor.

'The guy, by all accounts, seems to be extraordinarily capable – well educated, bright, hard-working, and to the extent you can be in these things, personable,' Geoffrey Pearson, the Canadian Ambassador to the Soviet Union, told a Knight-Ridder news reporter.† And then, as if reading the mindset that would prevail inside the Kremlin two years later, the diplomat said, 'Think what it would mean to have a vigorous, attractive figure at the head of the Soviet govern-ment. It would be a gold-plated political asset. In one stroke, the image of doddering, indecisive old men would be shat-tered.' Pearson, like Yakovlev, was amazed that the Ameri-can press didn't think it worthwhile to see and assess the man who would very likely soon run the Soviet Union.

The more lasting imprint on Mikhail Gorbachev, however, was his extended exposure to the person who would later become his alter ego, Alexander Nikolayevich Yakovlev. The two men had met as members of the Central Committee in 1970, but in 1973, Yakovlev had fallen foul of Suslov for his departures from 'the pretence of unanimity'† and had been sent off to soft exile in Canada to oversee the work of America-watching, the main function of the Ottawa ambassadorship.†

Early in Gorbachev's visit, the two men sat up all night together and hit it off famously. They found much in common: both had peasant backgrounds. Yakovlev was born in December 1923 in a tiny village near Yaroslavl, an ancient town on the Volga river. 'This peasant origin always leaves a trace,' Yakovlev told me. 'I think that country people are more responsive to human suffering . . . in a village you cannot refuse a beggar man. The cities are intolerant and

indifferent. In the village, people are more tolerant of those
who go to church or don't go to church.'

Like Gorbachev's grandparents, Yakovlev's father was a
private farmer who accepted the first chairmanship of the
local collective farm under duress. He later gave it up to
retreat into the woods as a 'hidden peasant', meaning one
who rejected collectivization.† Yakovlev's reaction at the time
– he was only thirteen years old – was self-protective: 'I could
have guessed some things, I had a little understanding, but
this was never in the form of political feelings,' which may
have been similar to young Misha's initial reaction when his
grandfather was imprisoned.

Their differences were just as important, and would later
make Alexander Nikolayevich attractive as a second self for
Mikhail Sergeyevich. Yakovlev was a true intellectual,
whereas Gorbachev, though he wanted to gather a circle of
intellectuals around him, was a natural politician. Yakovlev
was also a hero of the Front, who took awards for being
seriously wounded in combat. The harsh treatment of
soldiers shocked Yakovlev.

'That was the first blow against my total unconditional
faith in the justice of the regime,' he told me. 'What scratched
my heart were the very cruel measures used by the Soviet
Army on its own fighting men against minor cases of
negligence or mistakes. The real blow came after the war
when our prisoners-of-war began to return home from the
German camps and were imprisoned in camps of our own.'
Yakovlev himself had returned a cripple, the only reason he
could think of that the Party didn't retaliate when he spoke
out against these injustices. But, like Gorbachev, he hadn't
begun to see things clearly until 1956 and the secret Khrushchev speech.

Politically, Yakovlev had become a man of the world after
ten years in the West. He had been monitoring the American
news media and picking up Madison Avenue's slick political
packaging techniques (which he would later use to sell
Gorbachev to the West). He had also done a research paper

as an exchange student at Columbia University, back in 1959–60, on Franklin Roosevelt and the New Deal. 'Yakovlev has a more profound theoretical background than Gorbachev, and he's much more radical than Gorbachev – though he doesn't like to advertise that,' according to their colleague Alexander Bovin. 'He's really for democracy and pluralism.' And finally, Yakovlev was a homely, naturally acerbic man, not a crowd-pleaser; he would be content to stay behind the scenes while Gorbachev held centre stage.

Indeed, as the two Soviets barnstormed across the broad Canadian expanse in a small plane, Gorbachev behaved like a typical provincial, baby-kissing midwestern politician. But it was the private walks and talks between these two Soviets who both had non-standard ways of thinking that represented a turning point for Gorbachev. On similar walks with Andropov, Gorbachev had learned the grim realities of Soviet socialism: thus far the system had failed, it had to be restructured. Canada's bucolic farmland and booming economy were highly stimulating to him, and he listened eagerly as Yakovlev explained the way things worked in Canada.

Not that Gorbachev was undergoing a conversion experience; during one plane hop he was flipping through Canadian newspapers while Canada's Agricultural Minister, Gene Whelan, pointed out the full-page supermarket advertisements with their cut-rate price enticements and went into a riff on the wonders of free enterprise. Gorbachev stopped him with one of his stiletto pricks: 'Gene, you don't try to convert me to capitalism, and I won't try to convert you to Communism.'†

Yakovlev liked Canada, and arranged a meeting for Gorbachev with Prime Minister Trudeau, a figure the Soviet Ambassador admired greatly. But he had more than a small chip on his shoulder when it came to Americans. He described the 'American mentality' to Gorbachev by telling him about an unpleasant encounter he had had with a young American ambassador originally from the business sector who arrived in Canada in 1966. He snubbed the Soviet

Ambassador for several months. Finally, at a diplomatic reception, the Mexican Ambassador had to lead Yakovlev over to the American diplomat and introduce him for the first time. According to Yakovlev's account, the scorching exchange went like this.

Said the American, 'So, you are the Ambassador of the country that is divided into concentration camps, that has enslaved China, Yugoslavia, Albania, and that insulates all of Europe?' 'Yes, I do represent such a country,' Yakovlev replied evenly. 'And you are the American Ambassador?' Yes, the man said. 'Is it your country where small babies are eaten alive? Where you kill old people when they reach pensionable age? Where you use human beings as shooting targets?'

The American Ambassador shrank back under the barrage of ridiculous propaganda: 'How dare you insult the –'

'What else do you expect when the Ambassador of another country insults me?' snarled Yakovlev, and walked away.

'I think this is your American mentality,' Yakovlev told me, still smarting from the incident twenty-four years later.

He amended the story to say it doesn't speak for all Americans, that most are straightforward and have an open attitude. Nevertheless, Yakovlev's collected articles from his stay in Canada give a very negative evaluation of US policy (a posture which he continued to hold right up to the Geneva summit talks between then General Secretary Gorbachev and President Reagan). Reflecting a whole complex of ideas nurtured by Brezhnev, Andropov and even Chernenko, he cast the USSR as the peace-lover forced just to react to the military policies of the US – notably, to US missiles and military bases in Europe. But although these ideas were characteristic of his speeches, which were probably edited by the Politburo, he never denied that the US and USSR should be able to find common interests and a means toward restoring detente and engaging in mutual disarmament.†

Yakovlev's international views and early writings offered a whole new world perspective to Gorbachev. In the Soviet

Ambassador's mind the idea had already formed of a dialogue between the two superpowers on an equal basis, a dialogue necessary for the economic resuscitation of the Soviet Union. He was clear that the Soviet economy was going broke trying to keep pace with the arms race. He confirmed this in an interview with me, saying, 'In principle, my firm belief was based on the fact that the two countries, the US and USSR, must co-operate closely in the political field as well as in others.'

The two Great Russian peasants came to a meeting of minds that May of 1983: with the technology of war changing, the real contest for superpower status in the future would be an economic one. The US would still be the leader but there would be new players: Japan and Europe.† It was time to think beyond the Cold War and bipolar competition.

An enthusiastic Gorbachev went back to Moscow and began working through Andropov to clear Yakovlev's record and bring him home. When Yakovlev did return in 1983, he was named director of one of the most prestigious organizations in the country, the Institute for World Economics and International Relations. The post, which was usually reserved only for Politburo members, automatically made Yakovlev a consultant to the Central Committee on foreign affairs. Yakovlev also took over Suslov's old position as head of ideology and propaganda.

The closeness between Alexander Nikolayevich and Mikhail Sergeyevich would develop swiftly after that, to the point where it is probably impossible to say which one formulated what aspect of their overall policy rubric of perestroika. As American agribusinessman John Crystal affirms, 'Gorbachev has a very close relationship with Yakovlev, a social as well as an intellectual relationship.'

In the Land of Kings

All the lights are green when one works just beneath the Red Star of the Kremlin. The moment Gorbachev's heavily bolted handmade Zil limousine nosed into a central Moscow street, militiamen would materialize to hold up traffic for five minutes in all directions. Drivers were available in shifts to take Raisa to Moscow University, where she taught the philosophy of Marxism – making her what one might call a Limousine Marxist. And on weekends the couple's comfortably chauffeured car would race through the lights along Kutusavsky Prospekt on its way into the Land of Kings.

The road to the dacha colony of the bolshie shishki, or Kremlin big shots, is like no other around Moscow. Smoothly paved with well-painted traffic lines and high bright streetlights, it wends cleanly through a rich pine and birch forest – past the ghostly concrete domino blocks called 'New Buildings' where ordinary citizens live surrounded by a sea of gashed mud, garbage and concrete slabs meant for some abandoned construction, past the entrances to dimly lit, urine-smelling hallways and chipped tile floors, past women pushing prams in execrable parks and men walking their bent, broken mothers around, as if they were sleepwalkers in a labour camp – but all the lights are green for the bolshie shishki whizzing past to their splendid country houses to relax.

The Gorbachevs would be greeted by their chief bodyguard and welcomed into the grand marble entrance hall of a mansion provided for them by the state.† The enormous fireplace would be set by one of the staff, their favourite movies would be waiting in the projection room, a kitchen the size of a small house, with a separate underground cold room as refrigerator, would be stocked with delectable imported foods, should the couple wish to entertain at the thirty-foot-long dining-room table. Or they could simply relax on the vast glass-roofed verandah, in the manner of English lords or Kievan princes.

They weren't the only ones who lived in such luxury. An American president has the use of Camp David, but the Communist Party elite are treated to hundreds of Camp

Davids. Driving through this dacha colony one sees mile-
long fences of wood or brick, one after the other, with high
gates and listening devices and militia guarding entrances
surrounded by a generous periphery of empty forest to block
these mansions from the eyes of any stray motorist.

'Within this system nothing belongs to the individual,'
Boris Yeltsin points out in his book, *Against the Grain*. 'Each
"gift" – from a soft armchair with its numbered metal tag on
up to the bottle of normally unavailable medicine stamped
'safe' by the fourth directorate of the KGB – bears the seal of
the system. This is so the individual will never forget to
whom all this really belongs.' The KGB pays for it all. And
the state can take it all away the moment one breaks with the
'pretence of unanimity'. The recipients of such luxuries,
unless they are made of something other than normal human
stuff, come to depend on them, even to feel *entitled*. This was
Stalin's cunning design, says Yeltsin, to ensure the Party
elite would never have the will to challenge the Party's
power.

The changes championed by Andropov in 1983 didn't lay
a finger on this system of privilege, or on the centralized
bureaucratic system. Instead, he and Gorbachev attempted
through tightened discipline and punitive measures to
'require' the initiative they wanted workers to show. By the
summer of 1983 this campaign went to the desperate lengths
of announcing penalties for poor work performance and
drunkenness: workers would be fired on the spot and rehired
at only half their wage. Soviet workers, their living standard
ravished for decades to support a military superpower, only
grew more sullen and resentful – and drunk. In August,
Chairman Andropov addressed a congress of Party veterans
with Mikhail Gorbachev seated at his left side.

'We have not been vigorous enough,' Andropov admitted.
'We not infrequently resort to half-measures and have been
unable to overcome accumulated inertia. We must now make
up for what we have lost.' Andropov, by nature and generation a conservative, shunned the liberal word 'reform'. Yet

he now laid out plans to galvanize the bureaucracy by introducing economic levers such as prices and credits, and a new management structure. He even raised the issue of glasnost – or openness – which he said would bring the Party and government activities 'closer to the interests and needs of the people'.

He set 1 January 1985 as the target date to establish these sweeping changes, but he knew he would not live to see that day. 'My father foresaw very well that all the deeds he had just begun would have to be completed by the hands of another,' says Igor Andropov. Acknowledging it was time for a new generation to take over, he began endorsing his surrogate son, Gorbachev, as his chosen heir. His last televised words were those of a man confronting his own passing moment in the parade of history: 'Comrades, we have to admit, though it is not easy for everyone, that each new generation is in some ways stronger than the one before. It knows more. It sees further.'†

That autumn, Andropov repaired to a dacha colony on the outskirts of Moscow and began the long process of dying. He was semi-incapacitated for the final half of his fifteen-month regime. Suffering from dizzying fluctuations of blood pressure and the ravages of advanced diabetes, which had developed into chronic kidney insufficiency, he could scarcely walk. After doctors removed a kidney in early October, Andropov never re-emerged from his lavish hospital suite. Although he would have been surrounded by crystal chandeliers and oriental carpets and served meals on delicate porcelain (made in Leningrad exclusively for the Party elite), he was none the less expected to continue to run the country by remote control. A Soviet ruler literally belongs to the state body and soul; there is no question of resigning. His leadership would be supported by a kidney dialysis machine – and by Mikhail Gorbachev, who became the only link between the half-dead Andropov and the Party elite.

'Mikhail Sergeyevich was at my father's bedside every day and actually running the economic affairs of the country,' says Igor Andropov. 'At least it was a stable year, but we only moved out of stagnation by an insignificant degree.'

By this time, Gorbachev knew absolutely everything that Yuri Andropov could tell him. 'Now we know that the economy had approximately 500 billion rubles and, roughly speaking, it was going *from* the state *to* the state – a very serious problem of corruption which preoccupied my father from 1982 to 1983,' acknowledges Igor Andropov.

On his own, scrambling for solutions, Gorbachev asked to see the Minister of Finance, Tikhonov. For three hours the two men looked through the financial records. Shaken, Gorbachev demanded that the Food Programme be expanded.

'We don't have the money,' he was told by Tikhonov (who would resign from the Communist Party in 1990).

'It doesn't matter whether we have the money or not,' retorted Gorbachev, according to his old deputy Starshikov. 'The farmers have debts they can't pay back for a hundred and twenty years, but where are we going until then? Let's start modernizing. We must *change something*.'

Each time Starshikov travelled to Moscow and saw him, Gorbachev would shake his head and moan, 'We have strayed so far, it's a pity, we must lead our country back on track.' He confided in his old deputy that there were so few good people with educated backgrounds in the Party. And then, banging the table, he would exclaim, 'We *have* to pick ourselves up!'

In February 1984, Chairman Andropov gave up the ghost. It had been almost six years since Mikhail Sergeyevich had come to Moscow, to the rouged and golden city, and been catapulted into the Circle of Kings. His discipleship was ending with the death march of this last fallen patron and protector. It was up to him.

Gorbachev was now a heartbeat away from the leadership of the world's last empire.

V

Fourth Gorbachev:

The Great Persuader

1985–1989

For the dress rehearsal of his debut on the world stage Gorbachev chose as his leading lady Margaret Thatcher – an inspired choice. The British Prime Minister was almost as Russophobic as Ronald Reagan, with whom she had a 'close relationship' that was animated (according to top White House aides) by flirtation on both sides. Gorbachev cast himself as The Other Man.

But the object of winning over the lady in this triangle was geopolitical: Gorbachev wanted to show Moscow's new 'human face' to the West, to rekindle the cold ashes of Anglo-Soviet relations, and, most difficult and important, to use the British Prime Minister as a conduit to express his deep misgivings about America's space weaponry. Gorbachev would cast himself as the prince of peace, but the fact was, he had a concrete motive of national self-interest in trying to revive disarmament negotiations. His country was enfeebling itself to stay in the arms race and uphold the figleaf that made it appear a full-scale superpower. The Soviet military machine – a separate superstate unto itself – was cannibalizing the civilian economy. Eduard Shevardnadze would later disclose, as Foreign Minister, the cost of maintaining that machine: 'Clearly if we continue the way we have gone before – that is, to spend *one-fourth* of our

budget on military expenditures . . . we will ruin the country
. . . We simply would need no defence because a ruined
country and poor people need no defence.'†

If Gorbachev could convince Thatcher of his sincerity, she
might serve as a surrogate to soften up the American
President so Gorbachev could work on the central Soviet
foreign policy goal: ridding Western Europe of US missiles
and armed forces and persuading Reagan to pull back on his
pet Star Wars programme. Despite her lifelong enmity for
everything the Soviet Union stood for, and her previous
refusal even to send her Foreign Secretary to Moscow – 'I
don't want you to have anything to do with those bloody
Russians,' she told him – Thatcher was determined to be the
first Western leader to 'break through' to the next generation
of Soviet leaders.† She had sent out feelers to Moscow nine
months earlier, after Andropov's death. His successor, the
semi-comatose Konstantin Chernenko, certainly wasn't on
her invitation list, but the Foreign Office had picked out
Gorbachev and Grigory Romanov, the Party boss of Leningrad, as the two Politburo members most likely to ascend to
the top post.

Thatcher deliberately ordered a full-dress reception for
Gorbachev, as if he were already General Secretary. But the
Iron Lady was on her guard. She had warned of a 'massive
Soviet propaganda offensive' in a speech in Washington the
previous July, coolly predicting the Soviets would soon offer
'the alluring prospect of large reductions in nuclear weapons,
of a stable peace just around the corner, if only the United
States were to give up SDI [Star Wars], if only Britain and
France were to abandon their nuclear deterrents . . . if only,
in other words, we accept the Soviet view and give up our
own'. And she had already given her heart to 'Ronnie'. Her
Russian caller would have to challenge the Great Communicator at his own game – leadership through personal
chemistry.

From the moment his Ilyushin-62 jet set down at Heath-
row, Mikhail Gorbachev challenged every stereotype of the

Russian leader. Robust, informal, he bounded from his cabin with a woman who seemed to emerge, like Eve, from his ribs. Reporters were struck by the image of the Soviet leader's wife standing shoulder to shoulder with him at the top of the ramp. The only time Soviet wives had been seen in the past was when they were trotted out under heavy black veils to sniffle over their husbands' biers. Furthermore, Raisa Gorbachev looked drop-dead chic, her black Cossack coat tasselled in fur, her hair tinted reddish-brown, her eyes as focused and steady as a movie star's before the flashing cameras.

The couple arrived at Westminster Abbey in a black Rolls-Royce flying the Soviet hammer and sickle. As they entered the cathedral's Great West door, Gorbachev remarked, 'I feel as if I've been here before.'† He and Raisa talked knowledgeably about the architecture, then the Rolls purred across Parliament Square to the Victorian Gothic Houses of Parliament, where he and his wife again showed keen interest in the history and customs of both bodies. 'Are the peers paid?' he wanted to know as they stood in the opulent House of Lords. Quips he had aplenty, both good-humoured and intimidating. In the British Museum Reading Room, where Karl Marx had researched much of *Das Kapital*, he joked, 'If people don't like Marx, they should blame the British Museum.' But when a Conservative MP assailed him on Soviet persecution of religious groups, Gorbachev shot back, 'You govern your society, let us govern ours!' and returned the insult by touching on the boil of British relations with Northern Ireland: 'you persecute entire communities, entire nationalities'.† Yet seconds after the snap of temper he would soften into affability. The intuitive precision with which he played each moment was remarkable.

'It's nice to find a Soviet politician whose face moves,' cracked a Foreign Office diplomat after watching Gorbachev in action. 'Even when he scowls, you know where you stand.'†

And, the British marvelled, he was so astonishingly, well,

like us. He set off to be fitted for conservative Savile Row suits, choosing tailors to the royal family, Gieves and Hawkes. Raisa went flying around Harrods with her American Express card and snapped up a $1,780 pair of diamond stud earrings at Cartier. She was so unhesitant about stepping forward or speaking out, no one could quite believe it was her first official foreign trip. Reporters scribbled delightedly when she tossed out heavily accented English catchphrases ('See you later, Alligator'), and she played up to the cameras, collecting bouquets from the tabloids worthy of Jackie-O: 'charming', 'vivacious', and 'the star of British television'. She accepted the praise with all the poise and confidence displayed by her husband – and then, all at once, she vanished. Alarm had been expressed back in Moscow that the couple was fostering a personality cult, a serious taboo ever since the Stalin era.

On the fourth day of his week-long visit to London, Gorbachev gave a speech free of the red meat of anti-American invective that the West had come to expect (and that he had fed to a Moscow audience just before he left home). But the crowning glory of the trip was his first meeting with Thatcher.

She had decided to receive Mr Gorbachev at Chequers because it was 'homier', but in truth the Prime Minister's country residence fairly reeks of British history. As the Gorbachevs' borrowed Rolls slipped through the ornate gate, they were given the breathtaking vista, only accorded state visitors, of the long avenue leading to the house. The stage was set for a scene worthy of Congreve – or Chekhov. From the moment of his arrival, Gorbachev's body language conveyed a 'coiled energy' of raw power.† Thatcher came forward on the steps to greet him, firmly clasped his elbow and moved him into position for photographs. And at luncheon she monopolized Mikhail Sergeyevich, the two of them falling into such deep conversation that their roast beef was finally whisked away barely touched.

After the luncheon, Raisa was left to amuse herself. Mrs

Thatcher steered Mr Gorbachev towards the panelled draw-ing-room, where a pair of armchairs had been pulled up before a roaring fire. The Soviet Ambassador was excused; the only Russian aide admitted with the two was Alexander Yakovlev, who was left on a sofa like a wallflower, com-pletely ignored for the next three and a half hours.

Thatcher's political style is not unlike Gorbachev's. She too had taught herself how to exercise power by playing different roles, switching from the soft, breathy coquette voice – the signal for her young backbenchers to leap up and joust for her favour – to her nanny voice, all-knowing, simply telling you what's good for you (rather like Raisa). But as one of her parliamentary secretaries says, 'I've never seen her thwarted on a point of fact.' She was briefed to the teeth, as always, having learned that this Gorbachev fellow could recite Push-kin (just as she could recite Kipling) and, more intriguing, that he was frankly critical of the situation in the Soviet Union.

Gorbachev held up his end of the dramatic bargain. He had, as they say in the theatre, a 'luminous presence'.† He wasn't at all knowledgeable in foreign affairs, yet to Thatcher's delight he, too, loved a flat-out debate, and showed himself to be 'the kind of person who respects you if you give as good as you get'.† Thatcher and Gorbachev represented extreme differences of view, 'but each sensed the other was person with a vision, with a clear purpose and political courage – they are both tough people', according to former American Ambassador Rozanne Ridgway.† And there was much else they had in common: both had come to power from obscurity, both had overcome serious obstacles (Thatcher's lower-middle-class background, Gorbachev's dis-graced grandfather); and both displayed utter confidence bolstered by unquenchable energy.

As Mrs Thatcher later described it, 'We went in right from the top.'† After mentioning that he spoke with the full authority of Chernenko, Gorbachev never referred to the Soviet leader again. He snapped the rubber band off his note cards and raced through a list of points, some circled or underlined, and all in his own handwriting. The Russian railed against the folly of the arms race, repeatedly attacking America's Strategic Defence Initiative, and called into question Britain's acquiescence in US nuclear missiles in Europe. Thatcher came back with her well-honed argument that nuclear weapons had kept the peace for forty years, but she softened long enough to suggest that since Reagan was starting his last term, he might be more amenable to a reduction in East–West tensions and ready to talk about disarmament. Then it was back to hot and heavy argument.

This was how Gorbachev won her over, as Thatcher herself described later: 'President Reagan and I have always been close, but right from the beginning I found it very easy to discuss and debate with President Gorbachev in a very animated way. Neither of us giving an inch.' She loved the non-stop debate with this man. He didn't need statements or briefs or even advisers. She found him prepared to question accepted policies and positions, to argue it all out dialectically. He probed what she could tell him about the West and the lessons it might have for the Soviet Union. But not even the Queen of the West could have anticipated the turn their discussions would take.

He picked her brain on how he might decentralize the Soviet economy. And finally he questioned her on how Britain let go of her colonies and exchanged the Empire for a commonwealth. He must have had, even then, a similar idea in mind for shedding the Soviet satellites in Eastern Europe as a way of rescuing his desperate economy. The decolonization of the Soviet Union – at the time it was a stunning thought!†

In his readiness to consider extensive decentralization of power Thatcher saw the first sign of change in the whole paradigm of Soviet expansionism. It was this startling shift that prompted her to put her seal of approval on Gorbachev. But no small part in their historic relationship was played by the personal chemistry between them.

'Very often the chemistry works and she likes someone in the first few minutes,' I was told by one of her ambassadors, who like many men who work for her finds Mrs Thatcher 'sexually attractive, in a sort of packaged way'. In fact, the men who surround her have all learned 'how to handle her', according to Sir Ronald Millar, an obscure British playwright who has lasted fifteen years as a speechwriter for the Iron Lady. Millar, a sort of decaffeinated Noël Coward, says, 'We treat her as a woman. You have to be attracted to her, and that is not difficult.' Mrs Thatcher has admitted it: she likes to be 'made a fuss over by a lot of chaps'.

Gorbachev quickly picked up on the way Margaret Thatcher liked to be treated. He flattered her. He quoted her speeches back to her. He sat very close – sometimes their noses almost touched. Thatcher immediately responded. She has little patience with most men, brushing them off as 'a rather idle, sleepy lot'.† But this Gorbachev was so unlike the milksops in her House of Commons, whom she could easily cow by raising her voice and playing into the stereotype of the emotional woman.

Gorbachev never deferred, not on a point of debate anyway. She could work herself into a stuttering fury, but Gorbachev still wouldn't back down, though it would always be he who broke the tension with a quip. Once in a while Thatcher would get up and toss another log on the fire. But they didn't come up for air – even for a toilet break – during the entire three and a half hours they were together. 'I have never talked to any other Soviet leader like him,' Thatcher told reporters later, an uncharacteristic tone of wonder creeping into her voice.† As one of her ambassadors told me, 'she relishes Gorbachev as an *interlocuteur valable* – one worthy of her mettle'.†

Even though she warmed to Gorbachev, Mrs Thatcher still felt it was important not to 'go soft' on the Soviets.† She discovered that the Russian had a simplistic view of the United States; he had swallowed whole the stereotype that

the American President is dictated to by the 'military–
industrial complex'. Mrs Thatcher devoted the latter part of
their talk to persuading Gorbachev that her friend 'Ronnie'
was someone he could trust.†

From that day on, in each of their half-dozen meetings
over the remainder of the decade, accounts would concentrate on the intimate nature of their relationship. Even Soviet
spokesman Gennady Gerasimov, once asked to define the
basis of their relationship, smirked and told reporters, 'Personal chemistry'.†

The Queen of the West all but knighted Mikhail Gorbachev. Her grand proclamation to the world – 'I like Mr
Gorbachev. We can do business together' – virtually clinched
his ascent to power back home. She flew off the very next
day, on 21 December 1984, for a world tour that would take
her to Washington where she gave Reagan a full report on
the new man in her life.

After her departure, her Russian visitor had his motorcade
drop him at Downing Street. He walked up the tiny cobbled
lane alone and stood staring at the famous lion's-head door
knocker, almost like a love-sick swain. No sooner were the
aides inside alerted to this very unprotocol visit than Gorbachev was making off in his limousine.† He left London
having put Anglo-Soviet relations on an entirely new footing.
Now he could go home to crow about his successful audition
as the leader most able to cultivate a new image for the Soviet
Union, especially among the Americans, whose President
had characterized the Soviet Union as the 'evil empire'.*

If Reagan was the Great Communicator, Gorbachev was
the Great Persuader. Already he had successfully established
his style as a statesman – leadership through personal
chemistry.

---

* 'Evil empire' was, to many living inside the Soviet Union, appreciated as an
accurate phrase, and taken as welcome evidence that the West cared about
their government's abuses of its people. Glasnost, when it came, was seen as
an attack on the evil empire.

Two Faces

How did a mere member of the Politburo dare to conduct himself so confidently in the West, as if he were the General Secretary himself? Gorbachev had lost the power struggle following Andropov's death: at fifty-two, the Privolnian was still regarded as too young and untested, and so Chernenko was chosen Chairman of the Party. But the death processions of the ancient guard had been coming so thick and fast – Kulakov, Suslov, Brezhnev, Kosygin, Ustinov and Andropov all had died within six years – Mikhail Sergeyevich had only to wait. Once again, his old friend Mikhailova made him laugh at the situation.

'Misha, have you bought a season ticket yet for the funerals in Red Square?'

There was another possible reason he carried himself with such assurance. It is a hypothesis of researchers at Radio Free Europe that on his deathbed Andropov had sealed a secret deal with the Old Guard: if they insisted on clinging to power a little longer by elevating the incompetent Chernenko to General Secretary, Andropov demanded they make his protégé, Mikhail Gorbachev, Second Secretary.† (It is almost impossible to verify this hypothesis, since only a few Politburo members even knew Andropov was approaching his death! But Andropov's son confirmed in an interview with me that the dying leader exacted a power-sharing arrangement for Gorbachev.)

This arrangement continued from the time Gorbachev returned home from London until Chernenko's death three months later. During the interregnum, the Second Secretary calibrated to the finest point the kinds of political deals one needed to make to retain the favour of the Party guardians. The chief agricultural post had traditionally been a political – if not literal – graveyard for the unlucky soul selected. Gorbachev had now been steward of Soviet agriculture for six years, and the result was so abysmal one commentator made this slightly hyperbolic comparison: Soviet grain failures have set a record 'unprecedented since the Biblical days of Joseph and the Pharaoh in Egypt'.†

How did Gorbachev ride out such shocking failures unscathed? He kept a selective distance from Chernenko's more glaring follies. Raisa threw a fit over Chernenko's grandiose plan to turn Russian rivers around and send them south to irrigate drought areas,† and her husband publicly criticized a revival of land-reclamation. But even though Gorbachev personally loathed Chernenko, he praised him as 'an outstanding Party leader and statesman' and made certain to cosy up to him on public occasions. Peter Peterson, an American investment banker, once watched, transfixed, while Gorbachev walked arm in arm with the doddering old stooge. 'How could he lie, peaceful and unprovocative, under Chernenko?' Peterson wondered, deciding, 'It's his amazing self-control, and part of his brilliance.'†

In fact, Gorbachev had been socialized to show respect for Party tradition, Party hierarchy, Party monopoly of power and patronage. 'He had spent his whole career relating with the right people in the Party in a client/patron relationship,' observes the son of a KGB general, poet Sergei Bobkov.† Nadezhda Mikhailova makes even plainer his early appeal to the Party apparat: 'He was respectful of authority and followed orders. They wanted to use him as a young boy who would follow their way.' The Old Guard considered Gorbachev a child of his times, and he said or did little to discourage this misconception.

But the fires in Mikhail's mind were evident to select trusted colleagues he met behind closed doors, perpetuating the pattern of his university days. In the autumn of the Chernenko interregnum Gorbachev commissioned a group of academics from Novosibirsk, a city in Siberia, to write him reports describing and criticizing conditions in the country. These young economists were technologically sophisticated and Western-oriented – back in 1981, they'd even run computer models of Reagan's economic plans. Now they came back to Gorbachev with no less than ninety papers detailing the bleak economic reality behind the fantastic fabrications in official pronouncements and statistics. It was juicy raw material for a political platform. Gorbachev invited sociologist Tatyana Zaslavskaya to tell him more in person, and the head of the Siberian economists, Professor Abel Aganbegyan, was asked to give him the equivalent of tutorials on economics.

To dramatize the inefficiency of the central bureaucratic structure for his pupil, Aganbegyan used the example of shoe production. The USSR produced over 700 million pairs of shoes a year – more than three pairs per person.† In the US only 300 million pairs of shoes were produced, but they were sufficient. Why? Because the Soviet-produced stuff was of such poor quality that people were not satisfied; the minute a shipment of foreign shoes arrived in the shops from Czechoslovakia or Finland, queues would form, while the Soviet-made shoes sat on the shelves.

There were also high-level back-room studies of Lenin's sixty-year-old New Economic Policy and a search through early revolutionary ideas. The Bolsheviks, however, hadn't had an economic plan either. If answers were lacking in Russian history, they would have to cast about in more modern socialist economies and even in the West. Close interest was shown in the Hungarian economic experiment.† Gorbachev 'was strangely fond of academics',† notes a liberal consultant to the Central Committee. 'He thought they could actually solve the problems.'† In fact, he didn't implement the academics' strategies. He had nowhere else to turn: there were no professional economists or budget specialists in the Politburo, and certainly no one with actual experience in running anything on market principles who could weed through all the data and come up with an economic plan.

But to an American agribusinessman with existing Soviet investments to protect and potential new Soviet investments to make, Gorbachev made all the welcome noises of a modern Westernized leader. Dwayne Andreas, chairman of

Archer Daniels Midland Company, first met Gorbachev in November 1984, four months before his selection as General Secretary. The Soviet Trade Minister had impressed upon Andreas that this man was the one to watch: he would completely reorganize the Soviet Union.† Andreas claims that Gorbachev threw around phrases like 'we want to unleash market forces' and 'supply and demand'. He said he wanted to borrow a number of things from capitalism to make socialism work better. He mentioned wanting freedom for 'private farming'. Andreas was stunned. 'I got the very clear impression that his role model was West Germany, where about 60 per cent of the economy is owned by the government and about 40 per cent is private.'

And those weren't Gorbachev's only radical ideas. He spoke emphatically about wanting 'freedom to worship' and freedom of the press and freedom to travel. Andreas brought up the subject of the Baltics and rumblings of discontent in the other republics. Gorbachev jumped in with his own idea: 'I believe they should all have economic autonomy. The republics should not be run from Moscow.' His eyes blazed and his voice became charged with zeal. 'They should not be run from Moscow. We must liquidate Moscow centralized planning!' Such statements would have marked him at the time as a flaming radical.†

But Gorbachev had two faces, one for export, another for domestic consumption. Only three days before his dazzling world stage debut in London, Gorbachev made a secret speech in Moscow – in the manner of Khrushchev. Speaking to an ideology conference of Party insiders on 11 December 1984, he blasted the West. The capitalist world was suffering not only from a 'general crisis' but also a 'spiritual, ideological and moral crisis', he charged, and therefore the West 'has to manoeuvre and disguise itself, resorting to wars and terror, falsification and subversion'.

On the subject of the lagging Soviet economy, however, he presented himself as favouring reform. It smacked of a campaign speech and was in fact a replica of the basic

Andropov approach. 'Deep transformation' was necessary, not only in the economy but 'in the entire system of social relations'. Yet it was unclear how far Gorbachev supported actual economic restructuring. He did not pin his hopes for such a sea change on any disturbance of the political structure, but entirely on what he called 'truly revolutionary solutions' in science and technology. The problems were 'of vast dimensions' in terms of innovation and complexity, he said, and it would be 'a titanic task' to catch up.

Despite his Partyspeak vocabulary, he none the less got across the point that the enemies were those elements in the Party and state apparat that clung to a 'conservative mode of thought' and the 'reluctance to change proven work patterns'. He even dropped in a charge of 'hypocrisy'. Calling for increased discipline of workers he said heatedly, 'there is no other way of advancing', and indeed that 'without the hard work, commitment and complete dedication of each and every one . . . it is not even possible to preserve what has been achieved'. Yet, after all this alarmist talk, he wound up with a soothing promise that he would move slowly: 'Caution must be exerted,' he said, not to 'run ahead of the times'.

That was the manifesto of Mikhail Gorbachev on 11 December 1984. The emphasis on discipline hinted that what he had in mind, initially, was some kind of controlled and limited change from above rather than a radical, decentralizing reform giving scope to market forces. None the less, the speech was remarkably outspoken for a man who was still waiting for the other shoe to drop in the power struggle over who should eventually succeed Konstantin Chernenko. As always, Gorbachev proceeded with an almost blind confidence that he could persuade those around him to follow his vision.

Fooling Everyone

On the night of 11 March 1985, when Chernenko finally died, Mikhail didn't return home until three in the morning.

'I may be offered the job,' he told Raisa.†

The two went out for a stroll to talk it over. Gorbachev later told a reunion gathering of his university classmates that he was initially hesitant, because he would no longer be able to live as he had. (His classmates murmured sceptically.)† But after the nocturnal stroll with his wife, he was resolved to accept the number-one position in the Party – certainly the dream of his whole adult life.

All the waiting, all the years in Warm Siberia, all the flattery and hypocrisy and inactivity and doublethink had made this moment possible: Mikhail Sergeyevich would at last have his day. Following Andropov's death, two key Politburo members had voted against Gorbachev: Dmitry Ustinov and Andrei Gromyko. He'd worked to make sure that didn't happen again. He had focused on Gromyko, indulging the old man in his droning reminiscences at Politburo meetings, never interrupting him, even when Gorbachev's eyes glazed over. With Chernenko 'resting' (Kremlin euphemism for dying)† much of the time, Politburo meetings had often been chaired by the dynamic number-two man, and Gromyko observed he did it 'brilliantly'. As Minister of Foreign Affairs for a quarter of a century Gromyko had been privy to international opinion of the Soviet leadership, and its rulers had embarrassed him again and again, the elevation of Chernenko being the most blatant episode in this long farce. He saw a change was inevitable, and wanted to keep his position.

In the crucial twenty-four hours following Chernenko's death, Gorbachev's courtship of Gromyko paid off. He convinced the ageing diplomat to swing the Old Guard his way. Gromyko made a nomination speech that departed from all tradition, eschewing the usual dry enumeration of Party offices the nominee had held and how well qualified he was for the post. All Gromyko could talk about were Gorbachev's wonderful personal qualities.

He told the Central Committee that Mikhail Sergeyevich

was a man of strong convictions who said what was on his mind.† Praising his analytic approach to problems as 'brilliant', he claimed that Gorbachev also 'makes generalizations and draws conclusions', apparently a thought process rare enough among the leadership to be considered noteworthy. He added that the man could even speak without notes! (This had never been seen as a virtue within the leadership circle.) The seventy-five-year-old Gromyko represented the younger man as a near-genius.† His youth, too, was a plus. He hinted that Mr Gorbachev was prepared to stand up to older leaders, perhaps a reference to Ronald Reagan.†

The phrase for which Gromyko's nomination speech has gone down in history – 'this man has a nice smile, but he has iron teeth' – never appeared in the official text published in Party journals.† It only turned up in the Western press as attributed to Gromyko, although in twenty-five years the granite-faced Soviet Foreign Minister had not been known to utter a single poetic metaphor. His words must have been heavily edited by an unseen hand. Perhaps the KGB wanted to send a message to the West: Gorbachev may be a young unknown, but don't try to push him around.

In his maiden speech as General Secretary, Gorbachev droned on forever and perpetuated the old utopian socialist fantasies. Dedicating himself to pursuit of 'the struggle for the lofty ideals and great objectives of Communism' he mouthed the empty hypocrisies all over again: 'In the last five years the Soviet people's material and spiritual standards of living have improved markedly.' He marched out phoney figures to make his point. 'According to the statistics, the real per-capita income had doubled in the USSR in the past twenty years . . . permitted about 200 million people to improve their living conditions.' He didn't mention that the state had simply printed money until the ruble became virtually worthless, its value not tied to anything, and its convertibility to any hard currency unforeseeable. Or that the priority concern of the Party was the military state. And he wound up with a whopper of a false promise, even for a politician: 'By 1990 every Soviet family will have a separate flat with all modern conveniences.'

That was the smiling Gorbachev. Next came the iron teeth. He promised to clamp down on 'workers' negligence', which he argued was the reason for the poor quality of Soviet food, footwear, clothing and housing.† Gorbachev seemed determined to implant his own work ethic in the Russian people. Discipline was his first weapon. On 15 March, front-page editorials in all of the USSR's leading daily newspapers – *Pravda*, *Izvestia*, *Trud*, *Sovietskaya Rossiya*, *Krasnaya Zvezda* – spelled out the new General Secretary's intentions to the Soviet population:

SOVIET CITIZENS TOLD TO GET DOWN TO WORK.†

To the people, Gorbachev looked like all the rest; in his bulky overcoat and bearish hat he was just another of the remote and stony pillar-faces they had seen in the line-ups on the mausoleum during monotonous Kremlin rituals. And he sounded just like Yuri Andropov. Indeed, even at the April 1985 Party Plenum, later cited as the birthplace of perestroika, Gorbachev's speeches offered only warmed-over Chernenko ideas.†

Few Soviet citizens who watched and listened to this new ruler had any expectations of positive change. And most were too weary to care. The long, futile war still dragging on in Afghanistan had demoralized the country (in much the same way as the war in Vietnam affected the US) and the Soviet economy seemed impervious to improvement.

'No one imagined Gorbachev would be such a reformer,' groaned Geidar Aliyev, the former First Secretary of the Communist Party of Azerbaijan, when corruption charges caught up with him years later.† He and other reactionaries on the Politburo came to realize that the wool had been pulled over their eyes. Even the man who was Gorbachev's staunchest supporter on the Politburo, Alexander Yakovlev, would admit to journalist Dusko Doder, 'I knew that there would be changes, but if in 1985 you had said that all these things that are now happening would happen, I'd have given my arm that that was not possible.'†

The Western press was no more prescient about Mr Gorbachev. Serge Schmemann wrote in the *New York Times* on 3 March 1985: 'Nothing he has said or done suggests any greater degree of tolerance for unorthodox thinking than any of his colleagues . . .' and predicted, 'Foreign affairs is the field of Soviet endeavor least likely to change under a new generation.'†

In Bonn, reports from returning officials described the new leader as more 'pragmatic', 'flexible' and 'informal' than his predecessors, with 'a certain flair in dealing with Western public'. Others warned against 'confusing style and substance' and said his speeches indicated that he was no less dogmatic in maintaining official orthodoxy. No one predicted that he would move towards political liberalization. Some accounts mentioned that he had at least one daughter and one granddaughter but acknowledged that nothing else was known about his family or background.†

Radio Free Europe reported that he was picking up where Andropov had left off, and had drawn up a 'check-list' of priorities: reinvigorate the stagnating Soviet economy and restructure Soviet relations with Warsaw Pact allies.†

Virtually all the initial assessments of Gorbachev turned out to be wrong.

Cork on a River

Gorbachev is a highly intelligent and prodigiously energetic person who grew up within the repressive Stalinist system, where family and ideals were repeatedly betrayed. He was aware of it, he quarrelled with it, but he did not choose to fight it and risk ending up in the gulag. He not only survived but thrived under the political reward-and-punishment system of Brezhnev's depraved indifference. So, by the time he reached the pinnacle of power, he was a product of his interaction with that system, and to some degree deformed by it.

What Gorbachev brought to that isolated and treacherous environment was an incredible mission to know, and the patience to wait for his moment. Amazingly, he emerged after twenty-five years of relative silence with romantic ideals and the creative energy to pursue them. But what happens when the man who has always worked from the inside, within a despotic system, gets to the top?

'When a person like Gorbachev sees real life and its injustice – and prepares himself to fight it at the same time he wants to participate in it – he consciously develops a talent for compromise,' says his old classmate and Komsomol colleague, Dmitry Golovanov. The savvy Muscovite says it was this very quality that swung the kingmaker, Gromyko, to Gorbachev's side when the crucial Politburo vote was taken.

Gorbachev's mission was to save the socialist system by changing it, and thereby perpetuate the 'leading role' of the Communist Party. He did not seek compromise in the sense of submission to the status quo. His was a more cunning form of compromise, whereby he set up a reactionary platform and a reform platform and walked the tightrope between them, reversing his direction in mid-air whenever he was caught in a tight spot. For such a strategy he would need a fall guy on either side of him. He brought Boris Yeltsin from Sverdlovsk to Moscow, where he set him up as Moscow Party boss and used him as his liberal counterpart, while Yegor Ligachev, a hardline First Party Secretary from Tomsk he named to the Politburo, sufficed nicely as a reactionary sop for the hardliners.

In addition to his own natural talents – personal chemistry and the power of persuasion – Gorbachev as high-wire artist relied more and more on three tactics: surprise, compromise, improvise. These became the mainstays of Gorbachev's political repertoire. They also allowed him to compose the central conflict of his life. Being by temperament a person excited by change and constantly in the process of changing himself, yet at the same a natural insider, lacking the rare courage to step outside the protective shield of the existing structure even when he knew it to be riddled with hypocrisy, Gorbachev had to keep these two opposing sides of his own nature in balance.

Any leader must hold in his mind two sets of ideas at once. The first is that he is only a *cork on the river of history*,† and most of the time he will simply be swept along on the surface by powerful forces and dark currents more complex than he will ever understand. The other idea is that *everything he does matters*, everything he says can result in change, every action he takes has a consequence. These two ideas are psychologically and intellectually contradictory, but a leader must try to keep them both in balance if he is to be effective. The thesis is nicely articulated by Peter Goldmark Jr, president of the Rockefeller Foundation, who teaches management leadership at Harvard University.

'It is important that a leader understand that there are more unruly, perverse forces at work than he will ever be able to tame, or else he will not be disciplined about picking his few critical moments' – those brief periods of relative calm when he has the possibility of influencing the course the river takes by maybe a few centimetres. 'However, to get anything done, he must believe that everything he does and says makes a difference. It's the key to motivating people to undertake something which is in their long-term best interest but which involves short-term sacrifice.'

Over time, inevitably, the second set of ideas overwhelms the first, Goldmark points out, and we see the leader believing more in himself and his own ability to persuade people, influence events and change human behaviour, and becoming less able to accept realistically where he stands in relation to the larger forces of history.†

Abroad, as a statesman, Gorbachev would ride the current of history, and have an enormous influence on the river's direction. But on the domestic front he was radicalized very slowly, incrementally, and all along, even as he mouthed wonderful new slogans, his concrete actions were rarely more than half-measures.

Building a Power Base

The newly elected Soviet leader had to turn his attention to building up his own power base. Since the Soviet system gave him neither the constitutional nor personal authority to bring his own followers into the leadership with him, the General Secretary had to accrue power by gradually pensioning off 'the old mafia of the Party apparat which might have eaten any General Secretary alive without so much as a hiccup, an operation Gorbachev handled with incredible finesse', according to Boris Yeltsin.

In July 1985 the new Chairman removed his patron, the ageing Andrei Gromyko, as Minister of Foreign Affairs and named him to the largely ceremonial Soviet presidency. In his place he put Eduard Shevardnadze, a former territorial Party boss from the republic of Georgia with a bland, hangdog face. Gorbachev and Shevardnadze had a close friendship dating back to the days when they met as teenage activists in regional Communist Youth League organizations. The Georgian had a reputation for being scrupulously honest. He had served as his republic's top police general and became famous for fighting the local mafia Party boss, exposing the underbelly of black marketeering with all the flair of a Soviet 1920s crimebuster, though not much success. He had literary interests, like Gorbachev, was non-ideological, like Gorbachev, had promoted unorthodox principles such as family farming and pay incentives to workers, like Gorbachev. And he was always asking 'Why?'

The reaction in Western capitals was 'Eduard *who*?' But

within several months this shrewd but completely inexperi-
enced figure became 'a sophisticated world statesman',
according to a senior Bush diplomat. Where the 'Grim Grom',
Gromyko, had been known in the West as 'Mr Nyet',
Shevardnadze made it his business to be 'Mr Da'. Western
officials delighted in his satiric southern humour, and his
personal modesty and integrity earned much respect for the
new team in the Kremlin. One American diplomat with
many years in Moscow went so far as to characterize the
Soviet Foreign Minister as 'following a very Christian altruis-
tic approach to the world'.

Not always. Shevardnadze, like Gorbachev, had made his
share of dissembling speeches that helped him thrive in the
moral wasteland of the Brezhnev era. (Later admitting he
had praised the Party leadership in those years, a tearful
Shevardnadze told his critics at the July 1990 Party Congress,
'This question is painful for me.')†

But like his new boss he worked non-stop, becoming
known around the Stalinist skyscraper that houses the
Foreign Ministry as the man who turns out the lights and
shuts the door. And he had no political agenda of his own.
He offered Gorbachev that most-cherished of qualities in
their uncorrupted clan: loyalty.

Anatoly Dobrynin, the former Soviet Ambassador to the
US, also had an office just down the hall from Gorbachev's,
and played an important role until his retirement in 1990.
But the other leg in Gorbachev's personal power tripod was,
of course, Yakovlev. Alexander Nikolayevich stayed behind
the scenes but was Gorbachev's co-author of the ideas of
perestroika from the start and sat at his right hand on almost
every foreign trip. An impressively educated man, Yakovlev
had an undergraduate degree from a Yaroslav institute, the
year of graduate study at Colombia University, a year of
training in social sciences at the higher Party school in 1966,
and finally earned a doctorate in historical sciences in 1967.
He was a veteran of thirteen years in the Propaganda
Department of the Central Committee, where he rose to

Acting Chief before his exile to Canada, and would later take Suslov's old post under Gorbachev. But as a power behind the Kremlin walls, Yakovlev was a totally new sort of animal.

'Yakovlev is the first member of the Soviet leadership in many years who is a real intellectual and a bold thinker,' I was told by the Leningrad political historian, Yakov Grodin. 'He was the first who spoke about common human values.' He quickly became very popular with the intelligentsia but had little influence with the worker class and was a stranger to conservatives. (He would later become the bête noire of hardliners and militant nationalists, who blamed Yakovlev for 'losing' Eastern Europe.)

One senior American diplomat in Moscow came to think of the new team as the 'Star Trek troika' – Gorbachev as Captain Kirk, the sage and driving force, Yakovlev as Dr Spock, the unemotional conceptualizer, and Shevardnadze as McCoy, the moral force. Three uncommon men, they had a 'titanic task' ahead of them.†

Man of the People

The blueprint for 'New Soviet Man', the personality implant devised after the revolution to express Marxist dogma, had conditioned people for decades to expect a 'free lunch', in exchange for submission to the Communist Party that 'gave' it to them (never calling attention to the deflated wages and repressive working conditions that created this free lunch). People had been taught *not* to buy and sell – that was 'speculation' – and to hide any nonconformist initiative or talent. In return, they never had to contend with mortgages, taxes, unemployment, rising prices or credit crunches.

'People here do not see the results of their work as a means to improve their life,' explains filmmaker Natasha Barchevsky. 'You can't buy an apartment, a house, go to a resort, there are no nice clothes, no tasty foods. So people do not know what they need money for. It's abstract.' Income levelling had become a way of life long ago. Brezhnev's grandson, Andrei, reduced the problem to a primitive epigram: 'In your country you struggle so that the poor will be rich, and in our country we struggle so the rich will be poor.' It wasn't so bad as long as everybody else was in the same boat; hence Soviets didn't try to 'keep up with the Joneses', instead, they tried to keep the Ivanovs down on their luck.

Gorbachev, in essence, had to figure out how to recondition a nation of freeloaders into wanting something badly enough to work for it. But what could he give them?

That raised the question of the second major stumbling block to reform. Given an economic system not based on the principle of supply and demand, there was no way to measure the value of goods or labour, and no way to provide concrete incentives. Forty per cent of the Soviet population – one hundred million people – lived at the poverty line and could be pushed over it with even a partial shift to a market system and the inevitable rise in prices.

Furthermore, there was the long isolation of the Soviet people from their own government and the rest of the world; they were not plugged into the information revolution, they had not travelled, they hadn't had the chance to participate as citizens in the social and political life of their nation, and their own history had been kept from them. People were alienated from the state, and Gorbachev knew it.

What was his vision when he took over? I asked his closest intellectual partner, the theoretician of perestroika, Alexander Yakovlev. 'In 1985 we looked around ourselves in a civilized manner, without any prejudice, and we began to speak of general human values as opposed to class interests.'

Thus were Gorbachev and Yakovlev in their earliest brainstorming sessions willing to depart from the first principle of dogmatic Marxism – class struggle. The atmosphere of trust between the two men had to be extraordinary, since in 1985, 'it would have been impossible to imagine that we would base our policies on universal human values rather than on class foundations', observes Dmitry Golovanov, then deputy director of the Soviet evening news programme, *Vremya*. He says the idea was proposed to Gorbachev by Yakovlev.

But what was Gorbachev's image of the Soviet Union he wanted to build? Here, Yakovlev was far more vague: 'To live simply, to do everything so people can live better and with more freedom.' The same sort of answer came from Gennady Gerasimov, Gorbachev's foreign spokesman.

'It was a very general vision – to make everybody happy,' he said, trying to keep a straight face. 'To create a society which gives equal opportunities to everybody to develop its inner potential. It's a socialist idea.'

That April, at a meeting of the Central Committee, Gorbachev discussed for the first time the idea of perestroika. As if still speaking with Andropov's voice,† he told the committee that the entire economy would have to be 'retooled', the notion of 'cost accounting' introduced and the price system made 'flexible'.† These were the cornerstones of the hybrid concept first vaguely sketched out by Andropov and echoed by Chernenko. The Party faithful seemed unimpressed. Successive leaders, one after another, had said much the same and nothing drastic had happened. And each successive leader had had his pet enemy: Stalin had the kulaks, Khrushchev had Stalinism, Andropov had corruption. Now along came Gorbachev with an attack campaign on his 'public enemy number one' – vodka.†

Drinking, for the Soviet people, was escape. Drinking, for the Soviet state, was big money. Its take from the sales of alcohol was about 50 billion rubles in 1984, double the gross receipts of the early 1970s, and representing about *one-seventh* of the planned state revenues of 366 billion rubles.† But drinking, for the corpus of the labour force, was also suicide; alcoholism took a terrible toll on health, productivity and parenting.

And so Gorbachev decreed fines and punishments for being drunk in a public place. Shops and restaurants were restricted on hours for sale of alcohol. Many distilleries were ordered to convert to producing soft drinks. The villagers in

Gorbachev's home town of Privolnoye took a vow to go dry. And the drinking age was raised from eighteen to twenty-one.

Months after these decrees, illegal distilleries were thriving, virtually every bottle of cheap cologne had disappeared from shop shelves, and sugar grew scarce enough to be rationed, since most of it was diverted for making moonshine. Waiting in line became a major occupation, cancelling out the benefits of reduced absenteeism; the lines grew long and loopy and became known as 'Gorbachev's nooses'. Fist fights broke out between customers. Already it was obvious that the obstacles facing Gorbachev had deep roots.

The new General Secretary wasted no time getting out from behind the forbidding Kremlin walls. Possibly taking his cue from the Great Communicator in Washington, he introduced a Western political ritual, streetcorner campaigning, or what became known as the 'walkabout'.

He walked among the narod, the common people, this boyish man, his brown eyes twinkling or smouldering, his passions palpable, his energy communicable, his spontaneity for a Soviet simply unbelievable. In complete contrast to his formal speeches, he didn't speak the stock pieties nor invite the usual pretences that work production and personal satisfaction were good. Quite the reverse. He pushed the narod to express their dissatisfactions, empathizing with their eternal struggle, and tried to turn these sessions into motivational homilies. Always accompanied by his wife, he argued and joked with ordinary citizens on the subjects of hard work, individual initiative and abstinence, in walkabouts from Tblisi to Vladivostok. In that rough seaport one day in 1986, the couple ignored pelting rain while they tried to explain to workers why the concept of self-accounting (which Raisa favoured) was good for them.

Shoulder to shoulder, on the same level with the crowd, Gorbachev listened while his questioner went on for several minutes about the differentiation in salaries: 'Why do

workers have to suffer such unfairness?' Finally he
interrupted 'I listened to you, now you listen to me. Don't
you want to know what the General Secretary is thinking?
Is it fair for workers to get money without producing
anything?' He continued: 'What you really need are good
shoes, decent furniture, goods. We're still paying the workers to produce goods but they're not being bought because
they don't work. Televisions don't work. And you know
how much a colour television costs. How can you live like
that?'

Pumping his fist, his body propelled forward, he acted out
their frustrations. Then the pitch: 'We need to move everybody over to self-accounting. The central government's not
going to bail them out. They've got to work from a real
budget.'

Raisa shook her head up and down vigorously.

Then Gorbachev leaned into his questioner's face, his voice
dropping to a very personal, confidential tone – a species
apart from past Soviet leaders who projected themselves as
gods – 'Look, if you think I can do it, forget it, it's not going
to happen. Everybody's got to participate.' The motivational
message boiled down to: ask not what Moscow can do for
you but what you can do for yourselves with Moscow off
your back.

Appearing in an automobile factory in Moldavia he had
the national media along with him to record a friendly
exchange with workers on what concrete measures would be
taken in the struggle against drunkenness. Raisa stood just
behind him wearing a Persian lamb fur hat, making herself a
lightning rod for the envy and frustration of average women.
Gorbachev told the workers of great strides: 'We've cut the
production of vodka by almost a half. I must tell you, where
I grew up, we decided to do away with the production of
alcohol and we did. We did away with it. Why don't you do
that here? Just close it down!'

He was smiling and informal but relentless.

'Each family must set their own rules for this sort of thing,' he exhorted. 'Then it goes to the factory, to the institutes, then to the city.' The workers looked appropriately impressed. He took his homilies in person to supermarkets, schools, hospitals, even turning up unannounced at the door of people's apartments.

The whole thrust of these little moral lectures was that of a coach. He was also the surrogate for a village preacher, and the very model of a self-improved Marxist man: 'To show the light it is necessary to burn yourself.' He actually listened to the people in the early days. It was an astonishing turnaround after a millennium of top–down relations between leader and led in Russia.

And he showed a knack for finding the humour in almost any situation. 'Let's talk straight with one another,' the Kremlin boss declared to the kolkhozniki at the Zavorovo state farm. 'I have something I want to say to you and the correspondents should communicate it to the whole country.' Gorbachev paused to give the cameramen time to set up. When the cameras were rolling, his bright brown eyes twinkled as he quipped, 'Isn't it time to bring the making of moonshine to an end?. . . These sorts of people belong back in the times when the dinosaurs lived . . .'

The farmers' chuckles were duly recorded on videotape. Farmers, auto workers, school and hospital workers, all became backdrops for lectures that would be beamed to an audience of over 100 million on the evening news show. Gorbachev was already a master of the media.

His genius for reaching out to people of all social levels won him many adherents. 'He is a very good actor,' explains Soviet sociologist Leonid Sedov. 'Even though the language he uses is the wooden language of Partyspeak, still, he knows how to talk to miners and to the intelligentsia, to Central Asian leaders and Western leaders, and there is something, well, *boyish* in his appeal.'

And after the somnambulant Brezhnev and doddering Chernenko, Gorbachev's abilities became a matter of national pride. 'Mikhail could actually talk with leaders from other countries as an equal on a wide range of topics: problems of foreign policy, disarmament, science and progress, agriculture and problems of changing the political system,' notes Mikhailova.

Making Much of the Military

When Gorbachev took power, he had the three pillars of Soviet society supporting him. The KGB was his clan, the Party was his parent, and the Soviet army, symbol and substance of Soviet power, needed him to help it modernize.

The army was staunchly behind him in the beginning, and that was useful, since 80 per cent of Soviet military men are members of the Communist Party. Because the USSR had isolated itself from the Western world, ideologically, it was shut out of world trade organizations and subjected to rigid restrictions on the purchase of commercial equipment and computers that could have any military application. Gorbachev was determined to turn this situation around. And the military, eager to modernize its systems and operations, approved – at first.

What many generals did not grasp is that this would involve a retrenchment on expansionism. Indeed, in his nomination speech Gromyko had sold Gorbachev to the Politburo on the promise that he would uphold the 'holy of holies for us all – that is, fighting for peace and maintaining our defences at the necessary level'. But, once in charge, Gorbachev didn't behave at all like previous guardians of the much-vaunted Soviet power. He had never been a soldier, he had no military orders, he never donned a uniform nor emblazoned his chest with medals, and four months after taking charge he sprang on leaders of the armed forces his plan to force retirement of top commanders.

And that was only the beginning of his heresy. Gorbachev would be the first Soviet leader to take complete and exclusive control over nuclear policy – up to then a responsibility at least shared with generals inside the military superstate.

Gorbachev diminished the political input of the military by dropping the post of Minister of Defence from the membership of his Politburo. He announced a unilateral moratorium on nuclear testing during his first summer, and followed it in rapid succession with proposals for sharp cutbacks in strategic weapons and a readiness, for the first time, to open the country to inspection of military installations for verification of disarmament agreements. Gorbachev's peace offensive was steadily eroding the pride and purpose of those with a military mindset.

But he didn't have to concern himself with unhappiness among his generals. It is a common misconception in the West that the Soviet military is a force in its own right. My Moscow connections continually stress that the army is irrelevant in the Soviet political power structure. The KGB would never allow the army to have any control over the Soviet nuclear arsenal.

In the summer of 1986, Gorbachev made two proposals that would cut to the very heart of the military's raison d'être. Conceding that their longtime enemy, China, was 'a great socialist country', he began making noises about reducing Soviet troops in Mongolia and along the vast Sino-Soviet border. And he offered to withdraw seven thousand Soviet troops from Afghanistan – the start of a pullout that would end by February 1989 in an agreement for total withdrawal.

He also made known in June 1986 his intention to convert a number of defence industries into production of consumer goods. This threatened the financial monopoly of the military: civilian factories would have to account for their costs, whereas the defence industries never had to account for the money to produce their arms. Nobody, including the government, ever knew exactly how much of the budget was spent on tanks and missiles.

'So we start to make conversion, it sounds nice,' says *Ogonyok* editor-in-chief Vitaly Korotich. 'But in Moscow we have more generals than the whole US army. They had the money in barrels, they simply grabbed it.'

There was also an outraged emotional fallout – from marshals and generals on down through the ranks – the gist of which was: we are trained to produce missiles to maintain Soviet power, now you want us to produce *table knives*! It was beneath their dignity. And the symbol of this ignominy was Raisa.

His Right Hand

In his autobiography, Boris Yeltsin opined that Gorbachev's chief problem in launching perestroika was that he was practically alone. Typical of a Soviet man to overlook the most constant and influential adviser Gorbachev has had since the start of his career – Raisa Maximovna.

Gorbachev almost never leaves home without her. She is his speech coach, his intuitive reader of people, his sounding board in all political affairs, and she is one of his three chief advisers on foreign trips, often sitting in on preliminary meetings in which the only other participants are Shevardnadze and Yakovlev. At the first Washington summit, Raisa stayed in the room with top officials perched attentively on a loveseat beside Ambassador Dobrynin while Gorbachev talked with Secretary of State George Shultz. And during their watershed trip to West Germany in spring 1989, she sat up with Gorbachev and his brains trust until four in the morning, asking questions and making comments as they digested what they had accomplished.†

At home, her word carries all the weight of a Soviet leader, although she has it transmitted through aides. A leading Soviet economist gave me a specific example of how Raisa issues her orders. She spoke in person to the chairman of a major industrial organization about hiring someone more progressive. Stunned, he told Mrs Gorbachev, 'If you want me to do this, I have to get official permission.'

'You will be called,' said Raisa imperiously.

Immediately thereafter, one of Gorbachev's aides phoned the chairman and repeated Raisa's directive.

Gorbachev's deputy in Komsomol work at the university, Lieberman, is unequivocal about the predominant position of Raisa: 'Raisa Maximovna is the alter ego of Gorbachev. She is always helping Gorbachev. He has other aides, but she is the most important – to look through the mail, to talk to him, to watch what he eats – everything.' Lieberman agrees with their other old friends who say, 'They're very much alike. Both love work.'

American journalists who have caught the couple sitting together at the Bolshoi Theatre remark at how Raisa chatters into her husband's ear all through the performance. It was startling to see her at the luncheon for American intellectuals during the Bush–Gorbachev summit in Wahsington. Positioned smack between her husband and Shevardnadze, she kept up a running-fire conversation throughout the meal – and the two men listened to *her*.

Some say she never *stops* talking. And one can sometimes see Raisa, sitting in the front row at Gorbachev's press conferences, dictating into a miniature tape recorder, presumably to criticize his performance and coach him later.†

In the Stavropol years, the Andropov family had been amazed to hear Mikhail Sergeyevich discuss his wife's research in knowledgeable detail, and even to brag about her. And Gorbachev's own brother once told journalists in Moscow that Raisa was the secret weapon that boosted Mikhail Sergeyevich to power. True or not, it takes the two of them to keep moving forward, despite the venomous feelings many Russians vent about their first Western-style First Lady.

The Gorbachevs frequently disagree, and then the arguments will blaze between them, but Gorbachev enjoys that; intellectual combat is his exercise, his only sport. Their old family friend, Grigory Gorlov, has heard them clash on international issues, as did Zdenek Mlynar when he visited them in Stavropol.

'She's really his right hand – she's involved in all of his

life,' my contact in Gorbachev's circle, Nikolai Shishlin, confirmed for me.

Raisa was a smash success in international eyes when she first stepped on to the world stage during the 1984 London trip, but for Soviet viewers she got off on the wrong foot – or rather, offended them by being underfoot at all. There had been no precedent whatsoever for a Soviet First Lady. Then along came the outspoken Raisa Maximovna, shown on TV stepping out of a Rolls-Royce in a splashy white satin ensemble and calling attention to her slender legs with four-inch-heeled gold-lamé sandals – even upstaging her husband! The British press had fallen upon her as a phenomenon, recording her every utterance, marvelling over her taste in clothes and her ability to discuss British literature, trailing her through department stores and delighting in the henpecked-husband act put on by Gorbachev when he reportedly joked, 'That woman not only costs me a lot of money but also a lot of worry.'†

Back home, Raisa Gorbachev became possibly even more threatening than perestroika. She seized the opportunity to give cultural lectures on TV; it wasn't what she said that bothered people, but the fact that she was speaking out at all. Eventually Soviet citizens would use their new freedom of expression to write letters complaining that Mrs Gorbachev keeps butting her way into places she doesn't belong.

The ultimate offence was that every time she appeared on TV, she'd be wearing a different outfit, and rumours of her wardrobe of fur coats began to sound like Imelda Marcos and her shoes.

'We women notice things that you men don't,' Soviet females wrote to newspapers. 'She changes her clothes several times a day, while we can't even afford to buy a simple dress. Where are the funds coming from to pay for this?' Journalist Arkady Vaxberg, whose newspaper is bombarded with such letters, says, 'Your man in the street is willing to accept the necessity of her presence abroad, but nobody can understand *why the hell she has to follow him around all over the country.'*

That was the one twist that took away from the otherwise gold-plated public-relations value of Gorbachev's popular walkabouts. Raisa followed her Mikhail abroad, at home, into official meetings, out on the street politicking, everywhere. Starting out three steps behind her husband, she soon worked up to walking shoulder to shoulder with him. And butting in. During a trip to the Ukraine, as Gorbachev took questions from a crowd (cleared, as always, by KGB officers) Raisa suddenly interrupted.

'Why are there only men here?' she demanded. Then she plunged into the clot of people and clamped down on the arm of a dumbfounded woman and dragged her to the front. 'Now,' she turned imperiously to her husband, 'now you can continue the conversation.'†

This sort of behaviour so violated Russian norms for wifely conduct, a whole stable of jokes began to grow up around Raisa. Mikhail and Raisa are talking. She says, 'You know, people are complaining that I travel together with you too much. Maybe I should travel alone. I'll go to the summit meeting without you.'

An old chestnut was recast for Raisa as well. On the night after he was named General Secretary, Gorbachev went to sleep with satisfaction. But he was awakened in the middle to the night by Raisa. 'Did you ever think,' she said, 'when you were a poor country boy growing up in the village, that one day you would be sleeping with the wife of the General Secretary?'

By 1989 Raisa seemed to be trying to soften her public image, but somehow she still couldn't seem to resist playing her Queen Bee role to the hilt. Pounced on during her Paris visit for lunching with Estée Lauder and hobnobbing with Yves St Laurent, from whom she accepted a silk print shawl, she cancelled her planned drop-in at Valentino's couture showroom in Rome during her husband's historic visit to the Pope and turned up instead to inaugurate an exhibition of

'Perestroika in Action'. Castigated by Soviets for wearing a fur coat in Armenia where the earthquake victims had no coats at all, this time Raisa knew exactly how to dress for an earthquake zone. She flew down to Sicily to make common cause with the residents of Messina, site of a terrible quake in the late sixties. The town hall was decked in red poinsettias for the arrival of the Red Queen – in her plain cloth coat.

'I have seen a blue sea, sun, olive groves, I have seen your crop fields and evidence of your culture – a culture of such high standing that it is seldom seen elsewhere,' she purred, holding her audience of several hundred spellbound. Her face was white as the moon in the television lights. A spidery burst of fine lines at the corners of her eyes and mouth were the only hints of her true age, fifty-two; she could have been ten years younger. Her words rolled off a voluptuous lower lip, but every utterance was held tightly in check by her thin short upper lip.

She ended up running the show. 'Izvinite!' she commanded – Excuse me! – when the ceremony was concluded before she had presented her gift, and everyone had to sit back down. Outside, the door stood open to the olive plush backseat of her limousine. Once the agents had stuffed bags marked 'Souvenir' in the trunk, she was off, hovered over by her own pair of great birds flapping their rotor blades.

One of the local big shots, Giuseppe Fermilio, whistled in amazement: 'I think *she* is the capo – Raisa, not Mikhail.'

In those rarefied circles of elite Soviet women who share a professional partnership with their husbands, Raisa is a role model and a figure of pride owing to her international celebrity. But the privileges and prestige enjoyed by Raisa are beyond even dreaming of for the vast proportion of Soviet women.† She has her own handmade Zil limousine, virtually a replica of her husband's, her own round-the-clock drivers, and her own bodyguards who prevent anyone coming close to her. Once, when a foreign journalist managed to slip through the cordon sanitaire and present her with a bunch of flowers, he tried to ask her a question about politics. Raisa cut him down with a remark that revealed her mentality as the wife of a long-time Party boss. 'If next time you bring more flowers, you'll get more information.' In fact, she has never consented to an interview.†

Although Soviets continually carp at her unnecessary snootiness, Raisa is more of a cultural and intellectual snob than she was in her college days. When she and Mikhail first lunched with Prime Minister Thatcher, he modestly referred to their status back home as 'common people'. Raisa took the royal prerogative and corrected him, 'No, you are a *lawyer*.'

During the first Washington summit Mrs Gorbachev was a guest at a luncheon given by Secretary of State Shultz. He introduced her to Teresa Heinz, a woman of polyglot European background born in Mozambique, to demonstrate America as a nation of immigrants. As the story is told in Selwa Roosevelt's book, *Keeper of the Gate*, Ms Heinz tactfully asked the Soviet First Lady about human rights; 'What do you think we can do together to find solutions to these problems?'

'What education do you have?' Raisa questioned her. Satisfied that Ms Heinz had gone to graduate school in Geneva, Mrs Gorbachev then told the table, 'I am a philosopher, and I will give you a philosophical answer. At the moment of birth, every human being has a human rights problem.'

She told Nancy Reagan the White House looked like a museum, not for human occupancy. At the National Gallery of Art in Washington she complained there were too few Russian paintings. And when she was given a private tour of the Vatican art collection in Rome, she sniffed at the Raphael Loggia. 'Oh, yes, Director Petrovsky has this Loggia at the Hermitage,' she said offhandedly, every bit the modern empress. (But she was correct. The entire room had been reproduced from a cork model and all the Raphael paintings in it copied under orders from Catherine the Great.)†

Raisa Gorbachev has been very active at home in resurrecting the artistic and cultural treasures of pre-revolutionary Russia. As the guiding light in the Cultural Foundation of the USSR, she even launched the restoration of estates belonging to czarist plutocrats, a movement that has mushroomed into an openly sentimental fascination by Soviets in how the rich lived, dressed and particularly *ate* under the czars.

But despite all her moralistic lectures, Raisa is known for doing very little to alleviate the cruel conditions that dictate the lives of most of her countrywomen – working at the heaviest menial labour and bearing children they don't want because they're denied birth control. (It has long been Soviet policy to encourage large families in order to build up the labour force.) She did attract Mikhail's attention to the shocking facts about abortion in the Soviet Union. Ninety per cent of Soviet women who become pregnant for the first time have abortions. A letter from the editor-in-chief of *Rabotnitsa* (Woman-worker), a popular woman's magazine, informed Mrs Gorbachev that abortions were being done without anaesthetic and that women often suffered infections and became sterile. Raisa showed the letter to her husband. He directed that 40 per cent of all money for medical care should be concentrated on mothers and children.†

Their beautiful daughter, Irina Viragovskaya, is a medical demographer who studies mortality at the All-Union Cardiology Studies Centre in Moscow, so she also makes her father aware of the grim prognosis for maternal and child health. Irina is married to a cardiac surgeon. Gorbachev also has two young granddaughters, whom he sees mostly on his annual holiday on the Black Sea. Paring down to shorts and a t-shirt, canvas shoes and a peaked cap, Gorbachev swings with the girls on a swinging chair and looks happily domesticated.

But the kind of influence Raisa has on him is looked upon as nothing short of insurrectionary in a Russia where wives, in history as well as now, routinely refer to their husbands as 'master'.

One incident I witnessed while I was doing research in Stavropol has stayed with me. A well-dressed couple was waiting for a lift. The woman, about thirty, looked quite attractive in her bare-shouldered sun dress, but bored and sour. Her husband's nose began to drip. He leaned down, picked up her skirt, and wiped his nose on it. His wife's sullen expression never changed.

Husband as 'master' is no joke in Russian history. Stalin had his wife murdered. He was only acting in the grand tradition of the Cossack national hero, Stepan Razin, about whom a famous song was written. It seems Razin fell in love with a beautiful princess and took her with him on his military campaigns. One night he was hugging her in his boat as it floated down the Don. But his people, even his guards, shouted from the shore that he had betrayed them by taking this woman on his campaigns; he was not a real man. Whereupon the Cossack hero 'proved his manhood' by standing up and throwing his princess into the river to drown.

Consider the reception of Raisa in this light, and the scandal it would create to hear her husband continually say, 'I'll talk to Raisa Maximovna about that, I'll ask her opinion, we decide everything together.'

Less than a year into his leadership of the country, Gorbachev was aware of the contempt ultimately expressed openly towards Raisa. Yet, like the Cossack hero, he insisted upon taking her with him on every domestic and foreign campaign.

Gorbachev told his old girlfriend, Mikhailova, 'I always ask advice from Raisa. Before I give a speech, she's my first listener.'

He calls Raisa 'my General'.

Even if the appellation was half in jest, it made Raisa a lightning rod for the resentful military. For the first time since 1973, the armed forces were not even represented by a full member on Gorbachev's Politburo.

Raisa created near-havoc when her husband took her with him aboard a nuclear submarine during their first trip to the Soviet Far East in July 1986. It was shortly after the announcement of military conversion. Raisa threw a tantrum before the boarding ceremony. The naval officers in the port of Vladivostok, their chests glittering with medals, stood in rigid salute waiting for their Party commander to board the ship. The commander of the Soviet Pacific Fleet marched forward to greet him – his uniform dripping with braid, epaulettes, stars, five tiers of medals, the whole works.

But what's this? A woman – walking up the gangway with him, in front of him, he's even letting her go first, the collar of her chic French raincoat flipped up, a silk Cardin scarf fluttering at her throat, her dainty feet perched on four-inch-high heels, the woman their chief calls his 'General' – on their nuclear sub!

'Greetings, Comrade Admiral!' Gorbachev said smartly. He was wearing a type of British squire's raincoat. He did not salute his fleet, but merely bowed his head.

The sailors, their chins stuck up in the air, looked ready to explode. Raisa stood, all five-foot-two of her, amid the grotesque missiles and grand phallic anti-aircraft guns. Behind her back, right there on Soviet TV, sailors could be seen making 'Get rid of her!' motions with their hands. Russian tradition has it that a czarina once visited a cruiser and, the next time it sailed, it sank, and everyone on board was killed. The sailors' reaction was not unlike that of Razin's guards: Gorbachev was betraying them by bringing a woman aboard a military ship, where no women were ever allowed. *Not a real man.*

The invasion of Raisa was a sign of the conversion, literally the conversion outlined by Gorbachev of defence industries into consumer-goods production, but at a deeper symbolic level it was a sign that he wanted to convert all of them, the glorious Soviet fleet, to the humiliated, degraded, demilitarized mush of a man who is under a woman's thumb. After Raisa's visit, according to a Pentagon source, the Soviet Navy decommissioned the sub.

But Gorbachev's new style of leadership – the post-heroic leader for a nuclear age who does not rely on military weapons as the source of power – would become substance as well.

THE GREAT PERSUADER ABROAD

Internationally, Mikhail Gorbachev would be an altogether new sort of leader for the nuclear age, which must of necessity redefine the concepts of hero and heroism.

Throughout history, leaders have based their authority on their military prowess. Greek and Roman societies were dominated by the warrior-leader. Alexander, riding into combat on his great steed Bucephalus, found the test of leadership not in politics but in pitched battle – storming cities at the head of his army until his body was covered with scars testifying to his courage and heroism. Similarly, Wellington rode along the ridge of battle in white buckskin breeches on his great charger Copenhagen until he had been seen by the whole British army. In the East, Genghis Khan made slaves of his soldiers and imposed his will by a ferocious alternation of brutality and reward, but his authority was always based on battlefield success.

The inner nature of heroic leadership was 'exemplary, risk-taking, physical, passionate', as military historian John Keegan points out, and the Alexandrian–Wellingtonian style of Western leadership endured well into the twentieth century.† Even in the modern era of 'total war' the leaders of democracies have made much of their personal military records. Churchill created the heroic mood that turned the tide of the Battle of Britain, not by reflecting the uncertain mood of his surroundings, but by being stubbornly resistant to it, and by creating the necessary illusion that dramatized the lives of the British people and transformed them from mundane victims into a triumphant force of history.†

Eisenhower was elevated to leadership in America as the military commander who had co-ordinated the Allied victory in Europe. Stalin made the Great Patriotic War the symbol of his godlike powers and used its ghastly toll to justify every sort of human sacrifice for a decade after the war. John Kennedy was mythologized in a book about his naval heroism, and attempted to demonstrate his mettle in the disastrous Bay of Pigs invasion. Even in this decade, Ronald Reagan invaded a tiny Caribbean island when his authority needed bolstering; Margaret Thatcher used the Falklands war to prove that a female leader could be every bit as tough as a male; and George Bush's approval ratings for his conduct of foreign policy soared for six weeks after he had dispatched the largest post-Vietnam war military deployment since 1945 to Saudi Arabia to face off Saddam Hussein.

For a man of George Bush's generation, heroic conduct in war is still the noblest sport the world affords, as I discovered when I interviewed Bush during the 1988 presidential campaign. He admitted, 'I get in trouble with my mother if I talk about being in combat,' although he clearly relished the chance to do so.† As an eighteen-year-old string bean of a suburban boy, Bush was the youngest pilot in the US Navy when he climbed into his single-engined torpedo bomber and sat on top of two thousand pounds of TNT, ready to be catapulted into the Pacific mists and moments later to meet heavy anti-aircraft fire. He did this on fifty-eight missions over the Pacific in the Second World War. 'I thought I was kind of a macho pilot,' Bush told me.†

He would later pull rank on Gorbachev face to face, when the Soviet leader suggested during their 1990 summit in Washington that the US was not sufficiently sensitive to the deaths of millions of Soviet citizens in the Second World

War. 'I reminded [Gorbachev] I was the only one of the two of us' who actually fought in that war, Bush said.† The sharp exchange epitomized the difference in generational consciousness between the two world leaders. Gorbachev, too young to join the Soviet Army, had been a civilian victim of occupation; for him, the war brought no heroism, only humiliation and the loss of adolescence.

Proud veterans or not, leaders of nuclear powers are faced with a dilemma. Aside from beating up on some tiny little country, they cannot responsibly validate their authority by resorting to the heroic props of battle that always provided legitimacy in the past. Security in a nuclear world is derived only from the certainty of retaliation, and so their hands are tied. That calls for a new form of command, characterized by Keegan as Post-Heroic Leadership: 'What is asked first of a leader in the nuclear world is that he should not act, in any traditionally heroic sense, at all . . . for all is changed, utterly changed.'†

Gorbachev does not wear the 'mask of command'. His weapons are his personality and his vision, and with them he has been remarkably effective in disarming his enemies. He has a quality of gaiety, he can banter and quip, and when the tempest swirls around him, he is deft at adopting the mask of equanimity. This display of utter confidence at the brink of chaos is another way of validating the leader's superhuman capacities, replacing the confidence of physical courage that was formerly the foundation of generals-turned-president.

But possibly the most essential quality of a post-heroic leader in the information age is theatricality. Alexander was an actor of consummate skill, and theatricality has always been an important element of any leadership style. But in a world connected by satellite, the leader who first sees how the pieces fit together and who can transmit that vision, in a calm and confident manner, over television, is the beacon that everyone wants to follow.

Gorbachev leads by virtue of both his intellectual agility

and his acting ability; he doesn't have to wear a military uniform to be seen as a powerful presence.

From 1985 to 1990, although his anti-alcohol and anti-corruption campaigns cast him in the role of top cop at home, the world stage gave him an ideal opportunity to hone that unique leadership style. As an international leader Mikhail Gorbachev had one clear long-term goal: to convince Europe to embrace the Soviet Union. He would change tactics often, sometimes even reversing himself; offer many concessions; and take some painful losses. But always he kept moving forward.

Breaking the Ice at Geneva

Pessimism hung over the preparations for the first summit meeting at Geneva in September 1985. The new Kremlin reasoning found it acceptable for Gorbachev to build up his personality cult abroad, as long as the film clips beamed back to the folks at home were carefully edited. Still, Gorbachev's advisers expected President Reagan to show contempt for the new Soviet leader's worldview; in their experience, the 'human factor' had no currency in foreign relations. Gorbachev himself told American industrialist Armand Hammer, 'Your President couldn't make peace if he wanted to. He's a prisoner of the military–industrial complex.'†

Reagan's advisers were equally apprehensive, worried about the actor–President's lackadaisical preparation for complex negotiations. They had provided him with a tutor, Suzanne Massie, author of a cultural and artistic history of Russia called *Land of the Firebird*, a book the President had been perusing with enjoyment.

At breakfast on the mornong of 19 November, literally hours away from the first face-to-face engagement between the two superpower chiefs, the members of Reagan's team were on the edge of their chairs waiting to give the President a crash briefing on strategic weapons. In strolled Ronald Reagan and began their meeting with the remark, 'I'm in the year 1830.'† Reagan was trying to understand the mentality of St Petersburg, the old czarist capital, and to understand the Russians through their history. Two members of his briefing team looked at each other and rolled their eyes. *Jesus Christ, what are we going to do now*? was the silent message, recalls former Ambassador Mark Palmer.

Palmer and the American Ambassador to Moscow, Jack Matlock, handed the President the 'talking points' they had prepared and watched him go, wringing their hands with apprehension.

But Reagan had come to Geneva with a plan. An exchange of letters with Gorbachev had suggested to the American President that he might be 'a different sort of Russian' with whom he might find common ground to reduce the risk of Armageddon.†

After the first formal meeting, Reagan suggested that he and Gorbachev take a break, as planned, and walk over to a carefully selected beach house where the two leaders could sit by the warmth of a fireplace, 'and take a few minutes to begin to know each other as human beings'. Ever the coiled spring, Gorbachev was out of his seat before Reagan finished his sentence.†

As everyone who worked with Reagan has said, it is impossible to be nervous in his presence. His hearing problems and his congenitally poor eyesight, which makes everyone look like a blur, give him a buffer against harsh realities, and probably contribute to his semi-permanently pleasant, quizzical, 'What are we doing here, folks?' look.† But in that first private exchange with Gorbachev, Reagan surprised even his own advisers. With only their interpreters present, he completely bridged the gap between himself and the Soviet leader. As reconstructed by the ambassadors, this was his pitch: 'They've given us twelve minutes. We're supposed to make the points they've prepared for us. But I want to say to you that we both, you and I, we were born in small towns that nobody ever heard of, and nobody ever expected anything out of either one of us. It's up to us now to decide whether we're going to prove the world wrong or not.'

Gorbachev sat forward eagerly. Reagan might be twenty-five years older and an American capitalist but he knew how to touch a common chord.

'Here you and I are . . . probably the only two men in the world who could bring about World War III,' Reagan continued. 'But by the same token, we may be the only two men in the world who could perhaps bring about peace in the world.'†

With great relish and obvious respect, Gorbachev said he was very pleased with this approach. They could indeed stay there as long as they wanted. Gorbachev then spoke with convincing passion, as he would later do with other American leaders, of nuclear war as a 'universal catastrophe' and 'the worst of crimes', since it could never be corrected. Forcefully, he referred to Reagan's famous statement that a 'nuclear war could never be won and must never be fought'. Then why were both nations building more and newer nuclear weapons when they could never use the old ones?†

Twenty-five minutes passed, as the anxious aides waited for their bosses to emerge. Not a word from the beach house. Don Regan, the President's compulsive Chief of Staff, ordered an assistant to break up the meeting, but nobody dared interfere. The twelve-minute break stretched into an hour and twenty minutes.† As the two men walked up the hill from their firelit sanctuary, to the amazement of their aides, each had already asked the other for another date – two more summit meetings. 'I couldn't help but think something fundamental had changed in the relationship between our two countries,' Reagan later wrote.

The success of the historic relationship between Ronald Reagan and Mikhail Gorbachev all started with that valence between their personal chemistries. It even sustained them in moments of conflict. At one point the two leaders reached an impasse. Gorbachev's exasperation had come to the boiling point.

'Let's pound our fists on the table,' he exclaimed.

'All right!' Reagan responded. And they did.†

By the third and final day Reagan thought they were in agreement on the main points. 'But Gorbachev was all over him by ten in the morning, asking more questions, he just doesn't stop,' chuckles Ambassador Palmer in recollection. 'Reagan was really exhausted.'

The two leaders were made for each other. Both excelled in negotiating through personality (although Gorbachev was eager to move on to specifics). Both believed in their own personal myths. And both expressed a romantic ideal of their homeland: Reagan was the cowboy, Gorbachev the Cossack.

By contrast, the personal chemistry between Raisa and Nancy, as the world soon learned, was poisonous. 'Mrs Reagan probably expected that Raisa would show a certain deference, and I think Raisa's mistake was that she is very sure she knows everything,' observes Palmer. Nancy herself could not believe the extent to which Raisa 'expected to be deferred to' – more than any princess, queen or first lady she had ever met.† In my view, the two women were cut from similar cloth: both possessed of grand ambitions but limited by their sex and generation to exercising power through the men they married.

Nancy Reagan, as a former movie actress, was not generous about sharing the limelight. Furthermore, during the major theatrical tableaux of summit meetings she functioned as her husband's director. 'Ronnie's main objective above all was to establish a personal working relationship with Gorbachev,' she later informed us in her book, by then free to claim credit for changing her husband's mind about Gorbachev and the evil empire.†

Raisa Gorbachev also sees herself as a partner in power with her husband, and she does not take kindly to being treated as the Wife. She expects to be listened to. 'From the moment we met . . . she never stopped talking. Or lecturing to be more accurate,' wrote Nancy Reagan; in her monologues on Russian history and the Soviet political system Raisa was fond of pointing out there were no homeless people in the Soviet Union, and 'She even lectured on the failings of the American political system.'†

In many of her subsequent conversations with Americans Raisa also showed an ingrained view of the US as the warmonger in superpower relations. A simple tour to a Swiss museum where restored watches and clocks were displayed would become a foil for her own lecture on how disarmament should be accomplished: 'This is what we should be doing, restoring things instead of destroying things.'† She was evidently a major factor in Gorbachev's decision to order conversions of certain defence industries into consumer production.

The abrasive 'Raisa factor' was subsumed, however, by Gorbachev's winning personality, and the two leaders left Geneva having struck up an unexpected glow of personal warmth. But arms control, for Reagan, remained only a talking point.

Quick-Turn Artist

Clearly charm would not be enough to blast the Americans out of their complacent stance. Gorbachev privately expressed his frustration over the Americans' slowness; they were 'choking on the endless discussions of dead issues'.†

So, after Geneva, he wasted not a moment in pushing for another meeting with his new American acquaintance. The stumbling block, as he presented it in a satellite TV broadcast to the world on 18 August, 1986, before leaving for his annual holiday on the Black Sea, was America's insistence on the escalating arms race and, more pointedly, Reagan's 'notorious SDI'. If he wanted to slow the arms race, he would have to corner Reagan tactically.

His efforts to jump-start his economy were not working, and he feared perestroika would be smothered in its infancy by his defence budget. Moreover, the Soviet military was in progressive danger of being left behind. In the West, breakthroughs in computer technology and artificial raw materials were put to 'dual' – commercial and military – use. For example, lap-top microcomputers (TAP) had become a mainstay of modern US warfare, allowing a new generation of computer-literate operators to play Napoleon by calling up map displays on a colour video monitor and adding or deleting troop movements, forests, bridges, towns, correlating intelligence data and simulating air strikes.

Traditionally, the Soviet military–space superstate was walled off from the civilian economy, and of course there was no 'private sector', no nerds in their garages dreaming up the next Yabloko (Apple) computer. And it was beginning to show. The ignominious defeat of Soviet fighter aircraft in the 1982 Israeli–Syrian encounter signalled in one startling incident how far behind Soviet electronic miniaturization had fallen. Shoulder-fired Stinger rockets given as part of Reagan's aid to anti-Soviet guerrillas in Afghanistan had again highlighted the dinosaur quality of heavy Soviet tanks and weapons.† Given the policy reversal on military spending initiated by President Carter over Afghanistan and broadened under the conservative Reagan administration, the Soviet leadership saw a real possibility that the US would outstrip its nuclear adversary with new breakthroughs in military technology.† For these reasons, Gorbachev had become obsessed with SDI.

Speaking over satellite that August, 'in particular to the government of the United States and the American people', Gorbachev accused Washington of using the arms race to 'exhaust the Soviet Union economically . . . impose hardships of all kinds on the Soviet leadership to foil its plans, including those in the social sphere and those for improving our people's living standards'. He announced that the Soviet Union would extend for another six months its unilateral moratorium on nuclear testing.

He had upped Reagan's ante. And he kept pushing for another round of nuclear poker with his American opponent.

Gorbachev got his wish two months later. He went to the mini-summit meeting in Reykjavik, Iceland in October 1986 prepared to put all the nuclear chips on the table and call Reagan's bluff. He made concessions to all the earlier major Reagan proposals and added to them 'drastic measures' – the elimination of all strategic nuclear weapons by 1996.†

It was a breathtaking gamble. And a shrewd gambit by which he sought to render Star Wars – designed as a defence against exactly that class of missiles – an anachronism.† Reagan was surprised and pleased.† He did not anticipate the 'catch', as Mrs Reagan described it: 'Gorbachev suddenly insisted on a ten-year ban on the development and testing, outside the laboratory, of our SDI. Ronnie was enraged.' The world saw the two leaders part scowling and assumed the worst.†

But close observers surmised that Gorbachev had been quite prepared to put forward a demand he knew Reagan would reject. When Reagan did reject it, the Russian had his diplomats poised to disseminate the blame for the apparent breakdown at Reykjavik on Reagan and his 'military–industrial complex'.† Then Gorbachev changed direction. In talking conceptually with Reagan, as the two leaders were discussing overall strategy on offensive nuclear weapons to the end of the century, Gorbachev had sensed that he could negotiate with this American President after all. 'Within the first two hours of dealing with him head-on, he discovered this was not a game, Reagan was serious about arms reduction,' according to a member of the US team. Gorbachev quickly adjusted his own thinking to living with SDI for the time being.† It was another example of his emulation of Lenin's policy of two steps forward, one step back. Lenin, too, had been a high-roller, making the most startling about-faces to gain and maintain power and pursue his revolution.

A senior American adviser registered amazement: 'He can turn on a dime'. Back in Moscow, the Soviet leader acted as

Gorbachev's ancestors were free Ukrainian Cossacks drawn to the southernmost wilds of Privolnoye.

1 and 2. Four-year-old Misha with maternal grandparents. *Above:* **Caked earth where the family hut stood.**

Sipa Press

Misha came to respect strong women from an early age.

3. Gorbachev with his mother, Maria Panteleyevna, next to Raisa.

He identified with the romantic Cossack ideal.
4. Teenage Misha, upper right, in Cossack cap, with comrades.

Grandfather Gorbachev was sentenced to nine years in the gulag, villagers recall.
5. *l to r*: **Nikolai Lubenko, Matilda Ignatenko, Alexander Yakovenko.**

6. Gorbachev at 17, fourth from left with classmates.

He was naturally argumentative.

7. Grigory Gorlov, family friend and district Party official, with author in Privolnoye.

8. The girl next door, Alexandrovna Yakovenko, in Privolnoye.

Theirs was a generation of tragic fate.

9. Nadezhda Mikhailova, Gorbachev's first girlfriend.
10. Gorbachev, age 20.
11. Reunion of Law School Class of '55.

He lived a double life at Moscow State University.

12. Engagement of Mikhail Gorbachev and Raisa Titorenko, 1950.
13. Natasha Rimashevska today, member of Misha's study group.
14. Nadezhda Mikhailova today, keeps in close touch.

'We worshipped Stalin as a god, an icon,'
says Mikhailova.

15. Stalin giving a radio address.

**16. Workers in Moscow's 'Dynamo' auto factory
listening to announcement of Stalin's death.**

The peasant from Privolnoye pleased, charmed, and mirrored his patrons.

Dmitri Baltermants

Dmitri Baltermants

17. *left* **Mikhail Suslov, right, with Nikita Khrushchev, 1955.**

18. At Suslov's funeral Brezhnev marches in front row centre, Gorbachev right behind him next to his patron, Andropov.

Brezhnev spawned a system of colossally casual corruption.

Dmitri Baltermants

19. Brezhnev dwarfed by Lenin, 1973.

20. Brezhnev kisses Rashidov, crime boss of Uzbekistan.

21. Gorbachev positions himself between the dying Brezhnev, centre, and his successor, Chernenko, to right, Andropov, last on right.

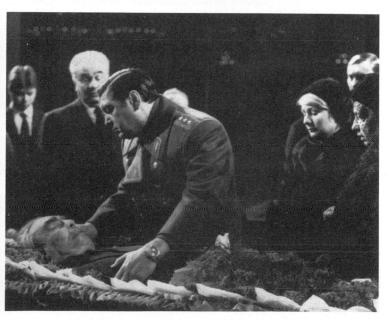

22. Malenkov pretends grief over Brezhnev's bier.

23. *Raisa Gorbachev sees herself as a partner in power.*

24. *The relationship between Gorbachev and Thatcher became 'passionate'.*

Co-opting the church became part of the campaign to legitimize his autocracy.

25 & 26. Soviet soldiers explore the monastery at Zagorsk.

He was expected now to play by democracy's rules.

27 & 28. Polling place laid out on the American model.

Mafia was the force controlling the scarcity.

29. Line outside my neighbourhood state store. 30. The 'market'.

Survivors of the Gorbachev era spoke of being 'perestroyed'.

31. Boris Gratchevsky and son with writer Natalya Daryalova.

32. Novelist Anatoly Pristavkin and wife Marina.

34 & 35. *My neighbours turned off their TV in disgust as Gorbachev organized his personal dictatorship.*

35. The apparition of McDonald's and the head of Lenin both loom over Gorbachev's Presidential Congress.

The tragedy of Gorbachev is he cannot finish his revolution.

his own spin doctor by presenting his case for 'truly large-scale proposals' to his people.

When the dust cleared, a quantum leap had been taken in the whole approach to disarmament: 'It was the first time in nuclear history that the two superpowers had talked about reducing, not just limiting, nuclear arms,' says Assistant Secretary of State Rozanne Ridgway, a member of the US summit working group. At Reykjavik the centrepiece of the historic agreement on INF (intermediate-range nuclear forces) went into draft form and the details were in place for the conventional-force reductions of today.†

How to Win Friends and Intimidate People

Gorbachev's leadership style naturally had flaws; most notably his tendencies to be overbearing and self-righteous. That same year, he had another confrontational meeting with a senior American political figure, Senator Edward Kennedy. After Kennedy left Moscow, an adviser suggested that Gorbachev might find it useful to read Dale Carnegie's book *How to Win Friends and Influence People*. (Most probably he had already read it; he subscribed to the Siberian *ECO* magazine, which had first published Carnegie's book in the mid-1970s.) A few weeks later a visitor noted that Gorbachev refrained from starting a meeting with the usual long lecture and made even more of an effort to ask his visitor's views in a flattering way.† Gorbachev never lets up on his lifelong efforts at self-improvement.

By January 1987, when he received a delegation of heavyweight American foreign-policy players, Gorbachev was a politician at the top of his game. Restless, driven, tough, he kicked off the three-hour session by throwing a 'zinger' as each official in the group, which was sponsored by the Council on Foreign Relations.†

First, he threw Henry Kissinger off balance with the insinuation that this year's anti-détente Kissinger was a different animal from the pro-détente Kissinger of 1972. Then, a razor-sharp edge of sarcasm in his voice, he 'thanked' former Secretary of State Cyrus Vance for the Carter grain embargo of 1980 and for the continuing US refusal to allow transfers of computer technology. It had forced his country to diversify its grain supply sources, he said, and to 'close the gap' in development of computer hard and software technology. By now, he claimed, the USSR was the equal of the West, at least in the defence area, even if they still lacked the ability to mass-produce these technologies. After confronting another Carter-era official, Harold Brown, the well-prepared provocateur leaned towards Jeane Kirkpatrick.

'And you, Mrs Kirkpatrick, didn't help matters with your "evil empire" speeches at the UN.'

The starchy conservative grande dame suggested that the General Secretary re-examine the record: her critical speeches had been prompted by the slashing attacks on US 'global imperialism' from then-Foreign Secretary Gromyko. But after three years, she said, the Soviet UN Ambassador and she had agreed to end this silly game.

With a rumble of laughter at this feisty riposte, Gorbachev leaned back, admitting he had not been fully informed on the point. 'The Soviet Union cannot correctly claim to be the possessor of all wisdom,' he nodded.

Then he was back on the attack again, demanding, 'Does President Reagan have the power to enter into an arms-control agreement with the Soviet Union, in light of the Iran controversy in Washington?'

After an hour of this, banker Peter Peterson was beginning to sweat. In thrall to the power of Gorbachev's personality, he scrawled a note and passed it to Cy Vance: 'Is this as tough a meeting as it seems to me?' Vance wrote back, 'Very much so.' So Peterson screwed up his courage and tried to change the direction of the discussion. 'Twenty years from now, how will history judge our two countries? Is it possible that other far nimbler countries, that are more concerned with far-sighted choices about their long-term economic destinies, will make our two countries look like a couple of dinosaurs circling each other in the sand . . .?'

BAM! Gorbachev brought his fist down on the table and smiled. 'Now *that's* a question worth discussing!' he exclaimed. All at once, the provocateur turned charming, witty, warm, engaging, and in no time he had even Jeane Kirkpatrick purring like a house cat.† His agile leap from confrontation to congeniality removed some of the sting of the first hour, says Peterson, but he had succeeded in conveying his most important message: 'I am in command.'

Aware that he was witnessing a great performance, Peterson was none the less flattered and enormously impressed: 'You have the sense that this man is in control of himself at all times. A man of magnificent internal discipline. And he controls everything around him – when, how, tone, agenda. He is a luminous presence, on a stage, even when he is not saying anything.'

Mikhail the Great

The relationship between the Soviet Union and the United States has always had a Romeo and Juliet quality; time and again the two powers have become infatuated with each other, until, precipitously, some breach of faith produces injured pride, self-righteous posturing, painful rejection, and it all ends badly.

Gorbachev, however, was more deeply attracted to the West than any previous Soviet leader. 'I think he's very much like Peter the Great – the same desire to benefit from the West, to be part of the West,' observed the former American Ambassador to Hungary.† By 1985, in the entire history of post-war relations, there had been only three summit meetings between heads of the Soviet Union and the United States.† Gorbachev would accelerate the tempo to seven summits in the space of the next five years. He would see Britain's Prime Minister just as often and make frequent trips to Germany and France.

Placing Gorbachev against the background of Russian history, Yakov Grodin, a scholar of eighteenth- and nineteenth-century political history, starts with the fact that 'He, like many others of our leaders, was ignorant in the past of Western political structures. But when he went to the West, since he is a very lively person and very impressionable, he liked them better than what he saw around him.' The scholar agrees there is a strong psychological parallel between Gorbachev and Peter the Great.

'Gorbachev sees a free Russia of European or even American style,' suggests Dmitry Barchevsky, the Soviet filmmaker who has Gorbachev's blessing to make a documentary about his revolution. 'He's seeking equality in wealth, equality in the good life. Before, we were equal in our poverty. It was good to be poor.'

The vision that is conjured up after talking to other Gorbachev confidants confirms this blend of rather vague, even utopian dreams taken from the Bolshevik revolution and a bold pastiche of the best ideas and institutions he has encountered on his many travels through Western democracies.

Gorbachev does not discourage comparisons between himself and Peter the Great. His yearning for the Soviet Union to be embraced as a part of Europe is plain. Raisa shares his Western orientation, and, as honorary chairman of the board of the Cultural Foundation of the USSR, she is devoted to recovering lost cultural artefacts from Russia's Europeanized past. Both Gorbachevs have been known to slip and identify themselves as 'Russian' – favouring their ethnic European identity – rather than by their politically correct identity as 'Soviet'. When Raisa was received by the Pope, for instance, Gorbachev introduced her, saying, 'This is the Holy Father.' Raisa, who made bold to wear bright Marxist red, presented herself in the manner of Catherine the Great: 'I am Raisa Maximovna, from *Russia*.'

Just as he'd unabashedly soaked up culture at Moscow State University from Mikhailova and Raisa, Mikhail Sergeyevich was not the least bit inhibited about reaching out for help to the West. And he would learn a great deal from his increasingly close relationship with Margaret Thatcher.

Thatcher's Tutorial

Gorbachev was searching for a formula to promote the dismantling of NATO in March 1987, when Margaret Thatcher arrived in Moscow for what turned out to be a mind-bending experience for both leaders. Although Thatcher had read and annotated every one of Gorbachev's interminable policy speeches, she was 'more nervous than I've ever been'.

Nervous or not, the Prime Minister looked ravishing as she stepped off the plane. Aquascutum had been commissioned to revamp her wardrobe completely: her hems had risen, her fine legs were shown off by spiky heels, and her English-rose complexion was richly framed by a Russian sable hat. (Her husband Denis had stayed behind. 'Pinkos', he is fond of telling friends, are not his cup of tea.)

The thirteen-hour tête-à-tête between the Iron Lady of capitalism and the iron-toothed man of Communism was unprecedented – the longest time Mrs Thatcher had ever spent with any head of state. As she explained, 'There are no what I call "diplomatic niceties" when I talk to Mr Gorbachev. We get right down to the nitty-gritty.'†

The two leaders clashed over the denuclearization of Europe. Assuming the combative pose that has won her the nickname 'Attila the Hen', Thatcher roundly dismissed the notion that Britain would join the United States in any nuclear-disarmament agreement.† Gorbachev needled her, raising the spectre of the public-relations contest to come. 'Let us assume that we begin the process of disarmament, remove medium-range missiles from Europe and reduce strategic offensive weapons by fifty per cent . . . while you continue building up your forces,' he proposed. 'Have you ever thought what you will look like in the eyes of the world public opinion?'†

Thatcher said she was sure Reagan would listen to her. That set Gorbachev off on Reagan and his frustration over their first two meetings. 'He doesn't know policy details!'† the Soviet leader complained, throwing up his hands. Mrs Thatcher could sympathize. Instead of reading his briefing books in preparation for the 1983 economic summit in Williamsburg, Reagan had watched *The Sound of Music* on TV. Thatcher, who had been fully armed with figures, later clucked to an adviser, 'You know, it's a pity about Ronnie – he doesn't understand economics at all.'† She and Gorbachev could share a laugh on that score.

(Although it should be said that in the end Reagan proved a better short-term economic strategist than either of the two others. His economy grew for seventy-four months, while Thatcher's economy ran into dismal inflation and Gorbachev's into disaster.)

The sessions between Maggie and Misha were so intense, they could scarcely tear themselves away for meal breaks or entertainment. They referred to each other always by their formal titles, but the subtext was very intimate. Locked in whispered conversation at a Kremlin banquet,† the Prime Minister and the General Secretary ignored the roomful of guests and pecked at their food, heads together, arms touching, eyes only for each other. On their night out at the Bolshoi they held up the second act of *Swan Lake* for twenty minutes, debating methods of grain silage. When they finally re-entered their box, Thatcher sat, resplendent in black lace, between Raisa and Mikhail. Raisa, highly displeased, was bent on elbowing her way into their discussions of Western nuclear policy.

'Not what you'd call a blushing violet, is she?' was Thatcher's acid assessment of Mrs Gorbachev.†

On her last night in Moscow, after an intimate family farewell dinner, Thatcher and Gorbachev ended up on a sofa drinking brandy and telling stories before another roaring fire. Her London intimates say Mrs Thatcher is at her best after midnight, and a couple of whiskies, when she lapses into her silky, sophisticated, woman-of-the-world voice, and bares her occasionally raunchy sense of humour.† With Mr Gorbachev, she felt comfortable enought to slip off her shoes and, as is her habit when her ear lobes start burning, to pull off her earrings.†

Over brandy, he paid her the highest compliment. He told her how much he valued her views and interpretations; he would be very grateful, given her special relationship with Reagan, if the Prime Minister would pass on his views to Washington.† He won her over, according to one of her ambassadors, by revealing his problems 'in a very human way'. He implied that he wanted to dismantle his Old Guard Communist Party apparat,† and the British leader saw in his troubles with the Party some parallels to her own problems with socialist trade unions. They could speak as revolutionaries, both determined to turn their societies upside down, both naming new systems of economic order (Thatcherism and perestroika). And she could teach him a thing or two.

The similarity in their temperaments, charged with the tantalizing difference in their sex, made each of them inflate the international importance of the other. For Thatcher, it was the most 'fascinating and invigorating' visit abroad in her eight years as Prime Minister.† Certainly the result would be astonishing: a new peace formula to replace MAD – mutual assured destruction.

'Thanks to these very warm and sincere meetings, we're growing closer and closer in our positions,' Mrs Thatcher later gushed on Soviet TV.† She saw her role with Gorbachev as his friend and tutor from the West. 'Anything we can do to go and teach them how to make decisions and how to do their own management . . . they come to England, they look at some of our great retail organizations, at the factories . . . et cetera,' she told David Frost in a TV interview. In early

1989, I asked Mrs Thatcher if she had given Mr Gorbachev a
'Thatcherism implant'.

She nodded, rather pleased with herself. 'I'm delighted
that he's realized that Communism does not give a higher
standard of living – it's only if you get more freedom that
you will get the enterprise, the initiative, to build up something on your own.'

Margaret Thatcher's belief that she was transforming Gorbachev into some sort of Soviet Malcolm Forbes was overly
optimistic. But there was at least one point on which she
profoundly influenced his thinking: how to Europeanize the
Soviet Union.

He argued forcefully that Russians are Europeans.
Thatcher resisted. 'Old Russia was united with Europe by
Christianity,' he pointed out;† the Ukrainians (his people),
the Russians, the Byelorussians, Moldavians, Lithuanians
and others had all made great contributions to European
history. He resented the attempt by some in the West to
'exclude' the Soviet Union from Europe.

Like lightning, Thatcher shot back that he should blame
Stalin's pact with Hitler for their exclusion, not the West. She
insisted that Britain and France had had to fight Hitler
'single-handed' because of the Nazi–Soviet pact, which kept
the Soviets out of the war until 1941.†

'Who handed over Czechoslovakia to the Nazis? Your
Chamberlain,'† Gorbachev thundered back. The British
rulers had had only one thing on their minds, he charged:
how to turn Hitler against the Soviet Union and crush
Communism.

Nose to nose, over a tiny table in an echoing Kremlin hall,
they shouted at each other, though, according to Thatcher's
aide Charles Powell, who was taking notes, the discussion
would shift just as abruptly to sunny agreement.†

Gorbachev explored his New Thinking on Europe with his
interlocutrice valable. He told her of his lively conversation
with President Mitterrand in 1985, during which he had first
picked up Charles de Gaulle's concept of a new Europe

stretching from 'the Atlantic to the Urals'. It had suggested to him a 'greater degree of integration'. Intense, Thatcher reminded Gorbachev there could hardly be an integration while his Eastern bloc was still barricaded behind the Brezhnev doctrine – under which the Russians claimed the right to crack down militarily if their allies needed to be 'taught how to live'.

Gorbachev condemned the Brezhnev doctrine. The iron curtain was 'archaic'. It was artificial to have a bloc-to-bloc confrontation in their, how to say it, their common European civilization, and suddenly – out of the tension and extraordinary personal chemistry – 'at the right moment this expression sprang from my tongue, by itself', Gorbachev wrote later. *'Europe is our common home.'*†

He hinted to Thatcher that his attitude towards Eastern Europe would be different and more liberal. They were both highly stimulated by this discussion, and Gorbachev took note of her warm response. 'I had been looking for such a formula for a long time,' he would dictate a few months later. It was a watershed. The expression, he admitted, 'came to have a life of its own'. The encounter with Thatcher had helped him to clarify his own ideas.

He lost no time moving forward. As early as April 1987, a month after that marathon debate, Gorbachev began to enunciate his vision for the decomposition of the outer Soviet Empire. Travelling to Czechoslovakia, choosing Prague because it lies exactly at the geographical centre of Europe, he announced his 'European theme' in a public address. Although the West paid little attention, Gorbachev began to suggest that each country in the Eastern bloc was free to go its own way. He had sympathized with the aims of the 1967 Prague Spring, and perhaps he felt a special shame about the Soviet crackdown that had resulted in the arrest and exile of his old friend Zdenek Mlynar. But the most pressing reason for the Prague statement was not social justice. He was eager to shift the dead weight of the dependent economies in his Eastern bloc.

Rejecting the isolated and expansionist view of his predecessors, he came to the concept of a 'contradictory but interconnected' world.† Prepared to remove the old ideological barriers between Russia and the West, he began taking actions to make his country compatible with the 'civilized nations', as he called the Atlantic club of democracies. He wanted admission to that club.

Both Thatcher and Reagan would exact a price from him. The Iron Lady's main concern was military security; she saw herself as the defender of the Atlantic alliance. Reagan's concerns were more idealistic and ideological; he wanted Gorbachev to let his people have democracy.

That December, on his way to Washington, where he and President Reagan would sign the historic INF treaty, Gorbachev made a stopover at the Brize Norton air base in Britain to see his favourite world leader. Thatcher waited in the sub-freezing wind on the tarmac without a coat or hat and in her highest heels – looking rather like Ingrid Bergman in *Casablanca* – to welcome him. They ducked into the back of her Daimler limousine and immediately began gesturing animatedly; in no time they were back where they had left off in Moscow eight months before.†

She was 'rock solid' on the need for effective verification before any signing of an arms-control agreement. It disturbed her that nobody was focusing on the Soviets' massive advantage in ground forces and chemical-weapons stocks. And she was alarmed that NATO seemed to have no resistance to Gorbachev's appeal. But she was reassured that her 'special relationship' with the General Secretary still worked. She dispatched him with her blessing (and sent a note to Reagan).

Thatcher could congratulate herself on being, 'in a very real sense, godmother to the Reagan–Gorbachev relationship'.† It was a role she relished. But, after seeing her Russian visitor off, she had second thoughts. Gorbachev might have been too seductive in creating an 'image of reasonableness', she mused. 'The Russian bear was easier to deal with when it looked like a bear.'†

Summiteer Extraordinaire

Gorbachev entered the White House cabinet room on 7 December 1987, determined to take charge. Before Reagan's team had even settled into their chairs Gorbachev had his leather notebook open and began firing off his handwritten points one after another, almost without pause. He kept up this electrifying oratorical onslaught for a full twenty minutes.

'Gorbachev had the clear initiative,' recounts Senator Howard Baker, who was then Reagan's Chief of Staff. 'I got a little concerned. Reagan appeared passive.'

Finally, the American actor interrupted. 'Mr General Secretary, I heard a story the other day . . .'

'I have to confess, I froze in my seat,' admits Baker. 'There were some Ronald Reagan Russian stories that I was not anxious for him to tell the leader of the Soviet Union.' But this was a basically harmless shaggy-dog story. Gorbachev let out a deep belly laugh, and Baker knew the world was safe for one more day.† Affirmed in his strong suit, Reagan then began reading from his prepared three-by-five cards and asserting his own agenda. Observers noted that, as in London, the Soviet leader didn't turn to his aides to ask for advice or instruction, not even once, during the exchange that followed.

Reagan repeatedly called the two countries 'adversaries'. Gorbachev kept romancing the Americans by referring to them as 'our partners'. Reagan was always on guard around Gorbachev, according to an intelligence analyst who sat in on their summit meetings – 'Reagan was a good actor but basically he had one act,' while Gorbachev shifts masks and tone like a consummate actor. And Gorbachev was equally versatile on substance. His intellectual agility led Baker to conclude, 'He's a master of give and take.'

At this, their third summit engagement, the two leaders agreed to eliminate two entire categories of nuclear weapons. The President's advisers, in disagreement over how to put

the right spin on the signing of the INF treaty to make
Americans appreciate this historic breakthrough, suddenly
realized that their work was being done for them. And being
done by Mikhail Gorbachev, in words that could have been
lifted straight out of a dozen Reagan speeches. The Soviet
leader cast the INF treaty as 'an unprecedented step in the
history of the nuclear age . . . the two militarily and strategi-
cally greatest powers have assumed an obligation to actually
destroy a portion of their nuclear weapons'.

Behind the nuclear newsmaker scenes, however, a psychological battle of wills was taking place. In their private
sessions, Reagan was acting like the young Russian's American uncle. (He repeatedly called the Soviet leader Mikhail,
although he never did get Gorbachev to refer to him as Ron.)
'There was enough of an age difference that it was almost
avuncular and instructive,' recounts Ambassador Ridgway.
Gorbachev's desire to be admitted to the Atlantic club was
palpable, but Reagan kept telling him that he couldn't have
an improved relationship with the United States if he did not
accommodate Western views on human rights. Reagan
always took the same theme, as paraphrased by Ambassador
Ridgway: 'If you want to be a successful society, then look at
these elements. It's human rights, it's openness, it's the right
to travel and share ideas.' Then the President would offer to
make available the names of thousands of refuseniks.

'By the way, it's in your own interest,' Reagan would wind
up his Uncle Sam pep talks, 'because successful societies are
open societies.' If the Soviet leader wanted to belong to the
club of Atlantic nations, the price would be 'a different kind
of society and different principles'.†

Gorbachev didn't like a lot of what he heard. He made a
fierce effort to control his temper during these tutorials from
Reagan, but he blew up repeatedly at Secretary of State
George Shultz.

'I've listened to enough of this, now you can listen to what
I think!' he shouted. And from then on, whenever he sensed

that the American Secretary of State was being condescending towards the Soviet Union, he'd have another 'showtime outburst', as the US negotiating team came to nickname his flashes of anger. He wanted Shultz to know that the Secretary of State wasn't of the same rank and that Gorbachev wasn't afraid of him.†

Yet even as he boiled over at the criticism, Gorbachev instructed his summit team to sign a statement 'in the back room', says Ambassador Ridgway. Never publicly issued, that statement committed the USSR for the first time to human rights reforms. It was the first of a stunning series of liberalizations Gorbachev would announce over the next year.

On his final, frenzied day in Washington, Gorbachev seemed to be everywhere at once – stroking members of Congress, gladhanding passersby, holding the world press at bay – and continuing to dazzle the normally blasé inside-the-beltway habitués of a city accustomed to foreign dignitaries. 'It's like seeing Lenin or Stalin,' gasped a set of Gorby groupies posted with binoculars on 16th Street. Then, en route to the White House for his final meeting with the President, Gorbachev's limousine suddenly put down mean screech marks.

'He's out!' a police officer hollered. 'He's shaking hands!'

Startled Secret Service men leaped up on newspaper vending machines to protect him. KGB agents growled at the crowd, 'Keep your hands out of your pockets!' Gorbachev exuded an aerosol of charm as he worked the crowd along Connecticut Avenue. An expense-account crowd rushed out on the balcony of the famed Duke Zeibert's restaurant and Gorbachev waved up at them, while the street crowd applauded and the television cameras whirred. That was the footage to reinforce his authority back home. Next, he let Vice President George Bush, then a presidential candidate, rub shoulders with him as the two posed, waving, like a triumphant campaign ticket.

Gorbachev kept the American commander in chief waiting

for an hour and a half. 'I thought you'd gone home,' Reagan quipped when the Soviet leader finally showed up at the White House.†

Making 'Em Jump

For all his eagerness to be accepted by Western leaders, Gorbachev was a formidable negotiator, alternately menacing and charming. There was no telling which style you were going to get from moment to moment, and this was the downside of doing a summit meeting with Mikhail Gorbachev. Reagan's jittery aides could be sure that at the last moment of the last meeting – it happened at every Reagan–Gorbachev summit – the Soviet leader would throw a spanner into the works. It was like tiptoeing around an unexploded firecracker.

During the 1987 summit, Gorbachev sprang his surprise at the end of the departure luncheon in the White House family dining-room. With the main course already cleared away, and no sign of Secretary Shultz or Minister Shevardnadze (not to mention the unexplained absence of Nancy and Raisa), Chief of Staff Baker began to twitch. He sent word to the cabinet room, where, it was assumed, the two teams needed only to sign off on the departure statement already buttoned up by their bosses.

'The Soviets have injected a new element,' said the written note sent back by Shultz.

Dessert was served. Still no sign of the statement that was scheduled to be read in ten minutes on the South Lawn. Baker fired off another note: 'I've got a perplexed President on my hands and a soon-to-be-angry General Secretary. What's happening?'

Shultz appealed for more time. Nonplussed, Baker covered the delay by suggesting in his soothing Tennessee drawl that the superpower leaders take coffee in the Red Room. President Reagan looked startled, Gorbachev puzzled.

'About that time, just for fun, as if we didn't have enough

problems, Nancy and Raisa walked in,' recounts Baker. Raisa had stood Nancy up for a tea at three, then kept stopping to talk to the press, and finally, upon entering the White House, made a derogatory remark about it seeming 'like a museum'. When the women finally appeared, the two superpower leaders hammed it up, looking down at their watches in unison and back at their wives with mock frowns.

By that time, there were only seconds left before the scheduled departure ceremony. Finally Shultz appeared. The negotiation had broken down over a comma, but a critical comma; depending on where the punctuation went, the ABM treaty would or would not permit testing in space for SDI. 'Gorbachev had apparently left word to negotiate for that one last item,' says Baker. As time ran out, and everyone's eyeballs began to pop, a 'paste-over' job left the question of SDI for the future.†

Gorbachev pulled the same stunt five months later in Moscow, over another issue that Secretary Shultz would only identify as 'significant'. In virtually the last seconds of the summit, as the principals stood up from the table after the final meal, Gorbachev threw a zinger at Reagan.

'Your people had agreed to this, Mr President. Why don't you agree to this?' Gorbachev's tone was petulant and his lips tightened menacingly. Reagan just stared at him, silent, for several seconds. Then he said, calmly, 'I don't believe we've agreed to that.'

A hurried huddle took place, right there, over the half-sipped coffee. After several minutes it was clear the American leader was not going to concede the point. Turning away in an attitude of disgust, Gorbachev snapped, 'Oh, all right.' But his indignation was well modulated.

'I have never seen Gorbachev *unintentionally* angry,' a senior intelligence analyst told me.

In fact, Gorbachev was often openly angry, especially when his opponent had no political power but a superior moral argument. He was often publicly angry with Sakharov, for instance. In the summer of 1988, during a televised meeting about the disputed territory of Nagorno-Karabakh, Gorbachev behaved shamefully towards the Armenian representatives, acting like an angry dictator. His anger seemed to break surface as soon as he was without rational arguments. Then he would become quickly hostile and verbally abusive.

After four days of straining to mask his exasperation with Reagan's lackadaisical approach, Gorbachev's patience had worn thin. Close observers say he regarded the American leader as a man with little command of detail. He was also furious that Reagan was cluttering the week with 'all sorts of propaganda gambits', instead of getting down to business.†

In his public appearance with Reagan, however, he let none of that show. As everyone who meets Gorbachev relates, he is like quicksilver in adjusting his personal chemistry to that of others. Madame Thatcher liked tempestuous debate, he gave her debate; if President Reagan liked happy talk, he'd give him happy talk. At the press conference just before their last session, he was all smiles and conviviality. Wearing a light Palm Beach-style suit, 'Mikhail' sat with his legs crossed in a relaxed, almost Californian style, close to Ron. So close, their elbows touched. Everything about his body language and his banter reflected Reagan's laid-back style.

Gorbachev announced that they had had a very substantial conversation on conventional arms. Reagan said he looked forward to real progress. '*If* the President takes advantage of the time left,' needled Gorbachev, but he looked endearingly at Reagan and chuckled as he said it. The elderly leader soaked it up. He began to reminisce about the good old times, at Geneva, when they'd agreed to pound their fists on the table. He looked pleased with himself. Gorbachev seized the mood and ran with it: 'Maybe it's again time to pound the fists on the table!' Reagan nodded: 'That's the way it is!'

Winking and smirking, the two nuclear potentates congratulated themselves on their wonderful relationship. By that night, Mikhail Gorbachev, who has spent a lifetime mirroring the people in power he wants to persuade, had Ronald Reagan eating out of his hand. Speaking at the farewell dinner in the Kremlin he fed back to the actor one of his own best lines: 'A nuclear war can never be won and must never be fought.' Looking into Reagan's eyes, Gorbachev said, 'And this is the understanding we have come to together.'

Admission to the Club

All this time the Soviet leader had been sponging up ideas and concepts from his Western counterparts. He became increasingly artful in his use of Western terms calculated to press the right emotional buttons, and raided quotations from America's greatest leaders in order to stake out the moral high ground for the Soviet Union.

For instance, in making a plea for a trade pact with the US, he lifted from Roosevelt's 'four freedoms' declaration of 1941, and said that, 'while liberating the world from fear, we are making steps toward a new world'.† Addressing people of both superpowers on the subject of nuclear disarmament, he rearranged Roosevelt's celebrated Depression-era aphorism – 'We have nothing to fear but fear itself' – which came out as 'No one can really scare us or scare you. We should fear only ourselves.'† It was vitally important to him to sound right. 'The world is listening to us . . .' he told a Communist Party congress. 'We want to show that our society is capable of being progressive.'†

His book, *Perestroika*, published in November 1987, was breathtakingly critical of every aspect of the Soviet system. Eager to hear what they longed to hear from the last great Communist leader, many Western readers assumed he had seen the light and realized that Communism was a noble philosophy that just didn't work. It almost sounded like he wanted to junk the system and start all over again. Few people seemed to catch the important omissions.

'We keep saying that Communism has failed, it's an

anachronism, but you don't hear Gorbachev saying those things,'† warns Senator Baker. 'We musn't let our own wish for changed circumstances substitute for the facts.'

Ambassador Ridgway sounded the same caveat. 'I think he is a deep believer in Communism. He is convinced it was betrayed, and if he could just get it back on track, he could show it is a better system.'

In a speech at the United Nations in early December 1988, he dazzled the world by setting out his vision of a new era beyond the Cold War. His delivery was subdued, but the power of his ideas came through even in translation. Gorbachev transmitted a sense of delight in being alive and in control at a time of seismic change that would shake up all the enemy stereotypes and security alliances of the post-war era. It almost seemed that he had a special vision, that he alone could see how the pieces of the new world would fit together. He evidently thrived on change and the very instability of things.

Living up to his reputation for surprises, he tossed out a 'Christmas gift'. He had decided to slash Soviet military forces by half a million men before the end of 1990. But it was a less publicized promise, made the next day in New York, by which he hoped to collect on his goal of membership in the family of modern civilized nations.

The Soviet Union, he promised, would bring its laws into conformity with the standards of the international human rights convention at Helsinki. Then he insisted that President Reagan and Prime Minister Thatcher respond before the end of the year.

Messages flew back and forth between Reagan in California and Thatcher in London all through that New Year's weekend.† They ticked off the requirements of the club: Let's see, change their legal code on human rights, practice of religion, right to teach religion, the right to emigrate within a predictable period – all right, he had done enough, they agreed. They would now say yes to an event of incalculable value in establishing the normalization of the

USSR in the eyes of the world: Moscow could throw an international human rights conference in 1991, and the Atlantic club members would come to the party.

The Soviet Union was in terrible trouble in Afghanistan. More than a million soldiers had been exposed to that demoralizing war,† 50,000 of whom lost their lives and another 150,000 who were injured, not to mention a drain of 60 billion rubles, as reported by an Estonian newspaper.

Conventional arguments in American academic and intelligence circles made the case that Moscow would never pull out voluntarily. 'Moscow has no tradition of delegating authority or building consensus among its communist satraps. It prefers *diktat* in dealing with subordinates, and it is suspicious of the Afghans,'† wrote Alvin Z. Rubinstein, a Senior Fellow of the Foreign Policy Research Institute, that winter. It was also widely predicted that if Soviet troops did get out, the Najibullah regime would immediately fall and guerrilla forces would sweep through the cities in months. Western experts were totally wrong on both counts.

Only leaders capable of exceptional statecraft can rescue a bleak loss and turn it into a moral triumph. Mikhail Gorbachev managed it in surprising the world with his pullout from Afghanistan. Foreign Minister Shevardnadze had unexpectedly visited Kabul in January 1988 and announced that Moscow 'would like the year 1988 to be the last year of the presence of Soviet troops', following up on Gorbachev's private commitment during the December summit to speed up efforts to reach a settlement before the next meeting with Reagan. For the first time since their exit from Austria in 1955, Russians prepared to withdraw voluntarily from territory they had taken in war. Gorbachev would later win the world's praise for his courage in admitting that Moscow's use of troops to overthrow an existing regime had been a 'crime against humanity' and 'an immoral war'. It was a performance of post-heroic leadership that far outclassed any

American president's handling of the equally immoral American war in Vietnam.

A year later Gorbachev was impatient to keep up the momentum towards his goals of easing the US military out of Western Europe and getting the West to pick up the tab for Eastern Europe. But although the Soviet leader might have succeeded in getting a ring through Reagan's nose, now he would have to win over a new American President: George Bush, inaugurated on 20 January 1989.

President Bush ordered a review of US foreign policy but gave his own 'apparat' no direction. After tying up hundreds of senior bureaucrats for seventy days, the report that came back reflected his lack of vision and priorities. It recommended no new initiatives towards the Soviet Union or Europe, no support for dramatic arms cuts, and concluded, in short, 'that the Soviet threat to us will decline no matter what we do'. It predicted, correctly, that the Soviets would place the highest priority on cultivating good relations with the United States.†

Bush, his alter ego, Secretary of State James Baker, and his Defence Secretary Richard Cheney, had all been believers in the détente period of the 1970s and felt burned by the abrupt end of that romance. They all believed that Ronald Reagan had 'gone foolish over Gorby' towards the end of his presidency,† as a top State Department official on the Reagan team told me. They still couldn't get over the image of America's most conservative President strolling arm in arm with the Communist Party boss through Red Square, in effect campaigning for him. In the spring of 1988, when the leftover Brezhnev–Chernenko functionaries had ganged up for a last charge at Gorbachev, he planned a showdown at an extraordinary Party conference. To give his 'friend, Mikhail', a boost, President Reagan had offered to fly to Moscow to play supporting actor.†

'We all had a good laugh reading the President's speeches,' said a Sovietologist in the administration. 'The Soviet leader couldn't have been more pleased if he'd written them himself.'† As late as April 1989, Jim Baker was still sceptical about Gorbachev's motives.

Again, Gorbachev would turn to Thatcher for help. He jetted to London that April – the first ever official visit of a Soviet leader to Britain – and stood behind Thatcher's heavily padded shoulders to take shots at Bush for dragging his feet.

By now the relationship between Gorbachev and Thatcher had become 'passionate', as spokesman Gennady Gerasimov described it, and each was increasingly prescient in identifying how the other could be of maximum benefit to their own prestige and worldwide designs. When they emerged from their long private talk, the TV cameras showed Thatcher tossing her head coquettishly, trilling with girlish laugher, seeming utterly secure in her feminine allure perhaps more than at any other time since her solemn and gawky girlhood.†

Just as he had won over Thatcher, Gorbachev was winning over her countrymen, and all Europeans, by giving them what they wanted – the promise of a nuclear-free continent. A poll published in the British press showed Gorbachev as the British people's favourite foreign leader, twice as popular as Ronald Reagan.†

The Soviet used his London stopover to rub in the contrast between Thatcher, a forward-looking leader who was doing brisk business with him, and the hyper-cautious Bush administration, still bogged down in 'prolonged evaluation' of superpower relations. 'There was no better place in which he could register such a political point,' confirmed one of Thatcher's ambassadors. Foreign Ministry spokesman Gerasimov put the point more forcefully: 'I think the new [Bush] administration tries to please everybody.'

Gorbachev followed up this initiative by inviting Secretary of State Baker into the Kremlin Palace for their first meeting, on 11 May 1989, and springing on him a surprise peace attack. The body language between the two men eloquently portrayed how far behind the pace of history the Americans had fallen. When the double doors were opened at either end of the great hall, protocol called for the two men to meet in the centre. Mr Baker sauntered in from his side, nonchalant, in no particular hurry. A buoyant Mr Gorbachev propelled himself from the other side, so fast that he was across the room and almost on top of Baker before the American knew it, thrusting out his hand to greet the visitor.† Then, after three hours of talks, the Soviet leader matched Baker's nonchalance by announcing, almost casually, that the next morning he would declare a unilateral withdrawal of 500 short-range nuclear weapons from Eastern Europe. With a NATO meeting weeks away, Bush's foreign policy team was caught off balance.

'It's clear that this man continues to hold a tremendous grip on the imagination of the world,' worried one senior Bush adviser. 'The general secretary threw out a lot of red meat.'† By now, there was no denying that Gorbachev was setting the East–West agenda. The American administration became obsessed with the public-relations problem.† Thatcher, on the other hand, was having serious second thoughts. She peppered President Bush with trans-Atlantic telephone calls to try to stiffen his resistance against negotiating with Gorbachev on short-range missiles. But even Paul H. Nitze, the veteran American disarmament negotiator, although he still saw Gorbachev as a dictator, warned that the US was in danger of being isolated within NATO by its refusal to accept the Soviets' proposal.

Bush was in a tizzy. He acknowledged that Gorbachev had gained an advantage in superpower relations by using the element of surprise. He admitted his own astonishment: 'Who would have predicted changes in the Soviet Union – perestroika and glasnost?'† Finally, under ridicule for showing timidity in the glare of Gorbachev's ground-breaking diplomacy, Bush called up to his Kennebunkport retreat a brains trust of his top officials and told them that he wanted to 'take a bold step' to meet the Soviet leader's initiatives.

At the end of May, Bush sent a letter to Gorbachev

proposing cuts in ground forces in East and West Europe that would remove ten times as many Soviet fighting men as Americans. NATO allies were quick to express approval for the President's apparent decision to compete with Mr Gorbachev for the laurels of peacemaker.

Thus had Gorbachev succeeded in engaging Bush in a contest for accomplishing exactly the objective the Soviet leader had set out to achieve back in 1984: to get the Americans and the Europeans to abandon their nuclear deterrents and accept the Soviet view of a new order in Europe and the world.

Next, the impatient Gorbachev made a watershed trip to Bonn in June, and there began an intense dialogue with Chancellor Kohl and the well-informed top officials of the West German government. In his very first meeting with the popular West German Foreign Minister, Hans-Dietrich Genscher, back in 1986, Gorbachev had proposed essentially the package that NATO would accept four years later: comprehensive arms reductions, an all-European security structure which wouldn't exclude the USSR, and serious transfusions of financial and technological aid to help the sick Soviet economy. Genscher, who had been born in East Germany and had always cherished the dream of a united Fatherland, got the impression even then that Mr Gorbachev might be willing to deliver the prize of German unity in return.† So in 1988 the Germans sweetened the relationship with the Soviets by arranging for a $2 billion loan earmarked to help Moscow modernize its industries.†

Now, in 1989, another window opened. Fired up with the possibilities for some sort of new German-Soviet alliance, Gorbachev sat up with ten of his travelling companions until two in morning. They turned over the mind-stretching possibilities stimulated by the meeting. 'Raisa was there with us too, listening, she made a few remarks, very appropriate ones,' says Rudolf Kolchanov, a university classmate of the couple and now an influential newspaper editor, who accompanied the Soviet leader. Later, when the others had left,

Raisa could act as Gorbachev's sounding board as he tried out ideas that would have been unthinkable, and certainly unspeakable, until the political groundwork had been laid.†

By this time the Soviet leader was heaping thousands of tanks, artillery pieces and personnel carriers on the altar of burnt military offerings. He was the first to propose the notion of troop reductions 'from the Atlantic to the Urals'.† Indisputably, Gorbachev was the most intoxicating suitor for Europe; and Bush, while a nice guy, was finishing last. As much of the world rushed forward, arms and spirits outstretched to embrace the freedoms that America enshrines, it was not the American President who succeeded in arousing love all over the world as an ally of revolution. The man being idolized was the last great champion of an ideology the world was rejecting.

That July, in an address in Strasbourg, Gorbachev publicly predicted 'the process of democratization' that would ultimately transform Eastern Europe. At last, Washington tuned in to the seismic shift. On his own trip through the infant democracies of Poland and Hungary that month, President Bush saw the scope of changes already in progress and heard unqualified praise for Gorbachev's sincerity. Delivering a speech in Mainz, Germany, he picked up on the Soviet leader's theme of a greater Europe and issued the call for 'a Europe whole and free'. And no sooner was he homebound on Air Force One than Bush wrote the first of a flurry of notes to Mikhail Gorbachev, this one suggesting an informal get-together which turned into the pre-summit at Malta in December.

The 'irrevocable act' of decomposition of his outer empire took place on 22 August, when Gorbachev explicitly encouraged the forfeiture of Poland.† He telephoned the leader of the Polish Communist Party and persuaded him to accept a minority position in a government headed by Lech Walesa's Solidarity. The engine of peaceful revolution was now set in motion.

Kissing the Wall Goodbye

In the autumn of 1989 the fires in Gorbachev's mind lit a blaze of freedom-seeking across the captive sub-continent of Eastern Europe. The exodus of young East Germans who slipped out the back door to the West via Hungary, Czechoslovakia or Poland had begun in August with a trickle. By early October the flow had swollen to the staggering rate of 200 people an hour† – an accumulated repudiation by almost 50,000 fleeing subjects of Erich Honecker's repressive regime.† The movement put tremendous pressure on Honecker to step aside, and Moscow seemed completely uninterested in bolstering the increasingly weak Communist leader. On 7 October, Gorbachev appeared in East Berlin for the fortieth birthday party of the Communist state. Protesters cried 'Gorby! Gorby!' and 'We need freedom!' With the whole world watching, the ossified East German regime celebrated its anniversary by clubbing with riot sticks the very workers it purported to represent. Though Gorbachev stood shoulder to shoulder with the stone-faced Honecker late into the night, he also emphasized his hands-off policy: 'First, I should tell our Western partners that matters relating to the German Democratic Republic are decided not in Moscow, but Berlin.'† Then he gave Honecker the kiss of the godfather and left Berlin.

Eleven days later Honecker was gone. Gorbachev's parting comment was prophetic: 'History punishes those who come too late.'†

Bells tolled from the churches of Budapest on 24 October as hundreds of thousands of Hungarians gathered outside their Parliament and shouted, alternatively, 'Russians go home!' and 'Gorby! Gorby!' They peacefully overthrew the 'socialist people's' label and declared themselves a republic. The next day Soviet Foreign Ministry spokesman Gerasimov gleefully pronounced the Brezhnev doctrine dead and used a classic American pop song to showcase the new, Westernized Kremlin policy – the 'Sinatra doctrine' – 'I did it my way.'†

The Communist Party of East Germany let go of its monopoly on power and on 9 November Honecker's successor, Egon Krentz, one of those fleeting figures of history, opened the border to the West. People the world over came home to the unbelievable spectacle on their TV screens of giddy East Germans dancing atop the Berlin Wall.

Czechoslovakia followed the East German pattern. A brutally suppressed student demonstration against neo-Stalinist policies on 17 November erupted in a non-violent revolution by students and artists. Within three weeks a new government was named with a playwright, Vaclav Havel, as the opposition's candidate for president.

Everyone, including the unprimed revolutionaries themselves, was shocked by the speed with which these regimes imploded – almost parodying a nuclear explosion – with the blinding flash of mass demonstrations followed by the internal collapse, the desiccation, the disappearance into earth of the towers of lies and deceit. Gorbachev had not engineered the events which led to the collapse of the Communist governments in Poland, Hungary, East Germany, Czechoslovakia, Bulgaria and Romania, but he had set the whole process in motion. In a mere six weeks – from the day the Wall opened to the death of Romanian despot Nikolai Ceaucescu – Stalin's dream of a Communist empire lay in tatters all over Eastern Europe.

The fever was spreading even into the Soviet Union. An audacious alternative parade shattered the sacred celebration of the Bolshevik revolution on 7 November 1989. It was the first time since the 1920s, before the rise of Stalin, that dissidents had marched in Moscow. They challenged the Party's monopoly on power. The banner at the head of the crowd proclaimed, '72 Years Leading Nowhere'. Demonstrators numbered only five thousand, but it was a sign that the bedrock under Soviet history was about to shift too.

Gorbachev was as ebullient as ever: 'We have to advance faster and faster,' he exhorted his countrymen that night over Soviet television, his eyes gleaming with adventure. He described his vision of a New Europe as 'a commonwealth of sovereign democratic states' to replace the divided East and West.

Peak of Triumph for the Post-Heroic Leader

The pinnacle of Mikhail Gorbachev's life may have been reached in that November of 1989. Since he had been largely responsible for the managed revolutions of Eastern Europe, his sincerity was now beyond question in the eyes of two of the other most powerful people in the world – the President of the United States and the holy leader of the world's Catholics. He would meet them both in Italy, back to back.

The Italians gave Gorbachev a welcome worthy of a Russian czar. A clattering of hooves on the cobbled stone of Rome's Quirinale Palace announced the grand entrance of gladiatorial horsemen with silver helmets tossing long black tails, looking just as they did centuries ago riding into battle. Outside the courtyard three heavily-bolted Zil limousines, flown in from Moscow, a red flag fluttering on the first, worked through the narrow streets. Shopkeepers came out to join all Roma for a street spectacle such as hadn't been seen in this indifferent city since President John Kennedy's visit in the sixties.

Out stepped a short, dumpling-shaped man with a half-moon of silver hair and a little smile: Mikhail Gorbachev, commander of the 4,250,000-man Soviet armed forces and a nuclear arsenal second to none – but who would have thought it? His gait was unsoldierly, no snap or fanfare in it. He was completely out of step with Soviet leaders of the past, or most leaders of history for that matter. Surrounded by symbols of the imperial power of ancient Rome, he was every inch the civilian, walking the length of the courtyard on foot. Yet every inch of him was commanding, by the sheer force of the acts which preceded him.

Presented to the fur-helmeted granatieri guard he did not salute. He merely bowed his head.

Stalin once asked, in swaggering belligerence, 'How many divisions does the Pope have?' But Gorbachev culminated his visit to Italy by crossing the square of St Peter's to seek an alliance with the Pope. Again he came on foot, looking the very embodiment of the post-heroic leader.

At the Vatican reporters watched open-mouthed as the vicar of Christ came out of his apartment to extend a personal greeting to the apostle of Communism. The previous day, mirroring the penitent mode preferred by the Pope, Gorbachev had made his 'confession' before the world for 'our mistake in treating religion superficially'. He had come prepared to atone for this mistake, telling the Pope of the new law on freedom of conscience he was shepherding towards adoption. Within moments, Gorbachev was literally rubbing elbows with the pontiff's white cassock as the two fell to laughing and chatting.

'I had substantial talks with His Holiness about politics and morality and about universal human values,' Gorbachev later said. And he was not too proud to admit the unthinkable for a Soviet leader, or almost any leader in world history for that matter, most of whom have normally preferred to lead a 'march of folly', in Barbara Tuchman's phrase, rather than admit a mistake.

'We no longer think that we are always right,' Gorbachev declared. He firmly discarded state atheism and totalitarianism and pledged his country to the 'principle of freedom of choice'.

He wore the mask of equanimity all through his visit to the Pope and the summit in Malta. Only up close did one notice the purplish folds of fatigue drooping like curtains over the bright stage of his eyes; only standing right behind him did one glimpse the raw dents on either side of his nose, where glasses had worked into the flesh. The night before he left for Italy he had been up until two at an emergency meeting of the Politburo – his nationalities problem boiling over in Armenia. But it is a unique quality of the man that the more things seem to fall apart, the calmer Gorbachev becomes. Some of his colleagues speak of his 'eerie detachment'.

'At a time of tumultuous change we have to remain confident and look to the positive results,' he said in Milan, his voice a steady, reassuring centre in the maelstrom of events, 'and decide which walls should be destroyed and which should be built.'

Bismarck once said that political genius consisted in the ability to hear the distant hoofbeat of the horse of history – and then by superhuman effort to leap and catch the horseman by the coat-tails † At that millisecond in the rush of history, Gorbachev's imagination seemed to be moving in perfect harmony with the restless spirit of the times.

'People want change,' he said with impassioned empathy. Then he underlined it, *'People want change everywhere . . .* they are demanding their politicians act.'

When Gorbachev moved on to Malta for his meeting with George Bush, it seemed that even the cautious American President had caught the fervour for global change. Bush and Gorbachev had got off to a rocky start in their relationship back in late 1988, when the President-elect took a high-handed tone with the Soviet leader. During a luncheon conversation where Gorbachev was being rather candid with his friend Reagan about the troubles he faced in pushing through his ambitious economic programme, Bush butted in, as if to show Reagan how tough he could be, demanding the Soviet chief tell the Americans if and when his reforms would succeed.

Gorbachev's stiletto appeared: 'Not even Jesus Christ knows the answer to your question.'†

'I don't think I was ever down on Gorbachev or negative about him,' Bush later said in an interview with the *Wall Street Journal*. 'But what . . . changed was the whole Eastern European scene. And we had communications with him during a lot of this period of change, quiet communications, letters that we didn't feel inclined to discuss a lot.'†

In Malta, President Bush would step forward as a full

booster of perestroika and the personal leadership cult of Mikhail Gorbachev. Apparently apprehensive about Gorbachev's habit of stealing the initiative, Bush came to what the press dubbed 'the seasick summit' armed with a dozen proposals for closing arms-control deals and pulling the Kremlin into the world economy, which he foisted on the Soviet leader almost before Gorbachev could open his mouth.

'I was going to ask you for specifics,' Gorbachev told Bush, probably mindful of his frustrations with Reagan. 'Now you've given them.'†

By March 1990, in his maiden speech as the first President of the USSR, Gorbachev pronounced with gusto the new manifesto of the post-heroic leader of a nuclear power: 'It is absolutely and forever excluded to use military forces outside the Soviet Union . . . with only one exception – in case of sudden attack from abroad.'

The Selling of Eastern Europe

The West would not grasp the magnitude of Gorbachev's grand strategy in courting the United States and Europe until the deal was done in the summer of 1990. It had taken him five years to persuade the US to begin reducing its nuclear commitment and negotiating the withdrawal of conventional forces in Europe and to convince Europe to take Russia under its wing.

'Back in 1987 we declared that we were champions of social choice in Eastern Europe,' I was reminded by Alexander Yakovlev in a later interview. I observed that 'No one imagined you would let go of Eastern Europe, it came as a total surprise to the West.'

With an ironic smile he said, 'This goes to say that Western political science and intelligence communities are doing a poor job.'

As late as the spring of 1988, at Columbia University, visiting political scientist Jan Gross from Emory University had proposed that Gorbachev was out to unburden himself of Eastern Europe, and that he would offer the reunification of Germany as a sop to the West. He was laughed at. The academic world in America, no less than its intelligence agencies, remained in the dark until after the Wall was breached.

Reagan's former Chief of Staff Howard Baker confessed in late 1989, 'I think Gorbachev knows what he's doing – he has an objective in mind, and it is probably imperfectly perceived by the West.'†

The broken and dependent economies of the Eastern bloc were an obvious burden to Moscow. Gorbachev was retreating from Europe, and he had to figure out how to take the US military presence along with him. The Soviet leader had tried to reverse the arms race by negotiation at Reykjavik in September 1986, and failed. By December 1987 Reagan was moving his way, but too slowly to head off Gorbachev's domestice débâcle. The INF treaty was in place, yet Gorbachev was getting nowhere on finding a face-saving formula for a pullback of his costly ground forces in Europe.

Throughout 1988, while American political leaders were caught up in the longest, nastiest presidential election campaign in memory, it seems that the hyperactive Soviet leader was laying the groundwork for a monumental swap. The one thing he had to offer the West, aside from modest disarmament, was a breach in the deadlocked containment of the Cold War that the Soviet Union, and only the Soviet Union, could make possible – opening the Wall. As long as the Wall stood, there would be no end to the Cold War, and glasnost and perestroika were merely slogans as far as the West was concerned. The Soviets knew that if they reduced tensions Western democracies could not keep up their military spending and the US would have to scale back its multi-billion dollar Star Wars programme; its citizens would demand a peace dividend. Gorbachev could set the whole process in motion with one calculated decision – to sacrifice East Germany. But, if he did so, the Russians would have to

be prepared to let the other Eastern bloc countries choose to
accept or reject socialism.

A month before the Wall came down, a source inside the
Soviet Communist Party Central Committee gave me an
intriguing prediction. 'A divided Germany will be changed
by the right of choice. The Soviet Union doesn't intend to
interfere into the domestic problems of Eastern Germany.'
He never showed the slightest surprise or displeasure over
the fate of Honecker or the non-socialist course taken by the
other former satellites. 'Gorbachev's policy greatly influenced
these changes,' he purred. 'The whole structure of Europe
before the millennium will be changed.'

Another high-level member of the apparat told me that
Gorbachev had intelligence information warning him of the
likelihood that, if Honecker was allowed to fall, no Communist leader would be acceptable in his place. 'But Gorbachev
was just interested in getting out,' says this economic consultant to the Central Committee.

And there was, indeed, a lucrative silver lining for Moscow
if the Eastern European countries threw out their totalitarian
regimes. Their economies ranged from sickly to terminal,
and that included the Potemkin economy of East Germany.
Always touted as the 'model economy' of all six satellites,
East Germany was so highly subsidized by its Soviet parent,
it would fall into a heap immediately after the Wall was
opened. (By January 1990 more than one thousand people a
day were crossing from East to West Germany, threatening
union by spasm – Selbstanschluss, or self-annexation – and
when the two countries' currencies were joined six months
later, the estimates by Western banks indicated that no more
than one-third of East Germany's outmoded industry was
salvageable.† If the West could be seduced into picking up
the mortgage on the near-bankrupt economies of the satellites, so to speak, the Soviet Union could go on preparing
the ground to move into a financially sound 'common
European home'.

President Bush and Secretary of State Baker were quick to

correct course and move with the tide Gorbachev had turned by allowing the collapse of the Wall. Seeing that unification was inevitable, they moved to facilitate it as soon as possible, taking care not to offend their man in Moscow whose political survival was Bush's openly stated objective.

But while much of the rest of the world was clucking over Gorbachev's loss of face in Eastern Europe, his inner circle was focused on the spreading malaise that could indeed topple him. 'Social disturbances' was the phrase they used again and again, meaning that Gorbachev's people were fed up with their standard of living. While he was busy jetting around the world collecting bouquets as a great statesman, his entourage staying in lavish hotels with food and service most Soviets could only dream about, their lives were growing every day meaner, dirtier, poorer. To the world perestroika may have meant the sunshine of peace and shared prosperity; to the Soviet people, perestroika was a sickness.

It was money from the West that Gorbachev was going for, and he needed it fast.

Living Off the West

'Get the hay in the barn while you can' was the compatible attitude of Chancellor Helmut Kohl, who needed Gorbachev's help on unification. The West German leader went to Moscow over the weekend of 10 and 11 February 1990 and sealed the fateful deal. Gorbachev agreed in principle to unification, and was assured that in return he would get what he wanted from Kohl: a reduction of overall German troops in a new unified German army plus a huge stipend.†
Gorbachev told Kohl of the hypocrisies of the French and British, both of whom had asked him to *prevent* unification.†

Thus was struck the new German–Soviet non-aggression pact, it being clear to both Gorbachev and Kohl (though not at all to the rest of the West) that the German–Soviet relationship superseded both nations' links to all other European players.†

'Yes, we predicted all the events in Eastern Europe,' Foreign Minister Shevardnadze would later acknowledge.† He and Gorbachev and Yakovlev may have made the same argument inside the Politburo back in 1988 that Shevardnadze mounted at the Communist Party Congress in July 1990: 'The concern over the process of German unification is understandable . . . [But] What is better for us: to have a million-strong West German Bundeswehr against us, or an army of a united Germany half this size? Our calculations show that in the current five-year period the sum-total peaceful dividend as result of the realization of the peaceful policy based on new thinking can make 240 to 250 billion rubles.'

Gorbachev wanted to sell Eastern Germany to save his own economy. This would mean he couldn't have Soviet troops in other Eastern European countries either, but that military presence was another redeemable asset. If he traded Soviet troop strength for billions of dollars of credits from West Germany, credits and investment from France and eventually all the Western allies, including Japan, would be likely to follow.

Indeed, in early summer 1990, West Germany together with France pushed a $15 billion aid package from the Western nations to help Gorbachev stir up the stagnant mire into which his half-hearted economic reforms had sunk. When they failed to get the US and others to join them in the bail-out, the Germans went ahead to negotiate the purchase of East Germany on its own terms – pledging a $3 billion down payment in credits and guaranteed loans to pay for the 380,000 Soviet troops still stationed inside East Germany.†

Behind the scenes, diplomats said, Gorbachev made no secret of his burning desire for Western aid. On 4 July 1990, Gorbachev sent a secret letter to President Bush asking for economic help, credits and technical assistance to 'tide over his economy for two years while its reform program comes into effect'.† A week later the world's seven richest democracies met for an economic summit in the deflated climate of a once-booming Texas. The meeting was dominated by the question, not of *if*, but of *how*, to help Gorbachev, and more to the point, *how much* to send him under what conditions. From a transcript of the meeting obtained by Mario Platero for *Il Sole – 24 Ore*,† here are the unpublished critiques of Gorbachev by half a dozen of the major world leaders.

President Bush, as usual, was cautious. 'For us, this is a very delicate matter.' Moscow was still pumping $5 billion a year into Cuba, the conventional-force talks were stuck, Gorbachev's government still hadn't introduced economic reforms, and on the whole, he said, 'Congress thinks . . . that the basic behaviour of Moscow has not changed drastically.' He recommended that all Western assistance be linked with programmes leading to a market economy, and that was prudent advice. The last thing the bedevilled Soviet population needed was more billions pouring into the pockets of the mafia chains that supported the corrupt apparat which had already brought them to penury and pre-revolution.

French President Mitterrand excoriated this approach as 'timid' and 'humiliating'. It was as though they were treating the mighty Soviet Union like Latin America or a small African country, he said. 'If we go this road we shall take the risk of losing Gorbachev as our interlocutor.'

West German Chancellor Kohl, who had come to the meeting hawking up to a $20 billion joint economic aid package for his friend Mikhail, affably agreed with Bush that linking aid to a concrete programme of reforms would 'make sure that Gorbachev will help himself'. He had already made his own arrangements.

Japanese Prime Minister Kaifu gave a brief, bloodless, bottom-line conclusion: 'The state of their economy is a disaster.' Although Japan would agree to making nice political noises about support for perestroika, 'we do not consider it appropriate to give financial help to the Soviet Union'.

Notwithstanding her affection for Gorbachev, Prime Minister Thatcher brought to the table the pennywise instincts of a shopkeeper's daughter who was plagued with her own inflation problems back home. 'When we help him we should also keep in mind their limits.' The Soviets *already* had $48 billion of international credit that they hadn't yet used, she pointed out, and 'they are certainly not lacking in resources – gold, platinum, oil, diamonds'.

But the transforming impact that Mikhail Gorbachev's personality had had on each and every one of them, in changing their image of the Soviet Union, was articulated in the poetic encomium he earned from Canada's Brian Mulroney: 'Mikhail Gorbachev knows each of us; it is as if we stood in front of a mirror; we see him, he sees us. He is a courageous man who is walking on a thread, waiting for our reaction . . . To say no would be wrong.'

The real question was: would the sudden infusion of Western consumer goods be used by Gorbachev's team to force bold reforms and a meaningful transition from massive military spending into building a civilian sector? Or would it simply support the same black crows of the corrupt bureaucracy in the style to which corruption had accustomed them, and allow them to postpone reform? Economist Judy Shelton, author of *The Coming Soviet Crash*, sounded a warning. 'We cannot take on 280 million permanent wards feeding off the West. The Soviets must solve these problems themselves.'† Western resources could only buy time;. but time was what Gorbachev needed more than anything else.

Leaving America Out of the Loop

In mid-July 1990, Mikhail Sergeyevich executed his most astounding mid-air pirouette yet. Bush was 5,000 miles away. Baker was in the air between Washington and Dublin, having predicted there would be no break in the impasse with the Soviets over Germany's status within NATO until the autumn. Even Downing Street was completely in the dark.

Gorbachev must have taken sweet revenge for Bush's backing and filling and Reagan's self-righteous lectures when he invited Chancellor Helmut Kohl down to his old stamping grounds in the Mineralnye Vody spa area for a one-on-one talk.

It was an intimate invitation. No other Western leader had ever seen Mr Gorbachev in the setting of his birth and rise through local Communist Party politics. Pointing up to the Caucasus Mountains on their walk through Stavropol, Gorbachev noted that he and Mr Kohl were starting at an altitude of 2,300 feet: 'We want to develop our relations further upward.'†

Gorbachev and Kohl were close in only one aspect, but it was a defining aspect: they were the first leaders of their respective countries too young to have experienced war as an adult. But Kohl himself had no idea Gorbachev was ready to give in. The signals from Moscow had been maddeningly contradictory. Gorbachev, using his confuse-them-with-contradictions strategy, had continually changed his conditions for agreeing to NATO membership for a new Germany. Kohl had brought a major concession on a voluntary limitation of military forces in a united Germany. He didn't even get to present it before Gorbachev staged his 'electric moment'.

Less than two hours into their first session Gorbachev told Kohl he was ready to move.† His price was massive financial and technical aid. The two continued late into the night haggling over the military details.†

The Soviet leader had whisked the German Chancellor by helicopter to the Caucasus resort of Arkhyz, where they spent the night. Operating again in the relaxed atmosphere of mountain walks and rain massages – where he had forged his ties with the top Kremlin brass as the maître d' of Mineralnye Vody – Gorbachev enveloped the German leader in a love bath. He even took off his tie and dressed in sports clothes, a sartorial hint from an always formal leader that something extraordinary was about to change. He walked

Kohl over ground that had nurtured him as a boy and had
been occupied by Nazi troops forty-eight years before.

By the time the two emerged for a news conference,
Gorbachev looked like his double: rotund but robust, like
Kohl, wearing a casual black Jaeger-type jacket over a white
polo shirt, just like Kohl. The two grinned and bantered like
the best of old friends.

After all the months of manoeuvring between Moscow and
the West over German unity, Gorbachev promised the skeleton force of unsuspecting reporters 'interesting news'. The
bombshell, of course, was that the Soviet leader had given in
completely on the issue of a united Germany remaining
within NATO.

'We are leaving one epoch in international relations, and
entering another period, I think, of strong prolonged peace,'
declared Gorbachev. And, in that stroke, he undid the last
tie in the terrible yoke Josef Stalin had brought down on half
of Europe after the failed promises of the conference at a
different Russian resort – Yalta – forty-five years before.

A gleeful Kohl called the agreement 'fantastic'. He
announced, 'All practical problems for German unification
have been cleared up.' Following on the 'intensive dialogue',
and the many 'meetings on highest levels, the telephone
calls, the mutual visits',† that Gorbachev had stimulated with
the Germans, starting in the spring of 1989, when he couldn't
get Bush and Baker to give him the time of day, Gorbachev
couched his historic announcement in terms of his unity with
Europeans: 'The work . . . that we did does not only touch
our two peoples, but all Europeans . . .' Then he virtually
boasted about beating Bush and Baker at what they think of
as their own game. 'I want to characterize the two last days
with a *German* expression: we made realpolitik.'

Finally, in the best Dale Carnegie tradition, he made his
negotiating partner look like the hero: 'Mr Chancellor, it was
you most of all who developed this idea.'†

Both he and Kohl grew in stature on the spot. Together, a
Russian leader, who saw himself as a non-authoritarian Peter

the Great, and a German leader, who later referred to himself 'as a modern Bismarck without the "blood and iron"', had written the ending to the Second World War.

Having begun his flirtation with the West by courting the lady behind the brass knocker at Number Ten Downing Street, Gorbachev wound up his wooing in the arms of the soon-to-be richest and most powerful leader in all Europe. It became crystal clear that the Germans and the Soviets were the leading forces in East–West realignment. The reaction from a major American foreign policy spokesman, Democratic Congressman Lee Hamilton, spoke volumes about the shift of axis in the post-Cold War world: 'I'm not saying that it's George Bush's fault, and I'm not saying that we have become a non-power.'†

But the fact was, the United States under Reagan and Bush had spent itself into the status of world's largest debtor nation, and in the process had lost its clout over Europe. As Representative Hamilton put it, 'we need to borrow money, and you can't say to your creditors, "This is what you're going to do."'

The new German–Soviet pact gave Gorbachev just what he and Shevardnadze had wanted: a ceiling on the armed forces of a united Germany that would render its army smaller than that of the existing West German army alone. With the promised withdrawal of Soviet troops within three or four years, Gorbachev implied, went Germany's agreement to push the American troops out: 'We take it that no other foreign troops appear there; here we have trust . . .' Gorbachev's international strategy had been a roaring success.

A better deal than Stalin ever dreamed of, this one committed the economic giant of Europe to act almost as the foster parent of the sickly and orphaned Soviet Union, with provisions for wide-ranging economic, political, cultural and even *military* co-operation. Of all the Western countries Gorbachev envied or admired, none had captured his imagination more than 'the rich and nice and civilized land' of Germany he had first seen fifteen years before. Now he had come closer than ever to making his dream of 'a common European home' a reality.

THE GREAT PERSUADER AT HOME

It would be hard to exaggerate the contrast between the Gorbachev who performed with such cool brilliance abroad and the emotional man who lurched in every direction in the attempt to perform a revolution at home. Soviets often use the metaphor of a ship without a firm commander, tossing from side to side, on an increasingly turbulent sea.

Gorbachev had no navigating plan when he set out in 1985 to decentralize the rigid Soviet economy with its monopolistic central command system. And five years later he would admit he still had no plan. He had 'hopes'.† Whereas in international policy he had a long-term strategy and kept moving towards it, in domestic policy he was ever a riddle of contradictions, not prepared to come to a decision on where he wanted to take the system and how far to move it from its socialist principles and original utopian Leninist ideals. He zig-zagged.

His supporters would complain later that he was poorly served by his advisers. Unlike his crack foreign-policy team, the new leader's Politburo was comprised of veterans of political work or career apparatchiks. Apart from Gromyko, their education consisted of a correspondence course in Shipbuilding or Locomotive Traction or ersatz degrees from an agronomy institute in Minsk or a railway technicum in Dnepropetrovsk.† The Party and government apparat had always fought to exclude specialists; what they wanted were dogmatists. As a result, no one at the top had any particular expertise, but they supported a strict interpretation of Marxism–Leninism.† The Politburo he inherited was also weighted by two-thirds with holdovers from the corrupt Brezhnev regime, several of them territorial Party bosses with their own clans and mafia connections. It would take Gorbachev four and a half years to get rid of the Brezhnevites in his Politburo.

Early on, he brought three loyal allies into his power elite. Nikolai Ryzhkov, who had earned his reputation as a factory manager and was always quick to praise Gorbachev, became in effect Prime Minister. The others, like Gorbachev, had been territorial Party bosses who had built their careers during the stagnation era: Yegor Ligachev, from the Tomsk Party organization in Siberia; and Boris Yeltsin, from the industrial city of Sverdlovsk, who was groomed to become Moscow Party boss and made a candidate-member of the Politburo. Although the two men held completely opposing conceptions of socialism, each was expected to force himself to utter the ritual phrases about the unity of the Politburo.†

Together with Yakovlev and Shevardnadze this was Gorbachev's inner circle, the brains of the ruling Party. And they operated within a closed loop. Questions would be referred to the apparat, which prepared a draft answer that then went back to the Politburo. Even in closed meetings of the conservative 300-member Central Committee, no one wanted to take any responsibility or initiative; its members would tell the General Secretary whatever they thought he wanted to hear. 'Gorbachev can pose questions very sharply,' says an economist who was invited to some of the Central Committee meetings. 'But he doesn't get hard facts for answers. So he could base his judgements only on their words.'

There was little debate on the Politburo either; weekly sessions would always begin with a discursive monologue from the General Secretary. Comments solicited around the table were expected to be brief, no more than five minutes. 'Yes, yes, very good . . . it will deepen perestroika . . . democratization . . . glasnost . . . pluralism – the new buzz-words,' as a disenchanted Yeltsin describes it.† After a hasty, emotional discussion, a decision would go back to the apparat to be implemented, and would die of resistance or inertia.

When Gorbachev tried to pry open the closed loop by bringing in non-political advisers, or revealing even a glimpse of his new ideas, the diehard conservatives who dominated the Central Committee immediately balked. For example, when Gorbachev's early economic guru, Professor Abel Aganbegyan, used the pages of *Izvestia* to float a trial balloon suggesting that it was time to start training young managers in Western-style business schools, a Central Committee official reacted with scorn: 'Such a path is excluded for us.'†

One rough estimate of the total number of bureaucrats in the Soviet Union is eighteen million,† of which about five million are leaders and have university or institute educations. The balance are employees of the apparat. All of the five million, provided with cars and drivers, special food stores and vouchers for secret health spas, were insulated from real life. Gorbachev sometimes talked about thinning out this bureaucracy by up to one-third. Soviets themselves use the image of black crows sitting on a tree branch. You can clap your hands, the crows will disappear, but within five minutes the branch will be filled with even more black crows. Without a competitive system, it seemed the eighteen million crows could never be driven away.† And so the new General Secretary decided to broaden his circles further.

The Media-crat

'Kremlin connections' they are called, those circles of ever-increasing exclusivity that constitute the Moscow Establishment. Three circles down from the top leaders, according to senior Soviet journalist Dmitry Golovanov, is a circle connecting to the Kremlin everyone who influences public opinion – newspaper and magazine writers, editors, journalists, novelists and poets, TV producers, filmmakers, artists, scientists, professors – about five or six thousand people in all. Known as the intelligentsia, it is a uniquely powerful force in Russia.

Back in the late 1970s, Sergei Bobkov, the KGB General who was then in charge of dissident writers, made an appeal to some of the repressed literary talents who had given up and decided to emigrate: 'Why are you leaving now? In the 1980s there will be a flowering of culture.'† Even then, the Andropov–KGB clan had been planning to cultivate the intelligentsia.

Now Andropov's successor wanted to bind the intelligentsia to him, and he knew the way to do it was to allow more freedom of expression. Routinely, once every three months, Gorbachev would call together thirty to fifty editors of the central newspapers: *Pravda*, *Izvestia*, *Moscow News* and so on. His purpose was 'to give directions to the press, and to listen to some ideas from journalists', says Viktor Starkov, editor of *Argumenty i Fakty*. 'He was extremely popular in the beginning,' says Gennady Gerasimov, then an editor of the well-read weekly *Moscow News*, who remembers the first such meeting. He and his editor-in-chief, Mr Labtov, listened to the vigorous young General Secretary describe his programme.

'Look, it sounds very good, but you have only so much time on your credit,' the senior editor told Gorbachev. 'It's not unlimited. You must deliver.' It was the 'cork on the river' message and it was prophetic. Given a sullen, protein-starved population that had heard preposterous promises before, Gorbachev probably had a credit line of three years, four at most.

On the whole, however, the give and take at his meetings with editors was mostly give, from Gorbachev, and the results were censored before they could be published. He used these sessions to school his propaganda forces in the new slogans: 'perestroika', 'break down inertia', 'show initiative', 'self-accounting'. He also enlisted them to follow him on his walkabouts and publicize his homilies on the anti-alcohol campaign.

As early as autumn 1985, the General Secretary began summoning select writers out of their safe niches to revive ossified magazines and literary journals that would represent the cutting edge of his new thinking.

'Get me Korotich,' Gorbachev reportedly ordered the First Secretary of the Ukraine.† Vitaly Korotich, a forty-nine-year-old state-approved writer, had become an unofficial patriarch of the youth of Kiev, good at giving pep talks to secondary-school students on doing their socialist duty. Korotich had survived, like so many of the writers who stayed through the Brezhnev era, by keeping his distance from the Centre and narrowing his scope. He tracked nomads in mid-Asia and lived with Eskimos in Arctic Russia until 'they forgot about me'. Granted the coveted permission in the sixties to make two brief trips to America, he had responded correctly by writing a scathingly critical book about the US, *Face of Hatred*. Now Gorbachev wanted the Party boss of the Ukraine to 'give to Moscow' his republic's favourite official author.

'You must take the editorship of *Ogonyok*' was the startling directive from the Writers' Union official who first summoned Korotich. *Ogonyok* was one of the despised fortresses of state chauvinism and anti-semitism. Korotich refused. Several times. Then he was called to Moscow by Alexander Yakovlev. 'All your life you have been fighting for cleanliness. Here, take the broom and do it yourself,' Yakovlev coaxed. The writer says he refused once more. Only when he was called before the secretariat of the Central Committee did he realize that Gorbachev was deadly serious.

'Why me?' protested Korotich, knowing that some of his friends had turned down the offer. It could be dangerous to be a propaganda operative for a reformist regime. The reactionary Politburo member Yegor Ligachev gave him an intriguing answer: 'We studied and sniffed you from all sides, and we learned you never had your own mafia. We need these kind of people.'

Korotich then asked a capitalistic question. 'Can I have enough money to pay good people?' The secretariat said yes, but it was Yakovlev's next words that amazed him and won him over. 'Please, never come to us asking what is possible to publish. Do your job.'

Korotich began to look for personalities who would write provocatively, 'not articles from some academy of science but *names* – this was very new for us'. He enlisted the most celebrated of all Soviet poets, Yevgeny Yevtushenko, to do anthologies, and poet Andrei Voznesensky to write about rock music, and progressive economic theorists such as Leonid Abalkin (always leftist but still Communist) to criticize the still-stodgy economic reforms. Abalkin was later adopted by Gorbachev.

Korotich was destined to emerge as a most courageous figure, eventually publishing truly startling investigative journalism about sacrosanct institutions such as the army and the KGB. It was an entirely new approach for a Soviet publication, and circulation exploded. Korotich was always walking the edge of censorship and Gorbachev's patience, but *Ogonyok* emerged in the forefront of the fight later waged by other democratic publications.

Another Gorbachev draftee was Grigory Baklanov, a mild-mannered writer of military history. 'When you're sixty-two, it's hard to change your life,' says the Second World War veteran, raking his fingers across the deep, damp furrows of his brow.† Baklanov (whose real name is Friedman) went against the wishes of his whole family and left his comfortable country life to accept a very prestigious post in Moscow, reviving the literary journal *Znamya*.

'I had to help change the way society thought, if that's possible.' Baklanov was realistic enough to know that people's thinking changes when their pocketbooks are fattened, and that this would not happen soon. But he believed that even good economic results wouldn't allow for a new political contract if people kept the same old mindset. He accepted the Gorbachev–Yakovlev philosophy that 'The press and fiction are supposed to make people understand that they really have to take power into their own hands.'

Gorbachev might call together any circle within the intelligentsia at any time in order to 'give his opinions' on an issue and invite questions. Even today, he sometimes picks up the phone and calls an editor directly, to sound him out on a move he is considering or to chew him up for not properly supporting perestroika. There is a direct line to the Kremlin in the office of *Ogonyok's* editor-in-chief. And Gorbachev, a 'quick and emotional man', according to Korotich, will suddenly be on the line.

'Hey, it's you? I want to cut you up in pieces!' Gorbachev might bluster, railing against some recent article. But several days later he will be back on the line with a 'normal, soft' tone of voice. 'Life is so short,' he'll say, 'I don't want to punish you.'†

The forces of light were now charged up to go forward and set off explosions of truth and awaken the sleeping population from their cocoons of fear. People began to sit up and take notice. This 'czar' was different. 'For the first few months Soviet people were hypnotized by these wonderful fantasies,' says a former Leningrad University language professor, Marina Minskaya. 'But the Russian people don't like someone who speaks nicely and gives sugary stories. After two or three months everyone felt nervous. Why does he talk so much? What does it mean?'

And it seemed he was on television (right after *Vremya*, the widely viewed hour-long news show that begins at 9 p.m.) every night. 'It was ten o'clock and Gorbachev would start to talk about arms control or make vague promises about perestroika,' says Professor Minskaya. 'People began to resent it. Too much repetition. They were impatient to get on to see their films.'

Only after the first year and a half did Gorbachev begin to come out of his rosy fog of vague and romantic dreams, having fallen foul of the Party bureaucracy. His pitch for infusions of new technology had run up against outside resistance from the West, and at home he found his own intelligentsia was afraid of computers, too proud to go through the stage of computer illiteracy! Already he was beginning to lose some of the good will that his walkabouts had engendered. His draconian measures to dry out the population and wake them up to hard work had, literally, poisoned the well. Desperate for any means of escape, people downed cleaning fluids and insecticides, anything containing alcohol, and hundreds died from poisoning. Factory workers also turned to hashish and other harder drugs, and for the first time the Soviet press began acknowledging problems of drug abuse.

What had gone wrong with Gorbachev's original version of 'making people happy'? With the easy contempt of hindsight, spokesman Gennady Gerasimov gave me this answer in May 1990: 'Stupidity. Inexperience. Amateurish approach. Lack of vision two days ahead. One of the most stupid things the new organization [Gorbachev and company] did was to try to make Russia dry. It created a big deficit in the budget. Extremely big deficit.'†

The anti-alcohol campaign pushed consumption of sugar three or four times above the health level because people used sugar to make home brew, continues Gerasimov. 'And they were so efficient in trying to make Russia dry that they not only shut down vodka plants, they destroyed vodka plants. They destroyed vineyards.' (One of the leading specialists on wines on the Georgian coast was so distraught over the destruction of vineyards that would take decades to recreate, he killed himself.) 'So now we don't have enough supply of vodka or wine, to say nothing of beer.'

Nikolai Ryzhkov, whom Gorbachev put in charge of the economy, had been a factory manager in the heavy-industrial belt of the Urals, probably producing armaments.† Ryzhkov would never favour market principles that are accepted all over the world. He was firmly entrenched in a system where the central 'plan' tells the manager how much of what to make and when, and where the concepts of a 'profit centre' or even a 'profit and loss statement' are utterly foreign.

Overall, Gorbachev's early attempts to tune up the economy had fizzled out with scarcely any traces of improvement. He found himself faced with a more formidable task than Lenin, whose New Economic Programme of liberalization in the 1920s was often held out as a model. But in those early years after the revolution the government still remembered how a market worked. 'Until 1917 it was the bankers, the financiers, the entrepreneurs . . . there were lots of people with brains. They understood things. But we lost them,' was the explanation, or excuse, given by one of the General Secretary's latter-day Presidential Council economists, Stanislav Shatalin.†

Even Lieberman – the most brilliant member of their law-school class, the man who once had to clear his own radical ideas with Gorbachev before daring to mention 'market principles' in a speech – had a sobering perspective. 'When Mikhail Sergeyevich came to power in 1985 he didn't know five-sixths of what he knows now,' Lieberman told me in early 1990. 'His first steps upset me. But two years later he began to understand where to go.'†

A Disastrous Life Accident

Two momentous events in 1986, one destructive and the other cathartic, forced Gorbachev to examine the ills of the Soviet system at a deeper level. One was an external accident, the other a subjective passage. Both affected him emotionally and started the wheels of his creative thinking churning more vigorously.

It had been one of his missions to boost the conversion of the country to nuclear power. His first five-year plan called with old-style Party bombast for a doubling of the nation's nuclear capacity. Two months later, at 1.23 on the morning of 26 April 1986, a state-of-the-art nuclear reactor in the Ukraine exploded. Its deadly cloud of radiation passed through the countries of Western Europe, irradiating the food chain and altering human cells, and raising the radio-active levels of iodine in milk as far away as America.†

The explosion was followed by a bureaucratic cover-up revealing a level of state negligence and deceit that shook the entire nation and brought Gorbachev down to earth. The unwillingness of anyone in the Chernobyl plant to take responsibility – an endemic feature of Soviet life – had led to an almost inevitable sequence of operator errors in a hazard-ous facility where no 'idiot-proofing' had been done to guard against human error. The incapacity of the centralized com-mand system to mobilize a prompt and efficient response to the disaster was another painful blow for Gorbachev. He did not stand in the way of the international pressure that forced admissions of such problems from high-ranking government officials, and in that decision he gave the first breath to glasnost. Chernobyl also opened up the issue of the callous-ness of the bureaucracy in poisoning the environment across a whole spectrum, whether it was chemically toxic foods, dangerous levels of heavy metals in drinking water, pregnant women delivering prematurely due to carbon dioxide in their placentas, workers being contaminated in coal mines, steel mills or oilfields.

Gorbachev was shaken by Chernobyl. It took him a long time to react, but two years later he moved to avert an even greater national catastrophe. Two respected writers among his Kremlin connections, Olas Adamovich and Daniil Granin, wrote to the General Secretary to tell him they had urgent information that contradicted the data he was receiving from the governments of the republics immediately affected. Gor-bachev called them in. They brought him a list given to them by academician Valery Legasov, an aide to the designer of the Chernobyl reactor.

Legasov had hanged himself. 'He told us that the following plants of the same design would also blow up – the one in Armenia, in Leningrad, in Lithuania and in Smolensk,' the writers reported.

Gorbachev's question was sharp. 'Why don't physicists write to tell me about this?'

'I asked Legasov the same thing,' said Adamovich. 'He replied, "The interests of the clan."'

Gorbachev's reaction was immediate and practical. He gathered together all the nuclear scientists to demand they tell him the truth about the safety of the country's nuclear power plants. They assured him all was well. According to Adamovich, 'with his peasant's cunning mind showing, he said to the scientists, "If everything's fine, then go to all these plants, check them, and give me your word when you return that they are safe."' Gorbachev knew very well that nobody takes responsibility for anything in the Soviet Union, so he insisted they sign papers agreeing that they would indeed be responsible. When the scientists returned, eleven of them insisted that the plants they'd visited be closed immediately.

The central government quickly and permanently shut down the nuclear power plant in Armenia and subsequently directed that five more reactors be taken out of operation. Four years later, Gorbachev directed the Soviet press to acknowledge the much wider consequences of the Chernobyl horror: four million people in the Ukraine and Byelorussia were currently living on nuclear-contaminated land, and more than 150,000 had been 'seriously affected' by radioactivity.†

An Emotional Turning Point

That autumn of 1986, Gorbachev would receive a more subjective blow. It was delivered by a movie, *Repentance*, a gut-twisting allegory of the Stalin terror made by a Georgian filmmaker, Tengiz Abuladze. The setting is a sleepy, lushly green town in the southern Caucusus that looks just like Stavropol, and what happens to the hero parallels the torment of tens of millions, including the family of Mikhail Gorbachev.

The mythical mayor of the town dies, and everyone expresses ritualistic grief at his funeral. But the corpse is dug up again and again, and placed each time in full, unavoidable view of the public. When the graverobber is caught, she turns out to be a woman who stands defiant but pure, all in white, and tells her accusers that the crimes of the dead man cannot be buried. She proceeds to tell the story of Varlam, the mayor, who symbolizes Stalin.

The movie flashes back forty years to a scene in which her father, then a young artist and a Christian, gains an audience with the mayor to plead for the saving of the town's oldest historical treasure, a sixth-century church. The mayor has given a directive that a scientific laboratory be built inside it, and the church's foundations are crumbling. The mayor defends his decision: nobody believes in God any more, doesn't the artist believe in progress, science? Destroy a church and you destroy the roots of the culture, warns the artist. The mayor smiles genially and offers a palliative: 'The experiments will be continued at a minimal level.' Eventually, of course, 'scientific progress' blows up the ancient church. This must have plucked at Gorbachev's sense of guilt over the explosion at Chernobyl. But he later confided that he felt an even more personal identification with the plight of the artist.

In a subsequent scene, the mayor calls upon the artist in his home. Half-drunk and boorish but also capriciously charming, he strokes the hair of the artist's little daughter and kisses the skirts of his gentle wife and feigns solemn praise for the artist's work. 'This is the kind of art we need, serious, deep,' he says, hinting only that 'our enemies' might regard such images as escaping from reality or leading to chaos. Between jokes and slobbered operatic singing and butchered Shakespeare, the mayor vows that 'Only a spiritual leader, a moral hero, can enlighten the people!' He obviously means himself.

The mayor also recalls the day he was appointed: he spotted the artist and his wife and daughter in the window

of their two-storey house on the town square. He remembers
that the little girl was blowing bubbles, and that the artist
shut the window instead of being attentive to his speech.

'I notice everything, so beware of me,' warns the mayor,
advertising his all-seeing godlike powers. 'Some blow bubbles while others track down enemies of the people.'

The mayor is a big heavy man in a black shirt, leather
braces and high boots. His head is narrowed at the temples
like a pear, or a sub-primate, and he wears a Hitlerian
moustache. His eyes squint behind tiny tinted pince-nez,
through which he constricts the world to his own hideously
distorted perspective. But he is everywhere, standing Mus-
solini-like in a jeep, singing and shouting and tracking down
souls to the ends of the earth, trembling with his obsession:
'We can trust no one . . . four out of every three people are
enemies!' He is the model of all despots. His ubiquitous
image, giganticized on placards, pursues the artist and his
wife into their nightmares.

Gorbachev sat through the private showing intently, until
the climactic scene: the artist is playing the piano while his
angelic wife sleeps fitfully in a chair near him. In the middle
of the night their intimacy is shattered by the ringing of their
bell. 'It's them! I'm sure it is,' gasps the wife. The secret
police step inside, planting their feet wide, faces hidden
behind helmets.

'Are you Sandro?' they demand. 'Come with us. It won't
be for long.'

While the secret police strip the walls of the artist's
paintings, their commander opens the piano with his heavily
black-gloved fingers and picks out a puerile and discordant
tune. He glares at the wife through the visor of his helmet.
The narrow eyes and pince-nez give him away. It is the omnipotent mayor; the anti-intellectual champion of unknowing.

Finally Gorbachev's iron self-control failed him. He
choked back his tears, as he confided later in private
remarks to several Italian Communist editors.† It was the
same story his grandmother had whispered to him about the

night his grandfather Gorbachev had been arrested, with the same capricious cruelty, the same uncertainty and stigma left on his family.

Seeing *Repentance* marked an emotional turning point for the fifty-five-year-old survivor of the Stalin era. Memories repressed for forty years must have been shaken loose and surfaced in all their dank and dreadful ugliness, but he used his inner discipline to confront the darkness and to extrapolate from his own reaction a decision about his society as a whole. Gorbachev gave a spontaneous directive to his aides: 'Make sure enough copies are made so that everyone in the country can see it.'

The film's key insight is offered by the character of the artist's daughter. Dressed in white, representing the conscience of the nation, she tells her accusers why she will dig up the body of the despot three hundred times if necessary. 'To bury him is to forgive him!'

Now Gorbachev had to answer the same moral dilemma for himself. Should he allow the lies of history to be exposed? Rip off the collective blindfold and expose the Soviet people to the hideous glare of truth, in the hopes they would have the inner strength to use their release from psychological bondage in a positive way? Gorbachev could not succeed unless he could persuade his country to come to terms with its own past. But Soviet society, forced into mass repression of memory, had learned to shift the moral responsibility for its problems entirely on to someone else. Perhaps they would hold *him* responsible for stripping away their illusions about the godliness of Stalin.

It was a decision he agonized over that winter, one that would have the most profound and untold consequences on hundreds of millions of people. He later admitted it was a turning point. Seingrimur Hermannson, the Foreign Minister of Iceland who met with Gorbachev in 1987, quoted him as saying that the hardest decision he had ever had to make was to 'expose the faults of the previous Soviet leaders'.†

*

The first glimmer of Gorbachev's willingness to dare democratization came only a couple of months after he had seen *Repentance* with a dramatic phone call to Gorky in December 1986, where Andrei Sakharov and his wife Elena Bonner had been kept in isolation from the world for seven years. The decision had been taken by the Kremlin, for calculated political reasons, to release the pair. Two months earlier, the Nobel laureate had sent the General Secretary a letter describing his banishment as illegal and unprecedented. He promised that he would 'make no more public statements, apart from exceptional cases when, in the words of Tolstoy, "I cannot remain silent."'

'Mikhail Sergeyevich will speak with you,' said a woman's voice when Sakharov picked up his hastily installed phone on 16 December 1986. This was the exchange, as recorded in Sakharov's *Memoirs*:

'Hello, this is Gorbachev speaking.'

'Hello, I'm listening.'

'I received your letter. We've reviewed it and discussed it. You can return to Moscow . . . A decision has also been made about Elena Bonnaire,' he said, mispronouncing the name.

Sakharov broke into his speech with an emotional outburst. 'That's my wife!'

Gorbachev said they could return to Moscow together, exhorting Sakharov to 'go back to your patriotic work!'

The physicist thanked the political leader. Still in mourning for a friend, the writer and political prisoner Marchenko, who was apparently killed by force-feeding during a hunger strike, Sakharov then spoke up for all those prosecuted for their beliefs. 'Everyone sentenced under those articles has been sentenced illegally, unjustly. They ought to be freed!'

'I don't agree with you,' Gorbachev said.

After a further, unsatisfying exchange, Sakharov was afraid he might say too much and so he spoke abruptly. 'Thank you again, goodbye,' said the prisoner to his liberator. He broke protocol by being the one to bring their conversation to a close. It must have caught the Soviet leader off guard.

Gorbachev had nothing left to say but 'Goodbye.'

That highly charged conversation was the harbinger of a power struggle between the two men and the conflicting forces of compromise and conscience they represented, a struggle that Sakharov would pursue even beyond the grave, through his memoirs. Sakharov tells us that at the time he felt no sense of joy or victory. Given his letter, his promise and the imperious tone of the General Secretary, it was all rather demeaning.↑

But for the General Secretary it was a different story. Reaching out to this man who carried the conscience of the nation – a man exiled for speaking the truth at the same moment Mikhail Sergeyevich was catapulted into power for being a disciple of doublespeak – would qualify as a personal act of repentance for Gorbachev. In a three-month period after Sakharov's release, about three hundred political prisoners were freed.*↑

New New Soviet Man

The release of Sakharov, together with Gorbachev's momentous decision to expose some of the worst horrors of Soviet history, initiated the campaign of democratization in January 1987. Having concluded that economic reform would not be possible without political reform, he determined that to galvanize the people behind perestroika would require 'drastic changes in thinking and psychology'.↑

'What Gorbachev did in the sphere of democratization and glasnost he did under the influence of Raisa,' emphasizes Vladimir Kvint, who, as a professor of the Academy of

---

* A year later, in December 1987, the total number of remaining political prisoners and people convicted for 'nationalism' or for 'religious' or dissident activities or in detention in psychiatric hospitals for 'crimes of conscience' was estimated at 2,500, according to Soviet historian Roy Medvedev.

Sciences and one of Gorbachev's team of Siberian economists, saw repeated evidence of Raisa's hand just behind the scenes. With propaganda genius Yakovlev to mastermind the campaign, Gorbachev set out to accomplish a complete psychological and spiritual remake of his people – a 'new personality with a new perestroika brain', as described by top Soviet space scientist Stanislav Fyodorov – or what could be called New New Soviet Man.†

It would be as carefully and brilliantly planned as any military campaign, but the army Gorbachev organized was a very different sort from the crushing columns of tanks or repressive secret police upon which his predecessors relied. *Repentance* was released in Moscow that January and shortly thereafter Gorbachev gave new marching orders to journalists. Gathering together his mass media in February 1987, he first congratulated them on the way they were presenting perestroika. 'It's good,' he said. 'The press is showing the new stage of restructuring as a difficult complex and dialectical process. That's how it is in real life.'† Then he coached them in the proper dialectic with which to present the corrections of formerly falsified events in Soviet history.

'History must be seen as it is. Everything happened, there were mistakes – grave mistakes – but the country moved forward. Take the years of industrialization or collectivization. That was life, reality. It was the people's fate, with all its contradictions – with achievements and with mistakes.'†

Gorbachev's domestic strategy was that of a lifelong expert in manipulation of public opinion. In his Stavropol years he was responsible for 'propaganda, ideology and agitation', and supervised local newspapers throughout the territory. Yakovlev, his right-hand man, had spent twenty-five years in the Propaganda Department and believed the Party had to take the initiative in the 'moral purification of [the people's] consciousness'.†

Yakovlev's view was that they should blame everything on Stalin. 'As a young man, I can remember that I met Communists, decent honest people,' he told me, recalling his argument. 'What Stalin did was to build some distorted dogma in which people were treated as pigs or great machines. When I read about the past, I grow bitter. But we must start telling the truth. I think it would be double immorality if you tried to build new illusions while pretending that things that happened in the past did not happen.'†

The building of 'new illusions' by the Party was an old story. Gorbachev and Yakovlev were themselves formed during the time when Soviet leaders claimed they were creating a New Socialist Man. Then, the illusion was that each man must sacrifice today to build the glorious future of Communism tomorrow, while in reality he was being used as a cog and condemned to futile work, appalling living and working conditions, and a shorter and shorter life. The fundamental postulates and principles of Marxism–Leninism had been implanted in him: the liquidation of individuality and personal property; the acceptance of state ownership and state responsibility for all social life; and the surrender of all ethnic, nationalistic and regional autonomy to a centralized authority. As rector of the Moscow Institute for Historian–Archivists Yuri Afanasev says with irony, 'We got rid of the market, we got rid of craven monetary relations – we've done exactly what the classics taught us to do. And now we've got it, just what we wanted, Marxist–Leninist-socialism.'

And so glasnost expanded into an unabridged publicity campaign to elaborate on and disseminate truths revealed by Khrushchev thirty years before. In his famous 'secret speech', delivered to the 20th Party Congress on 25 February 1956, Khrushchev attempted to obliterate the cult of his predecessor, the revered Stalin, for 'violating all existing standards of morality and of Soviet law', but his message was never published in the Soviet Union.

It became apparent to Gorbachev that working through the mass media and literary journals was insufficient. Again, he would have to broaden his circles, literally drafting the full spectrum of the liberal intelligentsia as his shock troops to disseminate the same message through the emotional mediums of novels, films and performance poetry.

Revolution of the Mind

Writers are the rock stars of the Soviet Union. Russian poets think a crowd of 10,000 panting to see them perform is, well, smallish. Poetry as performance art, pre-glasnost, was the most subtle, satisfying and subjective container for messages of half-truth in a society forced to live a lie. And so poets, followed by novelists, filled the roles of rock star, politician and priest and were worshipped by the masses because they came closest to being honest.

The writers of Gorbachev's generation had suffered most of their lives from the lack of a patron who would protect them. The brief 'thaw' during Khrushchev's early reign had inspired them to articulate the most serious social and political concerns of their society, but after his ousting they were once again abandoned and persecuted. Those who could bear the agony of pulling up the roots of language, and with it the very structure of thought that was the source of their prose or poetry, emigrated or defected. Others stayed behind and hid, or picked their morally treacherous way between acting occasionally as the brave bards of conscience and staying mostly on the right side of the KGB by engaging in agitprop or giving damaging denunciations of others.

'Orphans of literature' is how Anatoly Pristavkin always thought of his generation. A gifted novelist, Pristavkin was in his mid-fifties by the time Gorbachev appeared. 'First we crawled to one goal – to survive and exist – then we started crawling to another, to exist in literature,' he told me. 'But of course that orphanage didn't leave us in peace.'

Gorbachev and Yakovlev, or their aides, called many of the writers personally to enlist them in the patriotic duty of transmitting selected truths of history to the public. Suddenly these men and women were being asked to stand up and speak their conscience. Some could scarcely believe their ears. It was almost too good to be true, tantamount to a declaration that worship could resume. Every educated Soviet citizen whose home I have visited keeps his or her books enshrined in the central altar of the apartment – often glass-enclosed on lovingly home-made bookshelves and adorned with vases, dried flowers, even crucifixes – very much like the altars of the medieval monasteries that have survived in the countryside. And whenever they remove a book and caress it while they describe the precious contents for a visitor, I think of Pristavkin's metaphor: 'Literature is the expression of conscience and spirit of the people. Your friend can betray you, the woman you love can betray you, but a book – never.'†

In the front lines of Gorbachev's shock troops was Anatoly Rybakov, whose long-suppressed novel, *Children of the Arbat*, was launched as the opening salvo in a devastating campaign of psychological warfare to discredit Stalin and blame all the failures of socialism on one man. As Rybakov outlined the truth campaign to me one day, 'The worst thing Stalin did was to destroy agriculture and thus destroy the economy. We lost seventy million people in the last seventy years – thirteen million during collectivization, eight million during the civil war, twenty-seven million during the Second World War, and tens of millions under Stalin's repressions, but the most horrible losses were psychological and moral. One man did the thinking for everybody, and the rest stopped thinking. People have lived in fear for decades, they have to liberate themselves from the fear, and that won't change for a long time.'†

Rybakov, who had stayed while dozens of the most talented Soviet writers emigrated, became a pillar of the Soviet literary Establishment, even savouring the irony of winning the Stalin Prize in 1951. But his magnum opus, the autobiographical novel he wrote in 1969 about a young idealistic victim of Stalin, twice announced for publication in the Soviet Union, had each time been banned. Foreign editors offered to publish it.

'I refused, I waited,' gloated the Ukrainian-born Jewish writer when I visited him in the writer's colony of Peredelkino. 'I wanted this novel to be read by my people in my country.' He laughed and poured imported Harvey's Bristol Cream sherry for his editor wife and his visitors. 'So when the doors were finally opened, my book was first in line. It broke through, and all the others followed.' A robust seventy-eight in his black t-shirt, Rybakov has become the literary Picasso of the perestroichiki. More than seven million copies of *Children of the Arbat* have been printed in the Soviet Union.

These older writers saw their destiny as helping Gorbachev by 'changing the psychology of the masses', as Rybakov put it. It is standard operating procedure in the Soviet Union for leaders to use writers as propagandists to redefine the social contract between individuals and the state. 'So you see,' the now celebrated Rybakov sat back after another sip of sherry, 'we have to change the psychology of every man and woman – that's why we begin with novels, film, theatre, TV – this is the way Gorbachev sees the policies of the leader should awaken the initiative of people, so they'll say, "I want to start a co-operative," or "I want to own my own land."'

Yevgeny Yevtushenko, the Siberian wonder-boy, had claimed fame over forty years earlier, at age fifteen. He and Andrei Voznesensky were the most daring young writers among the Shestdesyatniki – the Sixtiers as they're known. They are the same generation as Gorbachev – who has admitted being affected by their poetry – and the same age, in their late fifties.

In recent years many Russian and Western readers have tired of Yevtushenko and Voznesensky, and neither has aged terribly well. But I found them in the writer's colony of Peredelkino giddy with the male post-menopausal zest granted by glasnost. Yevtushenko is a great tree of a man, too big for his house, his limbs flying about as if in a storm as he enumerates both the successes and great obstacles of the Gorbachev era. 'My life now is so crowded, I can't write poetry!' he squealed.

Sitting at his table, holding court, Yevtushenko evoked the sense felt by Soviet writers of furious participation in the momentous events of glasnost and perestroika. Yevtushenko had always gone out of his way to espouse his principles, shielded by his world-celebrated poetic gifts. He had spread his own celebrity over other beleaguered writers, making protests, hiding them in his dacha. But under Gorbachev he took on direct political leadership: spearheading Memorial, an association to trace and memorialize the victims of Stalinism; organizing the first Soviet PEN club; speaking out at the first Congress against Party privileges. Yevtushenko had become the ultimate public man.

When Gorbachev had to miss Yevtushenko's poetry reading at the Kremlin Palace of Congresses, he telephoned him personally – from the site of the earthquake in Armenia – to apologize. 'You know we have a tragic situation in Armenia now,' said the leader to the poet, referring to the first in a chain reaction of ethnic separatist revolts. 'What do you think we can do about it?'

'It would be better if there were Armenian representatives who would find their own solution, without Russians,' Yevtushenko offered.

'You are right,' he heard Gorbachev say.

Such conversations are the stuff of Norman Mailer's dreams.

If you are not afraid of being stung by nettles, you walk through shoulder-high weeds to find the door of the dacha assigned to Andrei Voznesensky. Suddenly he appears, all in white, gliding, arms outstretched, like a child's kite. Playful as always, the boy in him betrayed by a bulge at the waist and a rubberiness in the face, Voznesensky still acts the part of Pasternak's child protégé. He has never stopped being fourteen – the age at which he burst on to the literary scene with an ejaculatory inspiration.

Voznesensky invited us past the dacha's anonymous

exterior into a modernist interior that surrounds him with
self-images: drawings for giant phallic constructions, prints
created with Alexander Lieberman and Robert Rauschen-
berg. But his glass cabinet of writing notebooks is a dis-
orderly spill of distracted thought.

Hovering always a foot or two from him is his wife Zoya,
the hard-boiled organizer and agent for her husband, and a
successful sociological writer in her own right. Glasnost had
revolutionized their lives and even seemed to have revived
Voznesensky's faith. He had met two previous Soviet
leaders: 'I loved Khrushchev,' he admits. 'I thought he was a
liberal.' But once the poet was summoned to the Kremlin for
a tongue-lashing, he decided that Khrushchev was an ignorant, foul-mouthed man. 'A barbarian,' sums up Zoya,
who remembers the period of her husband's persecution.

Gorbachev, by contrast, is by far the most highly educated
Soviet leader since Lenin. Voznesensky was seated at the
General Secretary's table at the luncheon for President
Reagan held in December 1988 at the Writers' Union club.
Reagan read a few lines from Pasternak. Voznesensky leaned
over to Gorbachev and said he looked forward to publication
at last of *Doctor Zhivago*. Gorbachev didn't turn to an aide or
consult cue cards. He simply recited from memory two
stanzas of Pasternak's poetry. Voznesensky surrendered his
heart on the spot. And Gorbachev turned even this ultimate
social butterfly into a committed activist, putting him in
charge of the committee that rehabilitated and memorialized
Pasternak.

But at least one of the footsoldiers enlisted by Gorbachev
in his glasnost campaign, filmmaker Natasha Barchevsky,
came to see his shift to ideological reform as a tactical move.
Economic reform was too complex, lengthy and politically
charged a process, so Secretary Gorbachev switched strategies to concentrate on the psychological remake of the
people. 'Here he gained the full support of intellectuals'
circles and also international support,' she says. 'He became
respected all over the world for what he did in ideology, he

changed the thinking. That's why the economy is still at the bottom, and ideology has gone so far. It was easier to do with ideology than with economy.'

Searching for a Vision

In the middle of this great awakening, in the summer of 1987, Mikhail Sergeyevich dropped out of sight for fifty-two days. Usually, a great leader must face a cruel repudiation and retreat for a period 'in the wilderness' of self-contemplation and despair before he or she can return to make the ultimate transformation of the society. Gorbachev had to undergo whatever radical inner transformation he was prepared to make *while managing* a revolution.

Still, he did manage to hole up that August and most of September in one of his dachas, this one on the Black Sea, to write a book. The idea had been suggested to him by Michael Bessie, the American editor. At first, Gorbachev insisted on naming the book in true collectivist spirit, '*Our* Perestroika', but Bessie convinced him to drop the 'our' and write in a more individual voice. In thinking out and writing the book (with the help of Ivan Frolov and other aides) Gorbachev meant to set in motion the destruction of the Stalinist system of central command and political repression. In *Perestroika*, which became an international bestseller, he acknowledged: 'It is possible to suppress, compel, bribe, break or blast, but only for a certain period.'†

Gorbachev and his literary lieutenants were brutally candid about what had gone wrong with the noble ideals of Lenin. But what, I wondered, was Gorbachev's animating personal vision of the Soviet Union he would remake out of the ashes of such rough reform?

De Gaulle had an image of France as the cultural leader of Europe; Churchill saw Britain as a timeless embodiment of eternal, shining principles;† Reagan had a Technicolor vision of an America of unapologetic patriotism and old-time religion, constructed out of movies and archetypes of the past which exercised a powerful emotional pull on the public.

Gorbachev's international vision was not only grand, but he had a ready audience eager to embrace it. The two months he took 'in the wilderness', however, gave Gorbachev only a fleeting chance to formulate his image of what the Union of Soviet Socialist Republics should look like domestically in the twenty-first century, what kind of new economic deal and common ideology could bind so many disparate nationalities and ethnic groups under a common purpose. Gorbachev clearly did not have, as Churchill had, a cavalcade of history marching through his mind or a fixed moral universe from which to proceed. And consulting the history of reformers in Russia presented a bleak picture.

Soon after he became General Secretary, Gorbachev had ordered a review of the strategies attempted by Pyotr Stolypin, another famous top–down Russian reformer. From 1906 to 1911, as the powerful Chairman of the Council of Ministers under Czar Nicholas II, Stolypin tried to create a base of landowning peasants as a bulwark against the Bolsheviks and urban revolutionary groups. He was assassinated in 1911 by a former secret police agent, which gave rise to the suggestion that he had been done in by a political conspiracy. Even further back in the mists of history, Gorbachev had the example of Speransky, the gifted architect of Alexander I's imperial Russia (1801–25), who had been packed off to Siberia once the Czar changed his mind about reform.

Searching Russian history for a more successful reformist leader, one could point to Alexander II, the liberator of the serfs in 1861, but not even Alexander II had been as daring as Gorbachev. Despite his reforms, he never intended to destroy the ruling layer of the aristocracy. Gorbachev, by contrast, understood that many members of his ruling elite – the Party aristocracy – had to be disempowered.

Russia's misfortune is that her leaders always tried to programme her development. America grew naturally, like a tree. Gorbachev's greatest gift to Russia was to be the first leader who understood the necessity of a natural process. His New Thinking on perestroika at home was a dream of an entirely new social contract between leader and led: not by order or force but by consultation, he and his people would move through an orderly progression of stages to achieve full 'democracy within socialism'.

And with the crystallization of this romantic dream, the birth of a fourth Gorbachev took place. Having tested Andropov's vision, he was ready to become his own man, even to start undermining the very Communist Party apparat that had spawned him.

He escalated his reforms to a 'social revolution', announcing his intention for the first time in his book. Pacesetters like the sociologist Zaslavskaya, who picked up an early copy of *Perestroika* on travels abroad, were excited by the declaration of a social revolution, but to repeat such words among colleagues, even in late 1987, produced shock and disbelief.†

Gorbachev would make enormous leaps of thinking during 1987 and 1988, developing quickly, dramatically, instinctively rather than theoretically – which is most uncommon in Russia. Although he couldn't have understood fully what he was doing, he did perceive that his task was to make the rigid Soviet system flexible, able to bend to reality. The *process*, he believed, would change the Russian people from passive sleepwalkers to active participants in their society.

'Two centuries would not be too long for such a transformation,' says a senior American State Department analyst, staggered by the task Gorbachev dared to set himself.

But his people were not moving at anything like the pace Gorbachev was. For a thousand years – five hundred under the yoke of the Mongols–Tatars, and five hundred more from Ivan the Terrible to Lenin – the Russian people had no experience of liberal democracy or economic competition. And for seven decades under their Marxist masters they had been isolated from the civilized world, forbidden to travel to the West and insulated from the great currents of social, political, economic and spiritual thought. They had been thoroughly schooled in the belief that the accumulation of personal wealth – anything that smacks of monopolies or private ownership of the means of production – is evidence of oppression or corruption.

Grigory Baklanov, whose rallying-cry at the influential literary journal, *Znamya*, was to tell the truth about Stalinism, saw reader mail pouring in from every region and every social stratum that indicated that *30 to 40 per cent of the society was still Stalinist* in 1986. These people praised the order they had enjoyed under Stalin and equated democracy with crime. Even by late 1989, a national opinion poll showed that 40 per cent of the population still craved the return of a leader with a 'strong hand'.†

'We have a saying', lamented Baklanov, 'that only the grave will straighten out a hunchback.'†

'Now we are trying to solve problems that originated not in 1917, at the time of the October Revolution, but in the time of Peter the Great – 300 years ago,' says Yakov Grodin, a Leningrad scholar of Russian political history. The historian was emphatic in concluding, 'Gorbachev is in the most difficult position of all the reformers.'†

For the first three years Gorbachev engendered hope and infused the intelligentsia with his own insatiable energy and appetite for change. In this, as in maniacal commitment to work, he was not at all like most of his people. In fact, Gorbachev is an astonishingly anomalous personality in Soviet society – a congenital optimist, where pessimism historically shadows the Russian soul, and adventurous, full of ideas and initiative, where the reflexes of most Russians are more passive. He is a normal leader in a society that is still abnormal.

Indeed, one of his greatest contributions to Soviet history, no matter what happens in the future, stems from the most strikingly non-Russian facet of his personality: his unusual personal capacity to live with turbulence and not to be afraid of it. Even in the middle of a whirlwind of creative initiatives he always seemed to maintain his calm control, even detachment. Kissinger, who visited him in 1988, told me, 'Everybody who meets him, including me, marvels at his serenity.'

The Yeltsin Fiasco

During 1987 Gorbachev kicked up a great deal of dust. By creating a more assertive parliament and promoting a parcel of new laws, Gorbachev sought to transform a military–feudal state, based on fear and totalitarianism, into a more open political state based on laws and rationality.

At the same time the Soviet leader turned his attention to another near-impossible task: 'breaking the back of the bureaucracy'.† The place to start, he decided, was at the local level. He persuaded the Central Committee to give voters a choice of candidates in local elections, preparing the way for the creeping insurrection by which he would accomplish the purge of Old Guard Party committees. It was the first of a series of wily moves by which the leader manoeuvred many of the old Stalinists of his Party apparat out of the door. That June the first experimental multi-candidate elections were held in local districts, and the Party apparat began to feel the people's displeasure.† Inevitably, as Gorbachev struggled with writing *Perestroika* at his Black Sea dacha, the drumbeat of opposition from both the reactionaries and the progressives began to be heard back in Moscow.

Gorbachev consistently denied in public that perestroika had 'political enemies' or even 'opposition', upholding the standard Communist pretence of total unity.† Even as he launched purge after purge of 'old thinkers' in the Central Committee, army, KGB and regional Party machines, he kept steering a middle course between the reactionary Stalinists represented by Yegor Ligachev, and the radical reformers represented by Boris Yeltsin.

Ligachev, the Party's number-two man on the Politburo, that August called his own meeting of the leaders of the mass media and directors of the 'creative unions' to denounce certain publications and persons for 'showing a disrespectful attitude towards the generations who constructed socialism'. He vowed to put a stop to this 'one-way democracy'.† His targets were the feisty weekly magazines, *Ogonyok* and its editor Vitaly Korotich; *Moscow News* and its crusading editor Yegor Yakovlev; and the weekly *Nedelya* ('Week') published by the increasingly adventurous *Izvestia*. This attack by the Party's number-two man threw journalistic and intellectual circles into an uproar.

'Drunk with glasnost' was the accusation hurled on the front page of the sacrosanct newspaper of the Central Commitee, *Pravda*, on 21 August. Conservatives in major propaganda posts were now coming very close to attacking the General Secretary himself. Magazines that embraced glasnost were said to 'direct readers towards shabby tastes, towards a petit-bourgeois mentality that all too frequently coincides with amorality and the consumerism of Western mass culture'.† Historians were also attacked for the very reason that Gorbachev had unleashed them: 'they do not want to forgive Stalin'.†

From the opposite side of the political spectrum came a rocket on 12 September, a letter from Boris Yeltsin. It had been a year and nine months since Gorbachev had placed the hotheaded reformer at the head of the Moscow city Party organization. Now Yeltsin complained that little had been accomplished: 'Despite the incredible efforts you are making, the struggle to maintain political stability can lead to stagnation, to the state of affairs that we reached before, under Brezhnev.'†

Rumours were flying about the reasons for Gorbachev's long absence, but when he returned to the political scene on 29 September after the long vacation, all he said was, 'I can tell you, I earned it.'†

Galvanized into action by the great debate, Gorbachev prepared the ground for a climax to his de-Stalinization campaign – the speech he planned to make on the anniversary of the October Revolution. He had seen a screening of another devastating film, *Risk I*, which used documentary footage to show Stalin's concentration camps and which resurrected the banished Khrushchev and cast him in a rosy light as a betrayed reformer. Gorbachev learned that the film had been banned. In another of his god-is-calling suprises, he telephoned the filmmakers, Dmitry and Natasha Barchevsky, to ask if they would object to having their film shown on television. Astonished at his personal sponsorship, the filmmakers sat back while the movie was given massive nationwide promotion on the nightly news show before it was aired to an audience of one hundred million in October 1987.†

Outraged letters followed from daughters and widows of the men who had operated the concentration camp system, demanding, 'How could you defame our family name?' But just as many others whose relatives had perished in the gulag wrote in tearful thanks, 'Thank God that truth has finally started to come out.'

The General Secretary had already narrowed his own attack on Stalin to the peak of the Terror when his grandfather was taken: 'The Soviet people will never forgive or justify the repressions of the late 1930s.'† Then he submitted an advance draft of his keynote speech for the October Revolution celebration to secretaries of the Central Committee and Politburo members.

During the Politburo's discussion of the draft, Yeltsin got under Gorbachev's skin. The other members maintained at least the appearance of unanimity. Yeltsin was the misfit; he raised questions about the Party apparat, whose privileges and blatant corruption had been the target of his work. 'I still placed my hopes in Gorbachev, in the belief that he would realize the absurdity of a policy of half-measures and marking time,' Yeltsin would write later. 'I thought his pragmatism and natural intuition would be enough to tell him that the time had come to tackle the bureaucracy head-on . . .'†

Impetuously, Gorbachev shut off discussion and stormed out of the room, leaving the usually granite-faced Politburo stalwarts open-mouthed. But when he reappeared half an hour later, he still had not composed himself. He let go with a tirade of resentment, revealing how stung and pained he had been by the attacks on him in recent months. Although this rambling, 'almost hysterical', stream of consciousness had no bearing on Yeltsin's specific questions, Gorbachev directed his ire at the maverick Moscow boss and attacked his character 'almost in gutter language'.†

It was the beginning of the end, according to Yeltsin.

Gorbachev wouldn't even look at him or shake hands with him after that. Yeltsin sprang his own surprise attack on the General Secretary several weeks later at a plenum of the Party's Central Committee. Gorbachev had met with him beforehand and thought he had persuaded the malcontent to wait until the end of the year before resigning. Yeltsin's speech was brief and brutal, condemning the illusion of perestroika's progress and shattering the myth of unity within the Politburo. He tried to resign on the spot from the Central Committee, but the Party rules didn't allow it.

When it was time for the climax of the General Secretary's campaign to assign Stalin to infamy, with his three-hour condemnation speech in the Palace of Congresses, Gorbachev compromised himself. Bowing to the conservative criticisms of his speech draft, he represented Stalin's forced collectivization and accelerated industrialization as 'necessary' choices, referring only to 'errors' and 'mistakes'. And he went out of his way to state that radical reform of the Party did not cast doubt on 'its mission as society's guiding force.'†

At another Party plenum that November, in a fresh outburst of temper, he accepted Yeltsin's resignation as a candidate-member of the Politburo, calling him an 'immature demagogue' who had placed 'his own ambitions above the interests of the Party'. Yeltsin's precarious physical condition enhanced his appealing position as the underdog in this unprecedented public show of Kremlin bloodletting. Suffering from heart disease, he was taken from the hospital to the plenum heavily medicated, barely coherent and, some thought, on the edge of a psychological breakdown. Making speech after speech, the apparatchiks piled on to savage him. Constrained by tradition from attacking the General Secretary himself, they were using Yeltsin as a surrogate to rip apart the progressive aspects of Gorbachev's programme.

It may have been a chilling moment for Gorbachev, but he could not contain the forces he'd unleashed. The deed was done. Yeltsin's bravado earned splashy headlines around the world and secured his popularity with Muscovites, in particular with young people, who were given no place in Gorbachev's ruling circles. Gorbachev telephoned the burly radical and, according to Yeltsin, spitefully told him 'he wasn't going to let me back into politics'.† Ultimately, however, Gorbachev's personal vendetta would be foiled by his own democratization campaign. He had created Yeltsin as an heroic underdog, one who would mount an aggressive comeback on the left, constantly worrying the leader like a mad dog who won't let go of someone's leg.

Despite the fact that Yeltsin appeared to be closer in outlook to him than anyone else except Yakovlev and Shevardnadze, Mikhail Sergeyevich could not tolerate the maverick's open criticism of him. Gorbachev had almost no tolerance for dissent from within his own progressive clan. He seemed to believe that once he lifted the oppression, everybody in his ruling clique would come to the same conclusions. This is what revolutionaries usually think, which is why they usually end up hanging their opponents. They cannot believe that everyone doesn't agree with them. Increasingly, Gorbachev would brand those liberal activists who didn't fall into line dutifully behind him 'adventurists'. An eyewitness to a meeting where Lenin was challenged, back in August 1905, remembered the same intolerance, even the same words, being used by the founder of the Communist state. When someone in the audience referred to an article by his disciple Tikhonov, which contradicted him on a certain point, Lenin's yellow cat's eyes narrowed. With a crooked smile he cut him down: 'Tikhonov is a political adventurer, nothing more.'†

The Roosevelt Inspiration

After decades of force-feeding the Soviet people on anti-capitalist dogma, any talk of markets coming out of the Kremlin would sound like heresy. How to explain away the appearance that the Communist leader was turning into a 'creeping capitalist' and giving concessions to the West? It was time to adopt a new mask of command, a more international, Westernized form.

Gorbachev would adopt the model of Franklin Roosevelt's New Deal. 'The Great Depression of the thirties came about due to a dilemma in capitalism,' as Yakovlev explained the conception to me. 'Roosevelt managed to save capitalism by changing it. That is the idea of our perestroika, which is aimed at giving our society fundamental equality.'

Yakovlev admitted that the rallying cry of perestroika – 'New Thinking' – was inspired by Roosevelt's slogan. As an exchange student at Columbia University in 1959 Yakovlev had studied the FDR period. He was taken not only by the slogan but by FDR's 'methodology' in changing the system. He continually pressed Gorbachev towards adopting elements of a market economy, attempting to take the sting out of its association with Western materialism by arguing that the market is a 'pre-capitalist structure', it has no 'political colour', but that it has always been the basis for democracy. 'We will take everything we feel is useful from the West,' he told me. 'Production is more successful in America, labour and management relations are more harmonious in Japan, the social problem has been solved most successfully in Sweden.'†

In a triumph of pragmatism over ideology, Gorbachev came to accept that to save the Communist system he would have to reform it in some major way. The FDR model also suited his own unique qualities. 'His eyes are still open, he's still willing to learn and admit it when he doesn't know,' as Ambassador Ridgway observed of him in 1987.

Gorbachev was not an administrative type of leader, not one who came to power with a plan. Neither was Roosevelt. Gorbachev's New Thinking, like Roosevelt's New Deal, would also take twice as long to work as people expected. And like FDR, he took up plan A, tried it, and if it didn't work he was on to Plan B by the next afternoon. For those first three years, like Roosevelt, his authority as the leader was affirmed because he gave his people hope. It was all they had to go on while their society was turned upside down and they were suspended between belief systems.

'Roosevelt, like all great innovators, had a half-conscious premonitory awareness of the coming shape of society, not wholly unlike that of an artist,' as the British essayist Isaiah Berlin put it. He seemed to have antennae that registered the most subtle subjective changes in the emotional climate of the electorate.†

Gorbachev, too, seemed to have a half-conscious vision in his mind's eye. For antennae, he had the extraordinary sensors of the KGB.

Every day the Soviet leader has at least half a dozen contacts with the vast secret police organization. He starts his morning with tea and breakfast that has been scientifcally examined by KGB testers; he cannot eat or drink anything until the KGB has put its security tag on it – as a high Party officer, his body belongs to the state. Then he's taken by a KGB driver and bodyguards from his new dacha on Moscow's outskirts to his office in the Central Committee. The first reports he reads every morning are prepared by the KGB. Their analysis of the 'people's psychology' is taken from whatever crisis points they are monitoring through a blanket surveillance of mail and phone contacts in that area.†

Armed with these most penetrating data on subtle shifts in the emotional zeitgeist, Gorbachev is usually prepared to get out in front of any challenge or demonstration and say the right thing – without huddling with aides or waiting for polls. For all his reforms, Gorbachev's KGB operates with all its old methods unchanged.

The astute American Ambassador to Moscow, Jack Matlock, believes that Gorbachev works more from his immediate observations than from any profound study of history. 'He has the pragmatism to see that successful societies are those which have stimulated creativity at the bottom, that allow a diffusion of information and, therefore, a diffusion of decision-making. He looks at Germany, Japan, South Korea, the US, Britain – every country that has been successful in the modern technological age has these characteristics – and he wants to see the same characteristics working here.'

The Roosevelt analogy breaks down, however, on one crucial point. Roosevelt acted with the consent of the governed. By the very act of *not* choosing to throw out their leader during the Depression, the American people consented to *share* the risks and sacrifices their leader asked of them during a period of painful change. That is the very essence of democracy, and what makes it different from the 'democratization' handed down by the unelected leader of an illegitimate party, as in Gorbachev's Soviet Union. The simple fact that the US electorate can change leaders every four years builds in protection against the inevitable isolation from everyday reality, self-delusions and arrogance of the leader, and guards against the follies of utopianism.

Ship at Sea

In a private conversation in 1989, Gorbachev confessed to Henry Kissinger, 'It was easy to know what was wrong. It is very difficult to determine what is right.'†

The Soviet leader had apparently accepted by February 1987 that the source of the economic crisis was not merely poor discipline or slack organization in the field, it was the centralization of the system itself. State monopolies of the means of production were ruled by Communist overseers every bit as rapacious as any capitalist robber baron, but the difference was that, without competition, people only pretended to work and the system only pretended to pay them. Antiquated equipment broke down with no incentive to replace it, and huge quantities of goods never even reached the consumer, while the best items were diverted into the shadow economy in return for kickbacks to the bureaucrats.

In the heat of debate at every level of Soviet leadership, Gorbachev managed to get his initial reform programme approved by the Central Committee and enacted into law by the Supreme Soviet in June 1987 – a moment of clarity and apparent triumph. His goal was to transform the centralized command economy into a more decentralized economy by introducing some elements of a market system. He had pushed through the groundbreaking Law on Socialist Enterprise which made it possible for the first time – on paper, at least – for any of the nation's 50,000 business enterprises to reorganize themselves outside state control. They could make a profit and elect their own manager, but they would also have to pay their own way or go out of business. He emphasized that the entire structure of the central planning ministries should be radically changed to deprive bureaucrats of the prerogative of meddling with the details of these restructured enterprises. He described the economy as in a 'pre-crisis situation'.†

This early, oxymoronic concept of a 'socialist market' was the plan of Gorbachev's chief economist, Abel Aganbegyan. Its glaring flaw was that the state planning bodies still had complete control over how much money would be invested in an enterprise, which natural resources it would be given and at what price, and how it should compensate its work force.†

Even to this much reform the ministries put up a resistance; they wanted a 'policy in stages', and they had the support of the Party apparat. They proposed a leisurely seven-year timetable which would allow them to circumvent the Gorbachev legislation. Gorbachev compromised, accepting their disastrous timetable, even as he warned with great vehemence in June that 'the changes in the lives and the mood of the people surpass the Party's understanding of them'.†

Socialism is the economics of the lunatic asylum, as progressive Soviet economists began admitting to their American counterparts. A centrally planned economy is not just a badly managed version of a market economy but a whole different species, where prices are set arbitrarily, by commands issued to producers, and demand is decided by entitlements issued to consumers. With eighty million Soviets living below the official poverty line,† the 'price reform' Gorbachev talked about could quickly turn a 'pre-crisis situation' into a familiar disaster: mobs of people, unable to buy the essentials of life, taking to the streets and preparing the way for the return of a populist authoritarian regime.

In his attempts to grapple with this seemingly intractable set of problems Gorbachev faced an amorphous set of enemies: the troika of the Party apparat (with its mirror image in the government's planning bureaucracies), the mafias and Homo Sovieticus. At every layer of the bureaucracy officals were motivated to do their bit to frustrate reform. If you can imagine 441,851 Primary Party Organizations, supervising the nation's industrial enterprises, school districts and collective farms, suddenly being asked to give up their tin-hat fiefdoms to allow decision-making by the enterprises themselves, you'll have some idea of the size and invisibility of the enemies of decentralization. And all the institutions and forms and methods Gorbachev brought home from his travels to the West didn't seem to do much good.

In fact, Gorbachev's zig-zagging moves on economic reform, from radical to cautious to outright reversals, only made matters worse.

For example, in 1988, an attempt was made to force Soviet

enterprises to satisfy consumers by ordering factory managers to link wages and bonuses to their sales. But nothing
was done to set up competition between different enterprises
that might produce the same commodity, and no lid was put
on growth of the money supply. So, using their monopolistic
powers, enterprise managers and their patrons in the
bureaucracy simply switched from producing low-priced
items to 'improved' products like new models of refrigerators
or fancier sausages, and the government had to print more
money so people could pay the higher prices.†

The stark contrast between Gorbachev's brilliantly smooth
voyage on the high seas of international diplomacy and his
foundering ship on the river of Russian history was crystal-
lized in one day at the very end of 1988. A supremely
confident Gorbachev was standing between President
Reagan and Vice President Bush on Governor's Island in
New York, having just made a world-class appearance at the
United Nations, when the radiophone in his limousine
signalled an emergency. An earthquake had flattened several
cities and towns in Soviet Armenia.

Raisa was still wearing her fur and Mikhail Sergeyevich his
cashmere plaid muffler when the First Couple rushed to the
scene. Surrounded by a crowd of wretchedly dressed,
matted-haired, unbathed, distraught-looking Soviet citizens
in Yerevan, the Gorbachevs looked like visitors from another
planet. They no longer had any semblance of being Russian,
they were apparitions from *out there* . . . the illusory and
suspect West.

Gorbachev spoke slowly, thickly, about how 'we all feel
your tragedy'. He appeared as if he were about to cry. Then
he turned his words into an inspirational sermon, vowing 'In
two years we're going to rebuild everything.'

On the heels of this glorious socialist promise, the TV
interviewer asked an unexpected question: 'What's going to
happen with this informal Karabakh commission?' The reference was to a burning issue among Armenians, who had

signed a declaration demanding that the autonomous
territory called Nagorno-Karabakh, landlocked inside the
republic of Azerbaijan and populated mostly by their nationality, be reunited with the Armenian republic.

All at once Gorbachev's demeanour changed utterly. His
lips curled back, his eyes blazed and he began to harangue
the questioner as if to say 'How dare you!' He accused him
of being devoid of morality, how could he raise such a
question in the midst of such tragedy? Waving his arms,
almost breathless with anger, he demanded, 'Who is using
the situation of Nagorno-Karabakh?' He lambasted the leaders
of the Popular Front, saying that they were interested only
in their own power, inhumane, immoral. 'You should stamp
them as adventurists! Political demagogues!'

Gorbachev had suddenly dropped the mask of the solemn,
empathetic patriarch eulogizing at a family tragedy and
exposed his true face: that of a European Russian with no
tolerance, understanding or patience for dissension among
the many nationalities in the vast non-Russian portions of
the Soviet empire. Gorbachev was totally unprepared to deal
with his 'nationalities problem', as it would come to be
called. His constant references to a 'common European
home' left out something that could hardly be ignored in the
East – the fate of the vast central Asian republics, all five of
them, and the three republics in the Caucasus region –
Armenia, Azerbaijan and Georgia.

All politics is in the end cultural. During the time of the
czars Russia was called a 'prison of nations'. Even today,
Gorbachev presides over an empire comprised of 170 different nationalities and more than 200 languages and dialects.
The Ingush and Kalmyks and Balkars are deported nationalities, while two million Chuvash are Turks and two million
peoples of Dagestan are Muslims. While the Slavic population of Russians (145 million) and Ukrainians (44 million,
including others in the west with a heavy mixture of Polish
and German blood) comprises 75 per cent of the population,
the fastest-growing population group is descendants of the

vanished Islamic empires centred in middle Asia. With all the news about Lithuania, for example, it is easy to overlook the fact that the population of that Baltic state is only three million, compared to the sixteen million Uzbeks who populate only one of the Asian republics. Even farther to the east are scattered semi-nomadic tribes of Mongols, Chinese and Koreans.†

Gorbachev rarely travelled to the East and almost never referred to Soviet Asia. Both the Armenian earthquake and the Nagorno-Karabakh bloodbath to come were symbolic of the first tremors of an earthquake under his inner empire that Gorbachev ignored. These deeper darker currents of history soon began to disrupt the very equilibrium beneath the leader's neat legal reforms.

Crossing the Rubicon

Gorbachev's Stalinist opponents rigged the conditions for a coup d'état in March 1988, hiding behind the apparently innocent voice of a chemistry teacher who wrote a letter from Leningrad attacking the 'liberal socialism of the left'. Nina Andreyeva's letter was reworked by editors at the right-wing newspaper *Sovietskaya Rossiya* to give off clear chauvinistic and anti-semitic signals and was published as a rallying cry in defence of the Stalinist 'model' against any and all 'revision'. Once again, Ligachev called together the mass media, applauding the Andreyeva letter as an 'example to follow' for all editorial staffs. The lines of battle were starkly drawn. The editor-in-chief of *Izvestia*, Ivan Laptev, returned to his office obviously upset. He sounded the alarm that was heard all over the Kremlin circles that spring: 'The time to choose has arrived.'†

Gorbachev's supporters conducted an investigation of Nina Andreyeva's letter and proved that it was indeed instigated from inside the Politburo, courtesy of Ligachev. But Gorbachev couldn't attack the right-winger directly within the Central Committee, since Ligachev had the sympathies of a majority of its conservative members. So, in one of the many manoeuvres that have proven Gorbachev to be unparalleled as a Kremlin infighter, he held 'consultations' with different power blocs, in order to divide the conservatives against their champion. Then, after freezing Ligachev into a minority position, Gorbachev saw to it that he was stripped of some of his duties at an April plenum.† The shockwaves reverberated up and down the apparat. Gorbachev and his few trusted supporters on the Politburo agreed to keep their uneasy victory quiet behind the Kremlin walls. But his closest ally, Yakovlev, told a friend how dangerous and decisive a moment it was: 'We have crossed the Rubicon.'†

And on the other side Gorbachev's clan arrived not at safety but at the prospect of civil war, stimulated by a whole new set of contradictions.

In the first place, true democratization cannot coexist with 'selective' popular suppression. Second, full historical truth is necessary before people will believe again in a leadership that has relentlessly lied and cynically fostered false illusions in the past. Third, if the society was now to be based firmly on the rule of law, how could it be led by an illegal, non-elected Communist Party? And the final contradiction: four hundred years of expansionism and absolute centralized rule are inherently inconsistent with democracy; but if central power were taken away, would there be any country left?

Only three men on the Politburo, indeed in the entire leadership hierarchy, were willing to commit themselves to forging ahead with perestroika despite the perils of not knowing where it might lead. It appeared that the Star Trek troika of Gorbachev, Yakovlev and Shevardnadze was running the whole show. A top Soviet space scientist, Boris Raushenbakh, expressed exactly that view to me; it was confirmed by another of the Soviet Union's leading space scientists and former adviser to Gorbachev, Roald Sagdeev.†

Politically exposed, Gorbachev slowed down. Yes, he

indicated, we must make changes, but we cannot skip stages. And increasingly he took a detached, Solomonic position between the progressives and regressives.

Shift of Mood – 1988

Disenchantment began to set in during 1988 in key quarters: among the most progressive economists, intellectuals and younger writers. A chill was created between Gorbachev and the Siberian school of economists who had been his gurus since he came to power. As soon as they started to criticize his decisions as being only half-measures, they essentially stopped working with him. 'Gorbachev does not work with those who criticize his decisions,' say Vladimir Kvint, professor of economics, who worked before perestroika with Aganbegyan and later in Moscow with Aganbegyan and Abalkin. While acknowledging Gorbachev's great contribution in not getting in the way of the democratization forces, Kvint sees Gorbachev's 'main mistake' as trying 'to improve socialism. He still speaks about the Communist idea, and as a result he remains just a progressive Communist leader. By definition that leads to the precipice.'

The catch in the whole web of corrective measures Gorbachev announced, and what caused them to unravel from the inside or to be rejected by the people outside, was the fact that they were undertaken by the Communist Party and its closed system. His soft reforms were too weak to change the system, and were instead absorbed by it. The Party apparat and the black crows of the bureaucracy and the feudal clans of the provincial mafias maintained their resistance, and corruption spread like some fantastic tumour until it had infected almost everything.

'New Thinking', in fact, only accelerated the rush of the Soviet Union towards economic collapse, because in practice it was all half-measures.

The economy, which between 1985 and 1987 had been improving slightly, suddenly stopped and began reversing in 1988, according to Kvint.† The straw that may have broken th back of this feeble economic beast was the energy crisis that followed from a severe setback to nuclear energy development after Chernobyl.†

The reform economists generally give Gorbachev credit for only one clear success among his innovations: the Law on Socialist Enterprise that legalized the co-operatives, or small group businesses, coming as close as Soviet society ever had to private enterprise. Two years after co-ops were legalized, their output had mushroomed from 300 million rubles to 41 *billion* rubles, accounting for 80 per cent of the country's GNP. And the number of people caught up in the dynamic co-operative movement had swelled in the same two years from 70,000 to four and a half million.†

But this one vigorous limb was hardly enough to raise the whole ossified Soviet economy out of its stupor. Co-operatives were mainly organized around soft goods like restaurants and services; they didn't touch the country's industrial base. And the branch industrial ministries, those super-monopolies which are 'genetically opposed to any sort of market', held on to their power.† Furthermore, once co-operatives proliferated and a new class of entrepreneurs suddenly became more affluent under Gorbachev's policies, they became the focus of bitter resentment, reviled as 'speculators' and 'gougers'.

Politically, Gorbachev kept steering a middle course between the reactionaries and the radical reformers. 'But even by 1987 that strategy was exhausted,' says scientist Roald Sagdeev, who with a group of prominent intellectuals sent a letter to that effect to Gorbachev at the end of 1988. More and more, one heard from progressives that Gorbachev must be bolder, that he could not continue trying to please both sides simultaneously – the Party Establishment and the people. 'You can't ride two horses at once,' as Yeltsin expressed it.

Experienced Western observers, like Henry Kissinger with his ruthless Bismarckian approach to geopolitics, found the way Gorbachev played the power game nothing short of breathtaking. Kissinger acknowledged, however, 'There is almost no relationship between his destructive and his constructive efforts – almost everything he has done in the economic field is a disaster.' Gorbachev did succeed for four years in keeping his opposition divided and manageably weak. But the polarization between what is broadly termed the left and right radiated up and down through virtually every one of the ruling institutions, dividing formerly rigid hierarchies by generational and ethnic differences, as well as by the raw battle to preserve the power and perks once taken for granted as the right of the Party aristocracy.

Despite Gorbachev's attempts to limit the truth-in-history campaign to an exposé of Stalin, restless scholars were emboldened to take the inquiry beyond, questioning even the hallowed faith in Lenin and the very foundations of socialism itself. Historian Yuri Afanasev was one of the first to force uncomfortable questions. He called for a probe of what happened between 1917 and 1929, from the Bolshevik revolution through the period immediately following Lenin's death. If they didn't take time to answer these questions, warned the historian, Soviets would never understand why their society had ended up in this sorry condition.

'There'll always be this unresolved contradiction: if socialism is good, and we have it, then why do we have to rid ourselves of what we have?' Afanasev told me.†

'You have to keep in mind that these people [Gorbachev and Yakovlev and Shevardnadze] are in their fifties and sixties, they have been swimming in this *ocean of lies* for years and years, and it does have a lasting impact on them,' I was reminded by the young letters editor at *Ogonyok*, Valentin Yumashev.

By 1988, the political journalism that Gorbachev had fostered was the hottest and most disturbing medium of expression in the country. Soviets began gorging themselves on the details of their own degradation over seven decades; they wanted more and faster. The circulation of magazines like *Ogonyok* and *Znamya* mushroomed. Yet the awakening giant of curiosity was not reflected in activism by the public. People seemed almost paralysed in disbelief, or denial.

Once, the people had had the unshakeable belief that their country was the front line of the world proletariat, the embodiment of world revolution, and this gave their lives meaning. To be sure, they lived with ration cards then too, and shortages and spiritual poverty. But the young people I had met in the Soviet Union fifteen years before had a remarkably uncomplicated sense of themselves. They looked to no one to blame for their situation, only to their own energy and discipline to influence their destiny for the better – usually a lost cause. Nevertheless, one envied them the freedom from malice.

Gorbachev's revolution was stripping all that away. The naked truth, or at least half-truth, was there every night on the TV news, in the shocking attacks being made publicly in the parliament against government officials, in the stream of journalism set free to expose the abuses of Stalinism. Even *Pravda*, once mounted behind glass on the sidewalks and about as popular as an eye examination, even *Pravda* began publishing the first national public opinion polls ever seen by Soviets.

Bold young writers began pushing the boundaries of the social sciences, disciplines that had been gutted in the 1960s. They released statistics that would be of garden-variety grimness in the West, but were utterly shocking to the uninformed Soviet public: the high divorce rate, the uncontrolled rise in congenital mental illness due to parental alcoholism, and the revelation that one-third of all Soviet children were born out of wedlock. One talented novelist aged thirty, Natalya Daryalova, had attempted first-hand reporting on alcoholism by living with a young alcoholic couple whose five children had died in a fire after the parents abandoned them in their locked apartment. Daryalova wrote about the tragedy and its social causes in the early 1980s.

Editors finally dared to publish it in 1986, and Daryalova went on to expand her revelations of adolescent drug addiction, delinquency and criminal colonies for girls, in a groundbreaking book, *No Man's Land*.

But the hovering presence of the KGB was still evident even in the middle of Moscow, not to mention the provinces, where very few glasnost newspapers or magazines were seen. And the idea remained pervasive that everyone's life was being controlled, monitored by the Party thought police planted inside every workplace, or by the secret police with its vast and undiminished eavesdropping and mail-snooping apparatus. When dissidents spoke up in the press and no punishment followed, people didn't know what to make of it. Was Gorbachev genuine? How long would he be around? And what next?

A joke popular around that time had a Muscovite looking up from his paper and asking a friend, 'Did you hear the latest national poll results? Half the people are for glasnost. The other half are taking names.'

And so most of the people, who were already alienated from their government, slipped beyond cynicism. Oh to be sure, they would belong to the Party if their livelihood or privileges depended upon it. For example, all the crusading writers of perestroika belonged to the Writers' Union, an old Stalinist relic whose rules and membership are controlled by a politburo of non-elected hacks placed in power by the Party. But it offers writers a rather glamorous club where they enjoy decent meals and service, along with insurance and invitations to special sales and vouchers for holidays in the Baltics, and so on. When I had dinner at the Writers' Union with Tatyana Tolstaya, the great-grandniece of Leo Tolstoy, who had used the handsome mansion as his inspiration for Natasha Rostova's home in *War and Peace*, I remarked on how well Writers' Union members seemed to live. 'They're good Party members?'

'There is no such thing!' she snapped. 'No one believes in Communism any more.'

Perhaps the youngest prominent writer in the Soviet Union, Tolstaya is thirty-seven but looks much older. Her beautiful face is heavy, with deep black divots under her restless, unforgiving eyes. She smokes constantly and complains there is no caffeine in Russian coffee any more – 'They take it out.' Tolstaya admits she was born cynical, but her acute sensibility had already picked up the free-floating rage at every level of her society that would soon begin spilling into the streets.

Tolstaya's own rejection for membership in the Writers' Union had become a cause célèbre. She was young and cocky and a woman, and she dared to match wills with the irrational forces of censorship. One of the club's officials, who resisted admitting young talented writers, told Tolstaya that her generation of writers wasn't interesting. The official didn't understand why their poems were so complicated, poetry should come from the soul and the heart, 'and your prose is too fierce, too many cruel things in there'.

Tolstaya replied, 'Well, imagine, Irina, that the prisoner is let free from the concentration camp. As he leaves the gates, at that time nobody will have the idea to marry him.'

She refused to be intimidated. And she won admission.

Tolstaya invited me back to her home for real coffee. It is the first floor of a nineteenth-century house behind a newly working church, one of maybe a thousand empty run-down flats to be found in Moscow that could be fixed up for the homeless, she says, but nobody bothers. Tolstaya and her Greek husband are among the talented fortunates who have the hard currency to take advantage of the new freedom to travel, and these days she spends most of her time on teaching fellowships in America. But as for the tens of millions now on the economic or emotional precipice, she says she doesn't know how they survive. Even the rare hardy and energetic Soviet who starts a co-op gets slapped first with taxes, then with regulations that make it very hard for him to buy raw materials, and finally he must face bitter hatred and Jew-baiting.

'You have no way out. Some stay at home and watch TV, but they hear about the horrible ecological situation. Some start eating, but they hear they're eating poison. You are blocked. So people start hating. When the society as a whole becomes frustrated, it's very dangerous. Civil war is already going on. We are all tired and depressed. No one believes any more in the Communist Party. Yet we are all deformed by it.'

Dmitry and Natasha Barchevsky registered the same shift of mood in 1988. 'There was much more hope and sympathy with perestroika after the showing of *Risk I* than after *Risk II*,' say the filmmakers of their sequel. 'Many people, having not seen any concrete results that affect our way of life, such as availability of food and clothes, started to distance themselves from all the perestroika talk. They became disenchanted. Exactly one year passed between the two premières, and my impression is that people are getting tired of hoping,' observed Dmitry Barchevsky.

And yet, in the midst of all the criminal blight and civilian bitterness, a few unlikely blooms of independent thought and action were springing up among people who had been utterly passive or cynical before glasnost. Out of the ashes of Chernobyl had come a startling phoenix: an anti-nuclear movement that historian Zhores Medvedev credits with being the foundation for the 'people's fronts' in the vanguard of the democratic and secessionist movements in the Soviet Union.† Indeed, once glasnost opened the floodgates, what Soviets call 'civil society' – a whole new world of voluntary associations, independent of the formerly all-embracing state – rushed into being. By September 1987 a few thousand such groups had formed; by mid-1988, there were no fewer than thirty thousand informal groups involving millions of people.† The politicization of these groups would proceed slowly, very tentatively, since people were properly uncertain how long this new 'thaw' might last. But Soviet society now had a place for mavericks.

Last Romantic Socialist

Gorbachev believed, right up until 1990, that the titanic problems his country faced could be solved by mass psychotherapy. His faith in man as a rational being, eminently improvable, who given the proper conditions can be guided into rational acts, was the faith of a true Marxist. He needed only to offer himself as the moral guiding light, to explain things through his televised sermons. He and Yakovlev really thought that to create a new breed of exploratory, energetic self-starters 'All we had to do was to tell people that they are free, that they can do what they want, that they can say what they want, write what they want,' as Yakovlev confessed to Dan Rather on CBS in February 1990. 'But it turned out that most of the people were not so enthusiastic. I think we underestimated the effect of our past.'†

Then this master propagandist, who altogether had spent nearly twenty-five years in the ideology department, made a stunning and utterly ironic admission. 'The longer I was involved in ideology, the more I question our approach,' he said. 'We did tremendous damage.'†

But could a successful psychological remake of their people, even if ultimately successful, substitute for an admission that the *Communist Party itself* – not just its unworthy past leaders or its corrupt economic management – violated human nature? What's more, the two master propagandists had overlooked a basic tenet of Marxism. Karl Marx taught that economic relations are the basis of political ones. So long as people's daily existence did not improve materially, they weren't going to be good candidates for 'moral and spiritual reawakening'.

And so they had failed in the first five years to give birth to a New 'New Soviet Man' with a new perestroika brain. Yet Gorbachev still believed that he could return the Communist Party to the 'vanguard' of leadership towards glowing socialist ideals.

'You have to know Marxism, because it's political arithmetic, then you would understand that Gorbachev will only keep in pace with society,' I was told by his old college classmate Lieberman. 'This is where he is different from Lenin. Lenin used to go too far ahead and, when he realized that, he had to go back. As long as this society is still seized by all these old ideas and paradigms, if Gorbachev made one step ahead, he would be gone.'

In this regard, he had not changed much from his university days, when he always sat in the next to last row. As one of the radical Siberian economists saw Gorbachev's efforts at reform, 'He was never out in front; he was always, at best, in the last row of the avant-garde.'

His critics later lamented that as power exerted its hold over Gorbachev, he became more detached and remote from everyday reality – a moody, irresolute commander convinced of his powers of levitation – as if he were some supernatural being who could float above the turbulent seas he had stirred up, buoyed by the spiritual belief that his perestroika was developing broadly and would soon sweep the whole country.

As a leader Gorbachev is very much a process-oriented thinker, unlike Americans who are result-oriented. His approach is *I am moving towards something*. What is the something? *I don't know*. When are you going to reach it? *I don't know*. Is it going to be good or bad? *It's a dialectic, it's both good and bad, that's how it is in real life*. As a Marxist and believer in dialectical materialism, he has internalized its dogma that nothing is absolute except change itself: everything is a continuous interchange of forces that move and move and move. A content analysis of his speeches reveals this process-oriented thinking as his natural style. 'This is real life, movement, development, and thus every stage may have its own contradictions,' he told journalists in 1987. 'We must deal with this calmly, study it, decide things and educate people.'

He is stunningly smart. In fact, Gorbachev scored in the top 10 per cent of world political leaders on a Western psychological test of leaders' cognitive complexity. Where most of those studied describe the world in rigid black-and-white terms, Gorbachev shows in his speeches a remarkable tolerance for ambiguity and contradictions and an effort to find integrating solutions. This positive assessment by psychologists at the Institute of Personality Assessment at the University of California, Berkeley, is turned on its ear by Russian observers, however, who see Gorbachev's ease in tolerating conflicting points of view as a sign of weakness and doublethink, making him a man of half-measures.†

Perestroika started as a slogan for a new economic deal that would do away with the central command system created under Stalin. Gradually, its aim became expanded to mean 'a moral cleansing of society, and the opening up of creative possibilities for a free and all-round development of personality'.† The definition kept changing because Gorbachev kept changing. By 1990 he would be referring to this mass psychological remake as 'a revolution in our minds'.†

Being process-oriented gives Gorbachev enormous room to adhere to doublethink. He doesn't have to make a definitive decision, he doesn't have to say yes or no, because the process keeps going. And whenever his left-wing supporters in the intelligentsia pushed him to be decisive, to *act*, he could simply say, 'It's a process, this is life, this is reality.'

The process-oriented leader never has to make a firm decision. He seesaws, he drafts different advisers, he co-opts his rivals, he takes contradictory positions, but he never, finally, comes down with both feet on the side of any firm plan or principle. This was the trademark of Gorbachev as a domestic reformer.

There is both a touch of the infant god and a great deal of the actor in Mikhail Gorbachev. He believes in himself utterly, in his ability to convert anyone, anywhere, to his way of seeing things. And he believes in what he says – great actors do. He did not come to power a revolutionary by nature, but in reacting to the disastrous economic situation he inherited, he had to take up that role.

After searching Gorbachev's history from boyhood to the pinnacle of power for the moral and intellectual bearings that might have guided him, one has to ask: what did socialism mean to him? Americans don't articulate their ideology very often. They don't have to. The consensus around the principles enshrined in their Constitution is so ingrained, they simply don't question the fundamentals of their belief system.

Looking for the fundamentals by which Gorbachev is guided led me through a dizzying maze of good intentions and doublethink until I fell upon a shattering insight: there *is* no bottom line to the Soviet socialist ideal – it's a snake pit of hypocrisy. Stretched over this pit of hypocrisy, obscuring the depths of its lies, is only a rainbow of beautiful words and utopian dreams. And this is where Gorbachev's romantic nature comes into play.

'He still believes there is something pure at the heart of socialism,' related writer Olas Adamovich after a long soulful talk with Gorbachev about Solzhenitsyn. Adamovich uses the image of a cabbage. 'Gorbachev believes that if he takes off the decayed leaves there will be a healthy cabbage inside. The apparatchiks know it's dangerous to strip off the leaves, because it's rotten inside, it will all have to be thrown away. Gorbachev is the last romantic socialist.'

And so, Mikhail Sergeyevich, with his unshakeable confidence in his ability to persuade the people and maintain unity, kept on proselytizing, temporizing and improvising. His old Czech classmate Mlynar, recalling his friend's legendary self-confidence, believes that '*That* may even be his weak point – the tremendous self-assurance that makes him feel that everything will work out well.'

VI

Fifth Gorbachev:

Dictator for Democracy

1989–1990

'I feel like I've lived through three lifetimes in the last five years,' Gorbachev began telling Western visitors.† Since 1985, he had not only been living at three times the normal pace, he had also gone through three incarnations: from disciple to reformer, from reformer to revolutionary, and now from revolutionary to quasidemocratic leader.

In the heady days of mid-1989 he took the stage above a chorus of political neophytes he had created – the first Congress of People's Deputies – and gave a magnificent performance. This groundbreaking Congress followed on the heels of the first nationwide multi-candidate elections in the USSR since 1917. Work virtually stopped across the country for those electrifying ten days, beginning on 25 May, when the Congress convened. Soviets sat transfixed before their TV sets and watched a parade of newly elected deputies speaking out on a whole catalogue of pent-up frustrations. It was the first time the people had seen a living, breathing embodiment of the new institutions set up to grant them some voice in government.

In truth, those spring 1989 elections were far from the Western principle of 'one man, one vote'; Gorbachev's variation was to give ordinary people one vote, while members of the Party elite had two or three. A full third of the

'People's Deputies' seated at the 2,250-member Congress
were not elected by the people at all, but were nominated
instead by trustworthy 'public' organizations mostly controlled by the Party. In almost a thousand races, however,
there had been two candidates. And even in races where
they were presented with only one candidate, Soviets had
found a way to register their choice – by crossing out the
name. Many of those rejected, to their own and their Party's
amazement and embarrassment, were high-ranking Party
nabobs and arrogant anti-reformers. Despite harassment,
rumour-mongering and outright police diversion of voters
trying to get to rallies of independent candidates, a number
of outspoken voices had been elected.

Gorbachev simply assumed the role of chairman at the
Congress, and at first he resisted open debate. His air of self-
satisfaction was pricked right from the start, however, by the
man who would increasingly become a thorn in his flesh,
Andrei Sakharov. Acknowledging that Mikhail Sergeyevich
was the father of perestroika, and that there was no one else
in sight capable of leading the country, Sakharov nevertheless made clear that his support of Gorbachev was
'conditional' and exhorted the deputies to speak openly
about what had happened in the country during the past
four years. He insisted that Gorbachev himself 'should speak
both about the achievements and about the mistakes self-
critically'.†

Visibly lacing up his annoyance, Gorbachev responded
with genial resignation, 'Democracy is democracy.' Day after
day he sat above the crowd of deputies, almost saintlike in
his patience and self-control, listening to complaints about
everything from crooked co-operatives to unpaved roads in
remote republics, even allowing Sakharov a dozen chances
to come back to the microphone. Always attentive, he
maintained finger-tip control of the body of 2,250 delegates:
it was he who selected the soloists, timed their arias, set the
tempo, occasionally chided the discordant ones, and basically
orchestrated the whole Congress as if he were conducting

the chorus from *Aida*. Of course it didn't hurt that he could cut the sound to either of the two microphones with a flick of his wrist.

'Everybody agrees, tovarishchi [comrades]?' was Gorbachev's favourite line.

The deputies would respond to his persuasions on cue, in unison, with a long drawn-out 'Daaaaaah' – like children answering their teacher. An 'aggressively obedient majority', Deputy Yuri Afanasev dubbed the Congress in disgust.

None the less, taking the role of democratic leader exposed Gorbachev to unwelcome scrutiny. It tore the veil from one of the darkest moments in recent Soviet history – the atrocities committed in Tblisi on 9 April. A deputy from the southern republic of Georgia showed the Congress a home video of the terrible event, proving that peaceful dissent had been treated as counter-revolution.

The town square of Tblisi had filled with people demonstrating for Georgian independence. By 2 a.m., they were in an elated mood, dancing in front of the government building. Unseen, armoured troop carriers waited in silence; hidden behind them, paratroops of the Soviet army were poised to wield truncheons, sharpened shovels and tear gas. Just before 4 a.m. the Patriarch of the Georgian Church was authorized to give the only warning the happy crowd received: 'They have just told me that there is real danger if you stay here. It is possible that there are only a few minutes left.'

The people waited in silence. As the troops advanced, shoulder to shoulder, a young girl dashed out in front of the soldiers and threw open her arms, exclaiming in Russian, 'What are you doing?' A moment later she crumpled to the ground, and when people ran to her and carried her off, they saw the fantastic blooms of blood sprouting from her chest and mouth. She was the first of fourteen women who were bludgeoned or hacked to death in the next twenty minutes with a savagery bordering on the insane. When the killings and beatings were over, some of the Soviet soldiers swayed on their feet or leaned against walls or trees, as if drugged. Indeed, ambulance doctors on the scene later told the BBC they believed the troops were doped up, possibly with amphetamines.†

After the stunned deputies had seen the video, Gorbachev said lamely, 'I don't want to go into these details at the moment.'† He held to his excuse that he had known nothing of the order to send in army troops until he returned from a trip abroad the following day – a story later refuted by Yegor Ligachev, who chaired the Politburo meeting where the decision was taken and claims that Gorbachev was consulted.

Other, more personal, blows would be dealt Gorbachev at this first Congress. He heard his wife derided as a plotting Empress Josephine by a simple truck driver from Kharkov, who stepped forward and compared Gorbachev not to Lenin or Stalin but rather to Napoleon, who 'thanks to yes-men and his wife . . . went from a republic to an empire . . . Evidently, even you cannot avoid the flattery and influence of your wife.' This fearless prole ended defiantly: 'Put me to death, if you like, but I fear this path – and if this is so – the cause of the revolution is doomed to failure.'†

Gorbachev slowly measured out his reply: 'I accept your critical remarks [pause] as comradely ones. I am open to them.' This 'comradely' insolence was followed by another attack from a stock loader, who virtually accused Gorbachev of living like a king in a luxurious dacha built for him in the Crimea. The General Secretary's face settled into a mask of impassivity, but colleagues who had worked with him since the beginning sensed a deep inner turmoil. 'Of course, he expected some criticism about reforms,' recalls Tatyana Zaslavskaya, a close intellectual confrère. 'But when deputies spoke about him personally, he received a very hard shock. He pulled himself in tight.' Zaslavskaya saw it as a turning point.

When the General Secretary buttonholed a young upstart deputy from Moscow and privately cautioned him, 'Please, don't accelerate the process. You should be more moderate,' the deputy, Sergei Stankevich, saw up close the toll that Gorbachev's surface moderation was taking on this emotional man.† Blackened scythes of flesh beneath his eyes spoke of his fatigue, and he had to brace his arm on the table to hold himself up. 'The tension of the Congress was phenomenal and he was utterly exhausted,' Stankevich realized.

On the table in front of Chairman Gorbachev during these sessions was 'his ever-present glass of khaki-coloured liquid, a mystery to the nation', as the *New York Times* referred to it.† Other diabetics in the Party elite told me privately they think it is a homeopathic remedy he takes for his diabetes. To prepare it, water is allowed to stand overnight in a special Indian tumbler of sandalwood, which imparts properties that are supposedly tranquillizing to the nervous system. The brownish liquid is supposed to be drunk all day long. Stress and pressure, of course, are punishing for a diabetic, causing sharp fluctuations in the blood sugar. And Gorbachev was under extraordinary stress.

At the end of the thirteen-day marathon, his mask of equanimity slipped. The indefatigable Dr Sakharov had requested one last chance to speak. Gorbachev subtly cued the Congress to respond. 'Nyet!' the hall shouted in loud unison. When Sakharov persisted, Gorbachev magnani-mously offered him five minutes. But Sakharov's manifesto attempted to unmask Gorbachev's democracy performance. The physicist upbraided his fellow deputies for the 'extremely dangerous' oversight of leaving 'absolute, practi-cally unlimited personal power' in the hands of a single person, even if that person was the initiator of perestroika. He exposed Gorbachev's newly constructed legislature, the Supreme Soviet, as a 'screen for the real power of the President and the state and Party apparat'. When Sakharov began to speak on the painful subject of nationality problems and 'national oppression' of the republics, Gorbachev finally flew into a fury.

'That's all! Take away your speech, please!' he shouted,

cutting off power to Sakharov's microphone. Before being silenced, Sakharov gave a prophetic warning: 'If you float downstream singing lullabies to yourselves in the hope of changes for the better in the foreseeable future, the growing tension may explode in our society, bringing about the most dramatic consequences.'†

Gorbachev's actual purpose in permitting these elections and creating new quasi-parliamentary bodies had been to further his constant aim: restoring credibility to the Communist Party. A backlash against the Party as a whole was not at all what he had in mind. But the reforms that he had intended as a ventilation strategy to *take pressure off* the Party to share power in any meaningful way only *breathed life into* embryonic democratic and environmental factions. Along with popular fronts in the republics and independent trade union movements, these factions began in the summer of 1989 to spawn some impressive fledgling leaders.

Genie Out of the Bottle

'Our little fable of democracy' is how poet Yevgeny Yevtushenko described the whole exercise when I visited him that July. In Peredelkino, where the great men of letters live in the same row of dachas, go to the same clubs, and circulate protest letters from the sole copy machine (hidden in Yevtushenko's sauna), it was not difficult to sustain belief in the fable. 'Gorbachev, he is quite different, and now he's happily discussable,' exulted Yevtushenko, as a peal of church bells rang out over his praise. 'People are very unjust to him if they forget now everything good that he did. To paraphrase your astronaut, our elections are a little step of democracy, but a giant step for our country.' In his next breath the poet was insisting that I see a home video of his own crowning moment at the Congress – when he had shamed Gorbachev into voting against certain privileges for the Party elite.

On the heels of that first Congress, the radical deputies

formed a faction known as the Interregional Group. Insatiably curious about the nuts and bolts of how a democratic congress is actually supposed to work, a group of these younger men and women fell upon Senator Bill Bradley and a visiting delegation of American legislators and talked for hours about the US Congress. Their disenchantment with Gorbachev was already growing. Deputy Stankevich spoke of their puzzlement: 'Gorbachev's mind is unclear for us . . . We anticipated his actions would be more for the democratic group, but he's more moderate.'†

Meanwhile, the audience for the maverick publications into which Gorbachev had breathed new life was multiplying fast; ironically, it grew on the strength of articles attacking his policies and letters criticizing the General Secretary himself. *Ogonyok*'s muscle increased, from a 200,000-strong subscription list of mostly intellectuals in 1987, to a powerhouse of influence reaching into remote places with a circulation of 4,600,000 by spring 1990. The public had found a forum in which to protest against the most obviously hypocritical aspect of the Soviet system: Party privilege.

Gorbachev's own lifestyle was becoming that summer a blisteringly hot topic. At the Congress, disingenuously defending himself on the 'dacha question', Gorbachev had said, in a wounded voice: 'in my whole life, neither I nor members of my family have had dachas and do not have any personal ones.' In fact, he had at least four homes either in construction or expansion at the time, paid for out of Party coffers with free labour by state workers. Pictures and descriptions of these dachas began to leak out. The best builders, drafted to construct his ultra-modern country house in Thorosin in the Crimea, wrote a letter to *Ogonyok* calling it a disgrace, piggish, immodest; they described the multiple swimming pools and being bossed around by Raisa, who made them rebuild whatever she didn't like.† Gorbachev had also had a new house built for him in the Lenin Hills of Moscow, and the finishing touches were being put on a brand new dacha on the outskirts of the city, where he lives full-time today. It's a country house with lavish gardens and state-of-the-art electronic gadgetry, I learned from an aide to Gorbachev. How large? I asked. 'Rather big, rather big,' was the vague reply. How many rooms? 'It's impossible to count.'

Party privilege was also the major theme of the five thousand letters that were pouring into the offices of *Argumenty i Fakty* every day. The outrage was directed not just at Gorbachev, but also at his Politburo, and the hundreds of Central Committee members and the great bloated nomenklatura of ministers and vice-ministers and consultants and aides, all of whom lived the fantasy of full Communism while ordinary Soviets were guaranteed a little more than seven by seven metres of living space per individual. 'You have one Camp David but we have hundreds of them,' I was told by the editor, Viktor Starkov.

'Their focus is very narrow,' sneered spokesman Gennady Gerasimov, about his fellow citizens. 'You ask them about the next day, they don't know. You ask them about the next event, they don't know. You ask them about the next *block*, they don't know what's going on.'†

Not surprising, since the ordinary Soviets I met seemed to spend most of their time standing in queues. They had never had the freedom to travel, not even the freedom to move from one part of the country to another without bribing somebody or making a marriage of convenience to get the *propiska* for living space. Most still lived in communal apartments, two or three families sharing two or three rooms. Meanwhile, Gorbachev and his moveable court of hundreds of advisers and spokesmen were constantly travelling to Paris, Bonn, New York and so on. In Washington, they camped at the Madison Hotel and enjoyed sipping brandy in huge suites priced at a minimum of $500 a night, dining on roast pig and caviar at formal Embassy dinners, picking up contracts to write articles or books from foreign publishers, getting scholarships for their children to attend exclusive private schools, and buying the latest electronic goodies from a family shopping list. When they returned to Moscow, the airport baggage room looked like a discount electronic store.

Somehow, this didn't square with the lofty commitments to 'principles of social justice' Gorbachev continued to espouse in his speeches, not to the vast portion of the Soviet public which was barely surviving from day to day. Under Gorbachev 'The intelligentsia got anything they ever dreamed of and even more,' observed Arkady Vaxberg, a senior columnist for *Literaturnaya Gazeta*, 'but the population at large got nothing.'

The past five years had shaken Soviet society as elementally as a major earthquake. The people had lost their ideological footing; the structure of classlessness had crumbled; any notion of social justice was shattered – walls, ceilings, glass, the whole structure of life was tumbling down and each day brought fresh wreckage. While Gorbachev was busy courting the intelligentsia, the great industrial proletariat had been ignored. Suddenly that summer a spontaneous and uncontrollable revolution from below erupted in response to Gorbachev's revolution from above.

The threat first surfaced in July when men came up from the execrable coal mines of the Ukraine's Donets Basin and said they had had enough. The conditions of their short, brutish lives would be unimaginable in the industrialized West. The average life expectancy of a Soviet miner was forty-eight years.† Blackened in every crease of their bodies, they lived with no hot water and strictly rationed soap.† The promises of Marxism had brought them virtual serfdom. Strikes spread across Siberia, involving most of the nation's 2.5 million coal miners.† Their initial demands for better living and working conditions quickly escalated into something never before seen in Soviet history – outright political protests. These brave miners demanded an end to the Party's monopoly on power† – exactly what Sakharov had failed to goad the new people's deputies into doing.

'The miners' strikes must have been a very painful moment for Gorbachev,' says historian Yakov Grodin. 'He realized that all the power was not in the hands of the Communist Party – and he always believed in that before.'†

Another unexpected eruption had been sparked at the first Congress by historian Roy Medvedev, who attacked Soviet historiography's description of the 'peaceful' incorporation of the Baltic states into the USSR in 1940 as 'a lie'. Gorbachev's hand was being forced by revelations concerning the 1939 Nazi–Soviet pact, which had touched off a string of demonstrations in the Baltics. The secret pact had freed Hitler to invade Western Europe without having to fear a two-front war, and put the Soviet Union in collusion with Hitler to attack and liquidate Poland. Finally, the pact had psychologically disarmed much of the Soviet population, weakening their reaction to the crushing 'surprise' invasion of the Soviet western border in June 1941 – a blow about which Stalin had information he refused to believe.

Gorbachev named a commission, chaired by Yakovlev and including historian Yuri Afanasev, to study the question.

In July 1989, *Literaturnaya Gazeta* published a map, obtained from West German archives, showing the signatures of Stalin and Ribbentrop, Germany's Minister of Foreign Affairs, on a continent carved up into Soviet and German spheres of influence.† Gorbachev's stock rationale was that there had been no alternative to the Nazi–Soviet pact, but Yakovlev later admitted, 'My work in recent years . . . is morally exhausting, when the remains of millions of people continually haunt you. Socio-historical truth is needed.'† In bringing to light the protocols of the Nazi–Soviet pact, Yakovlev and Afanasev publicized a truth that had been known everywhere else in the world while it was ruthlessly kept from the Soviet people. For the last forty years, the USSR's vast losses in the Great Patriotic War had been used to explain the continuing backwardness of their country. To have this façade of patriotic self-justification stripped away was perhaps the most devastating aftershock of all.

Again, Gorbachev's slow, selective opening of the valves of truth would backfire on him. Most Lithuanians had believed all along that their incorporation into the union had been illegal. The publication of the protocols of the pact proved it. The stage was set for Lithuania's headlong rush towards separatism.

What to Believe In?

The summer of 1989 was the summer of disenchantment. Mounting disdain for the Communist Party was spreading even into the top levels of government. At a dinner in New York in August 1989, one of Gorbachev's image-makers, Nikolai Shishlin, was discussing the difficulties his boss was encountering in ridding the Party of its dead wood. How many of the Party apparat could Gorbachev purge without losing his own power base? Shishlin was asked. 'A million,' he answered casually. His fellow guests gasped. A million members of his own Party? 'They have nineteen million members,' Shishlin went on, 'so it's not a lot.' It was the word 'they' that hit me. Here was an official spokesman for the Gorbachev team, who spends his working weekends at a dacha on the Gorbachev compound, calling the Communist Party 'they'. It was symbolic of the increasing detachment and disbelief that ran throughout Soviet society about the prospects for a successful reformation of the system.

Gorbachev himself was a visionary only in the international sphere. At home, he seemed to have no idea how to navigate his society away from the shoals of a so-called planned economy towards the safety of some hazy shore of Swedish-style socialism.

'Hasn't he made the leap to seeing that a real market economy is the only hope?' I asked one of Gorbachev's image-makers that July.

'Not yet,' was the glum reply.

With his Ukrainian Cossack roots, Gorbachev comes from a different strain from the average Russian and has almost nothing in common with the more than one hundred other nationalities in his empire. Nor could the peasant Gorbachev get other Soviet peasants to identify with him. After decades of persecution and callous state neglect, nothing seemed to revive their desire to do what Gorbachev's own forebears had tried to do – work for themselves. They no longer trusted their government; even Gorbachev wouldn't *give* them back the land as private property, he would only grant them a fifty-year lease. Most, remembering past betrayals, refused to take it.

How could the Soviet people, after seventy-two years of adapting to an anti-human totalitarian system, recreate themselves psychologically, spiritually and physically to meet Gorbachev halfway? Their self-image was one of weakness, helplessness; they had no experience of sovereignty over their personal or collective destiny. They were accustomed to humiliation in every daily struggle. The belief persisted even among the most educated that the system had left them genetically weakened.

The brilliant ones felt stranded between the failed Communist blueprint for material well-being and the flawed capitalist dream, which they saw as deteriorated into spiritual indifference and hedonistic consumerism in the West. 'Before, we had two channels of belief – Communism and false romanticism – and they were secure,' the poet Voznesensky told me. 'Now nobody believes and nobody is happy. They are all feeling aggressive, looking for who to blame for the shortages and for the feeling of emptiness – what to live for?'†

Gorbachev was never a Kennedy-esque figure for the hip pacesetters in their twenties and thirties. 'He has no fans,' I learned from a young director of Leningrad's avant-garde TV show, *Fifth Wheel*, Sergei Sholokhov. Contemporary teenagers openly ridiculed the Party and taunted their parents and teachers for their passivity.

'No one knows what to believe any more,' my Intourist guide in Stavropol whimpered miserably that summer. 'Now we read in the paper that our whole Great Patriotic War was a lie.'

His fifteen-year-old daughter had looked him straight in the eye and said, 'Why didn't you tell us the truth of our own history? _How could you have lied to us for so long?'_ The father shrugged, silent with self-loathing. It was a scene multiplied in millions of kitchens across the country.

The generation of Gorbachev's parents was much worse off. 'My mother can't look at the documentaries they show now about the truth of Stalin's time,' a Soviet cameraman told me. 'She lived through it – it took away her tongue. Now she runs and hides her face in the pillow and begs me to turn off the TV. _The fear is in our souls.'_

Even Communist Party press organs were ruthlessly surveying the wreckage of everyday life. According to the first data of their kind ever published in a Soviet newspaper, a poll by _Pravda_ in July 1989, people learned that the social pyramid in the Soviet Union looks like this:

Rich	2.3 per cent
Middle class	11.2 per cent
Poor	86.5 per cent

What made this article so shocking was that it compared Soviet living standards with international ones, as opposed to comparing them to past Soviet living standards. The criterion which made the poll comparable, however remotely, to Western standards was that it measured the absolute level of consumer goods: cars, apartments, bikes, appliances, clothing. (It didn't include savings or investments, because seven out of eight Soviet citizens didn't have savings accounts.)

The article concluded that with 85 per cent of the Soviet population beneath the official poverty level, people would be easily swayed by extremist ideas. _Komsomolskaya Pravda_, the Party's youth newspaper, blamed the system, pointing out that before the 1917 Bolshevik revolution, Russia ranked seventh in the world in per-capita consumption, and now it was seventy-seventh – 'just after South Africa but ahead of Romania'.†

Simple amenities are beyond the reach of most Soviet citizens. Only 24 per cent of the population has telephone service. Even in Moscow it is not uncommon for a woman to have to walk a block from her apartment to draw water before she can begin cooking. 'So what have we achieved after all these years?' an economist, Anatoli Deryabin, wrote in the official monthly journal *Molodoi Kommunist*. 'What we have is equality in poverty.'

Gorbachev's answer to this depressing economic portrait was to remind people in every speech, 'The essence of perestroika is the socialist renewal of society.' Then he would repeat the mysterious mantra 'socialist market'. Nobody could figure out what it meant.

Manipulating the Mystical

In the crucial fissures of history, when whole populations are suspended over the abyss with their former faith or belief system shattered, all kinds of mysticism become popular. Into the moral vacuum left by the discredited Communist Party in the Soviet Union rushed mysticism, religious orthodoxy and quackery. This was not, however, a wholly natural phenomenon. The hidden hand of Gorbachev and his propaganda henchmen in the KGB could be spotted here and there, cynically manipulating this new psychological massage to serve their own ends of regaining mind control.

Consider the cult of Kashpirovsky, a hustling faith healer. Kashpirovsky offered televised mass psychotherapy and hypnotic suggestion to a society cut off from its religious foundations and abysmally short of medical care. In 1989, the immensely popular Kashpirovsky was also pulling in live theatre audiences of 1,500 people, all easily convinced he was their salvation. Believers would shake, thrash, tremble, as if under the spell of the supernatural.

The cult reached its peak when Kashpirovsky pulled the stunt of supposedly hynotizing an actress undergoing a televised operation in a city hundreds of miles away. While doctors made a forty-centimetre incision in her abdomen, without anaesthesia, the woman hung on to the healer's husky voice over a TV monitor – before 250 million viewers. The surgeon was afraid to start cutting. The mesmerizer issued stern orders, 'Begin. Begin now!' The surgeon cut. Kashpirovsky asked the actress, 'Do you feel like singing?' She sang. Later the actress admitted, 'I was in monstrous pain all the time.' Shortly thereafter, Kashpirovsky was taken off the air after being accused by some of his faithful of gross sexual exploitation.†

The fascinating background to this story is that Kashpirovsky's telecasts appeared on the sport/editorial channel, which is known to be a KGB operation.† Such mystics and proponents of extra-sensory phenomena were being 'sponsored' by the Gorbachev propaganda team.

The discredited Kashpirovsky's shoes were quickly filled by 'Doctor' Chumak, a ludicrous faith healer showcased on *120 Minutes*, the Soviet equivalent of the *Today Show*. Intelligent Soviets would actually sit transfixed before their TV set while this pudding-faced man wiggled his hands in hocus-pocus motions for ten minutes, supposedly dispelling their pain telepathically, one day zeroing in on their colons, the next on their hearts or livers.†

Of all the other-worldly comforts people sought, none was growing more rapidly than orthodox Christianity. The Russian Orthodox church had always supported the monarch. As Gorbachev became drawn more and more towards one-man rule for himself, with the KGB supporting the idea and Yakovlev trying to talk him into it, co-opting the church became an important part of the campaign to legitimize his autocracy.

In November 1989 Gorbachev made his historic pilgrimage to see the Pope and announce his freedom-of-conscience law. All over the Soviet Union, churches were given scarce resources to begin rebuilding. Onion domes were being regilded and painted in bright celestial blues, altars were once again covered with candles and notes to the deceased.

Before 1917 there had been 845 churches in Moscow; 426 were destroyed, and others closed or defaced. Now the remaining churches threw open their doors and rang their bells in a fever of newfound zeal. Religious activity also exploded in the Muslim republics of Central Asia, where mosques would begin to reopen at the rate of one a day in 1990.

The reaction of the people to this spiritual renaissance was overwhelming. Attending a mass, in the crush of standing bodies, one saw people straining to hear every utterance from the priest, many sobbing or clutching their sides, and one could feel their famished hope for deliverance from despair.

By the end of 1989, social economist Tatyana Zaslavskaya found a tremendous surge in the number of people who considered themselves religious. Her polls showed they had increased in one year from one-quarter to *one-half* the Soviet population. Fifty per cent of a population considering itself religious was normal in Judaeo-Christian societies, but in the Soviet Union? 'A rather shocking result,' commented the sociologist.

'Religion is something weak people need,' said the *Izvestia* columnist Alexander Bovin, reflecting the utterly pragmatic view common among Gorbachev's circle. Gorbachev's old friend Mikhailova was sickened by the cynical exploitation of religiosity to buoy up the power of the ruling Party elite. 'Religion always taught people to be obedient. People now don't know what to do with themselves. If you ask who considers himself a believer, they don't really know what it's about. It's the fashion. The Russian czars always relied heavily on religion to assure them respect from the people. I think there's some calculation of the same kind in our leadership.'†

That calculation only intensified as people became more and more disoriented. Indeed, by the summer of 1990, the Soviet government would arrange for American televangelist Robert Schuller to be broadcast over Central Television one Sunday a month, beaming his charismatic Protestant sermon from the Crystal Cathedral in California straight into the former heartland of state atheism.†

The Crime Binge

Moscow is a gaily coloured city in summer, its dusky red buildings iced in white and its apricot buildings roofed in a medley of bright greens. Trees cluster plentifully between the wide streets and broad boulevards that radiate out from Red Square. From the top of the Hotel Rossiya the view was splendid: the façades of 'Stalin Empire' skyscrapers looked almost convincingly classical; the Arabian-nights domes of St Basil's stood near the Kremlin's lighted red stars and waving red flag (fluttering indefatigably, I found out, with the help of a wind machine). Meanwhile, down below, hundreds of people wilted in the heat while they waited in a long queue at a kiosk labelled 'Drinks', only to be turned away – 'Nothing to drink!'

Th sizzle of frustration about to explode lay just beneath the surface. It was turning into a dog-eat-dog society. Every financial transaction was a struggle. A fake official price for every item existed alongside a real (black) market price, and in the breach was a free playground for racketeers.

It was as if the Soviet Union had suddenly been opened up as a giant sweet-shop just waiting to be looted. Since few honest citizens had any concept, much less experience, of profit-making, the new law on enterprise – regulated only by primitive law enforcement and a Party-controlled judiciary – attracted criminals like flies. All those who had learned how to turn a profit when it was illegal were naturally first with the knowhow when making money became legal. Brezhnev-era ruble millionaires saw in the new co-ops a chance to launder their ill-gotten gains. Crime bosses who formerly operated in the 'shadow economy' (private enterprises that would not be considered criminal in the West) set out to exploit the semi-open market, using brutal methods they had learned from operating in the underground or copying the

American mafia: protection rackets and contract hitmen to kill off competitors. These mobsters infiltrated the newly independent business enterprises and infected the new class of entrepreneurs.

During that summer of disenchantment I had several personal encounters that gave a peek at how rotten the cabbage of the system was from the inside. It would take me many more months to understand how this rot went to the heart of Gorbachev's own hold on power, but I would later look back on these encounters as clues.

Heads turned as Andrei Voznesensky's fashionable figure glided between the tables of the Elaine's of Moscow. Even Voznesensky, the ultimate social butterfly in his Cardin suit and grey silk cravat, blowing kisses and prefacing his remarks with a Hollywoodesque 'Dahling', had a coldly pragmatic view of the Soviet system. Talking about the owner of a co-op café in which we were sitting, he said, 'Dahling, nobody can be honest in his position.'

The café owner wanted to open a hotel, Voznesensky told me, 'but they're afraid it will be a bordello'. He explained that the retail-trade mafia places prostitutes in all the new hotels.

'The tourist hotels of Moscow and Leningrad are infested with crime,' a Soviet translator confirmed. One becomes accustomed to seeing black marketeers of all kinds, the small roaches swarming about the entrances waiting to change money or sell drugs or girls. I learned from the translator how to spot the top crime bosses, who sit in the restaurants gorging themselves on expensive food: 'They are always well dressed in expensive European clothes and look absolutely alien to this country – they want people to assume they're foreigners – but their faces are definitely Soviet. And they are dangerous. If you don't go along with them, they will have your restaurant burned down or you'll be beaten up. These mafia people have Uzi guns and Italian plastic mines, all the latest gear. Soviet police don't even have police radios. They can't trace anybody. They're useless.'

Aside from the bosses, the richest people in Gorbachev's Russia were the waiters in Intourist hotels and the prostitutes who worked the hotel restaurants and bars. Such jobs were for sale, as key ground positions in the mafia chain, and those who bought into them were 'taxed' by the crime bosses.

The Ginseng Beauty Salon started to fill up at 5 p.m. with breathtakingly beautiful young Russian women. They belonged to the 'nouveau riche' class and were catered to by this Finnish salon on Chernyshevsky Street. They might take a sauna or massage or have their roots retouched, but mostly they lolled around over coffee and cigarettes waiting for their night's work to begin.

A pride of prostitutes, quite open about their profession, they wore the latest European styles – outsized houndstooth-check men's jackets over tight jeans, brass-linked leather belts, butter-soft leather shoulder bags. I fell into conversation with a lean, lovely twenty-two-year-old by complimenting her on her expensive tourmaline earrings and slate-blue silk trouser suit. She said the earrings were from Italy and the suit she wasn't sure, maybe Austria, they were all 'gifts'. People of her 'circle', she said, got everything through their 'mafia' – the bosses who provided the girls with condoms, which were otherwise unavailable, and connections to the tourist trade.

The system depended on the prostitutes gaining access to the hotels for foreigners, which were legally off limits to Soviets. The young lady of the evening explained that she and her friends had to pay off everybody in the chain – the militiamen, the porter on the door, the restaurant manager – either by sleeping with them or cutting them in on their earnings. Then they could sit at a table and order a bottle of champagne and wait to be approached by foreign guests. Her primary clients were Germans and Italians. 'All the girls dream of meeting an American man, or any foreigner, who will take them away to live abroad.'

Meanwhile, they were expected to steal whatever they could. In America, the victim's first response would have been to call the police. In the Soviet Union it was an utterly futile act. Many militiamen are courageous and devoted to their work, despite very hard conditions of life, but others are not surprisingly in sympathy with the racketeers. Soviet police chiefs – so poorly paid they can't afford cars and often live in tiny communal apartments – can hardly be blamed for being as alienated and resentful as the criminals they're supposed to catch. In one year, Moscow's crime rate rose by 40 per cent, felonies by 75 per cent.†

A psychology professor I met at the University of Leningrad lamented the mounting materialism and greed vulgarizing the face of the nation beneath the last tattered veils of socialism. Expressing a common view, he saw the 'gougers' and 'money-laundering Brezhnev ruble millionaires' as setting the pace for others, particularly young people: everyone was grabbing for whatever they could get, wherever they could beg, barter or gouge to get it.

And they were proud of gouging! After a breathtakingly expensive lunch at Moscow's first co-operative café, Kreputkinskaya 36, I asked the assistant manager how he happened to be among the first to benefit under perestroika as a co-op operator.

'Because I understand the system,' he smirked. He had been a director at Intourist, the state travel agency. 'I was screwed by the system for a long time. And now' – he jammed an index finger into an opening in his fist – 'now I screw the customer!'

The openness of this perverse pride in becoming a mercenary capitalist was startling. I encountered it in full bloom in the writer Julian Semyonov, who is very well known for his thriller novels and screenplays about spies.

A millionaire long before perestroika, Semyonov was featured in *People* in 1987 along with photos of his lavish dacha. With a laugh like the ignition of a racing car and gold chains wreathing his neck, he combines relentless self-promotion with the compelling charm of a natural storyteller. His career was given a significant boost by his relationship with Yuri Andropov, who contacted him in the 1970s about inaccuracies in one of his film scripts. It's a story Semyonov loves to tell.

He got the call at home. The caller said he was Andropov.

'Which Andropov?' Semyonov demanded.

'You may have heard of me. I've just become head of the KGB.'

The writer gasped.

'I've read your novel about the KGB, and really admire you as a writer,' said Andropov. 'But this screenplay is so – KGBish.'

He invited Semyonov to come to the doorless Lubianka building to talk with him. After being admitted through one of the hidden subterranean entrances several blocks away from the KGB headquarters, and escorted to Andropov's office, the writer noticed a pile of literary journals, among them *Znamya* and *Novy Mir*, and many books which the chief had heavily annotated. Semyonov asked if he could send the secret police chief the manuscript of a novel he was working on. Andropov said he would be honoured. He returned it with only one comment: 'In this one paragraph, you're meaner to us than the CIA.'

Semyonov added a laudatory paragraph about the KGB. Later, when he was lambasted by KGB censors and informed that he would not be allowed to publish the novel, Semyonov told them, 'Well, I have one satisfied reader.'

'Who?'

'Andropov.'

Their eyes bulged. The novel was published as written, and that launched a cosy relationship between the writer and the KGB brass, which extended into the era of Gorbachev's leadership. Semyonov was among the chosen in Gorbachev's entourage, along with Korotich and Baklanov, when the Soviet leader flew to Washington for his first summit on American soil.

Semyonov saw most of his countrymen as hopelessly naive; he liked making money, and he was good at it. Now, he boasted, he and the 'godfathers' of the Crimea would put up a resort hotel using his reputation and his 'connections' in the KGB as protection. He had lots of pals among the mafia in the Crimea and Georgia; indeed, he crowed, stabbing his chest with his thumbs, 'I *own* the Crimea – all of it – so I'll put up the luxury hotels, you will be my guest.'

He waved around a decree signed by Prime Minister Ryzhkov, claiming that Gorbachev had dropped a word in the Prime Minister's ear. The document gave him the right to launch the first non-governmental enterprise, an international journal of mystery literature which he called *Top Secret*. It also granted him permission to open both a ruble and a foreign-currency bank account and to do business abroad. For these new Soviet entrepreneurs, perestroika meant more foreign travel and international fame. Semyonov had just signed with the famous Hollywood agent, Swifty Lazar.

'The Crimea is mine, all of it, mine.' His wristless hands pawed the air and his eyes blazed with the mania of a magnate in the making. Was this what Gorbachev meant when he talked about the new 'socialist market'? I left Semyonov wondering if I had seen the future of the Soviet Union and it was Tovarish Trump.

Six months later, across the street from my old hotel, I saw homeless people standing in line all day outside the glamorous new Estée Lauder boutique, holding someone else's place in exchange for a bottle of vodka. Gorbachev could pontificate all he wished about 'attempts to divide society into strata and set people at odds' being 'totally impermissible', but his foot-dragging policies were fostering an income stratification between rich and poor that was becoming almost as grotesque as the gap in the United States.

'Just in two months things have got much worse,' my driver complained when he met me at the airport in early September 1989. 'Sugar is rationed. You have to have coupons. But there's plenty of sugar in the stores so it's all an artificial deficit. Who's making it?' My driver was always using up his petrol driving around to look for more petrol. When he couldn't find a restaurant with anything left for lunch he often had to settle for a loaf of bread. The dingy film on people's clothes attested to the fact that the soap shortage was still in effect. 'What they give us stinks,' said the driver. The bathrooms of Soviets who have travelled abroad were crammed with precious perfumed soaps and shampoos from foreign hotel rooms. The latest deficit was tea.

A twenty-eight-year-old Moscow TV correspondent told me how he spent his Saturdays: making the rounds of his 'connections' at the transportation bays on the city's periphery – unloading areas for goods trucked in from the rest of the country to feed and clothe Moscow. These areas are off major highways, fenced in and heavily guarded, but with the right connections the correspondent could carry away crates of frozen meat and vodka and cigarettes, paying extra rubles and ensuring many fewer goods would make it to the shelves of state stores. Because he was a journalist, he had permission to travel abroad and could take orders for foreign goods – VCRs, motorbike parts, cassettes – to repay his connections.

The next level down in the black market was at the unloading docks right behind state stores. That's where my driver spent his Saturdays. Hearing a rumour about a shortage of cigarettes, he would rush to his friend at a loading platform and buy a dozen cartons. Multiply that by panic-buying all over the country and it accounts for a good part of the shortages. My driver boasted that sometimes he didn't even have to give his connections extra rubles. Poorly paid by the state, they just passed him a case for nothing. It was a passive–aggressive way to thumb their nose at the corrupt and utterly discredited system of government distribution.

When there's nothing in the stores, and everyone is making deals under the table to meet daily needs, should this be called corruption? Or adaptation?

In most parts of the world, what the Soviets called their 'shameful condition' might have produced a revolution long ago, but offsetting their frustration with the chasm between Gorbachev's rhetoric and the reality of their lives was one constant: almost no one wants to work.

A sobering statistic was released in one of the first comprehensive national surveys on Soviet attitudes, done by Zaslavskaya's National Public Opinion Research Centre: Only 37 per cent of Soviets said they would like to improve their income by working as hard as they could. A clear majority – 55 per cent – would prefer to make even *less* money than they do now if they could do easier work.

'Yes, of course, we are deformed,' my Russian friends nodded glumly when asked about this poll. Even Gorbachev spoke of the 'deformation of society'.†

The depth of hatred and resentment towards those Soviets who were striving to move up materially was brought home to me by the story of Boris and Galya Gratchevsky.

Boris, the originator of *Yeralash*, a delightfully satirical film series for children that had become a phenomenon of Soviet life, is a Jew and the grandson of a poor farmer who was among those drafted to clear the wild woods outside Moscow, today the site of the elite writer's colony Peredelkino.

His grandfather lived with other men in huts without water, heat, sanitation or adequate food while they broke ground for small plots to grow food to send to Moscow. To encourage them to stay in these harsh conditions, the state allowed them to keep their plots. All his life the grandfather dreamed of turning the hut into a real house with a few neighbours and maybe heat and water.

His son managed to get an apartment in Moscow, but of course he could not pass on the apartment and he had no other possessions or money and so he left the hut in Peredelkino to Boris.

Boris is in his early forties, an exceptionally warm and talented man and a famous person. In any developed country he would be living in luxury. He and his wife Galya, a mathematician who gave up her career to care for their family of four and who tirelessly combs the government stores and 'the market' for food and clothes, had a dream: to build their own home on the tiny plot left to Boris by his father. Excitedly, they constructed a wooden model of a house, a splurge of self-expression, a dream house.

They started construction three years ago, sinking all their savings into the project. Soon the work stopped dead: there were no building materials available. So Boris and Galya continue to live in their tiny Moscow apartment, entertaining friends at a table laden with hand-pickled vegetables, home-made salads and soups, cream puffs and coffee laced with pear brandy, everyone squeezed into seven square metres of space. Above them, on top of the china cabinet, sits the model of their dream house – a miniature reminder of their never-ending frustration. Boris despairs of ever finishing it, but if they ever do, he fears envious neighbours might burn it down.

'This is happening with people who come from the country and make a success and build a house: it's burned down. They build another,' said Boris. 'It's burned down again, so they give up and sink back into the mud with everyone else.'

'You cannot have more than the others,' added Galya. 'The psychology of the Russian people is so formed it would take generations to straighten it out, if ever.'

They did not see their children as a bridge to a better future. Their sixteen-year-old son wore jeans, Reeboks and a black leather jacket with an American flag on the sleeve, and kept a Walkman plugged into his ear playing Michael Jackson and Bon Jovi. He couldn't imagine living with his parents' passivity. The first chance he had to escape, he would be on his way to New York to film school. Having grown up under glasnost, he imagined the world as full of possibilities.

Boris shook his head heavily. 'They look on us as immigrants.'

Apocalypse Now?

By the second week of September 1989, fresh back from a month-long holiday, Gorbachev found the capital boiling with rumours of imminent disaster. In only two months the nation's mood had darkened as a whole web of external problems, together with people's inner psychological dislocation, appeared to spiral out of control. Many believed the reformers in the Kremlin had lost control. 'We're anticipating civil war' was a refrain so popular it entered the culture through a pop song by the group DDT.† People's fears and dissatisfactions were concentrated on Gorbachev – would he impose martial law? Would he survive? Would there be a Khrushchev-style putsch?

When their leader suddenly made a TV appearance to try to quell the rumours, it only set people's teeth on edge. Looking rested but sober, Gorbachev made a speech that did little more than reflect back to his people the tensions they felt: 'Everything has become tied together in a tight knot – the critical state of the consumer market, conflicts in relations between the nationalities, and the difficult, sometimes even painful, processes in public consciousness related to the overcoming of deformations and the renewal of socialism.' Life had not grown better during perestroika, he acknowledged, but worse, but he defiantly labelled the predictions of 'impending chaos . . . coup, or even civil war' as attempts at intimidation by 'people who would like to create an atmosphere of alarm, hopelessness and uncertainty in society'. He barely mentioned conservative opposition to perestroika, saving his remonstrances for those from 'the ultra-leftist corner' who were urging him to act 'just like that', by 'renouncing socialist values and conducting restructuring in a capitalist manner'.† The speech fell flat. *Renewal of socialism* was a tough sell. Nobody wanted to listen to explanations any more. 'Gorbachev is definitely losing his authority and popularity,' pronounced senior journalist Arkady Vaxberg.†

More pernicious was the spread of an entirely new consciousness for the Soviet people. 'For the first time in seventy years, they look at their leader and *they aren't afraid of him* any more,' as Vitaly Korotich put it. 'The bureaucracy is looking for a scapegoat – somebody who can be made guilty for the last seventy years – they'll never admit the system is to blame.' Characteristically apocalyptic, the *Ogonyok* editor feared that as more and more Party hacks were forced out of their privileged positions by citizens now armed with the vote, they would want revenge. To take the blame off Communism, they would turn to civil war.

Gorbachev 'is not tough enough' was the most commonly heard refrain. Even his old friend Mikhailova made a disparaging comment that autumn: 'Clearly he does not have enough of Stalin's toughness. He's too soft. A leader of such a wild country with uncultured people and ethnic strife must show firmness.'†

When Gorbachev warned at a Central Committee meeting that the conflict between Armenia and Azerbaijan could produce anarchy, he received loud applause from Party stalwarts for sounding more militant. Full-blooded Russians, who represent 145 million of the 285 million Soviet population, were particularly insistent that Gorbachev use a 'strong hand' in dealing with ethnic violence and uppity republics demanding independence.† Spokesman Gerasimov acknowledged that Gorbachev was in a bind: the population still craved a strong leader who would tell them what to think, 'but democracy, if it works, usually works without a strong leader.'†

He rejected a bold proposal to deal with his nationalities problem. I remember vividly my own wonderment the first time I heard the idea. I had been invited to dinner at the home of an expert on the nation's regional economy, free economic zones and joint ventures, Professor Vladimir Kvint. One whole wall of his dining-room was covered with a map of the vast Soviet empire. When conversation at the table turned to the possible violent break-up of the empire, I asked, 'What does the country really need and what can it give up?'

Professor Kvint leaped up to sweep his left arm across the far-flung northern Asiatic regions – dropping Vladivostok into the sea. 'Russia doesn't need this economically,' he said and swung his arm down like a scythe across the southern Asiatic republics – chopping out Uzbekistan, Tadzhikistan and so on. Then he swept his arm across the Caucasian republics (Georgia, Azerbaijan, Armenia), Byelorussia and upwards to lop off the Baltic states. 'You take all this away and you still have the biggest country in the world.' He pointed to the Russian Federation, which is the Motherland of the fifteen republics, and to the big red blotch that is Moscow, out of which thick red lines were drawn like spokes to show transport lines.

'This – the centre – and this – the Ukraine – these are the Russian core,' he said dramatically. 'But look how formidable the Russian republic is in itself!' He circled his arm from European Russia across the Ural Mountains and through Siberia stretching up to the Polar Circle. Russia has 92 per cent of the oil resources of the Soviet Union, 85 per cent of the coal, and is the only producer in the Eastern European countries of platinum and diamonds. 'Gorbachev should change the question from whether republics should be allowed to *leave* the Union to whether they should be allowed *into* the Union,' Kvint said prophetically that night in September 1989. 'And each republic should be free to decide. Forcibly keeping a republic within the Union is a crime against its people and against Russia, making it a colonial empire.'

Gorbachev dismissed the notion that he could abolish the Union Treaty (signed in 1922) and invite the republics to join the USSR under new, mutually beneficial conditions.† He kept *talking* about some vague new idea of federation, but he gave no hint that his inner empire could hope to obtain the freedom he'd allowed the Eastern bloc countries. When it was suggested to Gorbachev that he create a presidency, granting himself ascendancy over all other power structures, he rejected the notion as late as October 1989.

Gorbachev's Emotional Accidents

Then, Gorbachev began to have a series of 'emotional accidents', as my Soviet friends called them. Losing his temper repeatedly in public, lashing out at the progressives who thought they were on his side, lurching from contradiction to contradiction, his behaviour all that autumn and winter suggested an emotional volatility that could no longer be contained. Increasingly, he personalized his power struggles with those who disagreed with him or stood up to him.

'His skin is quite extraordinarily thin for a politician,' a friend in the Central Committee acknowledged.

When Mikhail Sergeyevich picked up a copy of a highly respected Moscow weekly, *Argumenty i Fakty*, in October 1989 and read that he, who believed himself to be the beloved parent guiding his people into a new century, was no longer the most popular political figure in the Soviet Union, he became livid. The survey ranked the popularity of members of the Soviet Parliament based on 15,000 letters from readers, and top ratings had gone to Gorbachev's most accursed antagonists – Andrei Sakharov and Boris Yeltsin.

'He was very emotional,' editor Viktor Starkov told me, describing the scene at one of Gorbachev's pep rallies for his media troops. 'By the end of the meeting he was really angry. He didn't scream but he turned very cold.' Gorbachev said stonily, 'If I were in the place of editor Starkov, I would ask to be retired.' Starkov tried to explain that it was not his own opinion, merely the opinion of some of his readers.

Gorbachev replied that 'it was impossible to judge anything by the opinion of the people, only by the KGB', Starkov remembered, a stark admission that Gorbachev still relied on his clan of secret police to gauge his people's thoughts and actions.† The editor tried to appease the General Secretary by agreeing that 'deeper psychological research' was probably needed. But Gorbachev was not to be soothed. Starkov was summoned to the Central Committee and ordered to resign from the post he had held for ten years.

'I can't express myself in the Soviet press, no one would publish it,' Starkov told Bill Keller of the *New York Times*, who broke the story.† Gorbachev's 'emotional accident' was televised in full, and Starkov's refusal to resign became a cause célèbre. He later had to publish a questionable poll by 'sociologists' showing Gorbachev as the most popular politician in the land, but he stayed in the job. The flap boosted the circulation of *Argumenty i Fakty* astronomically; by March 1990 it was the most popular publication in the world with a circulation of 31.5 million.† By that time, everything Gorbachev did to slap down glasnost seemed to backfire.

On the same day that he attacked Starkov, Gorbachev also privately blasted historian Yuri Afanasev, the ringleader of the Interregional Group.† It was suggested that Afanasev resign from the Communist Party. When he refused, he was added to a growing list of 'undesirable' people, including Yeltsin and other independent people's deputies, who were prohibited from appearing on TV or speaking through radio or newspapers. He had to turn to *Time* magazine to express his view: '[Gorbachev] is becoming more and more a leader of the Party apparat, he supports their kind of perestroika. That's why many people no longer believe in him.'

There is an iron law of revolutions: the more you change, the faster you have to change. The events in Eastern Europe had proven that the road from dictatorship to multi-party elections had no stopping places. What Gorbachev said constantly throughout the autumn of 1989 was, 'We must go faster, always faster.' What he did was drag his feet. Even as the spontaneous revolution from below leaped forward, with spasms of violence on the periphery and a youthquake of ignored thirty- and forty-year-olds flexing their political muscles in the cities, Gorbachev fell further and further behind the times.

Having given up the traditional tools used by Soviet leaders – force and fear – and committed himself to revolution by his own natural 'soft' weapons – propaganda and persuasion – Gorbachev needed more than ever to make haste. Even as his shock troops in the media and intelligentsia basked in their new-found individual celebrity, they knew the power of their lofty ideas was nothing compared with the raw power of rabid nationalism and anti-semitism.

Right-wing opposition to Gorbachev was taking increasingly ominous militaristic, even neo-fascist, forms. Party conservatives led by Yegor Ligachev lashed out at the press for attempting to 'blacken' and 'defame' the Soviet past. Many officers in the Soviet military were apoplectic about the speed of the withdrawal from Eastern Europe and the disintegration of the Warsaw Pact military alliance. Pamyat ('Memory'), a militantly nationalist society, was gaining adherents with its openly expressed hatred of Jews, the traditional scapegoats in times of adversity. The favoured insult for Raisa was 'yevreyka' (Jewess), and Dr Sakharov was branded 'an American kike'. The very word 'Jewess' is a curse word.

At a huge Pamyat rally in December a hysterical speaker stirred the crowd of 2,500 with a vicious attack on the liberal press: 'Mother Russia is screaming from every hill of our country. Why? The yellow press of Korotich is in the deep Canadian pockets of Yakovlev. If you help us to fight Yakovlev, I will kneel on my knees all night long.'† As Gorbachev's closest adviser, Yakovlev had become enemy number one for all those who were now calling themselves 'traditionalists'. They accused him of being Russophobic because he liked the West. 'But at a deeper level', admitted Anatoly Zalutsky, a columnist for right-wing papers and a Pamyat supporter, 'they hate Yakovlev because he's Gorbachev's man.'†

Near the end of 1989, while Gorbachev was flying around to various foreign capitals or indulging in temperamental outbursts at the results of his own glasnost, the black crows of the bureaucracy were making common cause with these Russian nationalists and anti-semites to create a powerful bulwark against reform, but Gorbachev never addressed the issue of anti-semitism or the menace of Pamyat. He concentrated his rebukes on the other end of the polarized political spectrum, where the strange fruits of democratization had a progressive colour. These independents were far more threatening to a political power structure that rested on an illegitimate authority established long ago by fear and force. The contradiction was catching up with him.

Gorbachev was being slowly poisoned by democracy.

Sakharov's Warning

'I am a Communist, a convinced Communist!' Gorbachev blurted out in an impassioned monologue to the second national Congress of People's Deputies in December 1989. 'For some that may be a fantasy. But to me it is my main goal.'†

The mood of curiosity and elation that had existed among the deputies at the first Congress only six months earlier was replaced by 'weariness and doubt'. Gorbachev himself was described by reporters as 'wary', 'temperamental', and 'testy'.† The contradictions in his position were glaring. He promised that 'We are carrying out perestroika on the basis of our own socialist principles,' but then his Prime Minister, Ryzhkov, announced that the government had decided to go back to the old five-year-planning methods which had led to the current economic stasis. The contrast was equally stark between the sunny, grinning, benevolent Gorbachev of summiteering fame, and the ill-tempered, often bullying Party boss who lashed out at his own law-making forum for doubting the torpid pace of his reforms. He snapped, sneered and pleaded with insurgents who attempted to question the Party's monopoly on power. Only a few deputies dared to come forward and raise the issue of multi-party politics.

'That's all, that's all,' Gorbachev would cut them off.

'Yesterday I stood in a queue to get a half-kilo of butter,' complained a citizen in a local newspaper. 'Then I came home and watched the Congress on television and realized why I would be standing in queues for the rest of my life.'†

The liberal deputies of the Interregional Group had been cowed into abandoning Andrei Sakharov's call for a protest strike to stress their challenge to Article Six, the constitutional guarantee of the Party's dominance. Yevtushenko managed to gain the rostrum and warn the Communists in the hall that 'You cannot gain prestige from a single paragraph,' referring to Article Six. 'Such authority should be earned daily.'

Gorbachev fumed.

At the last minute Andrei Sakharov, sixty-eight, heavy with the ravages of exile, shuffled to the podium to mount one last challenge. Undeterred by waves of groans from the Party faithful, he said he had a very simple proposal: to eliminate those articles, meaning the sacred Article Six, that were blocking the adoption of liberalized laws on property and land.

'I have the impression that you don't know how to implement your proposals,' snapped Gorbachev.

Sakharov offered to present a list of the articles.

'Let's drop the matter,' said Gorbachev.

The bent academician persisted, approaching the leader's lofty perch. 'I'll give you some telegrams I have received.'

Scowling ferociously, Gorbachev ordered, 'Come here, and I'll give you three folders with a thousand such telegrams.'

'I have sixty thousand,' countered Sakharov.

'That's all!' One last time Mikhail Sergeyevich silenced debate from his fearless antagonist. Listing slightly, Sakharov returned to his seat. Gorbachev then launched into a long, hot-blooded, desk-slapping tirade in defence of 'a mature Party' and its 'new functions as the political vanguard'. Even as he promised, 'We have to change everything,' he protested, in a voice revealing for its pleading tone, 'I am a Communist!'

Back in the spare apartment he used as a study, Andrei Sakharov sat down to write another speech, this time pressing Gorbachev to move more swiftly on the economy. 'Complete disbelief' in the Gorbachev programme would sweep through society over the next year, he predicted. The workers' distrust of their leader was deepening, he warned, adding, 'I think this distrust is justified.'

Dr Sakharov admitted he was having second thoughts about the 'mysterious personality' at the head of the nation.† 'Gorbachev is something of a paradox for me . . . The most favourable explanation is that he is a cautious man,' he mused, still trying to fathom the leader's hesitancy to accept political pluralism and genuine economic change. The less favourable explanation, he said, is that Mr Gorbachev may be 'guided by the tactical and unprincipled considerations' of classic Kremlin power struggles. 'That could not be forgiven.'†

That night he collapsed in the corridor, presumably of a heart attack. Sakharov's last words before he died were, 'Tomorrow there will be a battle.'†

Were Gorbachev's increasingly frequent tirades part of a strategy to keep the revolution at his tempo and steer clear of the chaos of civil war? Or were these 'emotional accidents' the sign of a beleaguered leader losing his own balance?

'He could control his temper until recently,' observed an astute Leningrad scholar of political leaders, Yakov Grodin. 'Now he starts losing his temper whenever he doesn't like something. He wants to show us his power.' His old classmate Lieberman was less sanguine. 'Misha always had a temper, but he is less and less able to control it.'

My hunch was that we were beginning to see the disintegration of his individual power and his inner control, leading him to grasp for ever greater – even quasi-dictatorial – external control. Events were now rushing past Mikhail Sergeyevich as if on some cosmic slide, scattering even

his powers of improvisation into a shower of quickly
extinguished sparks.

In mid-December the inner wall of monolithic Communism
that confined the fourteen non-Russian republics within
Moscow's control was breached by the little captive Baltic
republic of Lithuania. Its Communist Party was the first to
sever links with the national Party. Gorbachev erupted again.
He railed at those who wanted self-determination right away.
They were threatening to 'blow up' the Union, he scolded,
then he shut off debate, and stiffened his resistance to what
he perceived as a grave threat to his life's work. The renegade
secessionist movements, he prophesied, would sow 'discord,
bloodshed and death'.

One could hear and even see the wrenching conflict in
Gorbachev's escalating emotional outbursts during the long
Congress. 'We have to change everything,' he would decree
in one breath, even as he kept using the phrase 'within the
framework [of the Party]'.

His whole strategy in pressing for reforms was based on
the belief that the Communist Party would remain in power.
As the Party came under direct attack, Gorbachev could no
longer maintain a working alliance between the progressives
and the Stalinists. His constant pleadings for unity fell on
deaf ears, and he became more and more tense and irritable.
He was only able to conceive of working his reforms 'within
the framework' of his own psychological universe, that is,
within the Party structure – the surrogate father–mother–god
– that had sheltered and promoted him all his life. Because
he did not have the courage to step outside the Party
structure, he now became its prisoner.

The system protected him but also restricted his ability to
move with the forces of historical change he himself had
unleashed. The world was expecting this international hero
to be just as bold and progressive at home as he was abroad,
but as the control of the Party began to crack, so did Mikhail
Gorbachev. Trapped in the rubble of the 'tragic utopia'† from

which he had derived his power and charisma, Gorbachev was losing his authority and the respect of his people.

The dismemberment of the Communist Party was already well under way in five of his own republics – the Baltic states, Armenia and Azerbaijan. Indeed, the handwriting had been left on the Kremlin wall during the first elections, when local Party apparatchiks were rejected and humiliated. By the end of 1989 the Soviet leader was faced with the ultimate inner conflict: can a man destroy the very thing that nurtured him?

Challenged to strike down the law guaranteeing a one-party monopoly, he resorted to one of Lenin's tactics – threatening to resign. Then he gave a spirited defence of his mission to remake socialism. 'It's my life's work,' he said. 'It's my way of seeing things and I am not giving up.'

At the same time he admitted he had 'no clear-cut, detailed plan' to realize perestroika. As one conservative newspaperman in Moscow put it, 'He's like a Soviet cab-driver racing through the unfamiliar streets of Manhattan with five minutes to get to the airport.'

His contradictory statements were evidence of the internal conflict raging inside his own mind. Around the same time that he was publicly vowing, 'I am a Communist!' he confided to Margaret Thatcher, 'I don't even know if I'm a Communist any more.'† The ultimate chameleon, he would have to try to 'destroy himself' – in the best Leninist tradition – in order to be reborn yet again; this time, into the total pragmatist.

Losing Control

The first six months of 1990 were his crucible – the peak of inner psychological crisis. The centre was not holding, in any sense of the phrase. Gorbachev had lost control of at least five of his republics. His centralized economy was unravelling. And the centre of his Party had come apart. Gorbachev had reached the limit of what he could accomplish as a

Communist leader. The question was, could he remake himself once more? Or had he reached his limit to develop further?

Gennady Lisichkin, a member of the Supreme Soviet and a radical economist who had been enlisted by Gorbachev, cautioned against seeing Gorbachev as a post-socialist leader. 'It's most important to understand that Gorbachev is a Bolshevik, that Gorbachev is a Communist, that Gorbachev is a son of the Party. He has gone a long, hard way of development. The Gorbachev in Stavropol and the Gorbachev now in the Kremlin are *two different people*. You can compare him to Khrushchev in this regard. Khrushchev, who was a faithful son of Stalin, rejected with a lot of effort part of Stalin's bloody past. So Gorbachev makes one more step and rejects one more part of Stalin's heritage – remaining, unfortunately, a Bolshevik and a Communist.'†

The Communist Party was created as an avant-garde to realize the aim of seizing and holding power; that was its function and meaning, and holding on to that power for the Party and for himself – albeit under a different suit of clothes – remained Gorbachev's mission.

This would lead him to the ultimate paradox. In his quest for a means to reduce the centralization of power, he would actually amass more levers of power in his own hands than any Soviet leader since Stalin. He would rationalize this abandonment of democratization at the top as a temporary measure to save the country from chaos and save the Party from its own blindness. That was the lofty philosophical level of thinking we heard in his speeches. But power is its own witchcraft, and Gorbachev's best instincts were perverted by his increasingly frenzied fear of giving up control. That was the level of heart that explained his schizoid actions. Gorbachev's behaviour in the first half of 1990 was an exquisite exhibition of doublethink.

The ultimate test of his leadership would be in his handling of Lithuania. Rejecting pleas and warnings from the Kremlin, the parliament of that tiny republic made a defiant declaration on 8 December: to abolish the guarantee of power for the Communist Party and break from Moscow. Secession fever began spreading throughout the Baltic states.

Hints had been dropped in the past by Gorbachev, as early as his 1984 meeting with Mrs Thatcher, that the Soviet chief was flirting with a formula for offering autonomy to his more rebellious republics. Such progressive thoughts now seemed banished from Gorbachev's mind by the spectre of a political blacklash from Russians – even possibly from the Soviet military – if he dared to countenance a republic declaring independence from Moscow. He all but admitted that by crossing that line he would open himself to accusations that he had deliberately chosen the direction of 'dismembering the USSR'.†

And so, on Christmas Day 1989, Gorbachev closed his fist around the Union and declared, to thunderous applause from his ruling Central Committee: 'The current Party and state leadership will not permit the disintegration of the Union state.'†

In early January Gorbachev took one of the most desperate gambles of his career. Armed only with his weapons of personality and persuasion, he took his campaign to preserve the integrity of the Union to the streets of Lithuania. For three days he would argue and scold, demanding the people 'trust me' and stay in the Union while he and the Party worked out a better deal offering some increase in autonomy for the periphery. The strategy was to take the unruly republics' protests to Moscow as the source of their problems, and turn it all on its head. Let the upstarts realize that not only did Moscow depend on the republics, but the republics depended on Moscow for their very lifeline – the gas and oil pipelines that power their industries.

'The Central Committee session was only suspended while he made the trip, so it was an acute decision,' said Sergei Stankevich, a democratic deputy (later elected to the 'Mossoviet' or Moscow City Council). 'He anticipated attacks.'

But he had no idea of the depth of feeling he would encounter.

Surrounded in his first televised encounter in Vilnius by a curiously docile and expressionless group of people, Gorbachev implored them, eye to eye, to remain in the Soviet Union, warning that secession would mean economic calamity for Lithuanians. 'My personal fate is linked to this choice,' he said fervently. 'The two states must live together.'

Raisa glared at him, as if furious that he had chosen to make himself so humanly vulnerable, but he was the only one who spoke. Not a peep of challenge from the crowd – why?

'There are only special people on the streets since the first outburst in Krasnodar a year and a half ago,' I learned from Starkov, the editor of *Argumenty i Fakty.* 'You see the same people in different places, wearing the same clothes that the Party workers wear.' Starkov speculated that Gorbachev might not have known he was being insulated from reality. 'People from the apparat are so smart and cunning that they can do it. They know that the audience makes the king.'†
Clearly Gorbachev was not prepared for the drastically different audiences he was to confront in the next days.

That night, the real people came out into the central Cathedral Square of Vilnius and answered Gorbachev's entreaty with a terrifyingly hollow silence. They stood in the sodden dusk clutching candles, two hundred thousand of them, their faces waxen. For fifteen minutes not a sound was heard from this sea of bodies except the wet and laboured flapping of the flags of Lithuania, Latvia and Estonia. Demonstrators held up signs demanding 'freedom and independence'. The trappings of Gorbachev's authority were stripped bare by their unfearing faces. Then, bursting into nationalist songs, they shattered the silence and Roman Catholic churches struck their bells and the people were called to masses all over the republic to pray for the rebirth of their nation.†

Gorbachev moved his diplomatic campaign the next day to

a hall full of prominent intellectuals. Presumably the KGB expected they could organize a lively exchange between the master persuader and his natural tribe – the intelligentsia – with televised footage that would make it look like he was winning over the people. Gorbachev later admitted he expected this audience to be 'reserved and shy'. Again, he was badly misinformed.†

'You want to leave the Soviet Union or not?' he shouted at them, 'Yes or no!'

Da, da, da!

Their comeback struck him like a blow to the head. Gorbachev became enraged. Shoulders hunching up, skeleton shaking, he launched into a long, intimidating monologue. They talked right up to him. They didn't wait to be called upon. Gorbachev became further enraged.

'Where are you going to live! Where are you going to go!'

Some snickered. Wagging his finger, Gorbachev scolded them, treating them like children, telling them to take one baby step after another while Father Gorbachev led them by the hand through a deliberately tortuous constitutional process towards some vague rosy future he called a federation. This, after he had virtually admitted that the present constitution of the USSR wasn't worth the paper it was written on.†

'Do you know what a federation is or no? How do you know if you never lived in one?'

They ridiculed him. Rocking back and forth, this rotund and sputtering man looked for a flash like one of those souvenir Matryoshka dolls. 'Are you going to listen or not!' he shouted. All at once, apparently realizing he'd lost them, Gorbachev switched from being abusive to being charming. 'It turns out you speak up very quickly . . . Well, you don't think that we're enemies, do you!' No one answered him, but they quietened down. 'This is a dream, this kind of exodus,' he said gently. He was turning himself inside out to win their good will and beginning to get a response, until he tried to convince them that Lithuania was *less* independent before it was incorporated into the Soviet Union.

These mostly young men and women simply sat back in their seats, laughing in his face, and stopped listening to this silver-haired man from a dying era. For the first time ever, Soviet television viewers saw their head of state forced to use every ounce of his personal prestige and charisma to counter arguments against Moscow's control – and fail. For all his fabled mental agility, Gorbachev had shown that he could be outsmarted.

A music professor by the name of Landsbergis, head of the moderate Lithuanian national movement, told reporters that Mr Gorbachev's visit was welcome – it only boosted patriotic feeling – and that by lecturing proud Lithuanians so sharply, he might well have alienated some of the sympathy that existed before his visit.† Landsbergis got under Gorbachev's skin from the start.

After three days of wounding encounters, Gorbachev flew back to Moscow on Saturday, 13 January, his weapons of persuasion and personality exhausted. The rejection of Moscow's control was not confined to Lithuania. Independence fever had spread to neighbouring Latvia. In Soviet Georgia national-movement leaders were blockading the offices of the local Communist Party. Gorbachev returned home to even more alarming news.

Mobs of Azerbaijani nationalists had boiled over after a mass rally in Baku, where they demanded that the Moscow-installed Communist government resign, and they were on a rampage of pogroms against Armenian residents. Victims were being 'thrown out of windows and from houses, killed with iron bars, and stabbed with knives', witnesses later reported in *Izvestia*.†

Everything he had worked for appeared about to be swallowed up in the savagery of civil war between nationalities that Gorbachev had done his best to ignore. He was now forced to face the gargantuan proportions of his 'nationalities problem' and the grim facts he had ignored so long: that anti-Russian feeling was deep and endemic throughout the non-Russian Soviet republics; that millions of Soviet citizens saw the very political structure of the Union of Soviet Socialist Republics as illegitimate and were just waiting for their moment to bolt; and that the world's last empire, if it was not to implode through protracted internal civil wars, could only be held together by concrete economic progress, by political autonomy and, if all else failed, by military force.

'After deep soul-searching', Gorbachev violated every pledge he had made about perestroika being committed to persuasion over force and ordered five thousand Soviet army soldiers and six thousand Interior Ministry troops into Baku. As the cold-blooded indiscriminate killing of civilians in the streets began, the General Secretry dropped out of sight on 19 January, not to be seen in public for the next two weeks.

Another Metamorphosis

Holed up in his dacha on the outskirts of Moscow, Gorbachev had to figure out how to get ahead of the wave before the turbulence of history overtook him. He had fallen seriously behind the currents surging towards self-determination.

So it was not surprising to hear that Gorbachev was going through a 'rebirth'.

Another one? I asked.

'I'm quite sure there are several Gorbachevs,' Nikolai Shishlin enumerated matter-of-factly. 'One in Stavropol, another in Moscow, another in 1985, and another in 1987. And now,' he said confidently, 'there's a new Gorbachev.'

Was it a rebirth into the presidency?

He brushed off my naivety. 'The presidency is simply a suit.'

Shishlin said he sensed the latest rebirth occurring at the very end of 1989 and the beginning of the new year. He had recently been out to the Gorbachev compound where he was in retreat. 'The crisis is our own domestic problems. He saw that the government simply doesn't work. That's when he accepted the idea of abolishing Article Six and the idea of a multi-party system. He reached this point by himself.'

Perhaps the most extraordinary thing was that the *old* Gorbachev had survived so long, deviating his way through the mined waters of a majority consistently hostile to his reforms in all the key institutions of power in the country, and all the while reinforcing his own political position. But now, the ship of state on which that position rested had sprung a devastating leak. Gorbachev either had to go down with the ship, or have a lifeboat prepared for himself.

During those two weeks out of sight, brainstorming, with a parade of advisers whose limousines sped up and down the Rublyovskoye Highway to his dacha, Gorbachev decided to do an astonishing political somersault. He would propose that the Communist Party give up its constitutional monopoly on power as the guiding force of Soviet society. At the same time, he would open a crack in the window of pluralism by raising the possibility of legalizing rival politcal parties 'at a certain stage'.

Gorbachev only took this daring step after he did a volte-face on the extent of his own powers. His closest aides had been trying to convince him to create a presidency and grant himself ascendancy over all other power structures. He had publicly rejected the idea as late as October 1989. Yakovlev worked on him during the two-week retreat, and later indicated that Gorbachev had resisted the idea, believing that such a form of autocratic rule went against Soviet traditions. 'However, gradually, Gorbachev arrived at a conclusion that a consolidating force was really needed in our multi-ethnic state,' Yakovlev said in an interview in *Komsomolskaya Pravda*. He went on to make a claim of breathtaking doublethink: 'Mikhail Gorbachev is free from ambition. Moreover, he sometimes feels it as a burden.'†

The man who three months before had insisted that the 'salvation' of the USSR lay in involving ordinary people in politics, rather than concentrating unrestrained power in the hands of one man, was now prepared to demand that the Central Committee grant him 'plenipotentiary powers' to implement his policies.† 'Salvation' of the USSR was too loftily vague; Gorbachev's closest advisers were more immediately concerned with salvation for Mikhail Sergeyevich.

Their advice, revealed in a briefing paper prepared by Gorbachev's aides and published in *Le Monde*, was to move swiftly 'to impose a presidential system and to create a new type of Party'. They didn't suggest he *propose*, but *impose*, this radical shift of power. They gave him the strongest storm warnings that, if he didn't move swiftly, the country would risk civil disturbances 'worse than what happened in Tiananmen Square or in Romania'.†

But they wanted him to take an even more drastic step: to dissociate himself from the Party conservatives by giving up his position as Chairman of the Communist Party. In their confidential document his closest advisers warned Gorbachev that the Party and its leaders were rapidly losing the trust of the population. The urgent advice was that he should split off the post of head of state from Party leader. The same call was heard in the weeks before the Central Committee plenum from the new umbrella reform group, the 'Democratic Platform'.†

His aides argued that Gorbachev's skilful balancing act between right and left had exhausted its possibilities – no centre remained. The failure of his leadership to improve people's lives and the eruption of ethnic conflicts had so sharply polarized Soviet society that Gorbachev was satisfying neither the reformist radicals nor the traditionalist conservatives. His most ardent advisers had designed the presidency as a lifeboat, from which they wanted him to row away from the sinking ship of the Party.

The hour of decision had come. Gorbachev would have to decide whether he wanted to be the leader of perestroika for the people or leader of the Party aristocracy.

Co-opting the Pro-Democracy Movement

The walls of the Kremlin – synonymous with raw, red-stoned despotic strength – were faced squarely by hundreds of thousands of pro-democracy protesters on 4 February. It was the largest public rally in seventy years of Soviet power. The peaceful protesters themselves couldn't believe the swell of their numbers.

Vsevolod Revich, a science-fiction writer and film critic, left his apartment off Gorky Street that morning expecting to see perhaps 30,000, maybe even 50,000, people on the day of the first demonstration. When he turned into Gorky Street, he was stunned at the mass of bobbing heads and linked arms and thrusting banners calling for an end to the Communist lock on power. Bodies were swelling to overflow the massive width and length of this broad boulevard, all the way to the neck of Red Square!

'There had been no notices, no announcements, the whole thing was organized only by one person telephoning another,' he marvelled. 'I was amazed to find that *we* are well organized – the *liberals!*'

Actually, the Interregional Group of pro-democracy deputies who had organized this 'meeting in the streets' were given a helping hand by Gorbachev. The Stalinists led by Ligachev were close to gaining the upper hand in the ruling circle and openly demanding a purge of the leadership. Once Gorbachev learned that the whole tenor of the demonstration was to demand that he refuse concessions to the conservatives, he deliberately used the mass rally to warn his Party hardliners that they must change.† Announcements tantamount to a massive advertising campaign, were replayed on Central Television and Moscow Radio the day before, giving the time and place of the demonstration, while maps were published in official newspapers.

Police sealed off Red Square, but the leadership could not hide from the people. Radical reformers like Boris Yeltsin spoke out and were carried live on TV. Western newsmen beamed incendiary man-in-the-square interviews: 'There'll be no changes as long as this mafia is in control.'† Ordinary protesters walked right up to members of the Central Committee and challenged them as they emerged from a stormy emergency session on Lithuania.

The next day, 5 February, Gorbachev opened the Central Committee plenum by springing on the smug slugs of the apparat an historic statement announcing the reversal of the Communists' seven decades of ensured rule. His printed manifesto had been prepared in advance. It was the first inkling many hardliners had that they were targets. Mouths fell open as he spoke.

'In a society that is renewing itself, the Party can exist and fulfil its vanguard role only as a democratically acknowledged force . . . The CPSU naturally intends to fight for a position of being a ruling party, but it intends to do this strictly within the framework of the democratic process, renouncing any and all legal and political advantages . . .'

In fact, Gorbachev had no intention of giving up the Party's vast power base. It is quite possible to maintain Communism without a Communist Party. The Communists had vast land holdings, a treasure trove of patronage jobs, they controlled most of the press and TV, and they maintained a virtual chokehold on much of the administrative bureaucracy. 'Communism, in short, is a hierarchical organization, like the army, so there is always a watcher for every four or five people,' as the dissident writer Zinoviev explained it.†

'Gorbachev is categorically against the Communist Party having to campaign on a par with other parties for its seats in parliament,' I was told off the record by one of his close confrères. 'Even though he had to give in on Article Six, just now he doesn't have to worry. Other groups who want to form as parties have no platforms, no money, no organization or leadership. It will take at least ten years before any can gain momentum and rise to the level of the Communist Party.'

The debate was described by participants as one of the

bitterest in Party history. 'We spent three days trying to convince one another that black is black and white is white,'† Yakovlev told a press conference. But, in the end, only maverick deputy Boris Yeltsin, attending as a guest, voted against the decision to drop Article Six, presumably to register his dissent from any of Gorbachev's decisions.

Gorbachev's historic platform was carried unanimously. At the same time he got the Central Committee's approval to 'concentrate power in the hands of the President and cabinet'.† It was one more demonstration of his shrewdness as a politician. He could totally rearrange the nation's agenda to reflect his own political somersaults, and emerge from the bitterest debate with his own position reinforced – having prepared the result beforehand. 'Of course,' confirmed Gerasimov at a press conference. 'Otherwise he wouldn't have called the plenum.' The spokesman explained the philosophy that had led to the transformation of Gorbachev into a 'realist': 'If you can't beat 'em, join 'em. We must move with the tide, move with the people, and not be left behind by events.'

The Democratic Platform, an embryonic group of opposition forces which included the 400 dissenting deputies of the Interregional Group and many formerly non-political groups, predicted the Party would be split by summer. All political forces were in turmoil.

More than anything else, the people were tired. Many appeared to be terminally alienated from both Party and state. But even some of those who considered themselves cynically apolitical began to come alive in unexpected ways. The social organism began stripping away another layer after decades of impacted fear.

'We knew any economic change would create strong social shifts,' admitted the sociologist Zaslavskaya, 'but no one could have predicted the depth or width of this spontaneous and uncontrollable revolution from below in response to revolution from above.' She had been shaken by her own sensitive public opinion research. 'The initiative of peres-troika has gone over from leaders to masses – assuming unexpected, sometimes dangerous forms.'

The filmmaker Barchevsky took a more optimistic view of the disequilibrium: 'With Gorbachev, we don't understand yet what he's done. He has destroyed this world of enemies we were living in, and he accomplished that together with his wife.'

But the pitiable irony of it was, Gorbachev and his wife did not entirely welcome this throwing off of fear in people's souls. It was not something one man could control, nor one party. The experience of five years had shown that it was not enough to awaken the indifferent masses, but equally important to channel their energy. Gorbachev's revolution had become an epidemic of volition. The truth was, he didn't know how to direct it. He was beginning to reassess this concept he so blithely threw around – democracy – as evil.

Crack in the Godhead

Gorbachev's uncontrollable outbursts culminated, during a late February session of the Supreme Soviet, in a fusillade of insults aimed at the progressives of the Interregional Group. They had made public their disdain for his power-grab in proposing a presidency. They were hardly alone – the idea had pleased no important group in the population – yet Gorbachev singled them out for abuse.

'I know there are these feelings among deputies that it's all being plotted for Gorbachev, it's cheap demagogics,' he whined. The progressives applauded in acknowledgement. His voice turned harsh. He accused the 'democratic move-ments' of trying to create tension on the day of their big rally. His words were drowned in eruptions from the audi-ence. Then he charged them with 'organized blows' on perestroika. Hollering, whining, fuming – could this be Mikhail Sergeyevich – this moody, menacing, almost irrational ruler? He began to sound like Varlam, the despotic mayor in the film *Repentance*: '*I notice everything, so beware of me.*'

'I hear everything, comrades. Calm down! Be quiet!' ordered Gorbachev. The deputies recoiled at this highhanded treatment. Screaming now, virtually hysterical, Gorbachev issued repeated, futile orders for his audience to be silenced. 'What I think it to be necessary to say I'll say anyway!'

Over the uproar he warned, 'The situation in the country is very strained . . . We do not have years ahead but months.' Then he went back to hammering on those he depicted as undermining him: 'They want to persuade the people that the leadership is incapable . . . sow unbelief. They say Gorbachev's authority is going down.' His lips curled in contempt.

Suddenly he stopped speaking, rolled his tongue inside his lips, and then veered off into a stream of consciousness. 'Sometimes I have this crazy idea . . . to prove that nothing is plotted for someone, that I should withdraw my candidacy. I'm sharing with you, it's a crazy idea . . .' As derisive murmurs mounted, Gorbachev snapped back into his diatribe and accused the democratic deputies of trying to drive him crazy: 'They want to make the leadership come off the track. That won't work! It's a scheme for unstable people!'

Jaws gaped, deputies dropped their eyes. It was a shocking display of the leader's inner disquiet. The whole 'emotional accident', as shaken Soviets referred to it, was seen on national television.

As his confidante Frolov admitted, 'He knows a lot of people among intellectuals. He feels the need to attract these people, and deal with them.'† Yet, by choosing the progressive deputies for a tongue-lashing, Gorbachev was alienating his own most treasured tribe: the intelligentsia and politicized young urbanites.

'I've lost all hope in Gorbachev, even as a politician,' Yuri Afanasev told me the next day. The historian who spearheaded the Interregional Group saw Gorbachev's 'hysterical outburst' as evidence that the man was 'a politician without a future'.

By daring to criticize him, the democratic forces had become Gorbachev's enemies. Moreover, the structure of thought that was his habit of a lifetime, that is, accepting two contradictory ideas and *living with both*, was no longer possible. The forces demanding democratic change and the forces determined to block change had pulled so far apart that Gorbachev's lofty seat of power – the Apollonian throne from which he liked to play detached god – had been kicked out from beneath him. The contradictions were colliding even as the economy was in freefall. He would have to choose sides.

Intellectually, Gorbachev was clearly capable of great leaps of thought. We have seen how his vision of a modern Soviet Union embedded in a new world order was a profound and personal vision based, first, on a transformation in his own perception. Any revolution in thought first occurs in the minds of one or a few individuals who experience a flash of intuition; scientists often speak of the 'lightning flash' that suddenly permits them to see the pieces of a puzzle fitting together in a new solution. This is what must have happened in Gorbachev's mind, giving rise to his vision of a 'common European home' and a post-Cold War World.

Now there were glimmers that Gorbachev was attempting an intellectual leap of the same dimensions in his thinking about the political–economic system. He had adopted a brand-new radical pro-market economic counsellor, Professor Nikolai Petrakov, and was sitting through marathon sessions with him at the dacha.

But Petrakov stood at the opposite pole from Gorbachev's Prime Minister, Ryzhkov, who had only just announced the disastrous reverse to the old five-year-planning methods – with Gorbachev's blessing. This schizoid approach to economic fixes was characteristic of Gorbachev. From the beginning, he had picked up and dropped different economic experts, adopted and discarded totally contradictory measures, and even allowed opposing reform plans to be pursued simultaneously, all the while refraining from committing himself to one or the other. Just as he had taken up and dropped Aganbegyan and the 'Siberian school' whizzkids, in June 1989 he had co-opted a step-by-step reformer, Leonid Abalkin. Now he had dropped Abalkin to take up Petrakov as his 'personal economic adviser', the first ever professional economist in his inner cabinet. Again, he would levitate himself above the battle, leaving the fire-breathing Petrakov who favoured 'shock therapy' to slug it out with Ryzhkov, who represented the entrenched interests of the apparat.

For Gorbachev to make the transition to a free-market universe, his whole conceptual web would have to shift. 'The transfer to allegiance from paradigm to paradigm is a conversion experience that cannot be forced,' as Thomas Kuhn described the structure of scientific revolutions. Nor can such a shift be made a step at a time; it must occur all at once – like the gestalt switch.

I asked Shishlin, one of Gorbachev's global image-makers, if he, too, sensed in Gorbachev a man in massive conflict within himself, with his very identity as a political man ('I am a Communist, a convinced Communist') in disaccord with the forces of democratization. Or had the scales finally fallen from Gorbachev's eyes?

'This is a very difficult question – Gorbachev is really a true believer in socialist ideals.'

What was left of Lenin's ideas of social justice?

A self-mocking grin rippled across Shishlin's mouth. 'Look, Gorbachev understands that yes, it's possible to *preach* Lenin's ideas, but that it's impossible to *behave* like Lenin did in nineteen-twenty-one. It's necessary to behave in accordance with the realities of our country in nineteen-ninety.'

I said it still sounded like the script for a society of doublethink: preach one thing but live another.

'No, look, there is the problem of moral values.'

Gorbachev constantly harped on this in his speeches. I asked what was really meant by the phrase.

'Not to close the eyes on realities, not to repeat and repeat old stereotypes about capitalism and socialism.'

That sounded like a good start for a reborn Gorbachev, but how could he cleanse the society's moral values while preaching Leninism, if he himself didn't believe in it any more?

'He believes in Lenin's methods and moral qualities,' he replied uncomfortably.

Which methods?

Grasping, he came up with Lenin's last words: 'When he said we have to change all our thinking about socialism.'

'That's pretty vague, isn't it?' I said.

'Really vague, really vague,' he admitted.

By taking instruction from free-market advocates like Petrakov, it appeared that the leader was attempting to give himself an emergency brain transplant: removing Communism as his ideal and replacing it with the coldly pragmatic calculations of political survival. But that ideal had been the essence of his existence. So the core belief in his own mind, the psychic support for that calm centre that had always been his hallmark, was cracking open too – a much more serious fissure for a charismatic leader in the long run.

By definition, a charismatic leader is a believer; he must believe his act in order for his followers to believe in him. Gorbachev had been a god figure as long as he was able to connect the unconnectable. Often described as an enigma or a sphinx, he had remained resolutely *detached* from the turmoil his faint-hearted reforms had already caused, but if he were to take the breathtaking leap to embrace capitalistic tools to rebuild the broken Soviet economy, he would have to steel himself against the pain, frustration and fear of the unknown he would be imposing upon his society. For a man with 'emotionally coloured thought' who had never made the leap to believing in private ownership anyway, to remain detached and appear above it all was no longer possible.†

The godhead had cracked. The continuing outbursts of temper and loss of self-control in public were signs of his psychological inability to remain above it all and play god. In the glare of democracy the human Gorbachev was being exposed for the first time – he was not an icon, but merely another mortal fighting for beliefs he wasn't sure he still held, amid a cacophony of clashing forces.

Having opened the Soviet Union to the essence of democracy, he was expected now to play by democracy's rules. It was not his way. He was not brought up in anything remotely like such a system and he didn't know how to manoeuvre within it. Ned Kennan, an international political consultant for his own firm, KRC Research and Consulting, Inc., found the same paradox in Poland. Consulting with two of the leading characters in charge of managing the 'shock treatment' for Poland's new economy, the American asked what was their worst enemy now that Communism had been overthrown. 'Democracy!' they cried in unison. 'Every idiot can say something!'†

For Gorbachev, it was like becoming a refugee in his late fifties and having to learn how to operate in a brand-new language. He showed every evidence of feeling frustrated and humiliated – this was, after all, a man who for thirty years had been accustomed to the slavish obeisance offered to a Party boss. He found himself growing every day more infuriated by the slings and arrows of this outrageous thing called democracy, and that hardening intolerance was causing him to lose his detachment.

It also explained why he had an easier time dealing with the Party right-wingers. Although philosophically they were on the other side of the fence from him, they continued to respect authority and hierarchy and adhere to Party loyalty above all else. They didn't lead unruly demonstrations and embarrass him with insulting banners and give smart-aleck interviews to the Western media like the radical left. They were cut from the same cloth and spoke the same Partyspeak and accepted the same set of hypocrisies that had bolstered the system of personal power that had brought Gorbachev to the zenith.

'Leaders are not aliens. They were born and raised in an authoritarian society. They are the fruit of its fruit,' wrote historian L. Shevtosova in an important essay in *Izvestia* that February.† Probing the resistance of the leadership to real political pluralism, she referred indirectly, but powerfully, to the curse of Gorbachev: 'Power cannot cleanse itself from former habits, the stain of its birthmark.'

It was a thinly disguised reference to Gorbachev's birthmark, a glaring outward symbol of the inner mark on men and women conceived and nurtured on the placenta of the Communist Party. When Gorbachev was married at the age of twenty-four the birthmark was apparent in person but airbrushed out of the photographs. In many societies such a prominent birthmark often suggests that a person has been marked for something. Some people might say marked for greatness, but sociologists told me many Russian parents see it as the mark of the devil.

Russians are very superstitious. Those who thought that Gorbachev was deforming the country by pushing it into the arms of the West saw this mark as evidence of his curse. As Gorbachev grew older and his hair rapidly disappeared, more of his skull was visible, and the larger the stain appeared. It had always been something one noticed, but it didn't compel attention. Now it appeared to have grown and darkened, from wine-coloured to purple to the colour almost of dried blood, and with the smaller marks falling from the great blotch it almost looked as if his head *had* cracked open. Evidence of the struggle inside Gorbachev's mind was right there on his forehead.

However, the leader had many props to help him bear the psychic pain of being suspended between belief systems. When the Supreme Soviet served notice in February that the days of free dachas for Central Committee members were over – a sad sad day for the Party elite – the only two people who kept all their comforts were Gorbachev and his Prime

Minister. He continued to live in total comfort with the means to travel broadly and conduct planetary change with other global power-brokers. Gorbachev was living his life at three times the tempo of the ordinary Russian but he and a handful of his top advisers were utterly singular in this regard.

Soviet citizens increasingly looked upon Gorbachev as *not us* but *them*, a remote and out-of-touch relic of the past, and they saw the mark as a metaphor. The *stain of his birthmark* was to be leader of the Communist world – with all the blood and lies that go into that – at the moment in history when Communism was in defeat and retreat around the globe.

A Special Monster Called Mafia

Gorbachev told a Western visitor around this time, 'I can't listen any more to these economists' in the government. 'They don't know any more than I do.'

In truth, the Soviet Union already had an active market economy. The black market, or 'shadow economy', went far beyond raw, unregulated, buccaneer capitalism. Power was in the hands neither of those who controlled the means of production nor of the proletariat; it had fallen into the hands of those who control the means of consumption.

The ubiquitous conversation that covered almost any consumer desire in Soviet Union was this: 'Do they have it?' (telephones, foreign newspapers, juice, coffee, soap, sanitary napkins, condoms, nappies and so on).

'Yes, but you can't get it.'

Except through 'connections'.

Everybody had them. At the top there were the corrupt Party aristocrats and the dominions of ministers and vice ministers they had placed in government and protected. These bureaucrats controlled supply – by doling out the raw materials to all state enterprises – and demand – by setting prices and production targets. The corrupt Party chiefs and government ministers in the bureaucracy cultivated their connections among crime bosses, who in turn sold all the positions in retail trade and transportation to employees who made kickbacks.

The result was that goods were siphoned off from the state sector, where prices were fixed, and resold for a big mark-up either 'under the table' or on street corners. Black marketeers paid off workers in transportation and retail to divert truck-loads of goods of every kind, from wristwatches to refrigerators. 'There's speculation with everything – everything except for bread,' said the man charged with the mission of fighting the black market in Moscow, Colonel Shestopalov.†

The way the shadow economy thrives can be explained by the process of obtaining a car or an apartment in the Soviet Union: the state, which produces all the vehicles, allots a certain number of cars to each place of business (not including co-operatives), and each worker signs up and waits on a list. The same goes for apartments. There is a joke to describe the expected wait. A factory manager calls in a worker to notify him of the splendid news: his car will be ready for delivery in the year 2000.

'Ochen khorosho!' ('Very good!') the worker exclaims. He asks which month.

The irritated manager looks through his requisitions. 'You're scheduled for January.'

'Ochen khorosho!' the worker again shows proper appreciation. Then, pushing his boss's patience, he asks if he could know the date.

The exasperated manager looks once more at the requisition. 'The fifteenth of January.'

'Morning or afternoon?' asks the employee.

'What difference does it make!'

'The refrigerator is coming that morning.'

To speed up this process, people routinely turned to the black market or bribery. For example, as my neighbour explained, when it's a worker's turn to get a Volga, she goes to her superior with all her approvals. He says, sorry, he had to let that car go – she'll have to go to the end of the list.

Actually, her superior has either sold her car at three times
the price to one of the new co-op millionaires – who can
afford to pay the exorbitant price of 30,000 rubles – or to
somebody in his chain of 'connections'. If the wife goes to
the Party higher-ups to complain, she knows her chances of
getting the apartment she is waiting for will be nil – the same
superior has to give her approval.

Every time I came to the Soviet Union, I mentioned to
Mikhailova, there was less in the stores. People were becoming accustomed to ration cards and depending on their plants
or institutes to provide them with basic items through twice-
weekly 'distributions', making them totally dependent on
the powers-that-be for the necessities of life. Soviet consumers, having no experience with the laws of supply and
demand, saw no logic in a market economy. They simply
didn't connect prices with the availability or quality of a
product. As a result, they would sooner accept rationing,
bartering and the black market than they would price
increases.

People's real work would begin when they got home.
That's when they would get on the telephone to call their
connections and try to arrange for basic needs, like finding a
car tyre or antibiotics or ripe apples or a doctor, almost
everything. The most valuable connection was a Party boss
or a bureaucrat in the trade area. Since there were Party
bosses inside every plant and enterprise, the Party had a lock
on the people's loyalty that had nothing to do with ideology,
but everything to do with survival. I told Mikhailova that it
seemed to me there was a force controlling this scarcity.

'Mafia,' she hissed.

'It's become part of the popular mythology,' said the
respected sociologist, Yuri Levada. 'So far, nobody has seen
a Sicilian in the Soviet Union,' he chuckled. Yet, this name-
less, colourless, invisible contagion was spreading into every
corner of the society like a deadly leukaemia, and if people
didn't have a precise name for it, they had no doubt that it
was there.

'I define the mafia as the system of malaise related to the Centre, high up, and it's like a tumour spreading out,' Mikhailova elaborated. 'The situation is worse than even after the war.'

Less savvy Soviets, asked what they meant by 'mafia', told me, 'Maybe the same as your businessmen in the US.' Reactionary politicians seeking to protect their own scams were eager to render 'mafia' as synonymous with 'capitalist businessmen' or 'co-op operators', rather than to acknowledge what it really was – raw political corruption.

I asked Zaslavskaya if she thought the scarcity was being manipulated by reactionary ministers and their mafia connections – the theory being they had introduced rationing to scare people into panic buying and hoarding to ensure there would be even less food in the shops, all this to sabotage Gorbachev's perestroika by causing people to lose faith in the way their society was organized.

'It is my strong belief that these great difficulties with the food are being manipulated by the mafia,' she said.

She and her researchers had been stunned to discover, when they asked in repeated national surveys, 'Whose activity has made the situation in the country worse?' that a majority of Soviets named as enemy number one – the mafia. So the polling organization did another survey that spring specifically to probe what people meant by 'mafia'.

In the minds of Soviet citizens 'mafia' was inseparable from government. Specifically, people defined it as the corrupted Party apparat and state apparat (meaning ministry bureaucrats). But those are only the major participants. 'Mafia' is an enormous, interconnected chain. To understand how power in the Soviet government actually operates, imagine the five organized crime families of the US competing, not only for control of illicit enterprises, but for power and political influence within the central organs of the government. This is what makes 'mafia', as the term is widely used by Soviets, describe quite a different animal from what Americans and Europeans mean when they use the word. Yet 'mafia' clans have existed in the Soviet Union since Stalin's time and had flourished under Brezhnev.

Just think of the possibilities for corruption in a society where there is only one political party, which has unlimited power over the government and over patronage, which has no limit on its budget and no oversight on how it gets or spends money. At the top levels, the 'mafia' – criminal clans nourished in the same petri dish as the Party apparat – were, by Gorbachev's time, gene-spliced among the most powerful politicians.

Zaslavskaya's research confirmed my anecdotal sources: 'The first element of the mafia is corrupt Party and government officials. The second part is the workers and employees of the retail trade, at every level, who are obliged to pay money to the chain that kicks back to the apparat. It is impossible to work in this branch if you don't go along with the programme. You will be disposed of very cruelly.' Zaslavskaya estimated that at least 100,000 people were involved in the corrupt retail chain.

'But there's a third element of the mafia, without which it could not operate,' she added. 'The militia, prosecutors, courts, judges – all the law-enforcement agencies are bought by the trade people. So it is quite impossible to get social justice by appealing to the courts.' She said Westerners simply couldn't imagine the extent of injustice in Soviet courts. Criminals simply laughed at the notion of law enforcement.

People spoke of 'mafia chains'. There were no discernible ties of family or ethnicity within the newer mafia chains that had grown up in the Gorbachev era. The members bought their positions and shared no code of behaviour beyond the commitment to pay a bribe or kickback to the next person in the chain. Moscow alone had eleven such criminal groups.†

The scheme of bribes and kickbacks was intricately worked out. As Boris Yeltsin described it from his experience in trying to fight the Moscow mafia before he was muscled out of his post by Gorbachev, 'Each salesperson was obliged to overcharge the customer and hand a certain sum each day to his or her supervisor, who kept part of it for himself and gave part to the general manager of the store. Then the money was shared out among the management, from top to bottom. Every employee knew two or three people in the chain. In the wholesale trade there was another, much bigger, scale of kickbacks.' Yeltsin admitted he had never even touched the really big operators in the 'black economy' nor the top end of the mafia, with its links to politicians.†

Everybody was involved at some level: Party officials were paid off by the 'mafia', the 'mafia' bosses were paid off by the new co-op capitalists, and the law-enforcement agencies were bribed by both. A former Moscow police detective told a reporter for *Details* that in mid-1990 the police had the names of sixty-two of the people's deputies with proven links to mafia crime chains.

Yes, there were many new laws, but in practice nothing much had changed. 'It's an old custom of ours,' explained Viktor Savchuk, director of the Yaroslavl chamber of foreign trade. 'The Supreme Soviet passes a law that seems very progressive . . . but some fine print makes the ministries responsible for its implementation. Little by little, they succeed in clawing back many of the new freedoms.'†

Gorbachev was not dealing with the breakdown of retail trade by cracking down on crime. Instead, scarcity was being manipulated to bring the distribution of food and supplies increasingly under control of the Party. As the émigré writer Zinoviev analysed the situation, 'It is impossible to get food in shops. Many essentials are available only through channels operated by the Party, such as the "distributions" at one's workplace. The system is beginning to take on some of the characteristics of War Communism.' (War Communism or 'Military Communism' refers to the harsh and dictational methods, including rationing and enforced requisitioning, introduced during the Civil War period (1918–21) by the Bolshevik regime to engineer a revolutionary transition to socialism.) By October 1990, Stanislav Shatalin, a principal

Gorbachev economist, acknowledged both a rising crime rate and a 'militarization' of the economy.†

Entire underground department stores existed in Moscow. What's more, shopping by invitation had proliferated twenty times since 1986. Large enterprises or trade unions would be allotted scarce merchandise purchased abroad by the government and supposedly would invite their beleaguered workers to a special sale. But in practice union officials would *sell the right to buy*. They might trade for 200 rubles an invitation to buy a TV set costing 600 rubles.† Since there were many more rubles than goods to pay for them, when anything scarce became available, people quickly bid up the price. Inflation became uncontrollable.

Soviets, including my neighbours and friends, were enraged by this total breakdown in retail trade. Some progressive economists were of the opinion that it would bring Gorbachev down, that only a 'national salvation' or coalition government untainted by the mistakes of the previous five years could regain enough public confidence to undertake real reform.

The tragedy of Gorbachev's toe-in-the-water approach to decentralizing his economy, his failure to take the plunge into allowing private ownership and free-market industries and financial institutions, was that he had lifted controls just enough to create the ideal conditions for rampant corruption. Mafia bosses used their patrons in the ministries to purchase supplies at artificially low state prices, and then used the new laws to resell their products or services at rapacious prices. They gave free enterprise a bad name before it ever got off the ground.

Many Soviets knew only too well that, whatever it was called, there was something rotten going all the way to the top. Gorbachev could not be the only one in the country who didn't know what was really going on, and so long as he did nothing to attack the cancer at its centre, his dilatory attempts at economic 'reform' were doomed to be nothing more than distractions.

But by early 1990 the growing revulsion at mafia control of the economy would touch Gorbachev more personally and further threaten to cause his downfall. The scandal reached boiling point on the very eve of his Presidential Congress that March.

Mafia Cloud Over Gorbachev

'It's Gorbachev's mafia against Ligachev's mafia,' said the very smart, distraught woman who was the country's leading expert on the shadow economy. Tatyana Koryagina, a respected social economist, had worked in the economic institute, Gosplan, the central planning body for the state.

'There was an investigation about mafia operations in the northern Caucusus going back to the end of the 1970s,' she told me. 'Gorbachev's was the name that came up.'

Koregina waited for me to register shock.

Two investigators from the state prosecutor's office, Gdlyan and Ivanov, had submitted their explosive evidence to a parliamentary commission a few weeks before. 'They are in possession of four criminal charges against Gorbachev and one against Raisa, for bribe-taking while he was Party boss in Stavropol,' said Koryagina in her piercingly high-pitched voice.

'You realize that it is really dangerous for you now that you know, and you are writing about this topic, because the mafia will know,' she warned overdramatically.

What about her? Did she think her apartment was bugged? 'Of course.' We were sitting in her living-room with its bed and plastic-covered coffee table. The only visible reliefs from tawdriness were the big double cassette player and the VCR revered by her teenage daughter. Koryagina's survival tactic, she said, was to talk about the mafia at street rallies and to foreign journalists. 'Then, if they kill me, you will report it was a political murder.'

She acknowledged that the mafia probe of Gdlyan and Ivanov had become so entangled in politics that even the criminal investigators themselves suspected they were being used to discredit Gorbachev. The pair had been assigned in the late 1970s by then-KGB chief Andropov to do a thorough investigation of Party corruption. In 1987 and 1988 they had become media heroes for uncovering a bribery scandal in Uzbekistan which culminated in the conviction of Yuri Churbanov. Since Churbanov was the son-in-law of former General Secretary Brezhnev, he made a convenient target in the Gorbachev government's campaign to discredit the Brezhnev regime as corrupt.

But as the two investigators reached all the way into the current Politburo – implicating Ligachev in bribery – they suddenly found themselves accused of having broken laws and basing their case only on testimony from criminal suspects. If they had damning evidence on Ligachev, why didn't they publish it?

'Try to summon Ligachev to an interrogation,' Nikolai Ivanov would tell the press in defence of his predicament. 'Try to carry out a search of his workplace or his home – when the KGB is standing right at his side.'† The investigators themselves now suspected that the fresh charges they had received against Gorbachev were a 'provocation', planted by Ligachev's hardline faction within the KGB. Koryagina, who had worked on the investigation, echoed the findings of Soviet sociologists: 'Mafia has also infiltrated part of the KGB, the militia and the state prosecutors.'

She asked rhetorically, 'Why does Gorbachev go against everybody's wish and insist on making himself President? He feels that he's in danger, because of this plotting by Ligachev. He's looking for a way out.'

I asked her to explain how Gorbachev's mafia might have worked when he was territorial Party boss of Stavropol. 'He had a lot of guests, he wanted to entertain them,' she said. 'He needed to have presents, and he needed a lot of money to get those presents, so he gives favours to mafia and they pay bribes to him. Brezhnev was the boss and, remember,

Brezhnev liked a lot of presents. The more a person wants to please, the more he needs to have presents to give big shots, and Gorbachev was very eager to please. With leaders who make an easy and unnatural success in their careers, we must ask why.'

Koryagina cast the whole scandal as a power struggle between Gorbachev and Ligachev. 'Whichever man wins, it will be a tragedy for the country,' she prophesied, 'because nothing will change.'†

The mafia scandal had reached a critical mass in people's consciousness because of Gdlyan and Ivanov's campaign, although it came as no surprise to Soviets that Gorbachev might have dealt in bribes when he was a territorial Party boss. 'It goes without saying that Gorbachev is a mafia boss,' I was told by a savvy eighteen-year-old student in Moscow University's exclusive economic and diplomatic school. Her view was common particularly among young people. Nothing gets done at the top without bribes, they say, nothing.

Gorbachev's own behaviour contributed to the image. He saw himself as the *vozhd* – the supreme leader – and did not tolerate people who directly challenged him (Yeltsin, Landsbergis, Afanasev and so on). He ruled with only a couple of top lieutenants, appearing suspicious of everyone else, unwilling to encourage or promote a *team*, and he insisted on signing off on all government and Party appointments.

'But there's a universe of difference between him and Ligachev,' said an editor of the popular science magazine, *Znamya i Sila*, expressing a common view among progressives.† Many Soviets perceived the whole confused scandal as Ligachev's last-ditch effort to bring down Gorbachev.

Gorbachev must have been aware of his vulnerability: if he had attempted to get rid of Ligachev, the hardliner with allegedly strong mafia connections might have accelerated the smear campaign against Gorbachev. It was the only reasonable explanation for why he kept Ligachev on the

Politburo. It certainly wasn't because of his own love or the people's affection for this anti-perestroika Stalinist. A political popularity poll published in *Moscow News* that spring showed that 87 per cent of respondents hated Ligachev.

If it was a plot by Ligachev, he was using tried and true methods of Kremlin bloodletting. The mafia scandal had by now taken on huge proportions in the public's collective consciousness. And, in a society where truth is still a scarce commodity, the easiest way to kill off a rival is through slow death by the poison of rumour, dripped into the bloodstream of a nation of experienced paranoids. The KGB is expert in such methods.

The slow suffocation of retail trade was undermining Gorbachev's leadership. The most senior official photographer of Kremlin bosses, Dmitry Baltermants, who had studied and snapped almost the whole lot from Stalin to Gorbachev, was dead certain the shortages were the result of sabotage. That March his friend had gone to a neighbourhood store that sold watches, an item always in overproduction. Suddenly, shelves were completely bare of watches, and every week more goods disappeared from the stores.

'It's the apparat ministers and mafia – strangling Gorbachev,' he asserted. 'They want to make a putsch.'

Watching Gorbachev at Work

An emergency session of the Congress of People's Deputies was convened on 12 March, exactly five years and a two days after Gorbachev's appointment by the Politburo as General Secretary. The session had been called in great haste to adopt the draft law creating a presidency. Gorbachev wanted to 'impose' the presidency – without submitting to election by the people – and gather to himself powers that would include ruling by decree and the right to impose martial law or direct rule on any republic or region.

The Congress was a revealing spectacle. Official Moscow tingled with self-importance on the opening day. Fleets of special state cars with assigned valets and limousines of ascending sizes, depending on the status of the apparat member, flashed through the streets ferrying thousands of Communist Party members from outlying regions into the Centre.

Traffic was halted as they raced swifly across the broad snow-slick Stalinist boulevards, escorted by militia cars with blue lights flashing. Russians stopped to gape as they slipped through the austere red-brick gates of the Kremlin and stopped before a large modern structure known as the Palace of Congresses. The longest limousines pulled up at the side entrance of the Palace, where hugely corpulent men stepped out in blinding snow without even an overcoat, accustomed to being deposited never more than two steps from the door of their office or home.

Pro-democracy deputies were up in arms about this raw grab for supranational supremacy by one man. Just outside the main entrance the Interregional Group was circulating a handout: 'Everywhere people ask for direct elections of the president of the country,' it read. 'This procedure is anti-democratic . . . people ask for the right to choose for themselves.'

Inside the extravagant new palace, the huge disembodied head of Lenin towered high over the dais, a bas-relief in grey and black flagstone, the cracks between stones making it appear as if Lenin himself was coming apart. 'This face in some way haunts every Russian and suggests some sort of standard for human appearance, because it is utterly lacking in human character,' the émigré poet Joseph Brodsky once wrote.† Gorbachev took his seat in the centre of the enthroned praesidium, sober in a dark-blue suit, white shirt and red tie. His hair was no longer visible from a front view, only the massive ball of his cranium stamped with his trademark wine-dark stain.

His very first announcement sent a charge of electricity through the 2,092 deputies who filled every seat in the hall.

'The praesidium does not have a representative from Lithuania. The information we are getting from there is rather
alarming.'† Four days before, Vytautas Landsbergis, the
mild-tongued head of the Lithuanian popular front, had
been named President in his own right. Hours before Gorbachev opened this coronation Congress, President Landsbergis proclaimed Lithuania an independent state.

Gorbachev condemned the Lithuanian decision as 'illegal
and invalid', and with a cold slap ruled out negotiations:
'You cannot carry out negotiations with a foreign country.'
Behind the scenes Yakovlev was furious. 'Lithuanians
decided to make this decision early. They did this in order to
pre-empt the presidential institution,' he told me angrily.†

From the first day of the Congress to the last, four gruelling
days, Gorbachev orchestrated everything. The Presidential
Congress was entirely his idea. He was the only candidate.
He determined which deputies would speak, and for how
long, their remarks often having been censored in advance.
He alone could speak at any time. Some of the people's
deputies had complained last time about the hidden panel
by which Gorbachev controlled the microphones. Nothing
had changed.

Both Gorbachev and the KGB are masters of improvisation.
Later, when General Oleg Kalugin excommunicated himself
from the KGB and broke its code of secrecy, becoming a
celebrated insurgent, he said the secret police not only
manipulated the voting at the Congress, they could alter the
results. Since all the voting was now done electronically,
nobody in the hall could doublecheck the votes. Groups
don't trust one another enough to do a straw poll after the
fact. Furthermore, Gorbachev and other high officials wear
earphones, which is slightly sinister in light of the recent
revelations about Stasi, the East German secret police
modelled on the KGB. It was learned that beneath the
praesidium of the East German Parliament was a huge
underground room populated by Stasi people who fed their

leaders juicy tips on how to intimidate the participants and orchestrate the proceedings.

Several minutes before announcing the first break Gorbachev asked the technicians to 'prepare the voting devices'. Suddenly the hall emptied and the escalators were a stampede of deputies making their way to the vast eating hall on the top floor. Far more important to most deputies than parliamentary procedures were basic alimentary ones. Long tables had been laden with all kinds of goodies not available in the stores: sturgeon, red caviar, ripe apples, the best mineral water, sugar, cream and rich chocolate-covered cakes, all served up on gold-leafed Leningrad china – reminding the representatives of the system of privileges and status provided by the Communist Party.

Deputies swarmed all over the food and drink. There was none of the feverish caucusing or 'cloak-room' politicking seen during recesses of the American Congress or European parliaments; conversely, people scarcely talked. One was reminded again that with no other political parties, only one man had the power, and the majority of deputies belonged to his party. Without Gorbachev, the sun did not come up for them tomorrow.

The deputies were overwhelmingly men; not surprising, since more than 25 per cent of Soviets agreed that politics was the realm of men rather than women.† There were a little over one hundred female deputies among the more than 2,000 total, and they were obviously not yet comfortable with a political identity. Many wore form-fitting synthetic print dresses over tightly pinched waists and pitched forward on their very high heels, their legs showing through black net stockings decorated with kitchy-kitchy-coo bows or hearts. The military deputies, of whom there were a great many, hung together. Most wore multi-coloured plastic bars rather than the whole chandelier of medals that used to be the fashion under Brezhnev. The homogeneity of the mostly blond-haired, blue-eyed deputies was indeed striking in a congress supposedly representing 170 different nationalities.

Only a handful of them wore the Muslim caps, *tyubeteika*, of the Islamic Asian republics.

A waitress at my buffet table said gloomily, 'I'm so sorry for our country. These deputies – they're not the people.'

During the break I ran into Mikhailova, who was attending the Congress as a member of the working group of Gorbachev's Constitutional Commission. Ever the aristocrat, she looped an arm through mine and we strolled through the palace halls.

'Gorbachev is very nervous now,' she said worriedly. She enumerated the many troubles on his shoulders. Was he also worried about the corruption charges against him personally? I asked.

'He knows about these charges of criminality. It makes him nervous,' she confided, rushing to his defence and asserting her belief in his honesty. But she acknowledged that this was one of the reasons he was railroading through this presidency. While she favoured an indirect election to give Gorbachev the power of the presidency, she had no illusions that these powers would have any impact on improving the economy. 'The economy will not improve for another five years,' she said emphatically.

When the session resumed, Gorbachev took full advantage of the neophyte deputies' lack of parliamentary sophistication. He made up the rules as he went along. His spokesmen proposed that first they vote for the changes in the constitution as a whole, establishing a presidency and election procedure which would require a simple majority to pass. Only then would they vote on each separate amendment, which would then require a two-thirds majority to be changed.

Thus a historic overhaul in the constitution was hurtled with lightning speed past the befuddled deputies. Only afterwards did one representative dare to protest that he hadn't understood the voting procedure. He asked that the vote be taken again.

'It's just *you*, you don't understand,' Gorbachev tried to humiliate him. 'The others do.'

'No, it's not only me, many did not understand,' the man objected. Murmurs of assent rose in the hall.

Gorbachev jumped down the deputy's throat. The injured man gasped, 'I am ashamed, ashamed you could be so rude.'

'That's why you're a deputy,' Gorbachev scolded arrogantly. 'You're supposed to understand. This is parliamentary practice all over the world.'

Gorbachev pushed on to a discussion of the broad powers the President should have to declare a state of emergency in any republic and to impose direct rule. A military man raised an objection: there should be a distinction between the power of a president to deal with military threats and with civil disorders. Gorbachev cut off this debate as well. He declared simply, 'The President can declare temporary presidential government. We don't want to overburden the constitution with details.'

Deputies muttered restlessly. A sycophant stepped to the microphone to insist that 'Mikhail Sergeyevich knows in his own mind when it is right to use such powers.' Vigorously nodding, Gorbachev approved this paean to his own godlike wisdom. 'I ask you to work more,' he urged feverishly at 7 p.m. 'Let's finish . . . we can work day and night.'

By the third day Gorbachev had brought the Congress to the point of voting for one of four presidential candidates. The other three nominees kept coming to the microphone begging to be released. One was an army man, and the army deputies he represented were angry at their 'degradation' and 'humiliation' under Gorbachev. Another nominee was a militiaman, Bakatin, who said: 'I *plead* to have my nomination withdrawn.' When his appeal brought forth loud protests, he cried out: 'Nobody can be forced to be president!'

At 8 p.m., Prime Minister Ryzhkov, who had also been nominated, announced with finality, 'There can be only one nomination . . . Mikhail Gorbachev must be the first President of our great Motherland.'

One shame-faced deputy wailed: 'What happened? In all these years of perestroika didn't we find a single alternative? I speak to my own Interregional Group. Only Dostoevsky has no alternative.'

Progressive deputies from the Interregional Group were downcast. They were being outfoxed by Gorbachev's procedures. But their greatest handicap was their own timidity. 'We thought about leaving the Communist Party and starting a separate party before this Congress,' confessed the radical deputy representing Armenia, Galina Staravoitava. 'We decided to wait until summer, maybe we were wrong,' but, she admitted, the pro-democracy deputies simply were not unified. True, they were among the most highly educated and talented in the Congressional membership. Staravoitava herself was a brilliant ethnographer, but as politicos, their refinement worked against them. Gorbachev, with his peasant cunning, had them hogtied.

'We can't sit together,' said Staravoitava. 'They disperse us through the hall. We can't communicate. No one is allowed to get up and circulate.' I pointed out that some deputies had walked up to Gorbachev himself and handed him a note. 'But it isn't polite. It's not our style.'

On the final day, in all her imperious glory, Raisa appeared in the Palace of Congresses and sat in a box to watch her husband orchestrate his own coronation. Day and night during the tense sessions of the Presidential Congress, Raisa had watched everything on her TV set, a Gorbachev aide told me. She waited up to replay Mikhail's performance with him when he got home at night.

Now, peering over her box, her face was white with fury at the continuing challenges to her husband's monolithic power. She had the look of all ruthless wives who exercise piggyback power from behind their husbands' shoulders, the look that says 'If I were up there, the people wouldn't get away with this.'

Since Gorbachev had come under siege their symbiosis seemed more intense than ever. Mikhailova had told me,

'Raisa has more ambition that Gorbachev,' and Lieberman dubbed her Gorbachev's alter ego. The Soviet leader himself acknowledged Raisa's primacy in his conduct of life and presidency when he received a delegation of American congressmen that April. They asked, 'How can you cope with all this pressure?' His response was, 'Because of my parents, who gave me my genes, and my wife, who gives me support.'

In the crucial moments just before the vote to make Gorbachev president, 300 deputies from the Baltics decided to walk out. The insurgent deputies of the Interregional Group continued to sit still like obedient schoolchildren. As the voting machines were activated, one deputy was still pathetically petitioning, 'What *is* presidential government?'

Tension ricocheted through the hall. Gorbachev looked jumpy as the voting machines whirred. When the tally finally flashed on the monitors, first there were gasps, then the applause of relief. The gasps were for the cliffhanger of a victory in a country where 99.9 per cent landslides were once manufactured for Soviet leaders. Now, allowed a free vote, 495 deputies opposed Gorbachev, and almost a thousand others either abstained, walked off with their ballots to protest the undemocratic spectacle or refused to participate at all.

Without any competition, Gorbachev had attained his presidency with a victory majority of only 59.2 per cent.†

He proceeded to swear himself into office, no judge or parliamentarian to make it official. Mikhail Gorbachev simply left the stage and reappeared alone on the praesidium platform, looking suddenly larger than life. He splayed his fingers over the altered constitution, on which the ink had barely dried, and swore to uphold it. The whole procedure was reminiscent of a shotgun marriage.

People stayed up until 3 a.m. on the last night of the Congress – my Soviet neighbours no less transfixed than the American Ambassador – while deputies sharply attacked

Gorbachev for all the ills that had mounted under his leadership. It was the most attentively watched of the sessions; the people's voice finally was being heard. Gorbachev had promised with imperious calm that he would respond to the criticisms *after* he became president. Once having crowned himself, he dismissed the outcry calling him to account for his record. It was too late – he was already the dictator.

He did give an interminable speech. 'Perestroika has become the meaning of my whole life,' he said solemnly. He extolled his foreign-policy achievements as 'a turn of historic scope'. But the Soviet people paid no attention to Gorbachev's extraordinary leadership in the international sphere any more, it seemed nothing to them, so long as their lives grew more pitiable every day. My neighbour Irina turned off her TV in disgust.

The whole Party apparat had been paralysed by power-jockeying while Gorbachev created his presidency. Once the Congress was over, the bolshie shishki – big shots – had to slap together a new scaffolding beneath this pseudo-presidency by suggesting candidates for Gorbachev's new Presidential Council – essentially a handpicked surrogate politburo.

The most important impact of Gorbachev's triumphant seizure of the power of presidency was his move to put all the law-enforcement agencies, including the prosecutors, judges, courts and KGB, under his own direction. The polarization in Soviet society was mirrored by a serious split in the KGB and in the army. In the effort to keep these potential powder kegs from exploding, Gorbachev made his most trusted adviser, Yakovlev, the leader of his Presidential Council responsible for controlling all these security organs.

'Now that Gorbachev is a dictator of sorts, the KGB and prosecutors will be under his control,' said the shadow-economy specialist, Koryagina. 'He can close the bribery investigation.' And so he did. An order was issued from high in the Party leadership to silence Mr Ivanov.†

With the naming of his own Presidential Council, Gorbachev also rendered the Politburo impotent. Moreover, this council could not restrain him, because every person was appointed by his personal order. Four members were obligatory – the KGB chief, Defence Minister, Foreign Minister and Prime Minister – while all the others were appointed as if by the czar.

Moscow telephone wires were burning the night the sixteen names were announced: Gorbachev's progressive supporters were appalled. The council was packed with right-wingers and law-enforcement or military types, certainly not democrats – why? The worse offence was the appointment of Rasputin, a right-wing writer obsessed with eradicating 'Zionism'. Rasputin had been a highly respected writer until some years before when he had suffered a near-fatal accident which did some damage to his brain. 'After that, he became very paranoid and virtually stopped writing,' recalls a former editor at *Izvestia*, Andrei Malgin, who visited Rasputin in hospital. It was Malgin's impression that Raisa, who had invited Rasputin to accompany her and Gorbachev on a trip to the Far East, was responsible for the right-winger's appointment.†

Gorbachev was playing a game at which he is the expert – disarming his enemies by inviting them into his ruling circle, ostensibly to share power, but more importantly to share the blame when his halfhearted reforms fail. 'Yeltsin is Russian nationalist and Rasputin is Russian nationalist,' as spokesman Gerasimov explained the choice. 'Now Rasputin has his hands tied. Right? Because his position is co-opted.'†

Even Gorbachev boosters like liberal sociologist Leonid Sedov, who had enthusiastically supported the idea of a 'dictator for democracy', felt betrayed. 'Being one of the influential leaders of the intelligentsia, I do not think Gorbachev deserves any trust any longer,' Sedov told me.†

'Now his main aim is to obtain a personal dictatorship, at the same time as he pretends to democratize the system,' observed the disenchanted émigré writer, Zinoviev. 'Today he can promise democratization, tomorrow he can order his KGB forces to go into Azerbaijan and mow down Armenians, or troops into Tblisi to clean the streets of peaceful demonstrators.

'Every Soviet leader tries to organize a personal dictatorship,' Zinoviev went on. 'It doesn't depend on personality – Gorbachev is not alone – he is only on top of a huge pyramid that depends on his dictatorship to keep their own power.' It remained to be seen if this 'new suit' and the throne that went with it would enable Gorbachev to change his image in the minds of the people.

Bully of Vilnius

To demonstrate his new powers as President, Gorbachev roared at little Lithuania and tried to bring the recalcitrant Landsbergis to his knees. 'He needed to show authority,' confirmed a Gorbachev aide, at a time when waves of emotion and frustration were being fanned by self-appointed demagogues all over the country. It became a contest of wills.† Gorbachev could now threaten direct rule over any republic. Despite a series of intimidating moves by Gorbachev, the Lithuanian leadership held fast, insisting that international law gave them the right to secede.

From the moment at the opening of the Presidential Congress when the absence of the Lithuanian delegation had overshadowed Gorbachev's coronation, the whole tortured struggle between Moscow and Lithuania would be coloured by Gorbachev's visceral personal dislike of Landsbergis. Senator Bill Bradley picked it up when he and a Congressional delegation saw Gorbachev in April. 'Personal animosity distorts judgement,' worried Senator Bradley. 'Clearly, it's not in Gorbachev's historical interest to choke Lithuania. It creates an air of uncertainty about investment in the Soviet Union. If he's going to implement perestroika, there is going to be pain associated with higher prices, dislocations, unemployment, and if you're going to do that to a society, you need a consensual basis.'†

David simply spat in the eye of Goliath. Gorbachev's new best friends, West Germany and France, backed him up, scolding Lithuania, in effect: 'David, put down that sling-shot, you might hurt Goliath.' President Bush also refused to champion the pre-democracy, sounding somewhat lame for a superpower when he told Prime Minister Prunskiene, who herself had gone up against Gorbachev, 'If there was a constructive role for the US, of course, we should fulfil that, but there is not.'†

More than ever, Gorbachev seemed to take any actions against Moscow's control as a direct personal challenge to him. He had moved away from the first of those two contradictory ideas a leader must always keep in mind: that any leader is a cork on the river of the powerful forces of history, with a limited capacity to change their direction. He seemed caught up in the second idea: that everything he did mattered. Gorbachev had long since passed into that twilight of enchantment by power where a leader believes himself indivisible from the destiny of those he leads.

On 18 April President Gorbachev decreed that oil and gas lines be shut down to Lithuania. He was now dubbed 'the bully of Vilnius'. Was Gorbachev, like most Russian reformers before him, turning from a reformer into a repressor?

VII

Sixth Gorbachev:

Red Star Falling

Spring 1990

The concatenation of despair and hope I heard in the voices of my friends and connections during the late spring and summer of 1990 sounded like cries from victims of an earthquake. Hierarchical structures were breaking down in every sphere, a profoundly disorienting experience for people who have always waited for instructions. The state always took care of their work, the Party told them what to think. Now they didn't know what to do, didn't know who was in charge, didn't know which way to jump.

Dazed and disoriented, but often startled to find they were still functioning, the survivors of the Gorbachev era began to speak of being 'perestroyed'. Their perception of where this left them had a great deal to do with the generation to which they belonged.

A high-level assistant to Yakovlev dragged himself to have lunch with me on the last day of March. He was leading a life of almost the same intensity as Gorbachev. And up close he showed the ravages, some of which Gorbachev must have been suffering as he alternately attempted and resisted destroying himself. He arrived at the Savoy Hotel restaurant (his suggestion) in poor condition, and it soon became apparent that I was treating this super-apparatchik to lunch at golden ruble prices.

The atmosphere of the restaurant can only be described as resembling a whore's Valentine. The rose-coloured ceiling was garishly gold-painted with images of cupids and angels, the gilt behind the bar so new it was greenish. A marble fountain trickled in the centre of the room, and the long-skirted tables were set with self-important swirls of napkins and silver-plated cutlery, things never seen in Russian restaurants. The food was quite good Continental cuisine. At least the sullen waiter and the lousy service remained familiar.

'It's our Russian Baroque, full of wishes, dreams, fairy tales,' said the assistant, rolling his eyes upward at the infantile fantasies all over the ceiling – 'not what we need now.'

His breath was thick with stale cognac, his eyes watery grey puddles inside rubbed-red lids, his skin a ghastly blotch of blue and red with grey patches of oxygen-deprived tissue. His smile was wide, ironic, a mockery of mirth. Once upon a time, he must have been handsome. So many men of his age – in their fifties, Gorbachev's generation – were in the same terrible physical shape, many of them functional alcoholics. They had been living a roller-coaster existence since Gorbachev began his revolution. But being with this tortured man one had the sense, as I did with other 'children of the 20th Party Congress' like Bovin, Lieberman, Lisichkin, that this was the last dance. They were still holding on to their partner, the Communist Party, but at that second level of thinking, where they had always hidden away the truth, they knew the ball was almost over.

The man sat on the florid rose-damask banquette, hunched over, hang-dog, his voice barely audible, no energy, no conviction, scarcely any pretence left in it.

'It's a terrible time. The pressures are really growing, really growing, but in spite of all the problems, Gorbachev has made up his mind to face realities – real realities.'

But he'd had real realities pressuring him for some time now.

'I know, but now it's *really really* reality. He is into radical economic changes – real market.'

This insider's capacity to describe how and what changes that meant was severely limited; he didn't understand such economics, he explained apologetically, but he was sure that his superiors were 'just now constructing a new executive power and a new political system – to write a new model of society'. He scarcely took a breath. 'We don't want to call it a neo-bourgeois society,' he said, lapsing into a leer of self-mockery. 'Maybe we can call it neo-socialism.'

The words held no intrinsic meaning for him any more. 'Socialism', 'capitalism', 'market economy with socialist ideals', it was all a grab-bag of semantics. All he could repeat was the new line: 'Gorbachev is into radical economic reform.'

Although his aides had prepared his lifeboat, Gorbachev was refusing to jump, the insider told me. Apparently, the Soviet President had no more confidence in the fledgling institutions of democratization such as the Supreme Soviet than the people themselves, who suspected all along that the parliament was only another instrument of the Party's power and was heavily infiltrated by mafia members. So, against the advice of his closest advisers, Gorbachev had ruled out the option of resigning his Party leadership for another two or three years. (I later heard the same story from Yakovlev himself.) Crowning himself president had not stopped the leakage in the ship of state – it still had holes everywhere, and Gorbachev was imprisoned on this ship even though he knew it was sinking into the sea. Why?

'Because the Party is a real real political force,' said the official. The Party still set policy, controlled the state budget, gave orders to the army and worked hand in glove with the KGB. Having helped create the monster, Gorbachev couldn't see how he could leave its destructive power to anyone else.

Were Gorbachev and Yakovlev both still Communists?

'Communists, that's a title,' he scoffed.

Well then, were they both at least still convinced of the role of the Communist Party?

'No, they don't believe in paradise.'

If this insider was to be believed, the leader of the country and his right-hand man, the co-authors of perestroika, no longer had any further ideological or institutional loyalty to the Communist Party. Their ties to it were completely utilitarian. They couldn't jump ship because it was the only ship around, and because, above all, they were political survivors.

Alexander Yakovlev was still laying down the official line: 'It is wrong to blame the Party,' he later told me in a face-to-face interview. 'The blame rests with the system built by Stalin. There was exploitation of people's faith and sincerity, but this was practised by Stalin and his entourage. The Party has nothing to do with these actions.'

Just before we moved to a table, Yakovlev's aide free-associated about the failure of their psychological remake plan. 'In 1985 everything looked so simple. Declare freedom, declare human rights, tell people you are free people. They were trying to achieve a strange goal: to create a new man. Lenin did the same. And we received that man of Lenin's design' – a rueful laugh gurgled in his throat – 'lazy, no initiative, and rather aggressive.' He sneered now at the whole concept of psychological propaganda. 'It's impossible to create a new improved personality.'

When we sat down the man had to take off his bottle-thick glasses to study the menu, so closely his head practically grazed the table.

'Wine? Please, you are my guest,' I said.

'Only beer.' He shrugged, the eternal order-taker. 'It is necessary for me to go back and dictate some memos.'

He described some vague, delayed scenarios for monetary reform but said they would only, possibly, be introduced *after* the 28th Party Congress in July. I was surprised to hear how heavily freighted these schemes were with 'old thinking'; everything about Gorbachev's so-called 'new model of society' sounded like a loser, always a day late and a ruble short. Had there been any progress on a new all-Union treaty offering real sovereignty to the republics? The assistant said that when they were ready to 'reconstruct the destruction' of the Union and 'organize our country as a federal state', each republic would then have its chance – which meant more stalling and indecisiveness on how to deal with a Soviet Union spinning out of control. But of all the pipe-dreams the assistant relayed from his listening post inside the Central Committee, the most bizarre was the timetable.

'It is necessary right now to construct a whole new economic reform programme,' he said. 'It must be done in the next three weeks. Then everyone needs a vacation before preparing for the Party Congress in July.' He sat silent for a moment. I sat there open-mouthed. 'Oh, and by the way, the Summit.'

Theirs was a generation of tragic fate – born into the labour camp of collectivization, raised on the worship of despots; believers as boys in Stalin, who brutalized them, and then believers in Khrushchev, who failed them; toadies to Brezhnev, who bought their souls with doublethink while they watched the best years of their lives ebb away. Men like Gorbachev, Yakovlev and Shevardnadze were old when finally they had their day as revolutionaries.

Now Gorbachev was nearly sixty, the two faithful members of his troika had already passed into their seventh decade, and time had run out. They had begun their revolution from above with guts and great zeal, but they had come to history late.

'The tragedy of Gorbachev', his supporters began to murmur in May 1990, 'is that he cannot finish his revolution.'

Foreign Minister Shevardnadze looked close to tears at the Party Congress that summer as he described his generation: 'I wrote a poem dedicated to Stalin when I was seven years old. I believed in Stalin, and I believed in Khrushchev. I used to write letters to Khrushchev, and then he sent tanks to Tblisi, and 150 students died,' he mused in an elegiac speech.

To his bitter hardline attackers, who accused Gorbachev's Foreign Minister of losing everything for which the Soviet Union had fought the Great Patriotic War, Shevardnadze gave an emotional rebuttal: 'You can also accuse me of being born in 1928.'†

Yakovlev, too, was savaged by Party stalwarts at the summer Congress and turned on them with a devastating accusation: 'The Party still remains to a significant degree a prisoner of the system of social stagnation engendered by the regime of personal power.' Defiant amid the baying of wolves, he offered his resignation from the Politburo.

Gorbachev and other Andropov protégés such as columnist Alexander Bovin still could not let go of the philosophical rationale that had held together their divided personalities for the past thirty years. 'I am a Communist and it is a feeling deep in my heart – I believe Gorbachev feels the same way,' Bovin told me. With a touch of affected martyrdom, Bovin announced that for the past two years he had been contemplating suicide.

Even Yeltsin admitted to a Western reporter that 'I absorbed a lot from the system that is now so sick. I'm in the process of a self-revision, though I am a bit old for it.'†

Zdenek Mlynar, Gorbachev's closest friend from their student days, returned to Moscow that March for the first time in thirty-five years. The Czech patriot, arrested twenty years earlier by Soviet troops, expelled from the Party and exiled from being Alexander Dubček's deputy during the Prague Spring uprising, had for years been a non-person in the Soviet Union. Now, at last, he was watching Dubček emerge from degradation to a position in the new Czech and Slovak Federative Republic. He wasn't sure if Gorbachev would see him while he was in Moscow, but his old friend received him, and Mlynar spoke candidly: 'Something is very wrong, the shops are empty, Misha.' Gorbachev's response was sphinx-like: 'My conscience is clear.'†

Nadezhda Mikhailova, Gorbachev's old girlfriend from his university days, made a date to have dinner with me again that spring. I had almost given up waiting when finally she emerged from the subway, anachronistically aristocratic in a cornflower blue coat and white silk scarf. She was an hour late. 'One simply can't get a taxi in this city any more,' she warbled. 'I wish I had a car, but they are so expensive now – thirty-five thousand rubles – and they are going up to three times the price!'

Mikhailova's assessment of her beloved contemporary was mordant that night. 'I don't think Gorbachev grasps the tragic aspects of the situation. He has always been a roman-tic-minded man. He wanted to see what he wanted to see. Now, he believes in the charming influence of his own smile. He was met with a lot of hope, like a messiah, but things are getting worse. This worsening is being attributed to Gorbachev. His prestige and authority have dwindled.' Her last words to me were, 'This is a pre-revolutionary nation.'

The Awakened Generation

In fact, Gorbachev's democratization had begun to reveal the narod to itself. By daring to register their feelings in the first national opinion polls, the people were externalizing their secret inner lives for the first time and realizing: 'I'm not the only one!' Beginning with the miners' strike in summer 1989, the increasingly bold street demonstrations gave people first-hand proof that they were not alone and not powerless. The galvanizing effect of this realization on those in generations younger than Gorbachev's made Moscow kinetic with new-found energy in the spring of 1990.

It took a malevolent form among the youngest generation of Soviets, aged eighteen to twenty-six, who seemed cynical and empty. An enterprising young woman in her twenties who worked for me was completely open about the malaise. 'We're tired of not having enough opportunities, not having enough money, no real religion and no real beliefs. We're only concerned with money,' she said without shame. 'We *are* an empty generation.'

The system had for so long blocked talented people and the development of a civic culture, even students at the most elite universities in Moscow and Leningrad were apolitical. Young people from the provinces, where the economy was far worse, were streaming into Moscow by the hundreds of thousands to work as a subclass of impoverished migrants and live in hiding, in exchange for the promise of a residence permit.

Director Stanislav Govarukhin, whose shocking documentary on crime in the Soviet Union, *This Is No Way to Live*, produced standing ovations when it was shown to members of the Mossoviet (Moscow City Council) and the Russian parliament, told me that the entire younger generation, without exception, believes it is impossible to make a living by honest work.† Among the most seductive role models for young men are the toughs who work as mafia footsoldiers, strutting around in their leather jackets, Adidas tracksuit trousers and Reebok high-tops. Many of them go in for body-building or are Afghan war vets. Others, skinhead bouncers with mountainous physiques, stand just inside the doorways of the best co-op restaurants as protection for their criminal bosses inside.

Gorbachev's generation had become politically active as they reached their thirties, yet now many of the best and brightest thirty-year-olds were apathetic and pessimistic. 'They are alienated from politics because of this irony of democracy,' opined Deputy Sergei Stankevich, a thirty-six-year-old Moscow lawyer. 'They see that it is not a real election of the President, so they can't trust the political process, and they have no sense of stages.' The talented ones were occupied making satirical TV shows and opening co-operatives and laying down tracks to the West for the day they could say, 'I'm outta here.'

But something unexpected did happen in March 1990 – right under the nose of Gorbachev's railroaded Presidential Congress. Young radicals swept to power in local elections. Candidates with democratic platforms outperformed their own wildest dreams, and radical pro-market reformers took over the Moscow and Leningrad city governments, as well as several other major municipalities. Hallucinogenic, giddy, engorged with the sort of passion that spurts out in two forms – courage and anger – new voices were spawned, and suddenly, it seemed, the generation in their thirties and forties awakened.

It took a new kind of courage, for instance, for a literary editor to challenge his local KGB spook for a seat in the Moscow City Council. In the summer of 1989, when I first met Andrei Malgin, an intense thirty-one-year-old intellectual, he talked only about aesthetic values. He was trying to encourage younger literary talent by publishing their stories and excerpting their novels in the cultural magazine, *Nedeyla*, carried weekly within *Izvestia*, and by pushing the staunchly conservative Writers' Union to admit these startling new voices. He also wrote prolifically himself, with some 200 articles and two books to his credit.

Politics left him cold. 'Our generation began to work under Brezhnev,' he told me. 'We have the imprint of prisoners of a concentration camp. It makes the political opinions of my generation, at least the left-thinking writers, rather vague.' In September 1989 he was 'afraid of revolution in our country'.

Six months later Malgin was so swept up in politics that our lunch together at the restaurant Tren-Mos was completely taken up with a declension of the major forces and coalitions furiously contending for seats in the March elections. He himself was standing against nine other candidates for the post of deputy for his district, Sokolniki, to the Mossoviet. One of his opponents was 'our KGB', meaning the chief of the district's KGB office.

Malgin kept ringing doorbells, and soon had a little pack of teenagers running at his heels as volunteers. Election fever was high: voting notices prepared by the Democratic Platform umbrella group popped up on doorways everywhere, identifying all those who were democratic candidates. Election day was treated like a festive holiday. Whole families appeared at their district school, registered at long tables and stepped into green-curtained voting booths – all of it laid out on the American model – and finally, proudly, let their youngest child drop the ballot in the secret box.

Malgin beat the KGB candidate by 200 votes. Amazed and elated, he immediately threw himself into the run-off campaign, which he needed to win by 50 per cent. The main point in his voting programme was his promise to close the district KGB office – why should every small district of Moscow be haunted by its own secret police office? 'But I'm afraid I'll be accused of taking revenge on my rival,' he admitted. Indeed, an article did appear in the newspaper *Moscow Komsomol* charging that the young editor was 'persecuting' the KGB man!

Malgin looked very much the successful young politico the next time we had dinner. Wire-thin and full of nervous energy, the new Mossoviet deputy stood noticeably taller in his grey suit and turtleneck. As we ate in the boisterous gaiety of a Georgian restaurant, U Pirosmani, Andrei described a peak moment in his life.

The night after his election victory, a Sunday evening, he was walking in a deserted forest area in Sokolniki Park with his two-year-old daughter. At a remote walkway in the park, all of a sudden, he saw his KGB rival walking directly at him. Andrei, who had learned that 40 per cent of his own KGB file was completely fabricated, had already come to the conclusion he shouldn't be afraid of the secret police, because no matter what he did they would make up lies to discredit him. Still, coming face to face – virtually alone in a forest – with a KGB agent one has just beaten and humiliated is another level of fear.

'Hello,' said Andrei calmly.

A look of panic flashed across the KGB man's face. Like a roach surprised by the light, he turned and ran.

'He was more afraid of me than I was of him,' realized

Malgin, and in that moment he made a leap to the other side of the fear.

Andrei Malgin's election was part of a stunning power shift away from total control by the Party in the cities of Moscow, Leningrad, Lvov and Volgograd. The people chose a majority from a new crop of independent-minded politicians, and in Moscow they amassed a 60 per cent democratic majority in the Mossoviet and elected insurgent economist Gavriil Popov as the new chairman. On the tide of this incredible rush of events, the new gang in power began battling for its own voice in the press.

After three months, when it became apparent the Party would not give up either of its city newspapers to the newly elected city government, the Mossoviet decided to set up its own weekly journal, *Stolitsa* ('Capitol'), and pay out of their profits for the use of the Party's printing plant. Andrei Malgin was named editor. Triumphant, the young Turk told the *New York Times* he was certain that in winning the battle over control of the existing papers, the Communist Party had lost the war.

'We are going to be so sharp, so interesting to our readers, that we won't even be competing with [the Party's newspapers]. No one will want to read them any more.'†

Gorbachev's most important legacy will be the lifting of fear and the creation of a new political generation – people in their thirties and forties (considered young in the Soviet Union) galvanized by the chance to speak and act openly. They are not handicapped by the reflexes of the Gorbachev generation, which automatically saw the evils in democracy. The defining event for many of them was not one Communist leader secretly denouncing another, as it was for the 'children of the 20th Party Congress' politicized by Khrushchev's secret speech, it was their astonishment at their *own* concussionary strength when they dared to confront the entire Communist leadership, face to face.

God Brought Down to Earth

The month of May started out all wrong for Gorbachev. He and his Politburo marched out on to Lenin's mausoleum to review the annual May Day parade and found themselves up against chants of 'Resign!' and 'Shame!' from a fist-shaking column of protesters.

It was the first time the May Day demonstration – customarily an orchestrated show of worker solidarity by trade-union-sponsored demonstrators – had been opened to unofficial organizations. Gorbachev had consented to the participation of informal groups, and the new Moscow City Council was in charge of organizing the unofficial demonstration, the arrangement being that the marchers would keep their slogans 'decent and permissible'.†

The informal groups were met with parade music at the decibel level of a discotheque. Undeterred, they sent up a roar of cheers, not for Gorbachev but for the short, impish-faced man standing beside him, Gavriil Popov, the brand-new radical mayor of Moscow. Then the demonstrators held up placards with the picture of Boris Yeltsin. Gorbachev forced a smile and drummed his fingers on the rostrum. Having strongly discouraged the publication of opinion surveys on the relative popularity of Soviet leaders, this time he could not ignore the blatant evidence that among Muscovites his bête-noire was more popular than he.

'I felt uncomfortable carrying a Russian empire flag,' a young archaeology student in the pro-democracy movement admitted to me. Like many others, he had never been interested in politics and only a year before would never have dreamed of daring such direct action. Once inside Red Square, he made his way to the front lines and felt the jolt of excitement at being only twenty yards from the Soviet leader. 'It felt like a bullfight.'

Now Gorbachev put on his glasses and leaned forward to read the slogans: 'Dictator Equals a President Without Election', and 'Down with the Empire of Red Fascism', and

'Kremlin Ceaucescus'. He seemed especially disturbed by the banner, later shown in several TV broadcasts and mentioned in the newspapers: 'Gorbachev Is the Workhorse of the Mafia'. 'His lips were pressed together, tight and unpleasant,' recalls the archaeologist. 'And his KGB guards looked tense and helpless.'†

Raisa Gorbachev, half-hidden behind the mausoleum, was spotted bawling out the Moscow Communist Party leader, who had been in charge of the unofficial demonstration. When she had finished with him, the man huddled with the new mayor, but neither official attempted to suppress the crowd.†

After enduring twenty-five minutes of jeers and catcalls and the murderous show of slogans, President Gorbachev turned his back on the protesters and abruptly abandoned the mausoleum. The entire state and Communist Party leadership followed, sheeplike and stony-faced, to file back into the safety of the Kremlin. Never had they been so publicly humiliated. A wave of jubilation came over the crowd. The archaeologist would never forget the fleeting feeling of empowerment: 'They got scared. They ran away from us. The bull was suddenly gone from the arena.'

We won was the unimaginable news running around Moscow within an hour after the demonstration. The god had been brought down to earth. The democratic forces had proved to themselves they need no longer be afraid to challenge Gorbachev face to face. The shaken leader would immediately issue a presidential directive closing central Moscow to any further demonstrations. It seemed doubtful that he would ever again appear on top of the mausoleum. Gorbachev would now become a virtual prisoner inside his Kremlin.

Mikhailova was overcome with outrage at the humiliation dealt to Gorbachev by what she called 'a circus'. She said he had been stunned by the insulting slogans. His response was to use his new powers of decree to push through an unprecedented law making it a crime to say or write anything that would damage the 'honour and dignity' of the new Soviet President, with jail sentences of up to four years for violators. If the actions involved the use of the press or other mass media, the fines increased to 25 million rubles and imprisonment to six years.†

But the popular rage didn't go away. If people couldn't insult Gorbachev, they would desecrate the image of the father of the socialist revolution. The Party's deity, Lenin, would have a humiliating summer. Stoned, firebombed, smeared with paint, Lenin's sixty-foot hulk was finally ordered chopped down in Tblisi. The same fate befell the Moscow Lenin, the sentence passed by the progressive city council. Still, the rage spread over the summer, out into a tent city of rag-tag groups camping in the corner of Red Square next to the Rossiya Hotel, bringing their grievances to the foot of the Kremlin wall just the way peasants had petitioned the czars. A few blocks away, tens of thousands would line up every day outside the citadel of democracy – the golden arches of McDonald's – and wait four hours to make an offering of half a day's wages for an American burger.†

Losing Control of Russia

By the time I returned to the same Moscow apartment in May the situation had gone from worse to hopeless. In the six *weeks* from March to mid-May economic conditions had deteriorated as badly as in the six *months* from September to March. When I knocked on my neighbours' door to borrow an egg, the Peterhovs looked forlorn. 'Eggs, too, have disappeared. They haven't been in the shops for a month. Cheese is gone. Meat is out of the question. Sometimes we can't get milk now. Or butter. Well, we still have good Russian bread.' Bread cost 20 kopeks, a pittance that hadn't changed since the Second World War. With Irina away at a geological conference, the father and sons invited me to share what they could scrape together for dinner: frozen carrots and peas sautéd in mayonaise.

The economy was in a tailspin. I was almost bodily ejected from the corner state store for trying to buy butter. So drastic was the deterioration in the food supply, this sort of clash was happening on a much broader scale: district holding out against district, city against city, and republic against republic. Leningrad required passports to prove residence before one could shop there. Several important regions of the Soviet Union announced they would cut food shipments to Moscow in retaliation for a ban by the city authorities on shopping by non-residents.† The Soviet economy was breaking down into self-protective autarkic entities.

A top government finance minister told Mortimer Zuckerman, publisher of *US News & World Report*, that Gorbachev's programmes were causing the country's gross national product to decline at a rate of 10 per cent a year.† The economy was verging on total collapse, but many government ministers and mafia chains were making money hand over fist. Igor Andropov, son of the former KGB chief, described to me the despair of the secret police at their inability to stem the tide of crime: 'Nowhere are the hierarchies of mafia growing faster than in the Soviet Union.'

How was Gorbachev coping with all these blows? At the end of May, Alexander Yakovlev, his alter ego and closest adviser, made time to see me for a rare one-on-one interview. I arrived at the main building of the Central Committee complex on Staraya Square, the real citadel of power in the USSR, the place where the might of the Party's apparat is concentrated. I had become almost obsessed with finding out what lay inside this sanctum, where Gorbachev often works until late at night. I often wondered if he wasn't becoming a Wizard of Oz figure, pulling strings from behind the curtains, trying desperately to make some sound effects amid the roar of unruly forces let loose by his democratization. This would be a chance to find out.

The place is cavernous. The ceilings are high, the hallways broad and the windows veiled in floor-length pale silk draperies – but nowhere is there any real evidence of *work*. The hush is that of a vacuum. Even in the ante-room outside Yakovlev's office, no secretary is evident (although he has dozens of them), no aides tucked into corners with computers and phone banks and fax machines and printers spewing out miles of briefing papers, as one would see in any Executive Wing office at the White House. (I was told that there is another Central Committee building that houses computer equipment.) One large, chunky Russian-made typewriter sits on a table. The wood is always blond veneer, the walls empty, the bookshelves bare. Offices of Party officials are supposed to express their humility. The lavish appointments are saved for their dacha compounds, which are never seen by the public.

'We just talked to Mikhail Sergeyevich about that, there's no need to discuss it further,' said a Central Committee member who ducked in to take a phone call at the porter's desk.

Ushered into Yakovlev's large office, I was again overwhelmed by the cavernous emptiness. The only ornamentation was a twisted piece of metal on a stand. When I inquired about it, Yakovlev himself rose and limped across the room to put in my hands the fragment from a Soviet SS-12 short-range missile – destroyed on 12 November 1988, as the first tangible evidence of Gorbachev's and Reagan's agreement to reduce the superpowers' nuclear arsenals.

Alexander Nikolayevich has a massive head. His forehead protrudes as if his brain is almost too big for his skull. Deep lines flare above his eyes like lightning flashes. His skin is colourless, his sparse hair black as shoe-polish with fringes of white at the ears. When a smile breaks across his habitual poker face, a twinkle of sardonic wit enlivens his eyes, but, mostly, all the lines in his face drag downward.

He spent the first ten minutes closely examining my Sony BM-560 microcassette tape recorder. Then he walked over to his desk drawer and came back with *his* Sony tape recorder, and even more intently turned over the two machines in his meaty palms to see if by any marginal difference mine might be better. Satisfied that it was not, he was ready to answer questions posed in English, though he would speak only Russian.

No, he couldn't answer any questions about Gorbachev's character. 'I avoid giving personal characteristics for anyone, because we always turn out to be mistaken.' So we moved through his own life up until the present conundrums. I wanted to find out if the leadership believed the mafia malaise to be as central to their economic woes as the public and polls indicated, so I disgorged an interminable question. 'People say the number-one obstacle to perestroika is the mafia, by which they mean corrupted Party and state apparat. Is this entrenched mafia network trying to sabotage the supply of necessities in order to prevent you and President Gorbachev from gaining the consensus to pursue your ideas of a market economy? Or are there reactionaries in your leadership who favour scarcity, which leads to rationing and which people easily accept, which then leads back to political control by the Party?'

His thick grey and white brows flew upward. 'You have answered seventy-five per cent of your own question,' Yakovlev said. 'When we talk of mafia, we mean clan relations especially in the republics. Several clans have existed for thousands of years. I have to say there's been both satotage and outright resistance. And now the struggle will flare up over the market mechanisms since many people will be against them. First, members of the shadow economy will be against. Second, all lazy workers and all those who have preached a communism in which you are given everything and you don't give anything back.'

I went on to probe about the many members of the intelligentsia who had fervently supported perestroika and who felt Gorbachev had turned against them.

It was a raw wound. 'We are very respectful of the

intelligentsia,' he said defensively. 'All of us can be called intelligentsia. From perestroika the intelligentsia has received a lot of support.'

True, but did he worry that Gorbachev's enemies were poisoning his mind about his natural allies by giving distorted reports?

'We are not always stable people,' he replied, almost wistfully, 'we are eclectic, emotional and quick to react. We do something today and cry tomorrow.'

Yakovlev had once written that ultra-leftists were the curse of any revolution. Was this how he saw the Yeltsin forces?

'The ultra-leftists must be toned down or isolated,' he said darkly.

Isolated, how?

'Moral isolation.'

After this chilling answer, Yakovlev made an all-too-correct prophecy. 'The most most dangerous thing that could happen is a split in the left.'

At the end of two hours, I asked the number-two man in the country if he and Gorbachev ever combined work and relaxation by playing games, or fishing and hunting together like the famous Bush and Baker team.

'Absolutely not,' snapped the putty-faced intellectual in his strict three-piece suit. Bush and Baker could play games 'because they have no responsibility for economic problems,' he added with a touch of contempt, as if he were a scholarship student talking about a couple of rich dilettantes on the polo team.

'What is the pleasure in your life, Alexander Nikolayevich?'

'I don't know, I don't think about it,' he said hurriedly. Then, after a long reflective pause, he added, 'About the biggest fish is to change people's lives.'

Of all the intriguing things Yakovlev had said, the thing that stayed with me when I left his office was what he *hadn't* said. In two hours he had not once mentioned the name Gorbachev. I noticed the same thing when I interviewed the

well-known Foreign Office spokesman, Gennady Gerasimov.
Were these most intimate bellwethers of Kremlin power
beginning to distance themselves from a fatally weakened
leader?

The Bread Panic

Nearing the end of May, the government announced it
would begin the move to a 'regulated market economy' by
tripling bread prices. The last certainty in Russian life was
being stripped away. A wave of panic-buying swept the city.
My neighbours rushed over to warn me to get to the store
quickly, but it was afternoon, the shelves were already bare.
A month's supply of food was snapped up in three days.

Gorbachev's attempt to prepare his people for the pain
and sacrifice of a cold-turkey approach to economic overhaul
could hardly have been handled in a politically clumsier
fashion. He had put his Prime Minister, Ryzhkov, out front
to announce plans to increase the price of staples by 200 to
300 per cent. In his TV address on 24 May Ryzhkov sounded
uncertain, even scared, and gave no assurances that the plan
would work. Gorbachev, characteristically, registered neither
approval nor disapproval of the initiative, simply making a
nationally televised appeal to Soviet citizens to stay calm
during a 'tense, difficult and frankly speaking dangerous'
period.†

So preoccupied were Soviets with the miserable condition
of their lives, they paid almost no attention to the upcoming
summit meeting between their leader and President Bush.
On a trip to the provinces, Gorbachev grumbled that Soviet
citizens never bothered to ask him about foreign policy any
more. All he heard were complaints about inadequate
housing, food shortages, pollution. From the perspective of
Moscow, no one would have known that Mikhail Gorbachev
had lifted a finger to reverse the arms race and end the
Cold War. His foreign-policy achievements were totally

subsumed by the free-floating fury of a scavenging population.

The new economic plan immediately came under fire from all sides. Liberal economists criticized it as timid, while Gorbachev's rival Boris Yeltsin attacked its reliance on price increases. Miners in the Ukraine reacted by threatening to strike.†

Finally, Gorbachev threw his weight behind the government programme. 'Everyone on the presidential council agreed that we cannot afford to go slow,' he said on TV – words the democratic forces had been longing to hear. However, he did not sound convinced. It was a startling change. The leader's supreme confidence, even the fighting spirit of his bullying lectures, seemed to be ebbing into uncertainty.

A charismatic leader must believe, if he is to persuade his people to sacrifice for the greater good. And as much as Gorbachev might sound the call to radical economic reform, he didn't really believe in a modern, full-blooded market. Always he pulled back towards the old forms. As he said in September 1990: 'Setting up a mixed economy in which state and joint-stock enterprises, co-operatives and enterprises operating on leasehold principles – but also, on a certain scale, private enterprises – will . . . combine socialism with the private interests of people.'† For months, the adjectives most often used in the Western press to describe Gorbachev's rare public appearances were 'tense' and 'halting'.

The Yeltsin Comeback

Into the leadership vacuum rushed Gorbachev's nemesis, Boris Yeltsin. He reappeared in Moscow on 17 May for the opening session of the Russian parliament, raring for a fight over political and economic control of the republic.

Head sunk in his hand, eyes downcast, Mikhail Sergey-evich sat in the balcony watching the historic moment. If Yeltsin won the presidency of Russia – a jurisdiction twice the size of the United States – he could turn it into a significant power base, and Gorbachev knew that the fate of Russia would determine the fate of the Soviet Union. For two weeks he threw himself into ferocious politicking to defeat Yeltsin, accusing him of being 'anti-socialist' and railing in a speech before the parliament that what Yeltsin was really proposing, under his banner of Russian sovereignty, was 'the break-up of the Union'. Legislators were astonished that Gorbachev would come before them and devote a long-winded campaign address to discrediting Yeltsin.

Gorbachev's fifty-eight-year-old former ally had made one disastrous trip to the United States only six months before. Scarcely off the plane in New York, the big blunt man began making naive pronouncements about the US that exposed his provincialism. Officials of John Hopkins University were shocked when they went to Yeltsin's hotel to pick him up for the address he was scheduled to give. Swaying, swerving, careening like a comic W. C. Fields character, Yeltsin was in no shape to give a speech. A quart and a half of Jack Daniels stood empty on his dresser.

'I'm afraid the eight hours' time difference has hit me,' Yeltsin told the university officials. The show went on and Yeltsin bluffed and bassooned his way through it, though even back in Moscow, where the videotaped speech was later prominently shown, he looked coarse and clownish. The incident led to a story in the *Washington Post* that did not play well at all in the Capitol.†

The contrast with the thoroughly Westernized workaholic Gorbachev couldn't have been more striking. The two men were both born peasants, both former territorial Party bosses from the sticks, but they had totally different characters.

A scantily educated working-class underdog, Yeltsin's habit of action is to throw himself at life. He is a hard-drinking, hard-living man of raw instinct who lives for the moment, champions the convenient principle, and appears to give little thought to his actions. Just as Gorbachev is marked by the stain on his forehead, Yeltsin's symbol is his deformed hand. When he was eleven years old, during the Second World War, he sneaked into an arms storehouse and stole a couple of hand grenades, just for the hell of it. One of the grenades blew off his thumb and half a finger.

But Russians, from the lumpenproletariat to the most erudite Muscovites, can relate to Boris Yeltsin much more easily than to Gorbachev. Not for Yeltsin the years spent cramming information and applying the gloss of European culture. He is a bellicose bruiser with a boxer's nose who adores sports, gets drunk, smokes too much, swears like a stevedore, ignores his heart problems and is widely rumoured to have been caught by his mistress's husband and thrown in the Moscow river – all marks of stand-up Soviet masculinity. Soviets see him as a 'real' man, whereas Gorbachev, who shuns sports and affects the mannerisms of Western leaders, is increasingly criticized for being 'weak', 'indecisive', and 'under his wife's thumb'.

Muscovites also knew Yeltsin as the man who brought the first bright colours to their city by introducing the first City Fair, now an institution, during his brief stint as Moscow Party boss. He had tried to understand the city, not from behind the safety of his Party car, but by bolting through the streets and exposing some of the bloodsuckers in the lower levels of the mafia chains. He also earned a reputation for being dictatorial and impatient;† still, people remembered these traits fondly, since Yeltsin had used them to throw old Party hacks out of their jobs.

Most important, Yeltsin was not afraid to stand up squarely to the Communist Party. In the heady atmosphere of rebellion that spring, Yeltsin was able to capitalize on the Gorbachev-baiting. He deflected criticism for having received representatives from the hysterically anti-semitic Pamyat in 1986, saying he didn't then know what they stood for, but that now 'I can only spit on them.' A natural street politician, Yeltsin adopted an anti-Centre populism which suited his antagonistic temperament and authoritarian soul.

As the third round of voting for the presidency of the

Russian parliament came up at the end of May, Yeltsin's fifty–fifty chances for election eclipsed even the food crisis as the topic of discussion on street corners and around kitchen tables. The word running through the Moscow intelligentsia was, 'Boris has developed enormously, he's not the same man you saw in the United States last September.' People scarcely took notice when Gorbachev left town for his summit meeting with President Bush.

The Soviet President learned the results of the vote on an overnight plane trip in Canada. Yeltsin's narrow victory was a crushing personal humiliation for the leader of the Soviet Union. It seriously crippled his power over the republic that embraces more than half his country's population, three-fourths of its territory, and its greatest natural riches. What's more, he learned that the newly elected Russian President was planning to greet him on his return with a declaration of sovereignty asserting the right of the Soviet Union's largest republic to run its own affairs.

When Gorbachev deplaned in Ottawa that morning, he was hit with questions about the Yeltsin triumph. He gave a prickly reply. 'If he is indeed playing a political game, then we may be in for a difficult time.'†

Gorbachev had nobody but himself to blame for Yeltsin's strength. It was the Soviet leader's own thin-skinned reactions that had given Yeltsin an image as the underdog. By throwing Yeltsin off the Politburo and repeatedly attacking him as a 'rogue' and 'adventurist,' Gorbachev had further romanticized his rival's rough and ready image and channelled the massive free-floating frustration of the Soviet people towards an alternative. However, there was more to Yeltsin than his attraction in being Not Gorbachev. He had touched deep emotional chords in the Russian people.

Russian nationalism was the belief system that could substitute for the Communist Party – that was the truly revolutionary insight – and Yeltsin's movement saw it. This revolutionary insight would work only if the leader was prepared to give up the perfidious Union and regroup as Great Russia with a loose but voluntary commonwealth of independent former republics. While Gorbachev balked, Boris Yeltsin had the nationalist bluster to catch the tide and move with it.

Yeltsin would play Pied Piper and lead a procession of the most attractive new political children of perestroika, Mayor Popov of Moscow and Leningrad Mayor Anatoly Sobchak among them, out of the Party in late June. These new talents and others in the progressive coalition helped soften Yeltsin's demagoguery. Ultimately, the new Russian President would throw over himself the moral cloak of Alexander Solzhenitsyn, shepherding into print Solzhenitsyn's manifesto calling for the dissolution of the Soviet Union and the creation of a pure Slavic state.† And with this thunderbolt from the reactionary romanticized past, Yeltsin's forces stirred up the deepest undertow in the Russian soul – the yearning for an ethnically pure identity and a top–down society ruled by a duma of the professional classes.

Recharging Abroad

The June 1990 summit opened on a bright and sunny Washington spring day, but Gorbachev for obvious reasons started out in a sombre mood. Speaking to a luncheon gathering of American intellectuals, artists and entertainers at the Soviet Embassy, Gorbachev delivered an extraordinarily frank appraisal of his problems back home. He acknowledged that he was trying to 'figure out how to proceed' with his experiments with democracy and a free-market economy. After the luncheon, former Secretary of State Henry Kissinger said the Soviet leader had impressed him as being 'extremely serene and at peace with himself'.

But a new, almost pathetic need to reassure himself of popularity showed through Gorbachev's remarks at that same luncheon: 'Recently, I was pleasantly surprised on my birthday to receive fifty thousand messages of congratulation. Ninety-eight per cent of those were from the United States of America.'†

Bush, intent on improving his own 'personal chemistry' with the Soviet leader, insisted they spend their last day at Camp David. On the helicopter flight to the Maryland mountains, the Gorbachevs got their first eyeful of affluent American suburbia as they flew over Montgomery County and saw the lavish homes and swimming pools and fancy cars. While the President pointed out the areas of wealthy McLean with which he was familiar, Mrs Bush patiently explained to Mrs Gorbachev how mortgages work.

The further away from Moscow Gorbachev got, the more his mood seemed to lighten. On arrival at Camp David, he said, 'The most important thing is to go over the planet.'† The informal, feet-up atmosphere of Camp David is not Gorbachev's style, yet members of his entourage all took off their ties and put on Camp David jackets and sat around in the sunshine on the deck, jawboning like a bunch of vacationing suburbanites. The two leaders did not wrestle with the future of Germany or the problems of the Baltics, as the White House had envisaged; instead, they wandered across the globe, discussing, through simultaneous trans- lation, regional conflicts in Afghanistan and Cambodia, US complaints about Soviet backing for Cuba, and Cuba's role in supporting leftist rebels in El Salvador. Their talks, said Bush's spokesman, Marlin Fitzwater, were 'casual and lively' and often spliced with laughter. It was, he said, a 'kind of lean back and reflect' sort of day, not one for making agreements and issuing statements.†

Sure enough, Gorbachev obliged Bush by riding in his golf cart, walking through his woods, and even playing with his horseshoes. Bush saw the Soviet leader in a new light – as reflecting his own playful informality. As Bush said later, in defence of his unwavering personal support for the battered leader, 'I must say I enjoy dealing with him and I certainly don't dislike him.' On the international diplomatic front at least, Gorbachev had not lost his touch.

His mood continued to be buoyant as he and Raisa made their triumphal way across the United States, culminating in a love-fest in San Francisco. Gorbachev put on his super-salesman hat and made his pitch for new investment in the desolated Soviet economy to some of the leading figures of Western capitalism – computer pioneers Steve Wozniak and John Sculley of Apple Computer, the co-founders of Hewlett-Packard, heads of the Bechtel Group, and representatives of Chevron, which over the weekend had signed a joint venture to explore a potentially massive oilfield in Soviet Asia.

The next day, on a sun-splashed San Francisco morning, Raisa started off by briefly holding hands with Nancy Reagan on the balcony of the Consul General's mansion, while their husbands met inside. Wearing the same toned-down grey suit and fuchsia-pink blouse in which she'd made her show-case appearance at Wellesley College (where Barbara Bush shrewdly let her shine), Raisa seemed at last to have taken note of the criticisms of her lavish wardrobe and haughty manner.

She broke loose that afternoon, hopped a cable car, and then darted in and out of her Zil limo, auburn hair flashing, while San Franciscans scurried to snap her picture. Busily conducting her own sociological research, she priced the items in a mom-and-pop grocery, checked out how well Soviet Stolichnaya vodka was selling, then asked to be driven through Chinatown and up to Russian Hill. Finally, she admitted she was 'overwhelmed by this beautiful city'.

For her husband, the high point of their trip came after he gave a graceful loser's speech about the Cold War at Stanford University. He was followed by George Shultz, former Sec-retary of State and once his most nettlesome adversary at summit meetings. Not one for flowery speeches, Shultz stopped in the middle of his monotonal remarks, turned directly to Gorbachev, and said, 'You light up the landscape with your ideas. You are a great leader. You have a key part to play in this drama – *we need you, Mr Gorbachev*.'

Here the Soviet President was, beleaguered on all sides, fighting for his political life back home, having just come from battling Washington for a trade agreement, being counted out on all sides, when suddenly, in the most public way, a man of George Shultz's stature reached out and offered him this heartfelt statement of support. Gorbachev looked overwhelmed. He raised a hand to his eyes and appeared to brush away a tear.

The American experience – the affection and respect and appreciation for what he was trying to do and the relaxation of seeing something of this once-forbidden land – may have given him a second wind, but it was a private event he attended on his return home that seemed briefly to restore Gorbachev's legendary composure.

Reaching Out for Reassurance

On 17 June, even though he was exhausted, suffering from a bad cold and a high fever, and expected to chair a Politburo meeting at 4 p.m., Gorbachev went to a class reunion. Not even Raisa tugging on his sleeve could keep Mikhail Sergey-evich away from this gathering of his oldest friends from Moscow University.

Mikhailova, his one-time girlfriend, had been twisting his arm to attend. 'Good boy, he kept his word!' she exclaimed when she spotted Gorbachev's bodyguards driving into the campus. Seeing Misha face to face for the first time in ten years, she was immediately reassured.

'He was well tanned, wearing an elegant new light tan suit – well, he just looked wonderful,' she later rhapsodized to me. 'He has grown into a polished political figure since I last saw him, but his simplicity remains, and his affability.'

Mikhailova thrust a bouquet of roses into his arms.

'Nadya,' he said, shaking her hand warmly.

'He didn't hug or kiss me, maybe because Raya was right next to him and he may have felt uncomfortable.'†

Then immediately he was jostled and smothered by four dozen others, all of whom wanted to hug and kiss him. 'We had all been a little apprehensive about the prospect of seeing Gorbachev,' admits Dmitry Golovanov, 'after not having seen him or spoken to him in a long while.' Given the wave of rude shocks he had received in recent weeks – humiliation at the May Day demonstration, panic over the government economic plan, having the Russian republic stolen out from under him by Yeltsin, an impending economic catastrophe even worse than the Great Depression in America – it seemed highly unlikely to them that Gorbachev would take the time for a social gathering with classmates he had not seen for a decade.†

But he had, and protocol went out the window. Golovanov stepped up and planted a kiss on Raisa's cheek. When Golovanov addressed his old friend with the formal 'Mikhail Sergeyevich', Gorbachev mocked him. 'What are you doing, it's Misha!' They were all impressed with his informality among them. He reached out for their love and support, and they gave it to their old friend willingly.†

'I'm so pleased,' Gorbachev mumbled thickly, 'I'm almost in tears. I embrace you all.'

Mlynar had come from Vienna, Golovanov from Bulgaria. 'But the reunion showed that we all still share a common language, based on our common experiences,' said Golovanov.

Raisa (or Raya as most of them called her) did not put on airs with them either. Again, she was wearing the same simple grey suit and pink blouse, but she did keep consulting her watch and saying to Misha, as if she were his manager, 'Twenty-five minutes remaining.'† Mikhailova made her way over to Raisa and sounded a personal appeal: wouldn't she *please* let Misha stay for their 'festive hour' and give a little speech? Gorbachev stayed.

He was sick, he was busy, he was going to be late for a meeting at the Kremlin, 'but the impulse was very strong in him to feel support from his old friends and classmates', observed Golovanov. They swept him off into the auditorium where their classes used to be held. The President tried out his old seat. Then he told his friends how tired he was of sitting in praesidiums and making speeches, how he just wanted to sit there in his own seat, like a student again. Finally he was persuaded to go up to the praesidium with Raisa and say a few words.

At first, he spoke lightheartedly, then he reminisced soberly about the night in 1985 when he had to 'ponder the decision' over whether to take the job of General Secretary. Raisa confirmed his account, nudging him again about the time: 'Seven minutes remaining.'

Gorbachev shifted gears into the subjective and gave something like a profession of faith. He reinvoked the sense of loss they had all felt at the death of Stalin, reminding Mlynar he had stood beside him in this very room and said, 'What will become of us?'† He seemed to Lieberman to be talking to himself, running through his ideas in his mind, as if to reassure himself they were still right. But he appeared unrepentant.

'I can't go against my father or my grandfather,' he told his classmates.† He said he aimed to create democracy and to cleanse the ideals of his forebears from the stigma of Stalin's crimes.

He mentioned that he was facing the Party Congress in a few weeks, amid predictions of explosive splits, and in a private conversation earlier he had told Golovanov that he was still constantly wrestling with himself about whether or not to give up the post of General Secretary of the Party.

' "Misha, we're with you!" we said, and he told us he felt our moral support,' as Mikhailova describes the chemistry. No one asked a question or raised any of the charges whirling around him. 'I did not want to spoil his mood,' says Mikhailova emphatically. 'He didn't come to us to get criticized.'

'He received a real zaryad – a real shot – of optimism, that seemed to recharge his batteries and restore his self-composure,' asserted Golovanov. 'I just saw my old friend in great form.'

Mikhailova, Lieberman and Golovanov were all certain of one thing: seeing those with whom he had spent his youth made it possible for Misha to be an optimist again. 'I think our reunion helped him find new strength,' says Golovanov. This embrace of unqualified support from his old friends played an important role in restoring the beleaguered President's balance. He went on over the next few weeks to manage a series of problems any one of which might have been insurmountable if he had let himself crack. He found a temporary solution to the stand-off with Lithuania; he reached out to Yeltsin; he regained firm hold of the Communist Party at its congress; and coming off that political victory he was able to meet with Helmut Kohl and write the end to the Second World War in exchange for billions in emergency relief from West Germany.

Only weeks after the reunion, Gorbachev completed the mission of his generation: he issued a sweeping decree denouncing the crimes of Stalin as 'illegal and contradicting all social, economic and human rights', and lifting the 'stain of injustice'† from millions of Stalin's victims. It must have given him great satisfaction.

The Survivor of His Revolution

If after all the personal power he had accumulated he could still appreciate the powerful and dark currents that move the river of history, Mikhail Sergeyevich must have known by then that he could not complete his revolution in his lifetime. It is beyond the wits and endurance of one man to communicate his vision and alter all the navigation charts and guide a whole new generation to the other side of the torrent. If what he intended to do above all was smash the walls of the isolated past and the prison of totalitarian fear, he was successful.

Perestroika, however, is an abject failure. Time is against him. Facing hardship and proceeding, always proceeding, had been the theme of his life. His dream was to cultivate the Soviet Union, as he had cultivated himself from a narrow peasant background, into a civilized and modern nation worthy of the respect of the international community. As he put it, 'we want to be organically included in the entire world economically', but he never did seem to accept why socialism failed or understand why capitalism works.†

In the international sphere, it is predictable that he will remain steadfast to the end of his era of leadership – educating, exhorting, sermonizing for the vision of post-heroic leadership: to leave behind the 'bankruptcy of militarism'† and 'to make sure that our country becomes more and more open to the outside world'† until the superpowers have learned too much about each other to revive the 'enemy image'† that fuelled Cold War confrontation.

Even as he was being written off at home as an 'irrelevant' player, the Soviet leader briefly regained his leading role on the world stage at a quick summit in August called by President Bush. The immediate purpose of that Helsinki meeting was to gain the acquiescence of the Soviet Union for the massive US troop build-up in the Gulf in opposition to Saddam Hussein, but it turned out to be a defining moment in world history: the leaders of the two plenipotentiary nuclear powers came together for the first time during a world crisis and pledged to work together to find new ways to protect the planet from power-crazy tyrants armed to the teeth by the superpowers themselves. When Gorbachev mentioned Malta and Camp David as critical meetings that had allowed the two leaders to develop trust in each other, Bush became radiant with pride.

Their joint press conference turned positively kittenish. 'I don't know if I would be allowed to tell you a secret here,' said Gorbachev, smirking. Bush turned to face him, mockingly agog and grinning ear to ear. Gorbachev related Bush's admission that for a long time the American government had taken the view that the Soviet Union had no business in the Middle East, and that now that view had changed. The Helsinki get-together appeared to launch a partnership that would begin with an increased Soviet role in Middle Eastern diplomacy.† The notion was still new, still fragile, but if it worked it could conceivably become a building block towards a new set of regional security structures tailored to the post-Cold War world.

Gorbachev may have been written off by many Soviets as 'irrelevant' in connection with resolving their private miseries, but the Soviet leader was still a figure of monumental power and consequence in the world. He and Bush, having taken each other's measure, continued to hold great potential for co-operation and progress between the superpowers to resolve what had appeared to be intractable regional crises – now Cambodia, next Cuba (as they had together, quietly, resolved the long war in Nicaragua), and ultimately a mutual search for peace in the explosive Middle East – a goal that had eluded world statesmen longer even than an end to the Cold War.

Bush used Gorbachev's exact words, from his 1988 United Nations speech, and called for a 'new world order'.† Some strange chemical reaction seemed to have taken place between him and the Soviet President. When George Bush wrapped up their meeting, it was as if with the intensity of his belief Mikhail Gorbachev had burned his image of a new world on to the retina of the President of the United States. The old Gorbachev magic was still in evidence.

VIII

Epilogue

Summer 1990 – January 1991

Mikhail Gorbachev was a late, great believer in the system that exalted him. Had he not been, he never would have attempted its reform. But he could only move so far, and he never did make the leap of thought to accept democracy or market economics. The strength of his belief in Communism as holding the promise of a new civilization – the very strength that raised him to the supreme position in the crumbling Soviet empire – became the blind spot that threatened to bring him down.

The process of democratization he had relied on to create a more dynamic society ran away with him. He was not prepared for the uncontrollable combustion of grass roots power lit by the fires of free speech. When he distributed much of his power to the Soviets, or local governing bodies, the whole system began to come apart. Why? Because the Soviet political system was prepared for rule by one party, and only one party. Once the Communist Party's monopoly was rescinded, under political pressure, every republic, region, city hall, and local two-bit soviet seemed to be declaring its 'sovereignty'. And newspapers no one had heard of were ready to jump up and criticize the chairman and president. It drove Gorbachev wild.

As each jubilant spasm of liberalization gave birth to regional democratic leaders, Gorbachev's own authority shrank. He sought more and more desperately throughout 1990 to engineer more paper powers for himself, reverting in the process to the old familiar institutions of control and repression out of which he came – the party *apparat* and the KGB.

His refusal to submit to a general election, or to step down as party boss once he had annointed himself President, revealed that 'democratization' was a tool to him, not a commitment. To be a dictator for democracy, of course, is an oxymoron, and the attempt paralyzed the leadership of President Gorbachev. Into the vacuum rushed his nemesis, Boris Yeltsin.

Head sunk in his hands, Gorbachev watched on 1 May 1990 from the balcony of the Russian parliament as Yeltsin won the presidency of Russia. On 8 June, Gorbachev nearly lost both his one-man rule and the Soviet Union. Yeltsin proclaimed the sovereignty of Russia's laws over the Union's laws, and the very next day Yeltsin audaciously moved to take control of all state banks in the largest republic. In a matter of weeks since he had opened the struggle for control over the Russian republic, while the new Soviet President was off summiteering in the United States, Yeltsin had become more powerful inside Russia than its national leader.

Simultaneously, the Soviet Union spun off into irretrievable break-up as a single nation. The Baltic republics had already declared their independence and refused to dissolve their own new body of laws. By September 1990, thirteen out of the fifteen Union republics had passed some form of declaration of sovereignty. Armenia was the first to call for its own army and security forces to replace the KGB. Others prepared to seize the conduct of their own foreign policy and send ambassadors to the United Nations.

Gorbachev and his men inside the Kremlin and the Central Committee, like Yakovlev and Ryzhkov, Shakhnazarov, Primakov and Abalkin, looked tired and shell-shocked to high-level Western visitors. At their wits' end about how to save the economy, they were just hanging on.

By contrast, Boris Yeltsin and his bright-eyed young brainstrusters – ten to twenty years younger on the average than the circle around Gorbachev – were bursting with energy and generating ideas day and night. Opening himself to their influence, Yeltsin had accepted wholesale privatization as the cornerstone of a new economy.

In Moscow Gorbachev was seen as an increasingly irrelevant figure, vainly issuing decrees which he was in no position to enforce. With astonishing speed, the Red Star who had dominated the world political firmament for five years began falling to earth like a burned-out comet. Still ready to improvise, Gorbachev made a peace pact with Yeltsin by mid-summer and gave nodding approval to the Yeltsin forces' 500-day plan for adoption of a market economy. It was an acknowledgement of his own total failure to achieve perestroika within the structure of the Communist Party.

At the same time, Gorbachev was being squeezed to breaking point by that mysterious concatenation of political and criminal forces sworn to preserve the debauched status quo. Ministers of the apparat had every interest in things getting worse. It was suspiciously coincidental that six weeks after Gorbachev finally brought down the Stalinist Ligachev and his mafia at the midsummer Party Congress, ousting Ligachev from the new diluted Politburo, the shelves of Moscow were empty of the last remaining staple of life. Despite the bumper grain crop of 40 million tons, Russian bread was gone from the market.

Hesitant to abandon the centrist position that had been the foundation of his political buoyancy, and aware that the negative repercussions of the traumatic 500-day plan could generate a politically fatal backlash from the right, Gorbachev reverted to his old strategy. He started seesawing again, insisting on a compromise between the radical plan and his government's go-slow plan. It was like trying to make a marriage between a hedgehog and a snake, scoffed Yeltsin.†

Moreover, Gorbachev seemed genuinely afraid that once he allowed the Centre to let go, nothing would hold – the whole nation would be sucked into a whirlpool of dizzying inflation, disastrous unemployment, civil disorder and the chaotic disintegration of the Union.

To place his dilemma in historical context, Gorbachev might be seen as the last of the great reformist tsars. The Revolution of 1917 left the tsarist empire largely intact. It seems to be Gorbachev's fate to preside over the disintegration of both the Russian Empire and Communism.

The chilling metamorphosis of Gorbachev the reformer into Gorbachev the repressor is not without historical antecedent. In fact, the Russian reformers who survived have nearly always used brutal methods. Peter the Great set the historical precedent: arbitrary rule only increased as reforms progressed. Catherine the Great, although she admired the Western Enlightenment, saw it as her dynastic duty to use an iron fist to hammer home changes from above and to discourage popular movements for reform. Gorbachev attempted a transformation no less stunning than Peter the Great's dismantling of the patrimonial state or the top-down revolution launched by Alexander II when he freed the serfs in 1861. But while Gorbachev's revolution has destroyed the ideology of the Bolshevik Revolution, he has not found the belief system to put in its place. An even closer parallel for his metamorphosis is Alexander I, who started out a reformer in 1801 but ended up a reactionary.

On the point of accepting the radical 500-day plan for transition to a full-blooded market economy in early autumn 1990, with progressives euphoric and relations between East and West warmer than the most Pollyannish among us might have dreamt possible only a few years before, Gorbachev began an abrupt retreat on all fronts.

Bitterly disappointed by his precipitous loss of popularity, lost and confused, Gorbachev allowed himself to be dragged back by the conservative barons of the Communist Party. For all the pounding it had taken during its brief exposure to the light of political competition, the Party was still the most powerful institution in the country, flanked by the KGB and the military. And Gorbachev has been consistent throughout his career: he will always sacrifice principle to go where the power is.

The crossroads was upon him – the moment of moral choice most ordinary mortals never have to stare bald in the face. On 17 November 1990 Mikhail Gorbachev was offered a pact with the devil.

That was the night of the 'black colonels'. A group of military hardliners offered to draft Gorbachev even greater presidential powers, provided he would use them to get rid of his reformers, restore central control over the economy, and issue a blanket decree authorizing the military to use force against civilians to 'restore order'. Gorbachev threw in his lot with the hardliners.

Why he made that choice will be the subject of speculation for years to come. According to his once-closest personal advisers, such as Foreign Minister Eduard Shevardnadze and economists Nikolai Petrakov and Stanislav Shatalin, Mikhail Sergeyevich was obsessed with the thought of losing power. Even worse was the nightmare of losing power to Boris Yeltsin. He had also come to the end of his own rope as a reformer. As the sociologist Tatyana Zaslayskaya saw it, 'He doesn't want those changes that are the logical extension of what he started.'

An unwavering retreat from liberalization followed with breathtaking swiftness. One after another Gorbachev turned his back on the political soulmates with whom he had come to power with such lofty ideals. And one after another they were brought down by the right wing, shattered and often suffering heart attacks. The worst of it was, Gorbachev seemed to be a willing prisoner of his brand new allies – hardliners in the military, the KGB and the Communist Party.

The West scarcely took notice, so busy was it authorizing massive infusions of aid to prop up the Gorbachev regime and ensure his continued support of the Allied military option in the approaching Gulf War. Ten days after it conferred on Gorbachev its most revered award, the Nobel Peace Prize, the West was left stunned by the resignation of Eduard Shevardnadze. In a highly emotional speech before the Supreme Soviet, the man widely respected as the conscience of the reform movement warned of approaching dictatorship.

Gorbachev, who had coolly informed his foreign minister the night before that he had better 'look for other opportunities', brushed off the dire warning. Facing his parliament, he looked to the left and said he saw no threat of dictatorship there; he looked to his right and said he saw no threat of dictatorship there either. Quipped an influential newspaper editor, Fyodor Burlatsky, 'The only place he forgot to look was in the mirror. It's a very big mistake, the same mistake I saw with Khrushchev.'

Gorbachev did not defend his friends. Becoming hostage to his former enemies, he stood suddenly alone, pushed and mauled with insults from both sides of the political spectrum. To please the hardliners with whom he had replaced reformers in his government, he hastened a crackdown. He sanctioned the slaughter of citizens in Riga, reimposed censorship on Soviet television, and ordered the unleashing of army and KGB goons to patrol the streets of Soviet cities. The cooperative movement – the one economic success of the Gorbachev years – was dealt a mortal blow when he decreed that the authorities could break in and search their books at will.

Reform would continue, the new best friends of Gorbachev promised. But what they had in mind were a strange sort of reforms, bureaucratic reforms, by which the old barons of the Communist Party who used to be the ministers and managers of huge state monopolies, could now move over to the 'privatized' sector where they would become the presidents and vice-presidents of huge cooperatives. Perestroika was over, finished.

President Gorbachev could remain in a position of leadership for some years, although his actual power was likely to be reduced to that of a ceremonial head of state: the international face of whatever was left of the Union. He was smarter than any other political figure on the spectrum, and always a moving star, not a fixed point in the political universe. If he made his peace with the republics, allowing a new union of sovereign states to form from the bottom up, he could still serve as a wise elder managing the historic transition to a Russian federation with independent parties competing in a parliamentary system. As they looked over the precipice, many Soviets were beginning to see Gorbachev as the only buffer between the colliding forces on right and left – a strong personality who must be kept in place.

That is a scenario of rationality. It ignores the irrational element that moves the players on the great stage of fools where high political drama is played out.

A tragic hero of Tolstoyan proportions, a rapidly ageing and tired Gorbachev claimed the killings in Lithuania in January 1991 were 'a tragic experience for me'. Ever the survivor, Gorbachev could cling to power as long as the forces of darkness find him useful to do their dirty work. But they know he is not one of them. What's more, he is dangerous to them.

Power was a floating thing in the Soviet Union at the start of the new decade. Like every other institution, the Soviet foreign policy establishment was split by Gorbachev's dilemma. When Iraq invaded Kuwait eight months later, Gorbachev and his former ally, Shevardnadze, still controlled foreign policy and placed the Soviet Union squarely on the side of America. But the military establishment seized on the Gulf issue as a way to destroy the foreign policy which 'lost' Eastern Europe and turned the Soviet Union into a shadow superpower.

Gorbachev already looked like a figurehead – rather like the red flag atop the Kremlin kept waving by its hidden wind machine. The country was indeed unravelling. The only question left worth debating, agreed Soviet and Western experts alike, was what would trigger the chaotic violence certain to follow. Whether it was many regional civil wars or one grand revolutionary explosion, it would be the first internal conflict in a heavily nuclearized superstate. The danger hung over Gorbachev and his people like a constant, threatening twitch.

For a cork on a river, he was a mighty force. Gorbachev had perceived the perverse forces at work in a nuclearized world, but he had the ridiculous confidence to believe he could tame them, and the discipline to pick his moment. In that brief period of relative calm between 1985 and the start of a new decade, this man whose temperature always seemed a little higher than normal saw the chance to reverse the arms race and ran the distance of three lifetimes in the effort to democratize his society.

Already, by the dawn of the 1990s, Mikhail Gorbachev had done as much as any man or woman in the twentieth century to change the flow of history. Whatever his ending, he would surely take his place among the giants. And yet, just as he had lived his life in doublethink, he would probably be remembered after his political death in riddles of contradiction.

Mikhail Gorbachev – the last romantic Communist, who put Communism on the trash heap of history. Mikhail Gorbachev – the man who changed the world and lost his country.

Source Notes

I Looking for Mikhail Gorbachev

'Several Gorbachevs': Author's interview with Nikolai Shishlin, consultant to the Central Committee, March 1990.

Harry Hopkins: Robert E. Sherwood in *Roosevelt and Hopkins: An Intimate History* (New York: Harper & Brothers, 1948).

A bold reformer: Radio Liberty research by Terry McNeill, 10/12/84.

Brezhnev, too, was underestimated: ibid.

No less dogmatic: CND/Specials, 12/3/85.

'Least likely': Serge Schmemann in *New York Times*, 3/3/85.

'Our rockets': Mikhail Gorbachev in *Perestroika* (New York: Harper & Row, 1987).

'The only polling': Author's interview with Vladislav Starkov, editor, *Argumenty i Fakty*.

II First Gorbachev: Country Cossack 1931–1949

'The artificial famine': Mikhail Sergeyevich Gorbachev's early years were described to me by friends, teachers and officials in Privolnoye: Alexandrovna Ivanovna Yakovenko (the girl next door); Grigory Gorlov (former district kolkhoz chairman); Matilda Ignatenko (Gorbachev's German teacher); Alexander Yakovenko (worked on combine with Gorbachev); Nikolai Lubenko (worked with Gorbachev's father); Tamara Unstentova (Gorbachev's landlady in Krasnogvardeiskoye); Yekaterina Chaika (chemistry teacher); Antonina Sherbakova (history teacher); Maria Grevtseva (biology teacher); Boris Gladskoi (classmate). Unless otherwise noted, my description of those years comes from these interviews and from my visit to Privolnoye.

In certain villages: Zhores A. Medvedev in *Gorbachev* (New York: W. W. Norton, 1986).

Over three years ago: Gary Lee in *Washington Post*, 19/7/90.

Fatal avalanche: Robert Conquest in *The Harvest of Sorrow: Soviet Collectivization and the Terror Famine* (New York: Oxford University Press, 1986).

'Military Cossack-style hat': Author's interview with Alexandrovna Yakovenko, September 1989.

'All the girls': ibid.

'Not much educated': Author's interview with Professor Chuguyev, professor of the Agricultural Institute of Stavropol, September 1989.

Terror and lawlessness: Zhores Medvedev in *Gorbachev*.

'Rich peasant': Mikhail Sholokohov in *And Quiet Flows the Don* (New York: Vintage Books, 1966).

The entire value: Robert Conquest in *The Harvest of Sorrow*.

'Kulak bastards': Vasily Grossman in *Forever Flowering* (New York: Harper & Row, 1972).

The stubbornness: Robert Conquest in *The Harvest of Sorrow*.

Special commission: ibid.

'Knocker': ibid.

Sentenced to nine years: Dusko Doder and Louise Branson in *Gorbachev, Heretic in the Kremlin* (New York: Viking Books, 1990), from Gorbachev's conference with editors at *L'Unità*.

'By chance': Author's interview with Nikolai Shishlin, November 1989.

Whose name meant 'porcupine': Author's interview with author Natalie Darialova.

38,000–40,000 people: Michael Heller and Alexander Nekrich in *Utopia in Power* (New York: Simon & Schuster, 1986).

786,098 Soviet citizens: *New York Post*, 12/2/90.

To crush those who resisted: *Mikhail S. Gorbachev: An Intimate Biography* (New York: Time Incorporated, 1988).

Grandfather Gorbachev worked for Suslov: Author's interview with Viktor Yasmann, Radio Liberty researcher who specializes in the KGB.

'Emotionally, my mother': Mainhardt Count Nayhauss in *Hamburg Bild*, 14/6/89.

Seven male relatives: *Mikhail S. Gorbachev: An Intimate Biography*.

War was sapping the life blood: Sovietologist Steven Cohen on MacNeill Lehrer, 5/3/90.

Lost twenty-seven million: George Bush at Washington summit as reported by Jack Nelson and James Gerstenzang in *Los Angeles Times*, 1/6/90.

'**From the age of thirteen**': Gorbachev interviewed by Tass, 18/5/89.
'**Let's go to the movies**': David Remnick in *Washington Post*, 1/12/89.

III Second Gorbachev: First-Generation Apparatchik 1950–1977

Mikhail Sergeyevich Gorbachev's university years were described to me by members of the class of '55 of the Moscow State University Law School: Dmitry Golovanov, Grigory Gorlov, Rudolf Kolchanov, Vladimir Lieberman, Nadezhda Mikhailova, Zdenek Mlynar, Natasha Rimashevskaya; and by Professor Alexander Zinoviev. Unless otherwise noted, my description of those years comes from these interviews.

'**Neatness award**': Doder and Branson in *Heretic in the Kremlin*.
The term apparatchik: Frederick Barghoon in *Politics in the USSR* (Boston: Little Brown, 1966).
Only sixteen universities: Author's interview wih Viktor Yasmann.
'**I like mathematics**': Gorbachev quoted in Doder and Branson, *Heretic in the Kremlin*.
The local KGB directorate: Boris Yeltsin in *Against the Grain* (New York: Summit Books, 1990).
7.5 million: author's interview with Viktor Yasmann.
Denounced for his drunkenness: Fridrikh Neznansky, Gorbachev's university classmate, interviewed by editors of *Gorbachev: An Intimate Biography*.
'**We should all sing**': *Cossacks of the Kuban*, Soviet film, 1950.
'**There's nothing we can't do**': ibid.
'**Not an authoritarian personality**': Author's interview with Zdenek Mlynar, classmate and close friend of young Gorbachev, today a professor at the Austrian Institute for International Politics.
Not more than 300,000 people: Author's interview with Professor Vladimir Kvint, member of the Academy of Sciences, editorial board of ECO and one of Gorbachev's team of Siberian economists.
184.8 million people: *Narodnoe Khozyaistvo, 1922–1972* (Moscow: Statistika, 1977).
6,882,145 were Party members: *Great Soviet Encyclopedia* (Moscow: 1958).
'**Lack of vulgarity**': David Remnick's interview with Zdenek Mlynar, *Washingon Post*, 1/12/89.
Related by marriage to Andrei Gromyko: Author's interview with Alexander Zinoviev.
'**A very poor family**': Raisa Gorbachev as reported by Patt Morrison in *Los Angeles Times*, 5/6/90.
The crowd spun out of control: Roy Medvedev, *Let History Judge: The*

Origins and Consequences of Stalinism (New York: Alfred A. Knopf, 1971).

'Were in tears': Gorbachev as reported by Paul Quinn-Judge in *Boston Globe*, 17/6/90.

Satisfying military service: Author's interview with Zdenek Mlynar.

'You come from Stavropol': Author's interview with Dmitry Golovanov, classmate of Gorbachev's.

Mikhail Sergeyevich's and Raisa Maximovna's years in Stavropol were described to me by friends and colleagues in Stavropol: Professor Chuguyev, Grigory Gorlov, Grigory Starshikov. And others: Igor Andropov, Andrei Brezhnev, Vladimir Kvint, Nadezhda Mikhailova, Zdenek Mlynar, former Ambassador Mark Palmer, Leonid Sedov, Alexandrovna Yakovenko. Unless otherwise noted, my descriptions of those years come from my visits to Stavropol, Mineralnye Vody, Pyatigorsk, Kislovodsk.

A single, tiny heatless room: Author's interview with Professor Chuguyev, Stavropol Agricultural Institute.

It was a shattering blow: Zhores Medvedev, *Gorbachev*.

'I did not work': Gorbachev interviewed on private life, Tass, 18/5/89.

'Nikita will be forgotten': Author's interview with filmmaker Dmitry Barchevsky.

'A middle peasant': Gorbachev, as quoted in *Mikhail S. Gorbachev: An Intimate Biography*.

The 'killer instinct': *Observer*, Munich, 12/11/84.

All references to Lyndon Johnson: Robert A. Caro, *Means of Ascent: The Years of Lyndon Johnson* (New York: Alfred A. Knopf, 1990).

'Not like a common guy': Author's interview with Grigory Starshikov.

Characterizations of 'unexpectedly' and 'demotion': Zhores Medvedev in *Gorbachev*.

Co-ordinating its activities: ibid.

Rubberstamped Khrushchev's plan: Doder and Branson in *Heretic in the Kremlin*.

Nothing of the country bumpkin: UPI, 17/7/78.

'Didn't have any patience with drunkards': Author's interview with Grigory Gorlov.

Gorbachev watched as his patron navigated: Zhores Medvedev in *Gorbachev*.

'Break Khrushchev's neck': Doder and Branson in *Heretic in the Kremlin*.

His wife's philosophy seminar: Author's visit to Stavropol Agricultural Institute and interview with Professor Chuguyev.

Basis for future scholarships: Marc Fisher in *Washington Post*, 14/5/90.

First recorded use of the term: Radio Liberty research by Andreas Tenson, 'The Changing Winds of Agricultural Policy in Stavropol Krai', 12/6/81.

'Raisa got a lot of enjoyment': Author's interview with Igor Andropov.

'They trust me': Author's interview with Grigory Gorlov.

Chosen by the KGB: Author's interview with Oleg D. Kalugin, retired KGB major-general.

'All the churches had been allowed to function': Author's interview with Archbishop Antony of Stavropol.

'Why are they persecuting Solzhenitsyn?': Account from author's interview with journalist Arkady Vaxberg.

'Raisa will help me read it': Gorbachev, as quoted by Doder and Branson in *Heretic in the Kremlin*.

Permission for foreign travel: Zhores Medvedev in *Gorbachev*.

A leftist French businessman: Doder and Branson in *Heretic in the Kremlin*.

His openness to the idea: Whole anecdote from *Mikhail S. Gorbachev: An Intimate Biography*.

Sadly pessimistic: Author's interview with Zdenek Mlynar.

She threw Mlynar out: ibid.

'Exchange' with the Communist Party of Italy: Author's interview with Adalberto Minucci, MP, Grupa Communista.

'About the German land': *Mikhail S. Gorbachev: An Intimate Biography*.

Resembling self-employment: All references to the zveno group and the Ipatov method are from Radio Liberty research papers by Andreas Tenson, 12/1/81 and 4/4/84.

Led the world as grain exporter: Maurice Dobb, *Soviet Economic Development Since 1917* (New York: International Publishers, 1937).

'The principles of zveno are destroyed': *Komsomolskaya Pravda*, 15/4/78.

Brezhnev himself praised: *Economicheskaya Gazeta*, 1978.

'The green blaze': *Pravda*, 10/5/80.

About 19,000 workers had to be drafted: *Izvestia*, 3/8/83.

'Many ways to hide': Author's interview with Soviet journalist Arkady Vaxberg.

A local god: Boris Yeltsin in *Against the Grain*.

A useful barter arrangement: ibid.

He was not chosen to succeed Khrushchev: Author's interview with Soviet Ambassador-at-large Igor Andropov, son of KGB chief Yuri Andropov.

Liked to impress visiting American officials: Author's interview with Peter Peterson, CEO Blackstone Group and member of Council on Foreign Relations.

Private performances: Author's interview with Andrei Brezhnev, grandson of Leonid Brezhnev.

Big Brows: Author's interview with sociologist Leonid Sedov.

Gogol, *The Government Inspector: The Theatre of Nikolay Gogol* (Chicago: University of Chicago Press, 1980).

No discernible ties of family or ethnicity: Yuri Schenkochikin, who covers crime for *Literaturnaya Gazeta*.

Large clans: Author's interview with Alexander Yakovlev, member of the Politburo and secretary of the Central Committee, May 1990.

Threw the man out: Doder and Branson in *Heretic in the Kremlin*.

Scrupulously clean: Author's interviw with Viktor Yasmann, Radio Liberty.

'No sympathy for the KGB': Andrei Sakharov, *Memoirs* (New York: Alfred A. Knopf, 1990).

29 rubles a month: Doder and Branson in *Heretic in the Kremlin*.

Only a cousin: ibid.

How warm and familiar Gorbachev was: ibid.

Collaborated with the secret police: Grey Hodnett, 'Mikhail Andreevich Suslov', in George W. Simmonds (ed.), *Soviet Leaders* (New York: Thomas Y. Crowell Company, 1967).

'Aggressive orthodoxy': Boris I. Nicoleavsky, *Power and the Soviet Elite* (New York: Praeger, 1965).

'Western-oriented population to adjust': Romuald J. Misiunas and Rein Taagepera, *The Baltic States: Years of Dependence 1940–1980* (Berkeley, Cal.: University of California Press, 1983).

'The grey eminence': Radio Liberty research by Alexander Rahr, 12/4/84.

Life expectancy was declining: *Gorbachev's Economic Plans*, study papers submitted to the Joint Economic Committee, 23/11/87. (Washington: US Government Printing Service).

'THE SUDDEN DEATH': Radio Liberty research, Christian Duevel, 18/7/78.

The youngest and ablest: Zhores Medvedev in *Gorbachev*.

Five to ten doctors: Boris Yeltsin in *Against the Grain*.

Wrote the medical report: Zhores Medvedev in *Gorbachev*.

IV Third Gorbachev: Disciple of Doublethink 1978–1984

'No interest in women': Author's interview with Vladimir Lieberman, law-school classmate of Gorbachev.

'Kulakov's unexpected death': Radio Liberty research by Christian Duevel, 18/7/78.

'Your sheep-breeding empire': Author's interview with Grigory Starshikov.

Last on a list: Red Archives, UPI News Service, 28/11/78.

'Breathtaking youth': Radio Liberty research by Christian Duevel, 28/11/78.

Several insiders: Author's interviews with Nikolai Shishlin, Gennady Gerasimov and Vladimir Kvint.

The promotion of the Stavropolian: Radio Liberty research by Terry McNeill, 10/12/84.

Sharply down: Author's interview with Professor Vladimir Kvint.

'It's another job altogether': Thomas Butson, *Gorbachev, A Biography* (New York: Stein & Day, 1986).

'What did they think they were doing!': Author's interview with Nikolai Shishlin.

A report sharply critical: Author's interview with Soviet economist Abel Aganbegyan.

An insupportable 22 to 25 per cent: Information supplied by William Safire of the *New York Times*.

More of a politician: Author's interview with Dmitry Golovanov.

Promote from obscurity: Doder and Branson in *Heretic in the Kremlin*.

'When he first came to work': Boris Yeltsin in *Against the Grain*.

'An open debate': Radio Budapest, 1/2/79.

Only 8 per cent of Soviet farms: Radio Liberty research by Terry McNeill, 10/12/84.

'Decentralizing agriculture': Jim Gallagher in the *Chicago Tribune*, 10/11/81.

'An inferiority complex': Author's interview with John Crystal, American agribusinessman and banker.

Below the minimum standard in protein: Radio Liberty research by Terry McNeill, 10/12/84.

My life, my whole life: Andrei Sakharov in *Memoirs*.

Several blocks: Author's visit to the Central Committee.

Make-work: Boris Yeltsin in *Against the Grain*.

A 'nervous condition': Author's interview with Igor Andropov.

Writing in *Kommunist*: Gorbachev, 6/7/82.

Calmly took notes: Author's interview with Abel Aganbegyan.

Gone from my chair: Author's interview with sociologist Tatyana Zaslavskaya.

'Difficult to tie him': Radio Liberty research by Carey Cavanaugh, 2/7/82.

'Aggregate of social relations': Alexander Zinoviev, *The Reality of Communism* (London: V. Gollancz, 1984).

'Indifference is their chief characteristic': Author's interview with Soviet novelist Anatoly Pristavkin.

Andropov refused to back down: Serge Petroff, *The Red Eminence* (Clifton, NJ: Kingston Press, 1988).

'We are such simpletons?': Donald Kimelman in Knight-Ridder Newspapers, 14/10/84.

Humorous banter: Albert Weeks in *Free Press International*, 5/3/84.

'Extraordinarily capable': Donald Kimelman in Knight-Ridder Newspapers, 14/10/84.

'Pretence of unanimity': Author's interview with Alexander Yakovlev, May 1990.

America-watching: *Gorbachev: An Intimate Biography*.
'Hidden peasant': Author's interview with Alexander Yakovlev, May 1990.
'Gene, you don't try to convert me': *Gorbachev: An Intimate Biography*.
He never denied: Alexander Yakovlev, *Realism Is the Ground of Perestroika: Selected Speeches and Articles from 1980–1989*.
New players: Japan and Europe: Author's interview with John Crystal.
The Gorbachevs would be greeted: Boris Yeltsin in *Against the Grain*, and author's interview with his ghostwriter, Valentin Yumashev.
'Comrades, we have to admit': Doder and Branson in *Heretic in the Kremlin*.

V Fourth Gorbachev: The Great Persuader 1985–1989

'Clearly if we continue': Foreign Minister Eduard Shevardnadze at Party Congress, 3/7/90.
'Those bloody Russians': Chris Ogden, *Maggie* (New York: Simon & Schuster, 1990).
'I've been here before': Radio Liberty research, 18/12/84.
'You persecute entire communities': *Gorbachev: An Intimate Biography*.
'Even when he scowls': James Kelly in *Time*, 25/3/85.
'Coiled energy': British Home Office aide as quoted by Chris Ogden in *Maggie*.
A 'luminous presence': Author's interview with Peter Peterson.
'If you give as good as you get': Neil Kinnock as reported in 'Western European Reaction to Gorbachev' CND/Specials, 12/3/85.
'Both tough people': Author's interview with Ambassador Rozanne Ridgway.
'In right from the top': Author's interview with Prime Minister Margaret Thatcher, *Vanity Fair*, June 1989.
He questioned her on how Britain: Sources close to the Prime Minister.
'A rather idle, sleepy lot': Author's interview with Thatcher intimate, British TV commentator Brian Walden.
'I have never talked': Chris Ogden in *Maggie*.
'Interlocuteur valable': Author's interview with British Ambassador to the UN, Crispin Tickell.
'Go soft': Margaret Thatcher as reported in 'Western European Reaction to Gorbachev', CND/Specials, 12/3/85.
Someone he could trust: Doder and Branson in *Heretic in the Kremlin*.
'Personal chemistry': Gennady Gerasimov to author Chris Ogden in *Maggie*.
Up the tiny cobbled lane: Doder and Branson in *Heretic in the Kremlin*.

Sealed a secret deal: Radio Liberty research edited by Andrew
    Wilson, 19/2/84.
Since the Biblical days: Radio Liberty research.
Turn Russian rivers around: Kerstin Gustaffson in *Norshenflammen*,
    Swedish Communist Party newspaper.
'His amazing self-control': Author's interview with Peter Peterson.
'Client/patron relationship': Author's interview with Sergei Bobkov.
700 million pairs of shoes: Author's interview with Abel
    Aganbegyan, and his book, *The Challenge: The Economics of
    Perestroika* (London: Century Hutchinson, 1988).
Hungarian economic experiment: Radio Liberty research.
'Strangely fond of academics': Author's interview with Nikolai
    Shishlin, March 1990.
'Actually solve the problems': ibid.
Completely reorganize: Account from author's interview with
    Dwayne Andreas, CEO Archer Daniels Midland Company.
'Liquidate Moscow centralized planning': Sources close to Prime
    Minister Thatcher, and Gorbachev in *Perestroika*.
'I may be offered the job': Author's interview with Nadezhda
    Mikhailova.
His classmates murmured sceptically: Author's interview with
    Lieberman after he attended Moscow State University reunion on
    17/6/90.
He had focused on Gromyko: Boris Yeltsin in *Against the Grain*.
A man of strong convictions: Author's interview with Elizabeth
    Teague, Radio Liberty researcher.
A near-genius: Zhores Medvedev in *Gorbachev*.
Stand up to older leaders: London *Daily Telegraph*, 19/3/85.
Never appeared in the official text: Zhores Medvedev in *Gorbachev*.
'Workers' negligence': Tass, 15/3/85.
'Get Down To Work': Radio Liberty research by Elizabeth Teague,
    18/3/85.
Warmed-over Chernenko ideas: Author's interview with Professor
    Vladimir Kvint, who attended.
'Such a reformer': David Remnick in *Washington Post*, 17/2/90.
'Given my arm': Alexander Yakovlev in interview with authors
    Doder and Branson in *Gorbachev: Heretic in the Kremlin*.
'Nothing he has said or done': Serge Schmemann in *New York Times*,
    3/3/85.
At least one daughter: Associated Press, 11/3/85.
A 'check-list' of priorities: Radio Liberty research by Elizabeth
    Teague, 14/3/85.
Cork on the river of history: Author's interview with Peter Goldmark,
    President, Rockefeller Foundation.
The second set of ideas: ibid.

'This question is painful for me': Foreign Minister Eduard
   Shevardnadze, as reported by Alison Mitchell, *New York Newsday*,
   8/7/90.
'Star Trek troika': Author's interview with Mike Joyce, Deputy Chief
   of Mission, US Embassy, Moscow.
Speaking with Andropov's voice: Doder and Branson in *Gorbachev:
   Heretic in the Kremlin*.
'Retooled', 'cost accounting', 'flexible': Abel Aganbegyan in *The
   Challenge: The Economics of Perestroika*.
His pet enemy: Zhores Medvedev in *Gorbachev*.
One-seventh: *Narodnoye Khozyaistvo* (National Economy), 1985.
She sat up: Author's interview with Rudolf Kolchanov.
Dictating into a miniature tape recorder: *New York Times* photo,
   10/9/90.
'Costs me a lot of money': *Gorbachev: An Intimate Biography*.
'Why are there only men here?': Kerstin Gustavson, *Norshenflammen*.
Beyond even dreaming of: Author's interview with filmmaker
   Natasha Barchevsky.
'Bring more flowers': *Norshenflammen*.
'Director Petrovsky has this Loggia': Author's interview with
   Professor Pietrangeli, curator of the Vatican collection.
Raisa showed the letter: *Norshenflammen*.

The Great Persuader Abroad

The inner nature: John Keegan, *The Mask of Command* (New York:
   Viking Penguin, 1987).
Churchill created the heroic mood: Isaiah Berlin, 'Winston Churchill
   in 1940', *Personal Impressions*.
'In trouble with my mother': Gail Sheehy, *Character: America's Search
   for Leadership* (New York: William Morrow, 1988).
'Macho pilot': ibid.
'I was the only one': *Los Angeles Times*, 1/6/90.
'What is asked first': John Keegan in *The Mask of Command*.
'Military–industrial complex': *Gorbachev, An Intimate Biography*.
'Reagan had come': Ronald Reagan, *An American Life*, Hutchinson,
   1990
'I'm in the year 1830': Author's interview with former Ambassador to
   Hungary Mark Palmer.
Nineteenth-century château: ibid.
Gorbachev was out of his seat: Nancy Reagan in *My Turn*.
'What are we doing here, folks?': Peggy Noonan, 'Confessions of a
   Speechwriter', *New York Times magazine*, 15/10/89.
'Here you and I': Author's interviews with Ambassador Jack Matlock
   and former Ambassador Mark Palmer.

'Nuclear war could never': Reagan Press Conference reported in *Washington Post*, 23/10/87.

Twelve-minute break stretched: Nancy Reagan in *My Turn*.

'Let's pound our fists': Mikhail Gorbachev and Ronald Reagan at joint press conference, 22/5/88.

'Expected to be deferred to': Nancy Reagan in *My Turn*.

'Ronnie's main objective': ibid.

'Never stopped talking': ibid.

'Instead of destroying things': *Gorbachev: An Intimate Biography*.

'Choking on the endless discussions': Jerry Hough and Merle Fainsod, *How the Soviet Union is Governed* (Cambridge, Mass.: Harvard University Press, 1979).

Shoulder-fired Stinger rockets: Ronald Reagan library.

The US would outstrip: Zhores Medvedev in *Gorbachev*.

'Drastic measures': Doder and Branson in *Heretic in the Kremlin*.

Designed as a defence: Chiesa and Medvedev in *Time of Change*.

Surprised and pleased: Author's interview with Ambassador Roz Ridgway.

'Gorbachev suddenly insisted': Nancy Reagan in *My Turn*.

'Military–industrial complex': *Gorbachev, An Intimate Biography*.

'This was not a game': Author's interview with Ambassador Roz Ridgway.

'First time in nuclear history': ibid.

Dale Carnegie's book: Author Louise Branson's interview with Ambassador Arthur Hartman in *Gorbachev: Heretic in the Kremlin*.

Throwing a 'zinger': Account from author's interviews with Henry Kissinger and Peter Peterson.

Jeane Kirkpatrick purring: Author's interview with Henry Kissinger.

'Peter the Great': Author's interview with former Ambassador Mark Palmer.

Only three summit meetings: Reagan Library.

Right down to the 'nitty-gritty': Doder and Branson in *Heretic in the Kremlin*.

Thatcher roundly dismissed: Sources close to the Prime Minister.

'In the eyes of world public opinion?': Ambassador Bassiouny interviewed by authors Dusko Doder and Louise Branson in *Gorbachev: Heretic in the Kremlin*.

'He doesn't know policy details!': Chris Ogden in *Maggie*.

'It's a pity about Ronnie': Sources close to the Prime Minister.

Locked in whispered conversation: Chris Ogden, *Maggie*.

'A blushing violet': ibid.

'raunchy sense of humour': Author's interview with Sir John Hoskins.

Ear lobes start burning: Author's interviews with Thatcher intimates.

Pass on his views: Chris Ogden in *Maggie*.

Dismantle his Old Guard: Sources close to the Prime Minister.

'Fascinating and invigorating': Margaret Thatcher at press conference reported by Doder and Branson in *Heretic in the Kremlin*.

'Warm and sincere meetings': *Vremya*, December 1988.

'Old Russia was united': Mikhail Gorbachev in *Perestroika*.

Fight Hitler 'single-handed': *Perestroika* and sources close to Prime Minister Thatcher.

'Who handed over Czechoslovakia': Mikhail Gorbachev in *Perestroika*.

Nose to nose: Chris Ogden in *Maggie*.

'Europe is our common home': Mikhail Gorbachev in *Perestroika*.

'Contradictory but interconnected': ibid.

Daimler limousine: Chris Ogden in *Maggie*.

'In a very real sense, godmother': Sources close to the Prime Minister.

'The Russian bear': *Time*, 14/3/88.

'I froze in my seat': Account from author's interview with Senator Howard Baker.

'A different kind of society': Author's interview with Ambassador Roz Ridgway.

He wanted Shultz to know: ibid.

'You'd gone home': *Washington Post*, 11/12/87.

'Paste-over' job: Author's interview with Ambassador Roz Ridgway.

'All sorts of propaganda gambits': Bill Keller in *New York Times*, 2/6/89.

'Liberating the world from fear': Don Oberdorfer and David Hoffman in *Washington Post*, 2/6/90.

'No one can really scare us': David Remnick in *Washington Post*, 2/6/90.

'The world is listening': Mikhail Gorbachev to Party Congress, 10/7/90.

'It's an anachronism': Author's interview with Senator Howard Baker.

Messages flew back and forth: Author's interview with Ambassador Ridgway.

More than a million soldiers: *Noorte Haal*, 24/1/89.

'No tradition of delegating authority': *Orbis*, Winter 1987.

'That the Soviet threat to us': ibid.

'Gone foolish over Gorby': Author's interview with Ambassador Roz Ridgway.

His 'friend, Mikhail': Strobe Talbott in *Time*, 4/12/89.

'We all had a good laugh': Frederick Kempe and Peter Gumbel in *Wall Street Journal*, 27/5/89.

'Solemn girlhood': Author's interviews with girlhood friends and classmates of Margaret Thatcher, *Vanity Fair*, June 1989.

Favourite foreign leader: *Sunday Observer*, 1/4/89.
A buoyant Mr Gorbachev: Thomas Friedman in *New York Times*, 14/5/89.
'Red meat': Gerald Bush in *New York Times*, 20/4/89.
Obsessed with the public relations problem: Robert Greenberger in *Wall Street Journal*, 17/4/89.
'Who would have predicted changes': George Bush at a press conference in Brussels, 28/5/89.
The prize of German unity: Craig Whitney in *New York Times*, 20/7/90.
A $2 billion loan: Reuters, 11/5/88.
'Raisa was there with us': Author's interview with Rudolf Kolchanov.
'From the Atlantic to the Urals': Serge Schmemann in *New York Times*, 7/7/89.
The 'irrevocable act': Don Oberdorfer in *Washington Post*, 23/12/89.
200 people an hour: *New York Times*, 7/11/89.
50,000 fleeing subjects: Peter Gumbel in *Wall Street Journal*, 6/10/89.
'I should tell our Western partners': Serge Schmemann in *New York Times*, 7/10/89.
'History punishes those': Gorbachev, as reported by Garrick Utley on NBC *Sunday Today*, October 1989.
The 'Sinatra doctrine': Bill Keller in *New York Times*, 25/10/89.
Horseman by the coat-tails: Isaiah Berlin in *Personal Impressions*.
'Not even Jesus Christ': Gerald Seib in *Wall Street Journal*, 2/8/90.
'Or negative about him': ibid.
'Ask you for specifics': ibid.
'Gorbachev knows what he's doing': Author's interview with Senator Howard Baker.
One-third of East Germany's outmoded industry: MacNeil/Lehrer News Hour, 10/7/90.
Get what he wanted from Kohl: John Newhouse in *New Yorker*, 27/8/90.
Prevent unification: ibid.
Superseded both nations' links: ibid.
'We predicted all the events': Eduard Shevardnadze at Party Congress, 4/7/90.
A $3 billion down payment: Serge Schmemann in *New York Times*, 16/7/90.
'Tide over his economy': Spokesman Gennady Gerasimov on National Public Radio, 11/7/90 and *Financial Times*, 9/7/90.
The unpublished critiques of Gorbachev: transcript from Mario Platero, *Il Sole – 24 Ore*.
'280 million permanent wards': MacNeil/Lehrer News Hour, 10/7/90.
'Our relations further upward': Serge Schmemann in *New York Times*, 16/7/90.

Less than two hours: Marc Fisher and David Hoffman in *Washingon Post*, 21/7/90.

Continued late into the night: ibid.

'All practical problems': Gorbachev–Kohl joint news conference in Zheleznovodsk, 16/7/90.

'Mr Chancellor, it was you': ibid.

'It's George Bush's fault': R. W. Apple Jr in *New York Times*, 17/7/90.

The Great Persuader at Home

He had 'hopes': Gorbachev at luncheon for American intellectuals, Washington, 31/5/90.

Their education consisted: *A Biographic Directory of 100 Leading Soviet Officials* compiled by Alexander G. Rahr, Radio Liberty, Munich, August 1984.

Any particular expertise: ibid.

Completely opposing conceptions of socialism: Boris Yeltsin in *Against the Grain*.

'It will deepen perestroika': ibid.

'Such a path': Vadim Zagladin as quoted by Serge Schmemann in *New York Times*, 26/3/85.

Eighteen million: Author's interview with Professor Vladimir Kvint.

Black crows: Peter G. Peterson, 'Gorbachev's Bottom Line', *New York Review of Books*, 25/6/87.

'Why are you leaving now?': Author's interview with filmmaker Dmitry Barchevsky.

'Get me Korotich': Account from author's interview with Vitaly Korotich.

'When you're sixty-two': Author's interview with Grigori Baklonov.

'Cut you up in pieces!': Author's interview with Vitaly Korotich.

'Stupidity. Inexperience.': Author's interview with spokesman Gennady Gerasimov, May 1990.

A factory manager: Alexander Rahr in *A Biographic Directory of 100 Leading Soviet Officials*.

'Until 1917 it was the bankers': Bill Keller in *New York Times*, 14/5/90.

'He didn't know five-sixths': Author's interview with Vladimir Lieberman.

As far away as America: Jay M. Gould and Benjamin A. Goldman, *Deadly Deceit* (New York: Four Walls Eight Windows, 1990).

Four million people in the Ukraine: Felicity Barringer in *New York Times*, 27/4/90.

He choked back his tears: Gorbachev in a conversation with Italian Communist visitors as reported by Doder and Branson in *Gorbachev: Heretic in the Kremlin*.

'Expose the faults': information supplied by Flora Lewis of the *New*

York Times, reported by Doder and Branson in *Gorbachev: Heretic in the Kremlin.*

Given his letter: Andrei Sakharov in *Memoirs.*

In a three-month period: Medvedev and Chiesa in *Time of Change.*

'Drastic changes': Mikhail Gorbachev in *Perestroika.*

'New personality': Stanislav Fyodorov interviewed by Dan Rather on CBS *Nightly News,* 4/2/90.

'Restructuring as difficult, complex': Gorbachev's speech at a meeting with executives of the mass news and propaganda media, Moscow, January 1987.

'History must be seen as it is': ibid.

'Moral purification': Yakovlev's speech at the Party congress, 4/7/90, *New York Times.*

'As a young man': Author's interview with Alexander Yakovlev, May 1990.

'Expression of conscience': Author's interview with Anatoly Pristavkin.

'The worst thing Stalin did': Author's interview with author Anatoly Rybakov.

'To suppress, compel, bribe': Gorbachev in *Perestroika.*

De Gaulle had an image: Isaiah Berlin in *Personal Impressions.*

'Social revolution': Author's interview with Tatyana Zaslavskaya.

A 'strong hand': Bill Keller in *New York Times,* 5/11/89.

'Straighten out a hunchback': Author's interview with Grigory Baklonov.

'Most difficult position': Author's interview with Yakov Grodin.

'Back of the bureaucracy': Bill Keller in *New York Times,* 13/5/90.

First experimental multi-candidate elections: *Washington Post,* 6/2/90.

Gorbachev consistently denied: Gorbachev in interview with *L'Unità,* 20/5/87, Medevedev and Chiesa in *Time of Change.*

Disrespectful attitude: Medvedev and Chiesa in *Time of Change.*

To 'direct readers': Vyacheslav Gorbachev, editor of *Molodaya Gvardiya* as quoted by Medvedev and Chiesa, in *Time of Change.*

'They do not want to forgive Stalin': Vyacheslav Gorbachev in *Time of Change.*

'Despite the incredible efforts': Boris Yeltsin in *Against the Grain.*

'I earned it': Gorbachev as quoted by Chiesa and Medvedev in *Time of Change.*

Massive nationwide promotion: Author's interview with filmmakers Dmitry and Natasha Barchevsky.

'Never forgive or justify the repressions': Gorbachev to the mass media, 9/7/87, reported by Tass.

'My hopes in Gorbachev': Boris Yeltsin in *Against the Grain.*

'Gutter language': ibid.

'Necessary' choices: Medvedev and Chiesa in *Time of Change.*

'Let me back into politics': Boris Yeltsin in *Against the Grain*.

'Political adventurer': Author's interview with Anatole Shub, USIA, from a personal experience of Shub's father.

'New Thinking': Author's interview with Alexander Yakovlev, May 1990.

Roosevelt, like all great innovators: Isaiah Berlin in *Personal Impressions*.

Half a dozen contacts: Author's interview with Viktor Yasmann.

'Easy to know what was wrong': Author's interview with Henry Kissinger.

Pre-crisis situation': Medvedev and Chiesa in *Time of Change*.

'Socialist market': Author's interview with Abel Aganbegyan.

'Changes in the lives and the moods': Medvedev and Chiesa in *Time of Change*.

Eighty million Soviets: Rair Simonyan, an economist at the Institute of World Economics and International Relations, as quoted in *New York Times*, 13/5/90 by Bill Keller. Figures for 1988, adjusted for inflation.

Force Soviet enterprises: Ed Hewett in *New York Times*, 25/3/90.

170 different nationalities . . . semi-nomadic tribes: Robert Goldston, *The Russian Revolution*, and *Report on the USSR*, Radio Liberty, 19/1/90.

'The time to choose': Medvedev and Chiesa in *Time of Change*.

Stripped of some of his duties: ibid.

'Crossed the Rubicon': ibid.

Only three men: Author's interviews with Boris Raushenbakh and Roald Sagdeev.

Between 1985 and 1987 had been improving slightly: Author's interview with Professor Vladimir Kvint.

The energy crisis: Zhores Medvedev, *The Legacy of Chernobyl* (New York: W. W. Norton, 1990).

From 70,000 to four and a half million: Author's interview with economist Vladimir A. Tikhonov.

'Genetically opposed': Characterization by Nikolai Petrakov on 19/2/90 when he was appointed Gorbachev's personal economic adviser.

'Unresolved contradiction': Author's interview with Yuri Afanasev.

An anti-nuclear movement: Zhores Medvedev in *The Legacy of Chernobyl*.

A few thousand such groups: Medvedev and Chiesa in *Time of Change*.

'Tell the people': Alexander Yakovlev interviewed by Dan Rather on CBS *Nightly News*, 4/2/90.

'Tremendous damage': ibid.

Gorbachev scored in the top 10 per cent of world political leaders:

Philip E. Tetlock, professor of psychology at Berkeley and director of its Institute of Personality Assessment and Research, *Washington Post* Insight, 17/12/89.

'Moral cleansing': Gorbachev USSR press kit for Gorbachev's visit to the Pope, December 1989.

'Revolution in our minds': Gorbachev's remarks at meeting with American intellectuals, 31/5/90.

VI Fifth Gorbachev: Dictator for Democracy 1989–1990

'Three lifetimes': Author's interview with Senator Bill Bradley.

Gorbachev himself 'should speak': Andrei Sakharov as quoted in FBIS *Daily Report: Soviet Union*, 13/6/89.

The town square . . . amphetamines: Account from BBC, *Bloody Sunday–Georgian Massacres*, 8/12/89.

'Go into these details': Gorbachev at Congress of People's Deputies, 25/5/89.

'Thanks to yes-men': FBIS *Daily Report: Soviet Union*, 13/6/89.

'Don't accelerate the process': Author's interview with Sergei Stankevich.

Khaki-coloured liquid: Francis X. Clines in *New York Times*, 22/12/89.

'Gorbachev's mind is unclear': *Inside Gorbachev's USSR with Hedrick Smith*, WGBH and Martin Smith Productions, Inc., 30/5/90.

The best builders: Author's interview with Valentin Yumashev, letters editor of *Ogonyok*.

'Their focus is very narrow': Author's interview with Gennady Gerasimov, May 1990.

Forty-eight years: Margot Jacobs in Radio Liberty, *Report on the USSR*, 10/8/90.

No hot water: ibid.

2.5 million coal miners: Felicity Barringer in *New York Times*, 22/1/90.

Demanded an end: Esther B. Fein in *New York Times*, 26/10/89.

'A very painful moment': Author's interview with historian Yakov Grodin.

The signatures of Stalin and Ribbentrop: *Literaturnaya Gazeta*, 5/7/89.

'My work in recent years': Alexander Yakovlev at Party Congress as reported in *New York Times*, 4/7/90.

'Two channels of belief': Author's interview with Andrei Voznesensky.

It was seventy-seventh: David Remnick in *International Herald Tribune*, 21/5/90.

Audiences of 1,500: Edward Kiersh in *Moscow Magazine*, August 1990.

Known to be a KGB operation: Author's interview with Viktor Yasmann, Radio Liberty researcher.

'Doctor' Chumak: Edward Kiersh, *Moscow Magazine*, August 1990.

'Religion always taught people': Author's interview with Nadezhda Mikhailova, May 1990.

American televangelist: Author's interview with Gennady Gerasimov, May 1990.

Rose by 40 per cent: Documentary film *This Is No Way to Live* by Stanislav Govorukhin.

'Anticipating civil war': Peter Gumbel in *Wall Street Journal*, 13/9/89.

'Tied together in a tight knot': Gorbachev on Central Television, 10/9/89.

'Losing his authority': Author's interview with Arkady Vaxberg.

'Stalin's toughness': Author's interview with Nadezhda Mikhailova, September 1989.

145 million of the 285 million Soviet population: Radio Liberty *Report on the USSR*, 19/1/90.

'But democracy, if it works': Author's interview with Gennady Gerasimov, May 1990.

92 per cent of the oil: Vladimir Kvint in *Forbes*, 3/9/90.

Gorbachev dismissed the notion: Vladimir Kvint in *Forbes*, 11/6/90.

'Only by the KGB': Author's interview with Vladislav Starkov.

'I can't express myself': Bill Keller in *New York Times*, 23/10/89.

The most popular publication: *Newsweek*, 4/12/89.

Privately blasted: Author's interview with Yuri Afanasev.

'Mother Russia': Author's interview with Anatoly Zalutsky and tape of rally, December 1989.

'They hate Yakovlev': ibid.

'I am a Communist': Francis X. Clines in *New York Times*, 26/12/89.

'Weariness and doubt', 'testy': Francis X. Clines in *New York Times*, 13/12/89 and 22/12/89.

'I stood in line': Francis X. Clines in *New York Times*, 22/12/89.

'Mysterious personality': Francis X. Clines in *New York Times*, 28/12/89.

'Something of a paradox': David Remnick in *Washington Post*, 17/12/89.

'There will be a battle': ibid.

'Tragic utopia': Pope John Paul in Prague reported by Clyde Haberman in *New York Times*, 22/4/90.

'If I'm a Communist any more': *Newsweek*, 18/12/89.

'Gorbachev is a Bolshevik': Author's interview with Gennady Lisichkin.

'Dismembering the USSR': Gorbachev's speech to the Central Committee, 25/12/89, reported by Quentin Peel in *Financial Times*, 18/1/90.

'Not permit the disintegration': ibid.

'The apparat are so smart': Author's interview with Vladislav Starkov.

Bursting into nationalist songs: Quentin Peel in *Financial Times*, 12/1/90.

'Reserved and shy': Gorbachev on Central Television, 11/1/90.

'You want to leave': Quentin Peel in *Financial Times*, 18/1/90.

A music professor: Quentin Peel in *Financial Times*, 15/1/90.

'Thrown out of windows': Quentin Peel in *Financial Times*, 18/1/90.

'Free from ambition': Alexander Yakovlev quoted in Tass, 13/3/90.

'Plenipotentiary powers': Gorbachev in Tass, 5/2/90.

'To impose a presidential system': *Le Monde*, 30/1/90.

Dissociate himself from the Party: ibid.

Helping hand by Gorbachev: Quentin Peel in *Financial Times*, 5/2/90.

'Mafia is in control': Dan Rather interview on CBS *Evening News*, 4/2/90.

'Always a watcher': Author's interview with Alexander Zinoviev.

'Black is black': Alexander Yakovlev on Radio Moscow, 7/2/90.

'Concentrate power': ibid.

'Among intellectuals': Quentin Peel in *Financial Times*, 30/12/90.

'Emotionally coloured thought': Quentin Peel in *Financial Times*, 20/12/89.

'Every idiot': Author's interview with Ned Kennan, international political consultant.

'Leaders are not aliens': *Izvestia*, February 1990.

Eleven such criminal groups: David Gurevich in *Details*, October 1990.

'Obliged to overcharge . . . links to politicians': Boris Yeltsin in *Against the Grain*.

'Old custom of ours': *Washington Post*, 7/11/89.

'Militarization of the economy: Chris Hedges in *New York Times*, 8/10/90.

'Invitation to buy a TV': Peter Gumbel in *Wall Street Journal*, 5/90.

'Try to summon Ligachev': Scott Shane in *Baltimore Sun*, 7/4/90.

'Whichever man wins': Author's interview with Tatyana Koregina.

'Universe of difference': Author's interview with Tatyana Chaikovskaya.

Watching Gorbachev at Work: The following excerpts from the Congressional debate are taken from the author's notes as well as partial transcripts and summaries by the FBIS *Daily Reports*, 13–16/3/90.

'Haunts every Russian': Joseph Brodsky as quoted by David Remnick in *Washington Post*, 5/9/90.

'Rather alarming': Gorbachev at Congress, 13/3/90.

'Pre-empt the presidential institution': Author's interview with Alexander Yakovlev, May 1990.

Politics was the realm of men: Boris Grushon of Vox Popula in presentation to World Associations for Public Opinion Research, Lancaster, Penn., 10/5/90.

59.2 per cent: *Time*, 26/3/90.
'Dictator of sorts': Author's interview with Tatyana Koregina.
'Very paranoid': Author's interview with Andrei Malgin.
'Yeltsin is Russian nationalist': Author's interview with Gennady Gerasimov, May 1990.
'Deserves any trust': Author's interview with Leonid Sedov.
'Needed to show authority': Author's interview with Nikolai Shishlin, April 1990.
'Animosity distorts judgement': Author's interview with Senator Bill Bradley.
'Constructive role for the US': President Bush quoted in *New York Times*, 4/5/90.

VII   Sixth Gorbachev: Red Star Falling: Spring 1990

'Being born in 1928': Alison Mitchel in *New York Newsday*, 8/7/90.
'Process of a self-revision': Bill Keller in *New York Times*, 23/9/90.
'My conscience is clear': Author's interview with Nadezhda Mikhailova.
By honest work: Author's interview with film director Stanislav Govarukhin.
'So sharp': Celestine Bohlen in *New York Times*, 11/6/90.
'Decent and permissible': Ivan Laptev, Chairman of the Council of the Union, ABC-TV, *Leadership in the 90s*, 7/5/90.
'His lips were pressed': Author's interview with student who attended demonstration.
Half-hidden behind the mausoleum: Mary Dejevsky in *The Times* (London), 2/5/90.
The fines increased: *Izvestia*, 24/5/90.
Half a day's wages: Mortimer Zuckerman in *US News and World Report*, 9/7/90.
Cut food shipments: *Washington Post*, 3/6/90.
At a rate of 10 per cent: Mortimer Zuckerman in *US News and World Report*, 9/7/90.
'Tense, difficult and frankly speaking dangerous': Celestine Bohlen in *New York Times*, 27/5/90.
Threatening to strike: ibid.
'Setting up a mixed economy': Gorbachev speech to the Central Committee, 17/9/90, Radio Moscow.
A quart and a half of Jack Daniels: Paul Hendrickson in *Washington Post*, 13/9/89.
Dictatorial and impatient: Sverin Bialer, Columbia University, in *Pravda*, 13/11/87.
'Playing a political game': *New York Times*, 30/5/90.
Solzhenitsyn's manifesto: *Komsomolskaya Pravda*, 18/9/90.

'**Fifty thousand messages**': Gorbachev's speech to American
   intellectuals, 31/5/90.
'**Go over the planet**': *Washington Post*, 3/6/90.
'**Lean back and reflect**': ibid.
'**Didn't hug or kiss me**': Author's interview with Nadezhda
   Mikhailova, July 1990.
Not seen for a decade: Author's interview with Dmitry Golovanov.
'**It's Misha**': Author's interview with Lieberman.
'**Twenty-five minutes**': ibid.
'**What will become of us?**' Gorbachev as reported by Paul Quinn-
   Judge in *Boston Globe*, 19/6/90.
'**Can't go against my father**': ibid.
'**Stain of injustice**': David Remnick in *Washington Post*, 12/8/90.
'**Organically included**': Gorbachev interviewed in *Time*, 4/6/90.
'**Bankruptcy of militarism**': ibid.
'**More and more open**': Gorbachev's meeting with American
   intellectuals, 31/5/90.
'**Enemy image**': Gorbachev interviewed in *Time*, 4/6/90.
'**Tell you a secret**': Bush and Gorbachev's joint press conference,
   Helsinki, 9/9/90.
'**New world order**': Bush at Helsinki, 9/9/90.

VIII   Epilogue – Summer–Autumn 1990

'**Hedgehog and a snake**': Francis X. Clines in *New York Times*, 9/9/90.
'**I am also afraid**': Bill Keller in *New York Times*, 13/9/90.
'**Every inch a king**': Shakespeare, *King Lear*, Act IV, scene vi.
'**Cut to the brain**': ibid.
'**In their genes a vision**': Quentin Peel in *Financial Times*, 26/9/90.
Two possibilities: Popov at a conference in Vienna on 'Central
   Europe on the Way to Democracy'. Reported in *The Economist*,
   7/7/90.
Authoritarian populist: Author's interview with David Aaron,
   former Deputy National Security Adviser.
'**The next Stalin**': Author's interview with Gennady Gerasimov, May
   1990.

Bibliography

Aitmatov, Chingiz. *The Place of the Skull* (New York: Grove–
 Weidenfeld, 1989)

Aganbegyan, Abel. *The Challenge: Economics of Perestroika* (London:
 Hutchinson Education, 1988)

Berlin, Isaiah. *Personal Impressions* (New York: Viking Press, 1949)

Brodsky, Joeseph. *To Urania* (New York: Farrar Straus & Giroux,
 1988)

Butson, Thomas S. *Gorbachev: A Biography* (New York: Stein & Day,
 1986)

Caro, Robert A. *Means of Ascent: The Years of Lyndon Johnson* (New
 York: Alfred A. Knopf, 1990)

Chekhov, Anton. *Collected Works, Volume 3* (Moscow: Raduga
 Publishers, 1989)

Chekhov, Anton. *Lady with Lapdog and Other Stories* (New York:
 Penguin, 1964)

Cohen, Stephen F. and Vanden Heuvel, Katrina. *Voices of Glasnost:
 Interviews with Gorbachev's Reformers* (New York: W. W. Norton,
 1989)

Conquest, Robert. *The Great Terror: A Reassessment* (New York: Oxford
 University Press, 1990)

Conquest, Robert. *The Harvest of Sorrow: Soviet Collectivization and the
 Terror-Famine* (New York: Oxford University Press, 1986)

Doder, Dusko and Branson, Louise. *Gorbachev: Heretic in the Kremlin*
 (New York: Viking, 1990)

Gogol, Nikolai. *Dead Souls.* (London: Penguin Books, 1961)

Gogol, Nikolai. *Plays and Selected Writings* (Chicago: The University
 Press of Chicago, 1980)

Goldston, Robert. *The Russian Revolution* (New York: Vallentine Books, 1966).

Gorbachev, Mikhail S. *Perestroika: New Thinking for Our Country and the World* (New York: Harper & Row, 1987)

Gray, Francine du Plessix. *Soviet Women: Walking the Tightrope* (New York: Doubleday, 1989)

Gromyko, Andrei. *Memoirs* (New York: Doubleday, 1989)

Hough, Jerry and Fainsod, Merle. *How the Soviet Union Is Governed*. (Cambridge, Mass.: Harvard University Press, 1979)

Keegan, John. *The Mask of Command* (New York: Viking, 1987)

Klose, Kevin. *Russia and the Russians: Inside the Closed Society*. (New York: W. W. Norton, 1984)

Kohler, Phyllis Penn, (ed.). *Journey for Our Time: The Russian Journals of the Marquis de Custine* (Washington: Gateway Editions, 1987)

Kuhn, Thomas S. *The Structure of Scientific Revolution* (Chicago: University of Chicago Press, 1962)

The Lay of the Warfare Waged by Igor (Moscow: Progress Publishers, 1981), English translation of epic poem dating back to 1187.

Massie, Robert K. *Peter the Great: His Life and World* (New York: Ballantine Books, 1980)

Massie, Suzanne. *Land of the Firebird: The Beauty of Old Russia* (New York: Simon & Schuster, 1980)

Medvedev, Roy. *All Stalin's Men: Six Who Carried Out the Bloody Purges* (Garden City, NJ: Anchor Books, 1985)

Medvedev, Roy and Chiesa, Giulietto. *Time of Change: An Insider's View of Russia's Transformation* (New York: Pantheon Books, 1990)

Medvedev, Zhores A. *Gorbachev* (New York: W. W. Norton, 1986)

Medvedev, Zhores A. *The Legacy of Chernobyl* (New York: W. W. Norton, 1990)

Naisbitt, John and Aburdene, Patricia. *Megatrends 2000: Ten New Directions for the 1990s* (New York: William Morrow, 1990)

Ogden, Chris. *Maggie: An Intimate Portrait of a Woman in Power* (New York: Simon & Schuster, 1990)

Owen, Richard. *Comrade Chairman: Soviet Succession and the Rise of Gorbachov* (New York: Arbor House, 1986)

Polyanski, Nikolai and Rahr, Alexander. *Gorbatshow, Der Neue Mann* (Munich: Universitas, 1986)

Rahr, Alexander, (ed.). *A Biographical Directory of One Hundred Leading Soviet Officials* (New York: Westview, 1990)

Reagan, Nancy. *My Turn: The Memoirs of Nancy Reagan* (New York: Random House, 1989)

Reed, John. *Ten Days That Shook the World* (New York: Bantam Books, 1919)

Roosevelt, Selwa. *Keeper of the Gate* (New York: Simon & Schuster, 1990)

Rybakov, Anatoly. *Children of the Arabat* (New York: Little, Brown, 1988)

Sakharov, Andrei. *Memoirs* (New York: Alfred A. Knopf, 1990)

Sanders, Sol. *Living Off the West* (Lanham, Md: Madison Books, 1990)

Scherer, John L., (ed.). *USSR: Facts and Figures* (Florida: Academic International Press, 1984, 1985), vols 8 and 9.

Shelton, Judy. *The Coming Soviet Crash* (New York: The Free Press, 1989)

Sholokov, Mikhail. *And Quiet Flows the Don* (New York: Vintage Books, 1966)

Talbott, Strobe, (ed.). *Mikhail S. Gorbachev: An Intimate Biography* (New York: Time Incorporated, 1988)

Tolstaya, Tatyana. *On the Golden Porch* (New York: Alfred A. Knopf, 1989)

Voznesensky, Andrei. *An Arrow In the Wall: Selected Poetry and Prose* (New York: Henry Holt, 1987), trans. Antonina W. Bouis.

Yeltsin, Boris. *Against the Grain* (New York: Summit Books, 1990)

Yevtushenko, Yevgeny. *Wild Berries* (New York: Henry Holt, 1989)

Zhegulin, Anatoly. *Blackstone* (Moscow, 1988)

Index